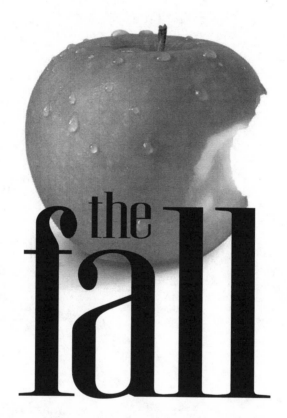

the fall

The Insanity of the Ego in Human History and the Dawning of a New Era

New Edition with Afterword

STEVE TAYLOR

First published by O-Books, 2005
Reprinted 2010
This edition published by iff Books, 2018
iff Books is an imprint of John Hunt Publishing Ltd., No. 3 East Street, Alresford,
Hampshire SO24 9EE, UK
office1@jhpbooks.net
www.johnhuntpublishing.com
www.iff-books.com

For distributor details and how to order please visit the 'Ordering' section on our website.

Text copyright: Steve Taylor 2005

ISBN: 978 1 78535 804 3
978 1 78535 805 0 (ebook)
Library of Congress Control Number: 2017951331

A CIP catalogue record for this book is available from the British Library.

Design: infograf.co.uk

Printed and bound by CPI Group (UK) Ltd, Croydon, CR0 4YY, UK

We operate a distinctive and ethical publishing philosophy in
all areas of our business, from our global network of authors to
production and worldwide distribution.

the fall

The Insanity of the Ego in Human History and the Dawning of a New Era

STEVE TAYLOR

New Edition with Afterword

BOOKS

Winchester, UK
Washington, USA

CONTENTS

FOREWORD

OVER THE YEARS I have been fascinated by the prehistoric murals that adorn the caves I have visited in many parts of the world. I have been struck by the absence of images of warriors or warfare in the paintings. In this remarkable book, Steve Taylor explains this absence. He maintains that the worldwide myths of a Golden Age or an original paradise have a factual, archaeological basis. There was a specific point in pre-history when things "went wrong" – that is, when warfare, patriarchy, social inequality and similar developments became widespread. Until that time, human societies were generally peaceful and egalitarian, and individuals experienced a sense of psychological well-being and connection to the cosmos. This is not merely conjecture or wishful thinking; Taylor marshals an impressive, wide-ranging body of evidence to make his case.

The transformation began about 4000 BCE, due to dramatic changes in climate in central Asia and the Middle East. These changes made survival more difficult and produced a sharpened sense of individuality among the areas' inhabitants. Taylor refers to this as the Ego Explosion, maintaining that this is the fundamental difference between the descendants of these peoples (such as modern Europeans and Americans) and the remaining indigenous groups such as the Australian Aborigines and the Native Americans. He sees this sharpened sense of ego as the root cause of war, male domination and social oppression, as well as other traits such as theistic religion. He makes the case that rather than showing a continual progression (as some historians would like to believe), in many ways human history is marked by a degeneration.

After his detailed analysis of the long, sorry saga of violence and oppression that makes up recorded history, Taylor still manages to take an optimistic view of humankind's future. There are, he believes, many signs that we are entering a new historical phase, one that he calls the trans-Fall era. Recent developments such as more egalitarian relationships between men and women and a healthier regard for the human body and nature provide some hope for the future.

Taylor's ideas are provocative, and never fail to captivate the reader. It is my fervent wish that his important book will have a wide audience and reach the individuals and institutions that mould public opinion and behaviour. In a world where the very existence of humanity is threatened, Steve Taylor offers a visionary yet practical path out of the morass that distorts human nature.

Dr. Stanley Krippner
Professor of Psychology,
Saybrook Graduate School,
California

INTRODUCTION

FOR THE LAST 6000 years, human beings have been suffering from a kind of collective psychosis. For almost all of recorded history human beings have been – at least to some degree – insane.

This seems incredible because we have come to accept the consequences of our insanity as normal. If madness is everywhere, nobody knows what sane, healthy and rational behaviour is any more. The most absurd and obscene practices become traditions, and are seen as natural. It becomes "natural" for human beings to kill each other, for men to oppress women, for parents to oppress children, for small groups of people to wield massive amounts of power and dominate massive numbers of other people. It becomes normal for people to abuse the natural world to the point of ecological disaster, and to despise their own bodies and feel guilty for experiencing completely natural desires. It becomes "natural" for human beings to try to accumulate massive amounts of wealth that they will never need, and to endlessly chase after success, power and fame – and also somehow "natural" that, even if they do manage to gain wealth and status, they never find contentment and fulfilment anyway, but remain constantly dissatisfied.

The aim of this book is to discover where this madness comes from, and to find out if it really *is* natural to human beings. We'll look at a great deal of evidence suggesting that earlier human beings were, in these terms, much more 'sane' than us. And even until recent times there were many parts of the world where the kind of pathological behaviour I've just described didn't exist.

All of this insanity was the result of an event which I call The Fall – a collective psychological shift which large groups of people underwent around 6000 years ago, as a result of an environmental disaster which began in the Middle East and central Asia. A new kind of human being came into existence then, with a more defined sense of individuality, and a new way of experiencing life and perceiving the world. In some ways the new human type was an advance – it brought technological advances, for example, and the civilisations of Sumer and Egypt (and many others afterwards). But it also gave rise to social pathologies such as warfare, male domination and social inequality.

We will see that before the Fall human life seems to have been fairly carefree and pleasant, even joyful. But after it life became "nasty, brutish and short," so full of misery that countless generations could only endure it by convincing themselves that it was just a brief stopover – to grin and bear as best they could – before they ascended to an eternal paradise. But perhaps now, as I discuss in the final section of this book, we are turning a full circle, and returning to a kind of sanity. Over the last few centuries – particularly since the eighteenth century – there have been signs of a re-emergence of all of the old "pre-Fall" characteristics. There has been a re-emergence of democracy and equality, of respect for nature and the human body, of an awareness of the essential spiritual reality of the cosmos, and so on. These characteristics perhaps haven't yet become as dominant as "fallen" ones, but they're certainly gaining in strength as time goes by.

The years I've spent researching and writing this book have been an inspiring voyage. I couldn't have completed the journey without the help of a large number of guides. I'm particularly grateful to Riane Eisler, Gerhard Lenski, Christopher Boehm, Robert Lawlor, Richard Heinberg, Brian Griffith, Elizabeth Baring and Jules Cashford, Richard Rudgley, Elman R. Service, Margaret Power and Christopher Ryan, not to mention the many authors of scholarly papers – particularly in the field of anthropology – whose work I've drawn on. I'm also grateful to Stanley Krippner and Christopher Ryan for their extensive comments on the manuscript. But perhaps most of all, I'm grateful to James DeMeo, whose book *Saharasia* provided me with a key to understanding the environmental causes of the Fall.

This book talks a lot about what we've lost, but also – hopefully – about what we can do to get it back. If there's just one thing that you, the reader, take away from these chapters I hope it's the idea that *it doesn't have to be like this*. The last 6000 years have been a schizophrenic nightmare from which we are finally beginning to awake. If this book can, in however small a way, contribute to this process of awakening I will be more than happy.

Also by Steve Taylor

Making Time (9781848310018)

Waking From Sleep (9781848501799)

Out of the Darkness (9781848502543)

Back to Sanity (9781848505476)

The Meaning (9781780993034)

The Calm Center (9781608683307)

The Leap (9781781809211)

Spiritual Science (9781786781581)

Edited by Steve Taylor

Not I, Not other than I: The Life and Teachings of Russel Williams (9781782797296)

PART ONE

THE HISTORY OF THE FALL

1

WHAT'S WRONG
WITH HUMAN BEINGS?

IF ALIEN BEINGS have been observing the course of human history over the last few thousand years they might well have reached the conclusion that human beings are the product of a scientific experiment which went horribly wrong. Perhaps, they might hypothesise, other aliens chose the earth as the site for an experiment to try to create a perfect being with amazing powers of intelligence and ingenuity. And create this being they did – but perhaps they didn't get the balance of chemicals exactly right, or maybe some of their laboratory equipment broke down half way through because, although the creature did possess amazing intelligence and ingenuity, it also turned out to be a kind of monster, with defects which were just as great as – or even greater than – its abilities.

Imagine if you had to draw up a balance sheet for the human race, listing our positive achievements on one side and our failures and problems on the other. On the plus side there would be the amazing scientific and technological feats which have made us the most successful species in the history of the earth - the advances of modern medicine, for example, which have doubled our life span, massively reduced infant mortality rates, controlled ailments which made life a misery for our ancestors (such as toothache, deafness or short-sightedness), and controlled diseases which killed them, such as smallpox or tuberculosis. Then there are our feats of engineering and building – 100-storey buildings, aeroplanes, space travel, tunnels underneath the sea. And then the incredible advances of modern science, which have enabled us to understand the physical laws of the universe, how life has evolved, to uncover the chemical structure of living beings and the physical structure of matter.

The plus side would also include the magnificent achievements of human creativity. The symphonies of Mahler or Beethoven, the songs of the Beatles or Bob Dylan, the novels of Dostoyevsky or D.H. Lawrence, the poems of

Wordsworth or Keats, the paintings of van Gogh – in their own way, all of these are just as impressive as any great building or scientific discovery, if not more so. There, too, would be the wisdom and insight of great philosophers and psychologists, which has helped us to understand our own psyche, and our predicament as conscious living beings.

And if, as some scientists believe, the only real purpose of life – for all living beings – is to survive and reproduce, then the human race has been massively successful in this regard too. Analysis of DNA suggests that all human beings alive today are descended from a group of a few hundred to a thousand people who left Africa 125,000 years ago. In just 125,000 years, therefore, this group of human beings has increased in number to a staggering 5 billion.

However, it seems to be a law of nature that great development in one area is offset by a lack of development in another. Great talent always seems to go hand in hand with great deficiency. Think of the great creative artists, like van Gogh or Beethoven, who paid for their genius with mental instability, depression and a lack of social skills. Or think of the archetypal absent-minded scientist who forgets to tie his own shoelaces and can't remember his grandchildren's names. Genius always has a price, it seems.

But the best illustration of this law isn't any individual human being but our species as a whole – because the bright side of the human race's achievements is balanced by a devastating and depressing dark side.

THE DARK SIDE OF HUMAN HISTORY – WAR

As well as being the most successful species in the history of the earth, the human race has been by far the most destructive and violent. It's impossible to read any history book – dealing with *any* period of history over the last five thousand years – without being shocked by what the historian Arnold Toynbee called "the horrifying sense of sin manifest in human affairs."[1] For most historians, history begins with the civilisations of Egypt and Sumer, which emerged at around 3500 BCE. And from that point on, right until the present day, history is little more than a catalogue of endless wars: conflicts over boundaries, raids to win slaves or victims for sacrifice, invasions to win new territory or increase the glory of the empire. In fact, these outward reasons for fighting aren't so significant, since the *real* cause of it all is the inner *need* which human beings have always had for conflict.

It's sometimes said that war is "natural," either because of certain chemicals (such as a high level of testosterone in men, or a low level of serotonin) or because we're made up of "selfish genes" which are determined to survive at all costs and make us compete against other individuals or groups for resources. But there are two important facts that contradict this view.

The first is that war is completely unknown amongst the rest of the animal kingdom. There are some primates who show a degree of aggressive behaviour, such as gorillas and chimpanzees, but even they are nowhere near as war-like as human beings. Their small degree of war-like behaviour only seems to occur when their natural way of life or their habitat is disrupted. This appears to have been the case with the chimpanzees of Gombe in Tanzania, who were famously studied by the primatologist Jane Goodall. They have been used as the basis of a "demonic male" hypothesis, suggesting that male primates – including human beings – are genetically programmed to be violent and murderous.[2] However, it's now clear that the violence of the chimpanzees at Gombe is the result of social and environmental disruption caused by human beings. As Margaret Power points out in her book *The Egalitarians*, Goodall's own early studies of the chimpanzees showed a lack of violence.[3] It was only later, after their feeding patterns had been disrupted, that they began to be aggressive. Recent studies of other chimpanzee groups in their natural environment show them to be extremely peaceful.[4] As the psychologist Erich Fromm noted, "If the human species had approximately the same degree of 'innate' aggressiveness as that of chimpanzees living in their natural habitat, we would live in a rather peaceful world."[5]

But most other species are even more peaceful than primates. Of course, many animals kill other species for food, but aside from this, as J.M.G. van der Dennen writes in his book *The Origins of War*, "Genocide, genocidal warfare, massacres, cruelty and sadism are…virtually absent in the animal world."[6] Apart from the killing of prey and the occasional practice of infanticide, the only type of violence which occurs amongst animals is what van der Dennen calls "ritualised interindividual agonistic behaviour" – in other words, aggression between the members of groups, usually connected to dominance or mating issues. But even here, actual fighting is quite rare. In fact, most animals go to great lengths to avoid real conflict. As the zoologist Glenn Weisfeld notes, "The animal usually threatens its opponent initially, as by hissing, vocalising, teeth-baring. Attack comes as a last resort."[7] And even if fighting does take place, animals also have appeasement signals, or displays of submission (such as when a dog rolls over), which abruptly end the fight before any killing occurs. Human beings are one of the very few species that does not have these instinctive inhibitions against killing, and are the only species that practises collective aggression and attempted conquest of other groups. In Erich Fromm's terms, whereas animal aggression is "benign and defensive" – only occurring when survival interests are threatened, and rarely going beyond threats and warning signals – human aggression is "malignant."[8]

The second reason is that, far from being "as old as humanity," war is actually a relatively recent (at least in terms of our whole history as a species) historical development. There is still a general assumption that early human beings were primitive "savages" who were much more aggressive and war-like than modern human beings – but archaeological and ethnographic evidence which has accumulated over the last few decades has now established that this isn't true. I'm not going to detail this evidence here, since it's one of the main themes of the next chapter, but there's now a general agreement amongst scholars that so-called "primitive" human beings were free from inter-group aggression and also from much of the "interindividual" aggression which van der Dennen speaks of. Van der Dennen examined the data on over several hundred primal peoples and found that the majority of them were "highly unwarlike," with "war reported as absent or mainly defensive," while the others only had "allegedly mild, low-level and/or ritualised warfare."[9] While another scholar, the anthropologist R. Brian Ferguson, has written that, "the global pattern of actual evidence indicates that war as a regular pattern is a relatively recent development in human history, emerging as our ancestors left the simple, mobile hunter-gatherer phase."[10]

As we'll see, warfare only seems to have begun at around 4000 BCE. Since then, however, as if to make up for lost time, human beings have turned large parts of this planet's surface into a constant battleground. Until the nineteenth century, European countries were at war with one or more of their neighbours for an average of nearly every second year. Between 1740 and 1897, there were 230 wars and revolutions in Europe, and during this time countries were almost bankrupting themselves with their military expenditure. At the end of the eighteenth century, the French government was spending two-thirds of its budget on the army, while Prussia was spending 90 per cent.[11] Warfare actually became slightly less frequent during the nineteenth and twentieth centuries, but this was only because of the awesome technological power which nations could now utilise, which meant that wars were over more quickly. In actual fact, the death toll from wars rose sharply. Whereas only 30 million people died in all the wars between 1740 and 1897, estimates of the number of dead in the First World War range from 5 million to 13 million, and a staggering 50 million people died during the Second World War.

And, of course, at the same time as war between different human groups, there has always been conflict within individual groups. Internal conflict has been as rife as external. Members of the ruling classes have continually battled with one another for power, religious groups have continually fought over their beliefs, and oppressed peasants have frequently rebelled against the ruling classes. The Roman Empire was so riddled with in-fighting that to become emperor was practically to condemn yourself to a premature – and usually a terrible – death. Of the 79 emperors, 31 were murdered, 6 were forced to kill themselves, and several more disappeared under suspicious circumstances after feuds with enemies. And in terms of class conflicts, historians have estimated that in medieval China there was a major peasant revolt almost every year, while one 60-year period of Russian history (1801-1861) saw 1,467 revolts.[12]

PATRIARCHY

It's possible, I believe, to say that there have been three main characteristics of human societies throughout recorded history (although, as we'll see later, there were peoples in some parts of the world who this doesn't apply to). War is the first of these; the second is patriarchy, or male domination; and the third (which we'll examine in a moment) is social inequality.

Feminist readers might already have objected to my statement that "the human race" has always waged war. In actual fact, only half the human race has waged war, since war has always been an almost exclusively male occupation. And in a sense men have always fought against women too. As well as being a catalogue of endless wars, the last few thousand years of history have been a story of continuing brutal oppression of women by men.

It has been suggested (by the sociologist Steven Goldberg, for example, in his book *The Inevitability of Patriarchy*[13]) that patriarchy – or the dominance of men over women – is inevitable too, because of the higher levels of testosterone which men have, which makes them much more aggressive and competitive than women. But in actual fact, again, this view is contradicted by the fact that patriarchy is a relatively recent historical development. The artwork, the burial practices and the cultural conventions of human societies from the Palaeolithic and early Neolithic periods of history (that is, the Old Stone Age and the early part of the New Stone Age) show a complete lack of evidence for male domination.[14] Women seem to have played just as prominent a part in these societies as men, and to have had exactly the same kinds of freedoms and rights. Many of these societies appear to have been "matrilinear" and "matrilocal" – that is, property was passed down the female side of the family, and on marriage men went to live with the bride's family. In addition, in some cultures children would take the mother's name rather than the father's. We'll also see that there are many primal peoples who have similar practices, and no traditions of male domination.

Like war, patriarchy only seems to make its first appearance in history at around 4000 BCE. In large parts of the world since then, however, the status of women has been only a little higher than that of slaves. In almost every society in Europe, the Middle East and Asia, women were unable to have any influence over the political, religious or cultural lives of their societies. It was taken for granted that they weren't fit to, since they were, in the words of the misogynistic philosopher Schopenhauer, "childish, foolish and short-sighted...something intermediate between the child and the man."[15] Women often couldn't own property or inherit land and wealth, and were frequently treated as mere property themselves. In some countries they could be confiscated by moneylenders or tax collectors to help settle debts (this was, for example, a common practice in Japan from the seventh century CE onwards). In ancient Assyria, the punishment for rape was the handing over of the rapist's wife to the husband of his victim, to use as he desired.[16]

Most gruesomely of all, some cultures practised what anthropologists have called ritual widow murder (or ritual widow suicide), when women would be killed (or kill themselves) shortly after the deaths of their husbands. This was common throughout India and China until the twentieth century, and there are still occasional cases nowadays. In India, the wives of Brahmin men would throw themselves – or else be thrown – on to their husbands' funeral pyres. According to Hindu tradition, once her husband dies, a woman becomes incomplete and sinful; she is a social outcast and cannot remarry. As a result, women sometimes chose *suttee* as a better option.

In Europe and North America, we're now used to a degree of sexual equality, but elsewhere women are still effectively slaves. In many countries – particularly in the Middle East – women live in seclusion in their own quarters, and can't go out unless accompanied by a male relative. If an unmarried girl has sex – even if she is raped – there is the possibility that she will be murdered by a male relative. In Saudi Arabia, women must wear a black gown – the *abaya* - which covers them completely save for a slit for the eyes. They can't drive a car or ride a bike, and can be stoned to death for committing adultery, while a man is permitted to marry four times.

In addition to this institutionalised oppression, women have continually been subjected to actual physical violence. In many cultures, female adultery, sex before marriage and abortion were punishable by death. In China, women were permanently deformed and disabled by having their feet bound, partly because men considered this erotic and partly because, as one Confucian scholar wrote, it would "prevent barbarous running around."[17] Wife-beating appears to have been common everywhere, and even to have been regarded as necessary. Women were seen as emotional and undisciplined creatures who needed to be taught self-control through violence.

Perhaps, however, there's no better symbol of the low value of female life and the domination of men than the widespread practice of female infanticide – that is, the killing of baby girls. This was rampant throughout Europe until recent centuries. During the ninth century, for example, the European population is estimated to have averaged three men for every two women, mainly because of infanticide. By the fourteenth century this had risen even higher, to 172 men for every 100 women.[18] Similarly, a scholar has estimated that in nineteenth century China, in some districts as many as a quarter of the female infants were killed at birth.[19] And perhaps there's no greater sign of the hostility and mistrust of men towards women than the state-sanctioned mass of murder of European women as "witches" that took place during the middle centuries of the last millennium.

SOCIAL INEQUALITY

It's not simply a question of men dominating and oppressing women, though. Men have always dominated and oppressed each other too. The third main characteristic of human societies over the last few thousand years has been the massive inequality which has always filled them, and the rigid classes and castes which have existed, with vastly different degrees of wealth and status.

Once again, as we'll see in Chapter 2 of this book, inequality and social oppression seem to have been absent from the earliest human societies. And in Chapter 4 we'll see that there are many contemporary indigenous societies which are egalitarian, with no classes or castes, an equal distribution of food and goods, and democratic decision-making processes. However, since 4000 BCE history has also been the story of the brutal oppression of the great mass of human beings by a tiny privileged minority. One of the world's first class systems was developed by a people called the Indo-Europeans – the ancestors of the Romans, Greeks, Celts and most modern Europeans and Americans. By the time they appeared in the Middle East and central Asia in the fourth millennium BCE, they had already divided themselves into three classes: the priesthood, the warriors and rulers, and the producers of economic wealth (which included merchants, farmers and craftsmen). And as they migrated into new lands and conquered the peoples who inhabited them, they added a new class to their social structure, consisting of the peoples they conquered, and who from that point on would be ruthlessly oppressed and exploited by them.[20] A similar social system developed in ancient Sumer in the third millennium BCE. The majority of property was owned by a small number of men (women weren't allowed to own any, of course), and a class system developed in which, as the historian Harriet Crawford writes, the royal family and the priests "controlled large numbers of men and women who worked for wages of food and other necessities and who do not seem to have been free to move away, nor did they own any land of their own."[21]

A similar social structure to this has operated throughout Europe, the Middle East and Asia for most of our history. This tiny privileged minority might only make up 1 or 2 per cent of a country's population, and yet own most of that country's wealth and land, and have complete control over political, economic and legal decisions. According to the sociologist Gerhard Lenski, the rulers and governing classes of what he calls "advanced agrarian societies" – which dominated

Europe, Asia and the Middle East from around 1000 BCE to the nineteenth century CE – typically had an income of more than half of their whole country's income.[22]   In England at the turn of the thirteenth century, for example, the average income of nobles was roughly 200 times that of an ordinary peasant, while the king's was 24,000 times as much. Similarly, in China in the nineteenth century, the income of an aristocrat was 10,000 times higher than an ordinary person's.[23]

In addition to owning most of their countries' land and wealth, the governing classes often actually owned the peasants who they dominated. This system of serfdom was common throughout Europe – especially Eastern Europe and Russia – and meant that the great mass of people were effectively slaves, who couldn't marry or even leave the estate without their landowner's permission. In nineteenth-century Russia, for example, the Czar owned over 27 million serfs, while noblemen sometimes owned as many as 300,000. Serfs could be called up for war at any time, leaving their farms to rot and their families to starve. Many landowners made use of what historians euphemistically call *le droit du seigneur* – their "right" to have sex with any of their serfs' brides on the wedding night.[24]

But even when peasants were nominally free and rented their land, their situation was usually little better. Landowners exploited them so brutally, with high rents, high taxes, massive interest rates, tithes, fines and compulsory "gifts," that, they were forced to give away at least half – and sometimes much more – of the value of the goods they produced.[25] As a result, while their masters basked in luxury and leisure, peasants lived lives of abject poverty and squalor, and often starved.

Other more direct forms of maltreatment were common too. Peasant women were frequently raped by landlords, and families were routinely separated if their master needed one or more of them to work elsewhere. Peasants were also liable to be brutally punished for insignificant crimes – stealing an egg or a loaf of bread, for example, was often punishable by death.

All of this was only possible because, in the same way that many men didn't consider women to be truly human, the governing classes saw their subjects as barbaric subhuman creatures who didn't deserve empathy or equality. Legal documents from medieval England actually refer to peasants' children as their "brood" or "litter", while there are estate records from Europe, Asia and America in which peasants are listed in the same category as livestock.[26]

What's wrong with human beings? These kinds of social pathology are so familiar to us that it's difficult to appreciate how strange and even insane they might appear to an impartial observer. After all, why *should* human history be such a terrible saga of violence and oppression? Why should human beings have this insatiable need to create conflict and to dominate and oppress one another? And why, as a result, should the lives of almost all the human beings who have lived over the past few thousand years have been so terrible, so full of misery and deprivation? Was life really meant to be as terrible as this? It's not surprising that the Buddha concluded that "life is suffering." It's also not surprising that the people who endured these terrible living conditions needed to console themselves with the belief in a glorious afterlife.

THE DARK SIDE OF THE HUMAN PSYCHE

But even all this – terrible enough though it is in itself – is only half the story. In fact, to be more precise, it's only the external half. So far we've been dealing with what you could call social suffering, which human beings inflict on one another. But there is another terrible price which the human race seems to have paid for its intelligence and creativity.

There is another kind of suffering, which comes from inside us: our psychological suffering. This is such a normal part of our experience that we usually don't realise it's there. But in its own way it's just as dangerous as warfare or social oppression. In fact, in a sense it's actually more dangerous since to a large extent – as we'll see later in this book - it actually *produces* these external problems.

The aliens who are observing us have probably noticed that that there seems to be something wrong with human beings as individuals too. They might ask themselves: Why do human beings seem to find it so difficult to be happy? Why do so many of them seem to suffer from different kinds of psychological malaise – for example, depression, drug abuse, eating disorders, self-mutilation – or else spend so much time oppressed by anxieties, worries and feelings of guilt or regret, and negative emotions like jealousy and bitterness? Or, more generally, why do so many of them seem to find it impossible to rest in a state of contentment, strive for happiness and never find it, and feel a general sense of being let down by life, as if the world has cheated them in some way?

Our animal cousins don't appear to have problems like these. They don't commit suicide (except in certain instances of over-population), take drugs or mutilate themselves. They don't appear to spend time worrying about the future or feeling guilty about the past. As the great American poet Walt Whitman wrote of animals, comparing them favourably to human beings, "they do not sweat and whine about their condition,/ They do not lie awake in the dark and weep for their sins…Not one is respectable or unhappy over the whole earth."[27]

Happiness is a subjective state, and it's impossible to be sure whether anyone experiences it or not. But it seems likely that early human beings, and the native peoples who have survived until recent times, had a more unified and peaceful kind of psyche than us, and lived in a state of relative contentment. Many anthropologists have been struck by the apparent serenity and contentment of native peoples. Elman R. Service says of the Copper Eskimos of northern Canada, for example: "The Eskimo display a buoyant light-heartedness, a good-humoured optimism, which has delighted foreigners who have lived with them."[28] The English anthropologist Colin Turnbull spent three years living with the Pygmies of central Africa in the 1950s, and characterises them as a strikingly carefree and good-humoured people, free of the psychological malaise that affects "civilised" peoples. To them, he writes, life was "a wonderful thing full of joy and happiness and free of care."[29] Similarly, Jean Liedloff, author of *The Continuum Concept*, describes the Tauripan Indians of South America as "the happiest people I had seen anywhere."[30] (In Chapter 4, we'll look at some more detailed evidence suggesting that native peoples in general don't experience as much "psychic suffering" as we do).

But at a certain point a giant transformation seems to have occurred. A giant can of psychological worms seems to have opened within the human mind.

SYMPTOMS OF DISCONTENT

If they looked a little closer, our aliens would see some very compelling evidence suggesting that there is something wrong with the human psyche. For example, there seems to be a fundamental kind of restlessness inside us, which makes it impossible – or at least extremely difficult – for us to do nothing, or to be in any situation where there isn't something external there for us to focus our attention on. Some 350 years ago the French philosopher and mathematician Pascal wrote that "the sole cause of man's unhappiness is that he does not know how to stay quietly in his room."[31] Nowadays, of course, staying in our rooms isn't so much of a problem for us, as long as we have television sets, computers or radios to give our attention to.

Think about everything you did yesterday, for example. It's likely that you spent the vast majority of the time you were awake with your attention focused outside yourself. Perhaps you read the paper or listened to the radio while you ate your breakfast, and listened to the radio in the car on your way to work (or read a newspaper on the train). For the next eight or nine hours your attention was mainly occupied by the tasks and chores of your job, and partly by chatting with your colleagues. Perhaps you listened to the radio again (or read the paper again) on the way home from work, and spent the evening watching TV, reading books, chatting to friends or playing sport (or combinations of these and other entertainments and activities). There were probably just a few moments when the parade of external stimuli halted and your attention wasn't occupied in this way – perhaps for ten minutes when you were waiting for your train, a few times when you were waiting for the kettle to boil or on the toilet, or ten minutes or so when you were lying in bed at night before you fell asleep.

The aliens would be amazed at some of the lengths we go to, to make sure we are never inactive and alone with ourselves. They would look at the housewives who vacuum their carpets, dust their ornaments and clean their windows every single morning, and the rich businessmen who still work 60 hours a week even though they could have retired years ago. Perhaps most of all, though, they would be amazed by our habit of watching television. If we were asked, most of us would probably say that we watch television because we want to relax, to be entertained, or to be informed about the world, and it's true that to an extent television does have these functions. But it's likely that the main reason why so many of us spend so much time watching TV is because it's the best method which anybody has yet devised of keeping our attention focused outside ourselves.

Again, this way of living is so normal to us that it's easy to forget how absurd it might seem to an objective observer. Why do these human beings have to *do* all the time, and seemingly find it impossible just to *be*? Why do they spend an average of 25 hours a week sitting in rooms staring at boxes with moving images on them, and try so hard to fill every other moment of their lives with activity or distraction?

It's as if we're afraid of ourselves, as if there's something in our own psyche which we don't want to face. And this fear certainly isn't groundless. There are some situations in our lives where it becomes very difficult for us to keep our attention focused outside ourselves, and when we suffer greatly as a result. This is one of the reasons why unemployment can have a terrible effect on people, making them feel frustrated and depressed. Psychologists' studies have found that unemployed people have a higher level of depression, suicide, alcoholism and drug addiction, more health problems and a higher death rate.[32] Retired people have similar problems. Studies have shown that, although there is a short honeymoon phase after retirement when the person feels a sense of freedom, this is followed by a period of disenchantment when he or she feels a sense of emptiness, low self-esteem and general depression.[33]

There is probably a variety of reasons for these problems, of course – the lack of social contact and affirmation, for example, and financial pressure – but it's likely that the main reason is simply the lack of activity, the fact that when we're unemployed or retired we're deprived of eight or nine hours of automatic activity and distraction every day. As a result, our attention isn't focused outside ourselves; it turns inwards, and we seem to confront a kind of fundamental disharmony or dissatisfaction within our own psyche. This is also probably the main reason why people such as pop stars or film stars – whose professions involve a great deal of inactivity or who have become so wealthy that they don't need to work – are so prone to drug problems and other kinds of psychological malaise. Despite their wealth and fame, they're just as vulnerable to the effects of inactivity as everybody else.

Similarly, studies by the American psychologist Mihaly Csikszentmihalyi show that the unhappiest time of the week for people who live alone is Sunday morning.[34] This fits with the strange fact that, from Freud onwards, psychologists have noted that nervous breakdowns are most likely to occur on Sunday mornings. We can presume that this is because Sunday morning is the time of least activity and least distraction during our weekly routines, when there is less than usual opportunity to keep our attention fixed outside ourselves. Or, as Csikszentmihalyi writes, "with no demands on attention, [people] are unable to decide what to do. The rest of the week psychic energy is directed by external routines...But what is one to do on Sunday morning, after breakfast, after having browsed through the papers?"[35]

THE MANIA FOR POSSESSION

The aliens would perhaps also be puzzled by the fact that we are, in Walt Whitman's phrase, "demented with the mania of owning things" – the way that so many of us devote so much of our time to trying to obtain material goods which we don't need and bring no real benefits to us. Why do human beings have this mania for buying new clothes, new jewellery, new cars, new antiques and ornaments, new furniture, when they already have enough of these things, and many have no function or use to them anyway? Why do they feel the desire to live in luxurious big houses, to drive the most expensive cars, to surround themselves with the most luxurious furniture, when a smaller house, a smaller car and simple furniture would suit their purposes just as well? As we'll see, the Native Americans were equally baffled by this aspect of the European psyche. As Sitting Bull said:

> The white man knows how to make everything, but he does not know how to distribute it. The love of possession is a disease with them. They take tithes from the poor to support the rich who rule. They claim this mother of ours, the earth, for their own and fence their neighbours away.[36]

In a similar way, an objective observer might be puzzled by the way that it's so important for many of us to be a "success" in our lives, or at least to be admired and respected by other people. Some of us put all of our time and energy into getting ahead in our careers, in the hope that we'll eventually become "special and important" people. Some of us dream of being famous pop stars and TV stars, certain that if we were our lives would be infinitely more satisfying, while many of us try to gain respect from others by wearing particular clothes, possessing certain objects (such as flashy cars, expensive jewellery or the latest fashionable furniture and kitchen equipment), going to certain places (such as "trendy" restaurants and clubs) or behaving in a certain way. The aliens might ask themselves: Why aren't they content to just be as they are? Why isn't it enough for them to just live their lives from day to day, doing what they have to do to keep themselves alive, rather than always feeling that they have to "get on" in the world and make other people admire them?

This wouldn't be so much of a problem if possessions and status could actually satisfy us. But part of the problem is that many of us are never satisfied with our lives as they are, and live in a permanent state of *wanting*. A new car or a new house might satisfy us for a short while, but then discontent arises again, and we want an even better one. You might feel satisfied for a short while when you become the manager of your company, when your first novel is published or when your song is played on the radio, but then the glow of ego-satisfaction fades and you start to hanker after a higher level of success.

And this never-ending cycle of wanting takes place in other areas of our lives too. Many of us feel an almost constant desire to change our lives in some way – to get a better job, find a new partner, live in a different house in a new area, improve our appearance. However, whenever any of these desires is realised, a new one takes its place almost straight away.

What's wrong with human beings? There seems to be a kind of psychological discord inside us, an inner discontent that continually plagues and torments us. To an extent we're all troubled souls like van Gogh or Friedrich Nietzsche, paying for our talent with psychological imbalance and turmoil. Again, it's not surprising that philosophers and writers have concluded that unhappiness is human beings' natural state, or that, in the words of Doctor Johnson, "man is not born for happiness."[37] In fact, the Buddha's statement that "life is suffering" refers more strictly to this internal suffering rather than the social suffering of war and oppression. (As one passage from the Buddhist scripture the Dhammapada states: "An enemy can hurt an enemy, and a man who hates can harm another man; but a man's mind, if wrongly directed, can do him a far greater harm."[38]) And again, it's very likely that this internal suffering has contributed to the dissatisfaction with life which has prompted human beings to console themselves in a belief in an idyllic afterlife. If we were happy we would be able to live with ourselves, to exist within our beings, rather than needing to constantly have our attention focused outside ourselves. Or as Pascal wrote, "If our condition were truly happy we should not seek to divert ourselves from thinking about it."[39] Similarly, if we were truly happy we wouldn't have to chase after external sources of well-being – such as possessions and status – as a compensation for our lack of inner well-being, and we wouldn't want anything apart from what we genuinely need.

THE ROOT CAUSE

This list of problems from the minus side of the human race's balance sheet is by no means exhaustive. As we'll see later, there are other kinds of social suffering besides the three major ones I've mentioned: for example, the hostile guilt-ridden attitude to the human body and sex which has run through the last few thousand years of history, and the sense of alienation from – and the desire to dominate – nature. I also haven't even mentioned a giant problem which stems from this attitude to nature, and which is perhaps the most convincing piece of evidence that there is something wrong with us: namely, our destruction of the environment. I'm not going to go into detail here, since the details are depressingly familiar to all of us, but perhaps, from the point of view of an objective observer, nothing would seem as insane as the way in which we are damaging and slowly destroying the life-support systems of this planet.

So what went wrong? Should we assume that human beings are just naturally violent, sadistic and discontented, so that there's nothing we can do about it, as the evolutionary psychologists (who tell us that war and patriarchy are the result of natural and sexual selection) and the physicalist scientists (who tell us that they're the result of hormones and brain chemicals) would have us believe? Or, as the myths of a "Fall" which are common to many of the world's cultures suggest, was there an earlier time of relative harmony, a time when these problems didn't exist, and a point when for some reason a giant change occurred, and we "fell" out of harmony and into social chaos and psychic disorder?

It's my intention in this book to show that this latter scenario is the true one, and that there really was a point in history when something went wrong with human beings. The amazing thing is that, although at first they might not seem to be connected (especially the social problems and the psychological ones), all of the problems I've dealt with in this chapter can be traced back to the same fundamental cause. This is even true of human beings' positive achievements as well, our creativity, ingenuity and technological and scientific prowess. The plus and negative sides of the human race's balance sheet are the positive and negative effects of the same phenomenon: namely, The Fall, or – to use a more precise term – the Ego Explosion.

2

THE PRE-FALL ERA

ONE IMPORTANT THING to remember about these social and psychological problems is that, as I've hinted, they haven't always been a part of human life. In fact, in terms of the whole of human history, they are a fairly late development.

For hundreds of thousands of years until around 8000 BCE, all human beings lived as hunter-gatherers – that is, they survived by hunting wild animals (the man's job) and foraging for wild plants, nuts, fruit and vegetables (the woman's job). Hunter-gatherer communities were small (with usually no more than a few dozen people) and mobile, moving on to a new site every few weeks or months when an area's supply of food began to dwindle. They were also – at least, judging by contemporary hunter-gatherer groups – fairly fluid, with a changing membership. As anthropologists such as Lee and DeVore[1] and Turnbull[2] have pointed out, contemporary foraging groups interact with each other a lot. They regularly visit each other, make marriage alliances, and often switch membership. Scholars used to assume that men provided most of the food in these societies, probably because it's so normal for the male to be the main breadwinner in our society. However, recent research (and observation of present-day hunter-gatherers like the Australian Aborigines) has shown that in actual fact women provided 80 to 90 per cent of food – a fact which has led some anthropologists to suggest that these peoples should be renamed gatherer-hunters.[3]

Another assumption we tend to make about life in prehistoric times is that it was tough and bleak, and full of hardship and suffering. And while there's no doubt that the hunter-gatherers' lives were very hard in some ways – with short life spans, for example, the danger of attack by wild animals, and a lack of protection from the elements and against disease – in other respects, their lives were actually easier than ours in the modern world. When anthropologists began to look systematically at how contemporary hunter-gatherers use their time, they discovered that, far from exhausting themselves in their search for food, they only actually spent 12 to 20 hours per week searching for it – between a third and a half of the average working week in the modern world! It was this that led the anthropologist Marshall Sahlins to call hunter-gatherers "the original affluent society." As he noted in his famous paper of that name, for foraging peoples, "the food quest is so successful that half the time the people do not seem to know what to do with themselves."[4] Or as Christopher Ryan points out in discussing Thomas Hobbes' famous summary of human life as "nasty, brutish and short," "There is every reason to conclude that human life in the Pleistocene [between 1.8 million years and 10000 BCE] was – relative to our own lives and even more so when compared with the lives known to Hobbes and his own contemporaries – rather low-stress, communal, peaceful and rich in many important ways."[5] Similarly, Robert Lawlor notes that Australian Aborigines who still live as hunter-gatherers only spend around four hours per day searching for food, and devote the rest of their time to leisure activities such as music, storytelling, artwork and being with family and friends.[6]

Research has also shown that – strange though it may sound – the diet of hunter-gatherers may actually have been better than many of ours in the modern world. Apart from the small amount of meat they ate (10 to 20 per cent of their diet) their diet was practically identical to that of a modern-day vegan, with no dairy products and a wide variety of fruits, vegetables, roots and nuts, all eaten raw (which nutrition experts tell us is the healthiest way to eat). This partly explains why most of the skeletons of ancient hunter-gatherers which have been discovered have been surprisingly large and robust, and show few signs of degenerative diseases and tooth decay. As the anthropologist Richard Rudgley writes, "We know from what they ate and the condition of their skeletons that the hunting people were, on the whole, in pretty good shape."[7] Studies by the physiologist Jared Diamond have shown that the hunter-gatherers of Greece and Turkey had an average height of five feet ten inches for men and five feet six for women. But after the advent of agriculture, these declined to five feet three and five feet one respectively.[8] An archaeological site in the lower Illinois valley in central USA shows that when people started cultivating maize and switched to a settled lifestyle, there was an increase in infant mortality, stunted growth in adults, and a massive increase in diseases related to malnutrition.[9]

Another reason for this is that the ancient hunter-gatherers were less vulnerable to disease than later peoples. In fact, until the advances of modern medicine and hygiene during the nineteenth and twentieth centuries, they may well have been less afflicted with disease than any other human beings in history. Many of the diseases which we're now susceptible to only actually arrived when we domesticated animals and started living close to them. Animals transmitted a whole host of diseases to us which we'd never been exposed to before. Pigs and ducks passed the flu on to us, horses gave us colds, cows gave us the pox and dogs gave us the measles. And later, when dairy products became a part of our diet, we increased our exposure to disease even more through drinking milk, which transmits at least 30 different diseases.[10]

What's even more interesting to us, though, as regards the thesis of this book, is that hunter-gatherer societies show little or no evidence of the problems which have characterised human life for the past few thousand years. The general assumption about early human beings which is least accurate of all is the myth that they were violent "savages" who constantly foamed at the mouth with aggression and went around bashing each other over the head with sticks. The truth of the matter could hardly be more different.

Archaeological studies throughout the world have found almost no evidence of warfare during the whole of the hunter-gatherer phase of history – that is, right from the beginnings of the human race until 8000 BCE. There are, in fact, just two clear and unambiguous instances of group violence during all of these tens of thousands of years. A cluster of sites around the Nile valley shows some signs of violence from around 12000 BCE. The site of Jebel Sahaba, for instance, has a grave containing the bodies of over 50 people who apparently died a violent death. And in south-east Australia, there are some signs of inter-tribal fighting – as well as of other kinds of social violence such as the cranial deformation of children – at several different sites dating from 11000 and 7000 BCE.[11] Lawrence Keeley's book *War Before Civilisation* purports to give several other examples of prehistoric violence and warfare, but all of these are dubious, and have been dismissed by other scholars. For example, Keeley sees cut marks on human bones as evidence of cannibalism, when these are more likely to be the result of prehistoric funeral rituals of cleaning bones of their flesh. He also interprets highly abstract and stylised drawings in caves in Australia as depicting battles, when they are open to a wide variety of other interpretations. In this way, as the anthropologist R. Brian Ferguson remarks, Keeley's "rhetoric exceeds his evidence in implying war is old as humanity."[12]

The lack of evidence for warfare is striking. In 1999, for example, three separate overviews of the archaeological evidence in different parts of the world were made, all of which showed no evidence of war during all of the Upper Palaeolithic period (40000 to 10000 BCE).[13] There are no signs of violent death, no signs of damage or disruption by warfare, and although many other artefacts have been found, including massive numbers of tools and pots, there is a complete absence of weapons. As Ferguson points out, "it is difficult to understand how war could have been common earlier in each area and remain so invisible."[14] Archaeologists have discovered over 300 cave "art galleries" dating from the Palaeolithic era, not one of which contains depictions of warfare, weapons or warriors.[15] Because of evidence like this, the archaeologist W.J. Perry has written, "it is an error, as profound as it is universal, to think that men in the food-gathering stage were given to fighting...All the available facts go to show that the food-gathering stage of history must have been one of perfect peace."[16] Even more plainly, in the words of another anthropologist, Richard Gabriel:

> For the first ninety-five thousand years after the Homo sapiens Stone Age began [until 4000 BCE], there is no evidence that man engaged in war on any level, let alone on a level requiring organized group violence. There is little evidence of any killing at all.[17]

We can also see evidence for this when we look at the peoples in the world who still live as hunter-gatherers, or at least who did until very recently. Some anthropologists advise against seeing contemporary indigenous cultures as representative of the cultures of the past, and this is true in the sense that every indigenous culture in existence has now been disrupted – and in many cases destroyed – by the influence of more "civilised" peoples. There is probably no genuinely indigenous or primal culture left in the world. But, at the same time, I believe it's valid to see these peoples *at the times when Europeans first had contact with them (and for a period afterwards)*, as a kind of window through which we can look back at the history of the whole human race. These were cultures which had been unchanged for thousands of years. As the anthropologist Robert Lawlor writes, for instance:

Traditional archaeological evidence holds that Aboriginal culture has existed in Australia for 60,000 years, but more recent evidence indicates that the period is more like 120,000 or 150,000 years. The Aborigines' rituals, beliefs and cosmology may represent the deepest collective memory of our race.[18]

There are also a great many similarities between contemporary and ancient hunter-gatherers. As far as we can tell, ancient hunter-gatherers had – for example – the same animistic view of the world, the same reverence for nature and the same egalitarian social system as contemporary hunter-gatherers. And in fact, most scholars accept that archaeological and ethnographic evidence are closely related. As the sociologist Lenski wrote, "Comparisons are not only valid but extremely valuable…The similarities are many and basic; the differences are fewer and much less important."[19]

And one striking feature of the hunter-gatherer peoples encountered by early European explorers and anthropologists – and of contemporary hunter-gatherers who manage to live something close to a traditional way of life – was the low level of warfare amongst them. A small number of tribes appear to have been fairly war-like even before European contact. This may be the case with the tribal peoples of the Amazon Basin in South America, tribes like the Jivaro and the Yanamamo (we'll look at these exceptions in more detail in Chapter 4). Many hunter-gatherer peoples also became much more violent once their troubles with Europeans began. This was the case with the Plains Indians, for example, and has happened in recent decades with contemporary peoples such as the !Kung of southern Africa. The !Kung were once extremely peaceful, but now – as a result of cultural disruption – they have a higher murder rate than most Western countries.[20] People who believe that "war is as old as humanity" often point to examples like these to show that war is natural, ignoring the fact that, in R. Brian Ferguson's words, "all around the world, what has been called primitive or indigenous warfare was generally transformed, frequently intensified, and sometimes precipitated by Western contact."[21] However, even nowadays it's still the case that, in Lenski's words, "the incidence of warfare [in hunting and gathering groups] is strikingly low. Certainly in those which have survived in the modern era, warfare is uncommon and violence between members of the same group is infrequent."[22]

This is generally true of the Australian Aborigines, for example. As the anthropologist Elman R. Service writes of one Aboriginal tribe, the Arunta:

> War in the sense of intertribal struggle is unknown. What fighting there is is better understood as an aspect of judicial procedure than as war. If a group, or family, feels wronged by an outside individual, it organises an expedition to avenge the wrong. It is important to realise, however, that arbitration usually occurs instead of actual fighting.[23]

One early anthropologist, William Graham Sumner, stated that none of the indigenous peoples he was aware of – including the Aborigines, the tribal peoples of India, of German Melanesia and Papua New Guinea – had warfare. As he summarised, "If we turn to the facts about the least civilised men, we find proofs that they are not war-like and do not practice war if they can help it."[24] While another early anthropologist, Branislav Malinowski, noted that although he had seen many different indigenous peoples show signs of anger, "the actual occurrence…of bodily violence is so rare that it becomes statistically negligible."[25]

Conflicts do occur sometimes, of course, but they are regulated or ritualised to ensure that very little violence actually occurs. When there is a quarrel between groups, what anthropologists call "tournament fights" are arranged, to give vent to hostile feelings. This is the purpose of the famous Eskimo singing contests, while other peoples use wrestling, or spear-throwing or head-butting contests.[26] One example of this "ritualised aggression" is described by W. Divale in his book *War in Primitive Society*.[27] In what he calls "advanced" tribal cultures, groups of "warriors" gather in a pre-arranged area, and, rather than fighting group against group, split off into pairs and "duel" against each other. Dozens of these duels can take place at the same time. One "warrior" shouts insults at his opponent, and then throws spears or arrows. However, actual killing hardly ever occurs, because of the distance between the individuals and because the warriors are highly skilled at dodging arrows. As Divale notes, "In the event that someone was badly wounded or slain, the battle would usually cease for that day."[28]

The important point here may be that hunter-gatherers are generally not territorial – that is, they don't think of a particular area of land as belonging to them and them alone, and don't aggressively resist anybody who encroaches on it.

As Burch and Ellanna put it, "both social and spatial boundaries among hunter-gatherers are extremely flexible with regard to membership and geographic extent."[29] And since they have no concept of territory they are obviously unlikely to fight wars to protect land or resources. Instead, they show what Margaret Power describes as "a lack of concern and possessiveness in regard to food resources."[30] This fits with the archaeological evidence, too, since, as the anthropologist Haas writes of pre-historic North America, for instance:

> The archaeological record gives no evidence of territorial behaviour on the part of any of these first hunters and gatherers. Rather, they seem to have developed a very open network of communication and interaction that spread across the continent.[31]

MALE DOMINATION AND INEQUALITY?

Patriarchy and social stratification appear to have been absent during the hunter-gatherer phase of history too. As the anthropologist Knauft has remarked, hunter-gatherers are characterised by "extreme political and sexual egalitarianism."[32] The fact that women provided so much of the tribe's food strongly suggests that they had at least equal status to men – it's difficult to see how they could have low status when they performed such an important economic role. The healthy, open attitude the hunter-gatherers had to the human body and to sex – illustrated by the nakedness of some present-day Aborigines and their frank attitude to sex – suggests this too, since, as we'll see later, the oppression of women is closely connected to a sense of alienation from the human body, and a negative attitude to instincts and bodily processes.

And, again, contemporary hunter-gatherer societies are notable for their lack of male domination. As the anthropologist M.A. Jaimes Guerrero states, "my own research indicates that almost all indigenous peoples, if not all at one time, were matrilineal societies before the European conquest and colonization."[33] That is, almost all indigenous peoples traced descent and ownership of property through the mother's rather than the father's side of the family, which is a clear sign of high female status. And as Ingold et al. note, in "immediate return" hunter-gatherer societies (that is, societies which live by immediately using any food or other resources they collect, rather than storing them for later use), men have no authority over women.[34] Women usually choose their own marriage partners, decide what work they want to do and work whenever they choose to, and if a marriage breaks down they have custody rights over their children. (We'll look at more evidence for this absence of patriarchy in indigenous cultures in Chapter 4.)

There is also some archaeological evidence to suggest that ancient hunter-gatherer societies were egalitarian, with no status differences. In archaeology, one of the most obvious signs of social stratification is grave differences – in size, position and the possessions which are placed in them. As we'll see, in stratified societies there are larger, more central graves for more "important" people, and these graves also have a lot more possessions in them. But the graves of the ancient hunter-gatherers are strikingly uniform, with little or no size differences and little or no grave wealth.

And, again, we can see a lot of evidence of the egalitarianism of ancient human societies by looking at contemporary hunter-gatherer peoples. Almost all contemporary hunter-gatherers show a striking absence of any of the characteristics that we associate with social inequality. The anthropologist James Woodburn speaks of the "profound egalitarianism" of immediate-return foraging peoples and emphasises that no other way of human life "permits so great an emphasis on equality."[35] Many primal peoples seem to live in a natural state of communism – a fact which Karl Marx himself realised, and referred to as "primitive communism." According to Lenski's statistics in *Human Societies*, only 2 per cent of contemporary hunter-gatherer societies have a class system, while private ownership of land is completely absent in 89 per cent of them (and only "rare" in the other 11 per cent).[36] In fact, there is very little ownership of anything. As Ingold et al. note, in hunter-gatherer societies, "people are not entitled to accumulate movable property beyond what they need for their immediate use. They are morally obliged to share it."[37] They give the example of the Hazda of Africa, who never own an "unnecessary" possession – such as a second axe or a second shirt – for more than a few days, and usually not more than a few hours. Their "moral obligation to share" makes them give it away almost immediately.

Foraging peoples are also strikingly democratic. Most societies do operate with a leader of some kind, but their power is usually very limited, and they can easily be deposed if the rest of the group aren't satisfied with their leadership.

People don't seek to be leaders – in fact, if anybody does show signs of a desire for power and wealth that person is usually barred from consideration as a leader.[38] The role of leader often rotates according to different situations. As Power notes, "The leadership role is spontaneously assigned by the group, conferred on some members in some particular situation…One leader replaces another as needed."[39] And even when people become leaders, they don't have the right to make decisions on their own. As Lenski writes, political decisions are not taken by the chief alone, but are usually "arrived at through informal discussions among the more respected and influential members, typically the heads of families."[40] Or as the anthropologist Jean Briggs wrote of the Utku Eskimos of northern Canada:

> The Utku, like other Eskimo bands, have no formal leaders whose authority transcends that of the separate householders. Moreover, cherishing independence of thought and action as a natural prerogative, people tend to look askance at anyone who seems to aspire to tell them what to do.[41]

At the same time, hunter-gatherer groups also have methods of ensuring that status differences don't occur. This is done by sharing credit and putting down or ridiculing anybody who becomes too boastful. The !Kung of Africa swop arrows before going hunting, and when an animal is killed, the credit doesn't go to the person who fired the arrow, but to the person who the arrow belongs to. If any person becomes too domineering or too arrogant the other members of their group gang up against them, or ostracise them.[42] As Christopher Boehm summarises, "This egalitarian approach seems to be universal for foragers who live in small bands that remain nomadic, suggesting considerable antiquity for political egalitarianism."[43]

There are probably some cultural reasons for this egalitarianism, of course – the mobility of the hunter-gatherer lifestyle, for example, which worked against the accumulation of property (since it would've been difficult to carry it from place to place). In addition, the small size of the groups and their lack of technology meant that there were none of the different social roles which can be the basis of classes or castes. But there's such a striking absence of social oppression that these factors don't seem to suffice as an explanation. As we'll see, it's likely that there's a much more fundamental reason – which is also the reason for the hunter-gatherers' lack of warfare and their sexual equality.

In other words, early human beings seem to have been completely free of the social suffering which has made the lives of so many millions of human beings a misery in more recent times. Although the fact that contemporary hunter-gatherers *appear* to be content suggests this, it's obviously impossible to say for certain whether their ancient counterparts were free of our psychological suffering too. Probably the only thing it's possible to say about them directly is that, since our obsession with material goods and with gaining success and status is largely caused by our psychological discord, the fact that hunter-gatherers apparently had no need for possessions and status *suggests* that there was no psychological discord inside them which they needed to compensate for. And since our inability to do nothing is also – at least to a large extent – the result of our psychological discord (because we need activity to escape from it), the fact that hunter-gatherers lived relatively inactive, leisure-filled lives might also suggest this.

It's important to remember that here we're dealing with a period of time stretching from the human race's beginnings hundreds of thousands of years ago until around 8000 BCE. The archaeological and ethnographic evidence overwhelmingly suggests that during the whole of this period human groups didn't wage war with one another, didn't dominate and abuse members of the opposite sex, and didn't oppress and exploit each other.

And this era of peace and equality didn't end here either.

THE EARLY HORTICULTURALISTS

At around 8000 BCE, beginning in the Middle East, human beings started to abandon the hunter-gathering lifestyle. Instead of foraging for plants they started to cultivate them, and instead of hunting animals they started to domesticate them. Nobody knows for sure why this happened, although the consensus is that it was due to a population increase, which meant that the hunter-gatherer lifestyle could no longer feed people. There's some evidence for this in Chinese mythology, which says that in ancient times people ate animals and birds, until the population grew so large that there were no longer enough to feed everyone. And at this point the legendary ruler Shen-nung taught the people how to cultivate plants. Environmental change may have been a factor too. The earth grew gradually warmer from 17000 to 8000 BCE, and the migration patterns of animals altered as a result.[44] This may have meant that our ancestors had to choose between following the animals to their new habitats or finding a new way of keeping themselves alive.

It's probably a mistake to refer to this way of life as agriculture, though. Agriculture means using a plough, and cultivating the same large fields for years on end. But these first "farmers" were really horticulturalists, or gardeners, since they used a hoe rather than a plough, and only cultivated small gardens, which they had to leave after a few years once they became overgrown with weeds. They grew cereals and crops, and domesticated other animals besides the dog (who had already been a part of hunter-gatherer groups). Women still had a major role – in fact, cultivating the crops was mainly their responsibility. It was men's job to clear land when new gardens were needed, and in some cases they continued to hunt. Although some large towns did eventually emerge, groups were usually still quite small – usually only around 150 people. However, the demands of tending to their crops and animals meant that they could no longer be mobile. For the first time ever, human beings settled down.

It's also probably a mistake to speak – as historians sometimes do – of a "Neolithic revolution," since the transition from foraging to horticulture actually took thousands of years. After beginning in the Middle East, it gradually fanned out into Europe, Asia and North Africa – and also developed independently in some places – but the process was so slow that horticulture only reached both Britain and China (in the far West and East respectively) towards the end of the third millennium BCE. At the same time, there were large parts of the world where people never made the transition – most of North and South America, the whole of Australia, and many other areas.

We've already seen that this transition had a bad effect in that the close contact with animals exposed people to a host of new diseases. It probably had a bad effect in terms of diet too. The hunter-gatherers had eaten a wide variety of foods but now people's diet was usually centred around two or three different types of grain, which meant a lack of nutrition and dietary balance. As a result, as Christopher Ryan puts it, "Throughout the world, the shift to agriculture was generally accompanied by a dramatic drop in the quality of people's diets severe enough to leave tell-tale signs on their bones which can still be read by paleopathologists."[45] These horticulturalists probably worked a lot harder than the hunter-gatherers as well, with longer hours and more demanding labour. Because of this it's not surprising that skeletons from the beginning of the farming era are smaller than those of the hunter-gatherers. They also show more signs of wear and tear, and people appear to have died younger.[46]

However, despite these drawbacks, the first phase of the Neolithic era – roughly 8000 to 4000 BCE – was also, it seems, a time of peace and harmony.

There are some authors and scholars who believe that the transition from the hunter-gathering to the agricultural (or, more strictly, horticultural) lifestyle was the point when the human race's social problems began. Jared Diamond, for instance, describes agriculture as "the worst mistake in the history of the human race."[47] The historian W. Newcomb suggests that "in a very real sense true warfare may be viewed as one of the more important consequences of the agricultural revolution."[48] In some ways, this view seems fairly logical. For example, we could say that now that people were settled down, they were able to accumulate possessions, which created differences in wealth and status. And at the same time, the settled lifestyle would lead to a "division of labour," with different sections of the group attending to food cultivation, storing and distributing crops, making houses and other buildings, and so on. In a similar way, we might say that the settled lifestyle made people more territorial, which – taken together with a new desire to acquire wealth – may have given rise to warfare. There is also the argument that the growth in population that caused the "agricultural revolution" led to warfare, since it meant that there weren't enough resources to go round any more, and different groups had to compete and fight for them.

However, the archaeological record doesn't support this view. Despite the differences in their lifestyle, the simple horticulturalists appear to have had the same basic social characteristics as the hunter-gatherers. As Riane Eisler summarises, "the prevailing view is still that male dominance, along with private property and slavery, were all by-products of the agrarian revolution...despite the evidence that, on the contrary, equality between the sexes – and among all people – was the general norm in the Neolithic."[49]

There is the same lack of evidence for violent conflict throughout the simple horticultural period of history as in the hunter-gather era. Graves don't contain weapons; images of warfare or weapons are still absent from artwork; and villages and towns aren't situated in inaccessible places or surrounded by defensive walls. It's true that some villages had ditches and fences around them, but these would've given very little protection from human invaders, and were probably to stop domestic animals escaping and wild animals coming in.[50]

Lenski's statistics for contemporary "simple horticultural" societies also contradict the idea that the sedentary way of life always brings war and social inequality. Although the settled lifestyle means that private property and private ownership of land become more common, and a small number (17 per cent) of the societies have a kind of class system (probably as a result of a division of labour), Lenski notes that none of this involves inequality. Contemporary "simple horticultural" peoples have the same lack of burial differences that we find amongst hunter-gatherers, and the same lack of powerful individual leader figures. As he writes, "The power of political leaders has been quite limited in nearly all simple horticultural societies…Social inequality is generally rather limited in most simple horticultural societies of the modern era."[51] Similarly, Christopher Boehm notes that many "people who live in permanent, settled groups that accumulate food surpluses through agriculture, are quite similar politically… These tribesmen lack strong leadership and domination among adult males, they make group decisions by consensus and they too exhibit an egalitarian ideology."[52]

And, in addition, the idea that social pathology is the result of the settled lifestyle is contradicted by the fact that the first human groups who appear to have developed pathological behaviour – peoples like the Indo-Europeans and the Semites who emerged from the Middle East and central Asia from around 4000 BCE – were not agriculturalists but nomads. There are also cases of contemporary nomadic peoples who are extremely war-like and patriarchal, such as the Bedouins of Saudi Arabia.

OLD EUROPE

Well then, if war and social inequality didn't come out of agriculture, then they must have been the result of civilisation – that is, living in cities. This is another popular argument, the basis of which is similar to the "agriculture is to blame for everything" theory. Inequality arose because of the division of labour and because a surplus of food and other goods developed, which led to different levels of wealth and status. And war came about because in cities governments became strong and centralised, which meant that they could control and organise large numbers of people.

But this argument can be easily disproved as well, since it's now known that many large towns developed during the simple horticultural period, particularly in the Middle East and central Europe, without apparently developing war or inequality. One of the most famous of these is the town of Catal Huyuk in southern Turkey, which was excavated by the archaeologist James Mellaart in 1952. Catal Huyuk had an estimated 7,000 inhabitants and flourished between 7000 BCE and 5500 BCE. In the 1,500 years of its heyday, it shows no evidence of any damage by warfare; in fact, there is no sign of any violent contact between human beings at all.[53] Catal Huyuk was apparently a multi-ethnic society, but there is no sign of any conflict between the different peoples who lived and worked there. Even though there was craft specialisation – including potters and toolmakers – the similarity of house sizes and graves suggests that there was little or no inequality. The town seems to have had sexual equality too: religious affairs were conducted by priestesses, with only a minor role for men, and there are a massive number of feminine images, which the archaeologist Marija Gimbutas and others have interpreted as images of a goddess. Women's high status is also suggested by the fact that their sleeping platforms were slightly larger than men's, and always in the same place – on the eastern side – whereas the position of men's wasn't fixed.[54]

Some Neolithic cultures reached such a high level of development that archaeologists have suggested that the traditional view that "civilisation" began in Egypt and Sumer in the third millennium BCE should now be revised. Marija Gimbutas has shown, for example, that a kind of civilisation flourished throughout south-eastern Europe during this period, which she calls "Old European" civilisation.[55] This stretched from Italy in the west to Romania in the east, from Greece in the south to Poland in the north, and covered Yugoslavia, Bulgaria and Hungary. There were many towns with up to several thousand inhabitants, who were highly skilled at engineering, crafts and art. Some of their temples were several storeys high, their houses had up to five rooms with furniture, they built the world's first drainage systems and roads, and practised crafts like basket weaving and pottery, and arts like sculpture and painting. They had specialist ceramicists, weavers, metallurgists and other artisans, and traded over hundreds of miles in goods like shells, marble and salt. They even developed a simple kind of writing too, which was mainly used for religious purposes.

What's most striking about the Old Europeans, though, is not what they achieved in technology, but what they were like as human beings. They seem to have completely lacked the need for conflict and war which characterises later European peoples. As Riane Eisler notes, closely following my description of simple horticultural peoples in general:

> Old Europeans never tried to live in inconvenient places such as high, steep hills, as did the later Indo-Europeans who built hill forts in inaccessible places and frequently surrounded their hillsites with cyclopean stone walls. The characteristic absence of heavy fortifications and of thrusting weapons speaks for the peaceful nature of the art-loving peoples.[56]

Another archaeologist, J.D. Evans, made a detailed study of Neolithic Malta, one of the southernmost points of Old European civilisation, and concluded that, "Insofar as we can judge from the evidence, no more peaceable society seems ever to have existed."[57] This was true of ancient Crete as well, which, because of its inaccessibility, was the pocket of Old European civilisation which survived longest, until around 1500 BCE. In the words of Nicolas Platon, who excavated the island for over 50 years, the Cretans were an "exceptionally peace-loving people," who somehow managed to sustain a state of peace at home and abroad for 1,500 years, while the world around them was raging with war.[58] Their towns didn't have military fortifications, their villas were built facing the sea, and there's no sign that the city-states of the island fought against each other or tried to conquer and dominate any other peoples. Eventually the Cretans were forced to develop weapons and to fight some battles in order to defend themselves, but even then their artwork doesn't idealise warfare and they only seem to have devoted a tiny part of their income to military pursuits.

Equally strikingly, despite the settled lifestyle and large towns, Old European society doesn't seem to have contained different levels of status and wealth. In Crete, for instance, there was, as Eisler writes, "a rather equitable sharing of wealth," the result of which was an apparent lack of poverty, with a high standard of living even for peasants.[59] There is little difference in the size of graves or in the goods placed inside them. Old European societies don't seem to have been run by powerful leader figures, since there are no unusually large graves containing massive amounts of wealth, and no depictions of leader figures in their artwork. In fact, the normal method of burial in Old Europe seems to have been communal. During the sixth millennium BCE in central and western Europe, the dead were placed in temporary graves until the beginning of winter, when they would be exhumed and reburied in a communal village grave.[60]

Patriarchy is even more strikingly absent from Old European society. Some observers have suggested that their culture (and that of Catal Huyuk) was matriarchal, but as with the hunter-gatherers, the truth seems to have been that the terms matriarchy and patriarchy had no meaning, since neither sex attempted to oppress the other. There seems to have been complete equality between the sexes. Old European societies were often matrilinear and matrilocal (that is, property was passed down through the female side, and a husband went to live with his wife's family after marriage), and their artwork often shows women as priests or in other positions of authority. There are also no differences in male and female graves. At the Old European site of Vinca, for instance, close to present-day Belgrade, there is a cemetery containing 53 graves, in which, as Gimbutas writes, "hardly any difference in wealth of equipment was discernible between male and female graves…In respect to the role of women in the society, the Vinca suggests an egalitarian and clearly non-patriarchal society."[61] And like the citizens of Catal Huyuk, the Old Europeans appear to have venerated the female form. Literally tens of thousands of female figurines have been found, showing naked women, often pregnant, with over-sized breasts and hips.

THE OLD WORLD

But these kinds of cultures were by no means confined to Europe. Wherever human beings made the switch from the hunter-gatherer to the horticultural lifestyle the same peaceful and harmonious conditions seem to have prevailed. Figurines and other feminine symbols have been found throughout the Middle East, as far west as Britain, and as far east as China. Horticulture spread to North Africa during the sixth millennium BCE, and there, as the historian and geographer James DeMeo writes, communities were "cooperative, productive and peaceful in character, without social stratification or strong man rule."[62] As elsewhere, archaeological excavations have found no weapons, and their art shows no signs of warfare. On the contrary, their artwork contains many scenes of dancing and music, and shows women playing an active role. As the archaeologist B. Davidson writes, women are depicted with "elegance and care – indicating the regard in which [they] were held."[63]

Similar cultures have been found as far away as China and Japan. According to Chinese legend, even after Shen-nung had taught people how to cultivate the land (that is, after the horticultural age had begun), "people rested at ease and acted with vigour. They cared for their mothers, but not for their fathers. They did not think of harming one another."[64] The reference to mothers here suggests that women had high status, which archaeological evidence confirms. As DeMeo writes:

> Archaeology has indicated an absence of militarism or significant social stratification among the earliest Chinese. The lack of significant caste and legends of high female status, plus textual prescriptions for abortion, suggests a fairly high female status for Neolithic China.[65]

In China, there are many legends speaking of a Golden Age before the time of constant warfare and social oppression, and archaeological evidence suggests that these aren't just myths. China's earliest villages contained houses all of roughly equal size, and as in ancient Europe, there are no defensive walls around villages, and an absence of weapons of war.[66] Women seem to have been the heads of clans, and children seem to have taken their mothers' surnames. As Brian Griffith notes, "the ancient word for family name (xing) is a compound of symbols for 'woman' and 'bear', suggesting a typical matrilineal totem-clan."[67]

Similarly, during the Neolithic period Japan was inhabited by a people called the Jomon, who lived as simple horticulturalists, cultivating rice. In 1992 Japanese archaeologists discovered a large Jomon town close to present-day Aomori City, which was occupied from 5000 to 3500 BCE, and contained over a thousand buildings. The town shows evidence of craft specialisation, trade, metallurgy and other skills. But again, the most striking thing about the town was that it showed no signs of damage by warfare, of defensive walls, of weapons, or of social inequality.[68] In fact, this is true of Jomon culture in general. As Professor Yasuda Yoshinori has written:

The society of the Jomon period had [a] marvellous principle
which later civilisations lacked: a respect for and co-existence
with nature. The principle of living within the cycles of nature
and maintaining social egalitarianism...[69]

OTHER CHARACTERISTICS

As with the hunter-gatherers, the fact that – despite their settled lives with some
division of labour – these peoples don't seem to have become obsessed with
accumulating material goods or with gaining status and power suggests that there
wasn't a fundamental unhappiness inside them which they needed to find
compensation for. In other words, they didn't suffer from "psychological discord"
to the same extent as us. These cultures also seem to be completely free of the
atmosphere of sin, repression and suffering which was a characteristic of later
Christian, Hebrew and Islamic cultures, for instance. Instead, there's an
atmosphere of lightness and joy, a sense of the sacredness of life and the beauty of
the world, which makes it difficult to imagine that they suffered from
psychological discord. According to Nicolas Platon, for instance, the artwork of
the ancient Cretans showed a "delight in beauty, grace and movement," and an
"enjoyment of life and closeness to nature."[70] Whereas later cultures were obsessed
with death and the afterlife, for them "the fear of death was almost obliterated by
the ubiquitous joy of living." While another archaeologist, Sir Leonard Woolley,
wrote that Minoan (or ancient Cretan) art showed "the most complete acceptance
of the grace of life the world has ever known."[71]

There are other important characteristics of these peoples which it's
important to mention briefly, and which also – suggesting, again, that there are
really no fundamental differences between them – generally apply to hunter-
gathering peoples. First of all, these peoples' attitude to nature seems to have been
very different from ours in the modern world. Whereas we're more likely to
experience a sense of separateness from nature and see it as a supply of resources
which we're entitled to exploit and abuse – and are seriously damaging our planet's
life-support systems as a consequence – these peoples seem to have had a strong
attachment to the natural world and a deep reverence for it. This is clear from the

artwork of the Old Europeans, for example, which, as Riane Eisler writes, depicts a "rich array of symbols from nature" which "attest to awe and wonder at the mystery of life."[72] These were practically everywhere in their villages and towns – images of the sun, of water, serpents and butterflies (as well as many goddess images) which were painted or drawn on the outside and inside walls of houses, in shrines, on vases, on bas reliefs, and so on. There are also numerous drawings of "cosmic eggs," and representations of the goddess as part human and part animal, which suggest that the Old Europeans had a sense of the interconnectedness of nature. These peoples obviously didn't have the capability to abuse and damage the environment – because of their small population and low level of technology – but it's clear that their sense of the sacredness of nature would have prevented them from doing this anyway. (This will be clearer in Chapter 4, when we look at contemporary "unfallen" peoples' attitude to nature.)

This attitude to nature was closely connected to both the hunter-gatherers' and simple horticultural peoples' religious life. An important difference between them and later peoples is that to them there was apparently no separation between religion and the rest of their lives, and no sense of the divine as being separate and apart from the world. To them God or Spirit was everywhere and in everything. This was obviously part of the reason why these peoples had such a deep respect for nature: because they saw it as an expression of Spirit. In fact, it's doubtful that the concept of gods – as higher beings who watch over the world and control its events – had any meaning to them whatsoever. It was only after 4000 BCE that people began to conceive of gods and goddesses. (The controversial matter here is whether – as Gimbutas and others believe – the Old Europeans and other Neolithic peoples worshipped a Goddess. However, as I will suggest later, this is really only an assumption with no real evidence behind it.)

There's probably another connection here with the hunter-gatherer and simple horticultural peoples' attitude to sex and their own bodies. Since they revered the natural world, it's not surprising that they had both a positive attitude to the natural processes and instincts of their own bodies, and lacked the sense of division from the body and sexual shame which characterises later peoples. Most hunter-gatherer peoples live their lives either mostly or completely naked, and, as we'll see later, their frank attitude to sex is startling even by present-day European standards. Archaeologists have also discovered a massive number of sexually explicit images and objects from the hunter-gatherer era, including phallic objects made of flint, figurines depicting sexual intercourse and the so-called Venus figurines, which show women in sexually inviting poses.[73]

We find the same explicitness in the art of the simple horticultural peoples of the Neolithic too – we've already mentioned, for example, the figurines showing naked pregnant women with grotesquely large breasts. According to the archaeologist Jaquetta Hawkes, Old European Crete was characterised by a "fearless and natural emphasis on sexual life that ran through all religious expression."[74] Cretan art is full of sexual symbols, and Hawkes believes that every spring there were sex ceremonies to celebrate the earth's fertility. Styles of dress were sexually explicit too. Paintings show women bare-breasted, and wearing what we would today call short "sexy" skirts. Men wore codpieces, and short garments which showed off their thighs and emphasised their penises. In Riane Eisler's view, this open attitude to sex "contributed to the generally peaceful and harmonious spirit predominant in Cretan life."[75]

THE EARTH 6,000 YEARS AGO

It's worth pausing for a moment here, to try to picture what the world was like at the end of the simple horticultural era, just before the Fall.

At 4000 BCE the world's population was still small – probably no more than 100 million. By this time horticulture had spread over large areas of the Middle East, Europe, Asia and North Africa, but had yet to reach western Europe or east Asia. Most of the earth's surface – including the whole of Australia, the Americas and most of Africa – was still inhabited by hunter-gatherer peoples. But as I've tried to show, the differences between the hunter-gatherers and the simple horticulturists were only superficial. They shared the same fundamental characteristics: peacefulness, equality, an absence of male domination, a reverence for nature and sexual openness.

From the evidence we have, it seems that this is how *all* human beings lived until 4000 BCE. In *Saharasia* James DeMeo uses the term "matrism" to refer to cultures which are "democratic, egalitarian, sex-positive and possess very low levels of adult violence." [76] He contrasts this with later "patrist" cultures, which "tend to inflict pain and trauma upon infants and young children subordinate the female possess high levels of adult violence, with various social institutions designed for the expression of pent-up sadistic aggression."[77] And until 4000 BCE *all* human societies, it seems, were "matrist." As DeMeo writes, "There does not exist any clear, compelling or unambiguous evidence for the existence of patrism anywhere on Earth significantly prior to c.4000 BCE." [78]

It sounds like paradise, and in a way – despite high death rates, a lack of medical care and other problems – it was. In fact, as we'll see in Chapter 5, this is exactly how it seemed to later peoples, who remembered this pre-Fall period of history in their mythology, as a Golden Age or an era when "The men of perfect virtue" lived. No human groups invaded other groups' territory and tried to conquer them and steal their possessions. There were no wandering bands of marauders who raided villages, and no pirates who lived by attacking coastal settlements. Everywhere the status of women was equal to that of men and nowhere were there any different classes or castes, with different degrees of status and wealth. Life was certainly hard in some ways, particularly for the converts to a horticultural way of life, but at the same time, a spirit of natural harmony seems to have filled the whole planet, a harmony between human beings and nature and amongst human beings themselves. Human beings may have been oppressed by nature to an extent, but they were free from oppression by other human beings. Human groups didn't oppress other groups, members of the same groups didn't oppress each other, and men didn't oppress women.

But everything was about to change. A seismic shift in history was about to occur.

3

THE FALL

FROM AROUND 4000 BCE onwards a new spirit of suffering and turmoil enters human history. It is now – and only now – that a "horrifying sense of sin" becomes manifest in human affairs. At this point, it seems, a completely new type of human being comes into existence, with a completely different way of relating to the world and to other human beings. In Riane Eisler's words, now comes "the great change – a change so great, indeed, that nothing in all we know of human cultural evolution is comparable in magnitude."[1]

It wasn't completely out of the blue. There had been warning signs over the past 1,000 years or so – occasional outbreaks of social violence around the Middle East and Anatolia (in Turkey), linked to temporary episodes of drought and aridity. Towards the end of the sixth millennium BCE, some sites in Anatolia – incuding Catal Huyuk – were damaged by fighting, leaving the bodies of massacred victims.[2] (Catal Huyuk was finally destroyed at around 4800 BCE.) Semitic peoples from the Zagros mountains invaded Syria and Mesopotamia, causing great devastation. Fortifications began to appear throughout the Middle East, and many sites show what archaeologists call "destruction layers."[3]

However, it was only from around 4000 BCE that social violence became endemic, with constant warfare, large-scale social oppression and male domination. As I've suggested, the root cause of the transformation seems to have been environmental. At around 4000 BCE what James DeMeo has referred to as "one of the most substantial environmental and climatic changes…since the close of the last glacial epoch" began to take place.[4] Synthesising a vast amount of research by other scholars, DeMeo has established that a process of desiccation – or drying out – affected the area of the earth which he calls "Saharasia." As its name suggests, this is the enormous belt of arid land which stretches from North Africa, through the Middle East, and into central Asia. It contains many of the world's deserts – for example, the Sahara in North Africa, the Arabian and Iranian in the Middle East. Between the deserts there are areas which, while not actually deserts, are extremely arid. In this way "Saharasia" makes up a more or less continuous arid zone, stretching all the way from the west coast of Africa to China.

Today Saharasia has very little vegetation, very little rainfall, few rivers or lakes, very little animal life, and is largely unpopulated. But thousands of years ago this wasn't the case. Until around 4000 BCE, it was a fertile semi-forested grassland, full of lakes and rivers and human and animal life. Archaeological excavations have discovered the remains of villages from areas which are now uninhabitable, a massive number of fossils of animals which could only have inhabited this kind of environment, and cave drawings of these animals as well as of vegetation (which are also evidence of human habitation, of course). In addition, DeMeo has shown that there were much higher levels of rainfall before 4000 BCE, and that "some of the now-dry basins of Saharasia were then filled to levels ten to hundreds of meters deep, while the canyons and wadis flowed with permanent streams and rivers."[5]

According to another scholar, Brian Griffith, at 9000 BCE the area of the Sahara desert was "the very portrait of a happy hunting ground. While much of Europe was still encased in ice, ancestors of the Europeans thrived in the green Sahara."[6] The area was like the savannas of Kenya, Griffith suggests, full of grazing antelopes and big cats.

The fertility of Saharasia before 4000 BCE was probably due to the retreat and melting of glaciers after the last ice age, which made sea levels rise. But eventually the glaciers shrunk and melted away, and there was no more moisture. Sea levels fell and, beginning in the Near East and central Asia, the area started to dry up. Rainfall decreased, rivers and lakes evaporated, vegetation disappeared and famine and drought took hold. Farming was impossible, and the lack of water made hunting treacherous. As a result, there was a mass exodus of animals and people from the region.[7]

As we've seen, the peoples who lived in the region while it was still fertile were – like all other peoples on earth before 4000 BCE – peaceful, non-patriarchal, and egalitarian, with a healthy, open attitude to sex and the body. But it seems that this environmental change had a devastating effect on them, both in terms of how it affected their way of life, and – most importantly – how it affected their *psyche*. In DeMeo's terminology, it transformed them from "matrists" into "patrists."

THE NEW NOMADS

THE MOST VISIBLE effect of the drying up of Saharasia, in archaeological terms, is that its inhabitants were forced to leave the area and seek out new homelands. Signs of these migrations appear all over the Middle East, central Asia and central and eastern Europe, as the "Saharasian" peoples moved into the areas inhabited by peaceful "matrist" Neolithic peoples. But what's most striking isn't these movements themselves, but the manner in which they occurred, and what we can tell of the behaviour and apparent character of the people who made them.

One of the migrating peoples was the Indo-Europeans, the human group which most modern Europeans, Americans and Australians are descended from. The homeland of the Indo-Europeans seems to have been the steppes of southern Russia, close to the Black Sea, which is part of the Saharasian region. When the area could no longer support them, the Indo-Europeans headed westwards through Europe and southwards towards the Middle East and Arabia. Later they moved eastwards too, through Iran, Afghanistan and eventually towards India (at around 1800 BCE).

The Indo-Europeans – or Aryans, as they have also been called – have been idealised as the founders of Western culture, and the first "true" Europeans. This was how the Nazis saw them, of course, and archaeologists like V. Gordon Childe have described them as being "fitted with exceptional mental endowments" and as the "promoters of true progress."[8] There are some ways in which this isn't *totally* inaccurate – it's probable that, because of their intensified sense of ego, the Saharasian peoples generally had slightly greater powers of invention and intellect than other peoples before them. But all in all, and particularly during the first phases of their migrations across Europe and the Middle East, the Indo-Europeans brought nothing but destruction. Far from bringing a new or higher culture of their own, they simply destroyed the Old Neolithic cultures which had developed thousands of years before they appeared. During the fourth millennium BCE, south-eastern Europe shows signs of massive disruption. As the archaeologist J.P. Mallory writes, this included

> the abandonment of the tell sites which had flourished for several millennia; the displacement of previous cultures in almost every direction except eastward [the direction which the

Indo-Europeans were migrating from]; movement to marginal locations, such as islands and caves and easily fortified hilltop sites such as Cernavoda 1...[9]

All of this is clearly evidence of a violent invasion, especially since, as Mallory adds, these changes coincide with "the continuous incursions of mobile pastoralists."

There is other archaeological evidence which shows that the Indo-Europeans were a violent and war-like people. They seemed to have lacked the reverence for nature which the Neolithic peoples had. Instead they revered war and violence. Their artwork contains very few natural images, but a massive number of scenes of war, violence and weapons. They apparently worshipped male warrior-gods, who they often depicted with weapons arranged to represent different parts of the body. As Marija Gimbutas writes, "Weapons obviously represented the god's functions and powers, and were worshipped as representations of the god himself. The sacredness of the weapon is well-evidenced in all Indo-European religions."[10]

The Indo-Europeans were also clearly a patriarchal people. Their culture was patrilinear and patrilocal (that is, property passed down through the male side and wives went to live with husbands' families) and their gods were exclusively male. They also seem to have given the world its first ever cases of "ritual widow murder." As Riane Eisler notes:

> For the first time in European graves, we find along with an exceptionally tall or large-boned male skeleton the skeletons of sacrificed women – the wives, concubines or slaves of the men who died. This practice...was apparently introduced by the Indo-European Kurgans into Europe.[11]

There are clear signs of inequality and social oppression too. For the first time ever, human beings have vastly different grave sizes, and are buried with vastly different degrees of wealth. There are large "chieftain graves" filled with luxury goods, suggesting that the Indo-European groups were ruled by "strongman" warrior figures; and much smaller graves with no goods, presumably belonging to the people they ruled over. We also find what seem to be the world's first ever instances of slavery. Archaeologists have discovered that, at some early Indo-

European sites, the female population was mainly made up of Old European women. This suggests that, as they invaded Old European sites, the Indo-Europeans killed the men and children but spared some girls and women, who became their concubines or slaves.[12]

At the same time, a people called the Semites – the ancestors of modern Jews and Arabs – began to leave their homeland in Arabia and to spread out over the Middle East and into North Africa.[13] The Semites were so similar to the Indo-Europeans, with the same war-like and patriarchal character, that some archaeologists have suggested that the two peoples stemmed from a common ancestor,[14] although linguistic and archaeological evidence doesn't support this. However, the reason for these similarities is clear when we consider that the Semites also came from the "Saharasia" region and were therefore subject to the same environmental pressures as the Indo-Europeans, which presumably affected their "psyche" in exactly the same way. They began to attack and conquer the Neolithic peoples of the Middle East and North Africa in exactly the same way that the Indo-Europeans did in Europe (and the Near East, since the Indo-Europeans spread into both areas).

It's likely that other peoples were involved too, such as the ancestors of those who later became the Finno-Ugric peoples, the Turks, the Scythians, the Mongols, the Shang and the Sarmatians. Traces of these peoples only emerge at later stages, but since they spoke non-Indo-European and non-Semitic languages but were all highly "patrist" and from the Saharasian regions, it's likely that they were descended from earlier peoples who were affected by the desertification of the area. They were probably also from central Asia, and although some of them went south and west, like the Indo-Europeans, most of them seem to have migrated eastwards. The Shang, for example, became the earliest invaders of China, arriving there around 2000 BCE.

All over these areas it was the same story. From 4000 BCE (or thereabouts – Marija Gimbutas dates the first invasions of Old Europe at 4300 BCE) the Indo-Europeans swept through Old European culture like a forest fire. As Gimbutas writes, "Millennial traditions were truncated, towns and villages disintegrated, magnificent painted pottery vanished; as did shrines, frescoes, sculptures, symbols and script."[15] From this point on everything is different. There are no more female figurines, no more artistic depictions of natural phenomena, and no more communal graves or whole communities with equal-sized graves. Now war takes precedence over nature in art, and death seems to take precedence over life. Weapons are found everywhere, and settlements are always fortified and walled. Here the historian P. Stern describes the impact of the Indo-Europeans in eastern and central Europe from 3500 BCE onwards:

> they were introducing violence to a part of the world that previously had been relatively peaceful. And along with ruthless invasions, undeclared warfare, and appropriation of women as their rightful spoils, they were developing a society in which masculinity was supreme. An insatiable desire for property and power, together with insensitivity to pain and suffering in themselves as well as in others, characterised everything they did.[16]

The Neolithic peoples of the Middle East met exactly the same fate. The matrist cultures of Mesopotamia (in present-day Iraq) and the Levant (the area of the Middle East which includes present-day Israel, Lebanon and Syria) were invaded and conquered by Semitic and Indo-European peoples. Meanwhile an Indo-European group called the Hittites invaded Anatolia, as a result of which, in DeMeo's words, "Fortress architecture appeared more frequently and female figurines declined in abundance or vanished altogether."[17] At roughly the same time, Semitic peoples invaded North Africa.

With their unfortified settlements and lack of weapons, together with their lack of military experience and non-aggressive character, the old Neolithic peoples were presumably helpless against these Saharasian peoples with their war technology and merciless cruelty. They were, in Gimbutas' words, "easy prey for invaders on horseback with long knives."[18] The same pattern of destruction and conquest occurs everywhere. Now, for the first time ever, war, social stratification and patriarchy became "normal." As Eisler comments, "all over the ancient world populations were now set against populations, as men were set against women and against other men."[19]

According to Gerhard Lenski's scheme of history, 4000 BCE was the point when the first "advanced horticultural" societies developed in the Middle East.[20] These were the first societies to use metals intensively, mainly as material for weapons. As Lenski notes, during this period "battle-axes, daggers and other arms appear in the grave of every adult male."[21] Lenksi sees their use of metal as the defining characteristic of these societies, but since this was mainly an effect of war – which created a massive demand for weapons – it's probably more accurate to see war as their defining characteristic.

Like many sociologists, Lenksi sees these new societies as the result of "social evolution," a natural progression which occurred as the simple horticulturalists gradually accumulated more knowledge and technological skill. But in historical terms this wasn't the case. As we've seen, it wasn't so much a question of a development from one kind of society to another, as of one being *supplanted by* the other, as the Old World peoples were invaded and conquered by the war-like Saharasian peoples.[22]

EGYPT AND SUMER

There were, however, some positive aspects to this new kind of psyche. At the same time as generating a new brutality and selfishness, it gave rise to a new kind of intellectual ability, and a new kind of practicality and inventiveness. Although some "Old World" peoples did reach a high level of technological development, after 4000 BCE the Middle East saw a sudden surge of technological development which quickly outstripped anything which had come before. As V. Gordon Childe wrote, "The thousand years or so immediately preceding 3000 B.C. were perhaps more fertile in inventions and discoveries than any period in human history prior to the sixteenth century AD."[23] These innovations included the wheel (which was quickly applied to carts and pottery), the plough, the use of animals to pull ploughs and wagons, wind-driven sailboats, complex new writing and number systems, and the calendar. As Anne Baring and Jules Cashford summarise in their book *The Myth of the Goddess*, at the beginning of the Bronze Age "a tremendous explosion of knowledge took place as writing, mathematics and astronomy were discovered. It was as if the human mind had suddenly revealed a new dimension of itself." [24]

These innovations came mainly from Egypt and Mesopotamia and led to the development of the famous ancient civilisations in these areas. Whether these were the world's first civilisations or not – as traditional archaeology has always maintained – depends on your definition of civilisation. If, like Marija Gimbutas, you define it as "the ability of a given people to adjust to its environment and to develop adequate arts, technology, script, and social relationships," then, as she suggests, "Old Europe" was clearly a kind of civilisation.[25] Traditional archaeologists, however, tend to think of civilisation only in terms of the kind of civilisations which have existed for the last 5,000 or so years. To be classed as a "civilisation," a culture has to have metal tools, social stratification, a large surplus of goods and wealth, a strong centralised authority, military power, and so on. But what we're really dealing with here are, in my terminology, pre-Fall and post-Fall civilisations. Old Europe and Egypt and Sumer (which was a part of Mesopotamia) were simply different *kinds* of civilisation.

This new kind of civilisation developed during the latter half of the fourth millennium BCE (with Sumer slightly ahead of Egypt). Archaeologists have never been able to conclusively answer the question of who the original Egyptians and Sumerians were. But evidence clearly suggests that the Egyptians who "civilised" the Nile region were immigrants from the desert areas. As Brian Griffith points out, in North Africa recorded history begins against the background of mass migrations out of a growing desert. He notes that "pre-dynastic Egyptians were a jumbled assortment of tribes, many of them recent arrivals from the deserts."[26] The first signs of social upheaval occur in the Nile region at around 3300 BCE when a people who called themselves "followers of Horus" established themselves as a ruling class. According to DeMeo, they "possessed many Semitic characteristics."[27] Their language shows that they weren't actually a Semitic people (or Indo-European either) but at the same time, it's clear that they must have had close contact with them, since they used many words of Semitic origins.

The origins of the Sumerians are vague too. However, since we know that they were migrants who arrived some time during the second half of the fourth millennium BCE,[28] there is a high probability that they were also refugees from desertification. This is suggested by very early Sumerian cylinder seals, which show similarities with the cultures of the Arabian and Syrian deserts.[29] There is a connection to Semitic peoples as well. Whoever the original Sumerians were, Semitic peoples were present as a minority amongst them from early on. As time went by, there was an increasing use of Semitic words, suggesting that the Semites were becoming more dominant, until eventually Sumer was largely a "Semitic" culture.[30] According to DeMeo, archaeological evidence suggests that "Settlements on the Nile and Tigris-Euphrates [the areas where Egyptian and Sumerian civilisation developed respectively], as well in the moister highland portions of the Levant, Anatolia and Iran, were invaded and conquered by peoples abandoning Arabia and/or central Europe."[31]

But in a way it's not necessary to make these connections, since it's clear, when we look at their cultures, that the ancient Egyptians and Sumerians were Saharasian peoples. Although they were only mildly patrist to begin with, their cultures were clearly closer to those of Indo-European or Semitic peoples than to those of Old Europeans and other prehistoric peoples.

We've already seen that social stratification was a feature of Sumerian culture. The Sumerians possessed a recognisably "modern" lust for material goods and wealth, which was completely alien to the non-possessiveness of hunter-gatherer peoples. As Samuel Noah Kramer has stated, "Sumerian culture fostered an obsessive drive for wealth and possession." Documents show an "obsessive concern…with grain-laden fields, vegetable rich gardens, bulging sheepfolds, milk, cream and cheese in profusion."[32] And this lust for possession created social inequalities. Royal graves contained vast amounts of wealth and are always at the centre of cemeteries, while there are large numbers of small and simple graves without any possessions, and these graves are usually found towards the edges.[33] Houseplans dating from the third millennium BCE also show that the size of Sumerian houses varied greatly. Some houses were large well-laid out "mansions," while others were tiny one-room hovels squeezed into gaps between existing buildings. According to the Cambridge archaeologist Joan Oates:

> Perhaps the most striking feature of Mesopotamian [the larger area which Sumer was a part of] social structure at all periods is the apparent lack of other than economic stratification. Society fell basically into two groups, those who owned the means of production, especially property in land, and those dependent on them.[34]

Sumer consisted of a number of cities (around 50 by 2500 BCE), all within 10 to 30 miles of each other in the area between the Tigris and the Euphrates rivers. The early kings of these city-states have had a reputation of being less brutal than those who came later, and this is probably true. Nevertheless, the city-states continually fought against each other, necessitating the construction of enormous city walls and the development of military technologies, such as horse-drawn "war carts." And by the first part of the third millennium BCE, savagery and military lust seem to have taken complete hold. As Joan Oates writes, dismissing the idea that the Akkadians (a Semitic people) who dominated Sumer at this time were not as warlike as later Sumerians:

> a close examination of the available texts reveals pillage and slaughter to be the common accompaniment of their expansionist policies. Nor does the war-scene from the well known "Standard of Ur" depict other than callous disregard for the slain and the cruel treatment of prisoners.[35]

At around 2400 BCE, the whole of Mesopotamia was conquered by the warrior king Sargon (who was also an Akkadian). Sargon was the world's first empire builder; he staged massive military campaigns (chronicles which have been discovered give details of at least 34 "great battles") and managed to expand his empire over vast areas of the Near East. A royal chronicle from that time describes how he achieved this:

> Sargon, king of Agade, the city of Uruk he smote and its wall he destroyed. With the people of Uruk he battled and he routed them. With Lugal-zaggisi, King of Uruk, he battled and he captured him and in fetters he led him through the gate of Emil. Sargon of Agade battled with the man of UR and vanquished him; his city he smote and its wall he destroyed. E-Nimmar he smote and its wall he destroyed, and its entire territory, from Lagash to the sea, he smote. And he washed his weapons in the sea.[36]

Despite all of this, there is some evidence which suggests that the early Sumerians weren't quite as patrist as the people who came after them, perhaps because they absorbed some of the matrist characteristics of the people they conquered. Early Sumer was clearly a male dominated society – originally land was owned by families rather than individuals (which itself suggests a less severe kind of patrism), but only the male members of the family had any authority in dealing with it. Later, individual ownership became normal, and while it was possible for women to own land, it was almost always in the hands of men. Nevertheless, women's status was higher than it became later. The early Sumerians' pantheon of gods included prominent goddesses (perhaps adopted from the matrist peoples who they conquered). Even as late as 2000 BCE there is a document from the city-state of Elam which describes how a married woman refused to make a joint will with her husband and passed her entire property on to her daughter.[37] All of this suggests that, as the historian H.W.F. Saggs writes, "The status of women was certainly much higher in the early Sumerian city-states than it subsequently became." [38]

The original Egyptians also had many female goddesses, and some status for women. Women could own their own homes, artwork pictured them as liberated and uninhibited, and tomb paintings showed them the same size as men (which is a sign of equal status). In fact, the ancient Egyptian word for wife, *nebt-per*, actually meant "ruler of the house."[39] However, from early on there are clear signs of a new tradition of male domination. As DeMeo writes, when the new invaders took control, "the status of women was instantly reduced to servitude and concubinage."[40] Upper class Egyptians often had several wives as well as concubines, and both were sometimes buried with them when they died.

Early Egyptian towns usually didn't have walls, and the state only had a small army, suggesting that there wasn't a great deal of warfare. However, the popular image of early Egyptians as a spiritual and peaceful people doesn't have much basis. The kingdom was founded through military conquest, when over the course of 200 years the "followers of Horus" conquered the peoples of the Nile Delta and Nubia, until finally, in 3100 BCE, the entire area was unified under the control of the first pharaoh, King Menes.[41] Rock art from this time is full of images of violence, and archaeologists have discovered evidence of large-scale burning of people, both of war prisoners and villagers along the Nile.[42]

Although they didn't stage massive campaigns to expand their territory until later, the Egyptians fought amongst themselves, especially during the periods when there wasn't a strong centralised government to bind them together. Different city-states fought for independence from the central state and for dominance over each other, and the situation became so bad that nobles often had their own private armies to protect themselves.[43] At the same time the Egyptians were continually fighting along their borders, to try to ward off the Asiatic peoples, Libyans and other nomadic tribes who constantly attacked them.

As in Sumer, a high level of social stratification seems to have been present in Egypt from the beginning. That there was inequality is obvious from the massive amounts of wealth that some graves contain, and also from studies of human remains, which have shown that after the civilisation began the protein intake of ordinary farmers decreased, suggesting a centralisation of wealth.[44] A small elite of nobles (who were exempt from taxes) owned massive areas of land, which the rest of the population worked on as serfs. Serfs had no rights over the land they worked, and could be called on to do "corvee" (forced labour) for the state at any time. This, it seems, is how the pyramids were built. Peasants would be called away from their land for perhaps several weeks every year to help construct them. And the pyramids themselves, of course, are a grotesque illustration of social stratification, the most extreme example the world has ever known of inequality of grave sizes and burial goods. As DeMeo puts it, "Enormous and magnificent structures were built at tremendous cost to house the corpses of dead kings, while the bodies of the commoners and slaves who built them were interred in communal pits."[45]

THE SECOND MILLENNIUM BCE TO THE PRESENT

Old European civilisation survived on some islands for centuries – millennia in Crete's case – after it had disappeared on the mainland, but even the most inaccessible areas fell to the new patrists eventually. The civilisation of Malta ended abruptly at around 2500 BCE, probably due to a combination of foreign invasion and natural disaster. Cretan civilisation lasted another 1,000 years, until the island came under the control of an Indo-European people called the Achaeans, who spoke Greek. Although the Achaeans took on some of the matrist ways of the islanders, a process of cultural disintegration began, in which, in Riane Eisler's words, "art became less spontaneous and free" and there was "a much greater concern with, an emphasis on, death."[46] The Achaeans ruled Crete for around four hundred years, until, during the twelfth century BCE, the island was attacked by another Indo-European people, the Dorians, who massacred its population and left its civilisation in ruins.

Similarly, Britain's geographical isolation meant that its ancient matrist culture remained undisturbed until around 2500 BCE, when the Beaker People arrived from mainland Europe. Whereas the Neolithic people before them had used communal graves, they buried themselves individually, and had the same grave differences as other Saharasian peoples. And whereas before their arrival there is little sign of war or violence, the Beaker People used their metal-working skills to make massive numbers of weapons, and built many hill forts and ring forts.[47] The same desperate fear of war which had filled mainland Europe spread to Britain. Villages were surrounded by high fences, and people (possibly the old Neolithic peoples trying to defend themselves against their new invaders) started to live on *crannogs* – or platforms – in the middle of lakes, connected to the mainland by wooden bridges which could be cut in times of conflict.

On the main Eurasian landmass, meanwhile, the Saharasian peoples continued migrating east and west. As we noted before, the Shang reached China from the steppes of central Asia (which had also become a near desert by this time) at around 2000 BCE. It's clear that they were a Saharasian people from some Indo-European and Semitic words they appear to have borrowed – for example, their word *khan* (meaning lord or priest) was close to the Semitic word *cohen* (high priest), while their word *bagadur* (meaning epic hero or god) is similar to the Indo-European word for god, *baga*.[48] But, again, this is also clear enough from the new culture they brought to China. The "Golden Age" of peace and sexual equality came to a cataclysmic end. As DeMeo writes:

> Like the militaristic groups who presided over Upper Egypt, Mesopotamia, and central Asia, [the Shang] engaged in a plethora of authoritarian, anti-female, anti-child practices: Divine Kingship, male gods, monumental tombs with massive grave wealth, human sacrifice, a military caste, slavery.[49]

Around 500 years later another people from the deserts of central Asia, the Chou (or Zhou), invaded China. They were even more war-like and socially oppressive than the Shang. With the aid of bronze weapons and chariots, they conquered massive areas in short spaces of time. They established themselves as a warrior nobility, living lives of luxury inside fortress-cities, while the peasants they ruled over lived in squalor outside. Under the Chou, patriarchy intensified even further, with "ritual widow murder" and female infanticide becoming even more common. As DeMeo notes, "Upper class women of the ruling Chou caste were greatly restricted and slaves in every sense of the word."[50] At first lower-class women still had a degree of freedom. They were free to marry who they liked, to divorce, and could dance and sing in public. But as time went by the Chou's anti-female attitudes spread to the general population, until Chinese culture as a whole became heavily patriarchal.

Around the beginning of the second millennium BCE, after conquering most of Europe, the Indo-Europeans started migrating eastwards. By 1800 BCE they had reached Iran (which is still Indo-European – or Aryan – in name), where they established themselves as a ruling class. During the third millennium BCE, the Indus valley region of northern India had been conquered by a people called the Harrapans, who probably stemmed from the deserts of the Middle East. The Harrapans established one of the world's earliest civilisations, using the indigenous Dravidian people of India as slaves. But now, at around 1500 BCE, their civilisation – which was already declining due to increasing desertification – was in turn overrun by invading Indo-European groups. The Indo-Europeans spread farther afield than the Harrapans, forcing the matrilineal and egalitarian Dravidians to the south. The Indo-Europeans brought their "caste system" to India – consisting of warrior-rulers, priests and producers of economic wealth – and the conquered Dravidians became a fourth class of serfs and labourers, the *Shudrus,* or untouchables. This caste system is still intact today, of course, and still features massive inequality.

And at the same as it was spreading farther, patrism was intensifying. In some cases – as we've seen with the Sumerians – Saharasian peoples absorbed some of the matrist characteristics of the Neolithic peoples they conquered. But by 2000 BCE, these lingering traces of matrism had disappeared. In Sumer there are no more instances of matrilineal descent or female inheritance. Goddesses had been a central part of early Sumerian religion, but by this time their status had drastically fallen, and they only appeared as consorts to male gods.[51] Now male "sky gods" reigned supreme. In mythology a new attitude of domination towards both women and nature is symbolised by new "hero myths" which feature individual men slaying serpents and dragons. And in reflection of this, the Sumerians began to develop what Jaquetta Hawkes calls an "ever-growing ferocity...of the punishments to be inflicted on adulterous wives or disobedient children."[52]

Social oppression and inequality seemed to have increased in Sumer after

2000 BCE as well. As late as 2300 BCE, a Sumerian king called Urukagina passed a set of reforms, one of which stated that the food grown on temple lands should be given to the poor, rather than – as had become customary - to the priests. (The reforms actually state that this was the way things were done earlier, suggesting that the practice dates back to pre-Saharasian times.)[53] But just 500 years later, another Mesopotamian king, Hammurabi, created his famous code of 252 laws, which are full of cruelty and brutality, showing a complete lack of empathy for other human beings. They state, for example, that any farmers who damaged their fields could be sold into slavery, and that a man could use his wife or daughter as security for a debt. Riane Eisler summarises the increasing patrism of later Sumer:

> The kinship structures were radically changed to fit a rigidly hierarchic system increasingly based on private property and the centralisation of political power in the hands of military leaders – Women were pushed out of political decision making.[54]

The nature of war changed at this time too. Before wars had been quite short, and fought by ordinary people, usually only after they had collected that year's harvest. But now kings and nobles started to think in terms of empire-building, and established professional armies who could go to war at any time in order to do this. As a result, war became even more frequent and even more savage. As we've already noted, Sargon of Akkadia was the first of these empire-builders, but by the turn of the second millennium BCE, the Middle East was filled with different peoples who fought viciously with one another to increase their territory and wealth, peoples such as the Elamites, the Assyrians, the Hittites, the Mitannians, the Kassites, the Canaanites, the Syrians and many more. At around 1600 BCE warfare also became much more important to the Egyptians. They formed a massive professional army for the first time too, and staged enormous campaigns to conquer new lands.

From this point on – right until the present day, in fact – the Middle East was a chaotic melting pot of warring peoples, who seemed determined to outdo each other's savagery. As Baring and Cashford note, "As the bronze age progressed, the incidence of war and the victims of war increased incalculably, until the time when the barbarism of Assyria extinguished what was left of the civilisation of Mesopotamia."[55] The Assyrians – who flourished between the 1200s and 600 BCE

– were perhaps the most bloodthirsty people the world has ever known. Practically every year for over 600 years, they staged military expeditions to conquer new lands or to extort more money and goods out of peoples they had already conquered. Anybody who failed to pay would be met with the kind of response described by one of the last kings of Assyria, Sennacherib (704-681 BCE), after his conquest of Babylon: "I left not a single one young or old, with their corpses I filled the city's broad streets."[56] Everywhere life was becoming more savage, more insecure, more full of violence and suffering. As the Iron Age began, at around 1250 BCE, the atmosphere over the Middle East was, in Baring and Cashford's words, "one of acute anxiety and fear of disaster" which "created a compulsion to aggression."[57]

In Europe the situation was similar, if not quite as intense. During the thirteenth century BCE, mysterious peoples who the Egyptians referred to as the Sea Peoples began to wreak havoc throughout the Mediterranean. They were bands of savage marauders who, in the space of just one century, caused more destruction than any other people before them, and ushered in an era of chaos and decline which lasted for around 300 years. During this one century, both the Egyptian and the Hittite Empires collapsed, the Mycenaean (Old Greek) civilisation was destroyed (including the city of Troy), and everywhere cities were destroyed and abandoned. Although natural disasters may have played a part, historians believe that the Sea Peoples were mainly responsible for all this devastation.

In central and western Europe, meanwhile, the Indo-Europeans fought against each other – the Greeks against the Romans, the Celts against the Greeks and Romans, the Germanic peoples against the Celts and Greeks and Romans, and so on. Saharasia was continuing to dry up, and new waves of Indo-European invaders (and other Saharasian peoples) kept migrating west to Europe, killing and conquering and causing massive upheaval. These invasions peaked between 300 to 600 CE, when what historians call the *Volkerwandergung* occurred. This was possibly the biggest exodus of people out of the Saharasian region in all history. Hundreds of different tribes – including the Goths, Franks, Vandals, Huns and Avars – fled from central Asia and descended on Europe, devouring the Roman Empire and forcing earlier Indo-European groups westwards.[58] It was this massive upheaval which created Europe as we know it today. Once the movement had settled, the contemporary ethnographic map of the continent was more or less in place. Save for the Finno-Ugric speaking peoples of Finland, Hungary and Estonia, Europe was now wholly "Aryan," consisting mainly of Germanic, Slavic, Latin and Celtic peoples.

Once the three great Saharasian religions of Judaism, Christianity and Islam had begun to co-exist – with Islam the last to come, midway through the first millennium CE – the potential for conflict increased even further. These religions codified the negative attitudes to sex, the body, women and the natural world which were part of the Saharasian peoples' psyche, and created a new kind of enmity and otherness: between believers and unbelievers, or the faithful and the infidels. In the Middle East the Semitic peoples had sub-divided into Jewish and Arabic tribes, and once the Arabs began to adopt Islam, the enmity between them grew so great that a conflict began which is just as savage today – and as apparently insoluble – as it ever was. The Muslims fought against the Christians too, and the Christians oppressed and killed the Jews. And once the Christians had had some time to sub-divide into different groups, they too started to fight against each other.

A similar pattern occurred in China. After controlling the country for several hundred years, the Chou's authority started to collapse in the eighth century BCE. China split into separate states, which waged war with one another. At first there were dozens of these but as they fought, certain states became more powerful and conquered and absorbed smaller ones, until finally – after 300 years – seven major kingdoms emerged. And then, of course, the kingdoms started fighting against each other, which they did for the next for the next 250 years. Finally, at 220 BCE, a people called the Ch'in established control over the whole country. But after only 15 years of their rule, civil war broke out again, and they were overthrown by a people called the Han.

And all of this savage fighting was, of course, accompanied by equally brutal treatment of women and of different social groups. The same psychological conditions which made human beings unable to live in peace with one another gave rise to a hysterically negative attitude to women and to sex. The ancient Hebrews forbade girls and boys from playing together, treated masturbation as a heinous crime warranting the death penalty, and saw it as a crime for a man to speak to or even look at a women who was on her own.[59] The Assyrians were as brutal to women as they were to their enemies. Assyrian women who stole from their husbands could be executed; if a woman gave shelter to a runaway wife both women would have their ears chopped off and if a woman went out without wearing her veil she would be flogged with staves.[60] Throughout the Middle East, India and China, women – particularly upper class women – lived in *purdah*, in seclusion in their own quarters, unable to talk to any men outside their family and unable to leave the house except with a male escort.

In Europe it took longer for this level of anti-female hysteria to develop – probably because it was farther away from the Saharasian "heartland" and so the influence of Neolithic matrism endured longer there. In fact, in a few places, where the influence of Old European culture was strongest, women continued to have a reasonably high status for centuries after the Indo-European invasions. In the Basque region of Spain, Celtic Ireland and northern Scotland, for example, women were free to marry and divorce and make friends as they chose, and often when a couple married they went to live with the bride's family.[61] But in "civilised" Europe women's status was almost as low as in the Middle East. In ancient Greece – where the idea of democracy supposedly originated – women couldn't own property, had no political rights, and were forbidden to leave their homes after dark. In ancient Rome women were excluded from social events (except as employed "escort girls") and when children were born the father was entitled to have the baby killed if it was a girl.[62]

With the spread of Christianity a stronger anti-female attitude took hold all over Europe. Men (particularly clergymen) began to see women as evil temptresses with a naturally sinful nature, who were easily influenced by – and often working for – Satan. This led to the catastrophic witch-craze of the Middle Ages, when, according to some estimates, during the years 1485 to 1784 at least 9 million innocent women were murdered as "witches," mostly at the behest of celibate clergymen. Bishops saw the rooting out of "dangerous" women – which often just meant women who were more intelligent, independent, wealthy or beautiful than normal – as a God-given duty, and boasted of the number they killed. The Spanish inquisitor Torquemada, for example, boasted of having over 100,000 people executed (nearly all of them women). The historian Gordon Rattray Taylor notes that the murder of women – together with other religious persecutions by the Spanish Inquisition – was responsible for reducing the population of Spain from 20 million to 6 million in two centuries.[63]

This is the history of the human race – century after century of violence, oppression and misery. We normally think of history as a forward movement, a process of gradual improvement and development. And there's no doubt that in some ways – particularly in terms of technology, medicine and science – the human race has progressed massively. But when we compare the period of history we've looked at in this chapter with the one we looked at in the last, it's clear that the main event in human history is a sudden, massive *regression* – a dramatic shift from harmony to chaos, from peace to war, from life-affirmation to gloom, or from sanity to madness.

But this isn't the whole story. There were large areas of the world to which this social insanity *didn't* spread, and which remained largely free from patriarchy, war and social oppression until relatively recent times. It's these "unfallen" cultures which we're going to examine in the next chapter.

4

UNFALLEN PEOPLES

BY 300 BCE patrism had completely covered the Eurasian landmass. It reached Ireland – the most westerly point of the landmass – in 1200 BCE, when the Beaker People crossed over from England. And in 300 BCE it finally reached the equivalent point in the east, when the Yayoi people migrated to Japan from Korea, and conquered the matrist cultures of the Jomon and the Ainu.

At this point, the spread of patrism was complete, at least for the time being. There were still some large pockets of old Neolithic peoples scattered across Europe and Asia, such as the Etruscans and the Basque people in Europe and the Dravidians in India. But most of them had been affected by their contact with Saharasian peoples, and had fallen away from matrism to some degree. It was only in a few inaccessible and inhospitable areas that pre-Saharaisan peoples lived on in their original state – the Lapplanders of northern Scandinavia, the tribal peoples of Siberia and Mongolia, or the tribal peoples of the forests of India, for instance.

Outside the Eurasian landmass, however, it was a different story. In fact, it's actually questionable to say that "fallen" Saharasian people dominated the world at this time. Until around 1600 CE, roughly half of the earth's surface was still occupied by "unfallen" peoples – that is, peoples who didn't originate from Saharasia and hadn't been negatively influenced by contact with peoples from the region. This was certainly true of Australia, and of most of North and South America. This was also the case with many smaller island areas, such as the Pacific islands of Micronesia and Polynesia. And also of Africa to a large extent – although its case is quite complex, since it was subject to patrist influences from quite an early stage.

The differences between the world's native peoples and modern-day Saharasian peoples (that is, peoples like Europeans, Americans, Chinese and others who are descended from the groups which left the Saharasian regions thousands of years ago) is one of the main themes of this book. We're going to be continually referring to these, and so I don't want to examine them in exhaustive detail at this point. But it's clear, even from the most cursory analysis that – apart from some special cases – the cultures of native peoples did retain the same basic "unfallen" psyche as the Paleolithic and Neolithic peoples of Europe, the Middle East and Asia, and that as a result they were largely free of war, inequality, hostility to sex and the body, and other patrist characteristics.

There were some exceptions to this, of course, which are mainly the result of two different factors. On the one hand, there are groups of primal peoples who apparently became patrist because of environmental factors, like the Saharasian people themselves. This seems to be what happened in the Middle East at around 12000 BCE and in south-eastern Australia between 11000 and 7000 BCE. In both cases, warfare and other kinds of social violence coincided with a period of intense aridity.[1] The second case is much easier to identify, and is of primal peoples who transformed – usually quite drastically – in relatively recent times, as a result of their encounters with European colonists.

THE ABORIGINES

We've already seen that the Australian Aborigines were extremely peaceful and that even the small amount of conflict which did exist was highly ritualised and involved little bloodshed. And the Aborigines were also highly egalitarian. According to the anthropologist Robert Lawlor, theirs is "an open society in which people actively share everything with each other."[2] Bands and tribes don't have chiefs or leaders, and there are no laws or penalties for crimes. The elders make most important decisions, and therefore have some authority, but the rest of the tribe are free to disagree with them. As Lawlor writes, "Beyond the kinship convention, no other law enforcement is required in Aboriginal society…Tribal elders receive great respect, but they do not have an authoritarian or judicial role."[3] In the absence of a legal system, when conflicts between individuals or groups do occur they are usually settled at an open forum, where the disputing parties sit together and air their grievances. These meetings are repeated until a solution is mutually agreed.

At first sight aboriginal societies might seem to show some signs of patriarchy. Men can have more than one wife – although in practice most have only one – and after marriage a wife usually leaves her own clan to go and live with her husband's. But this apparent patriarchy is only superficial. Polygamy as the Aborigines practise it is completely different from the polygamy of Islamic cultures, for instance. To a large extent, it's only the result of economic and social convenience, since the Aboriginal custom of men marrying at a fairly late age means that there are always more unmarried women than men around. Women usually get married shortly after puberty, but men wait until their mid-20s, sometimes even until the age of 40. Women are thought of as being somehow "complete" as they are, with a naturally mature understanding of life, and so are considered ready for marriage straight away. On the other hand, men have to "complete" themselves, gaining their understanding of life through a long process of initiation, and are only allowed to marry once they have done this. As a result – because some men inevitably die before they reach marrying age – there is always a higher potential wife to husband ratio, and men sometimes marry more than one woman to balance this.

In addition, these marriages involve none of the sexual domination and possessiveness which characterises Saharasian cultures (especially ones which allow polygamy). The Aborigines have a startlingly free and easy attitude to sexual relations, and in practice women are actually polygamous too, since it's normal for them to have affairs. Young wives often have "sweethearts" of their own age, while older women often offer their own kind of initiation, by giving young men their first sexual experiences.[4]

Women have their own initiation rites too. These aren't as long or complex as men's, but again, they don't need to be, since women are thought of as already possessing the spiritual knowledge which men are trying to gain. As Lawlor writes:

> Women in aboriginal societies seem to have an unspoken understanding that in the nature of things, the masculine psyche is secondary to, or removed from, the ground of organic creation. They accept that the fragile male ego requires constant external reinforcement, and they instigate and support male ceremonies that shape the male psyche so that it may function positively in nature and society.[5]

Some of the apparent patriarchal tendencies of Aboriginal society are also the result of colonial influence. Until recently the role of women was underestimated – and even ignored – because of the Aborigine tradition of keeping men and women's business separate. Early anthropologists (all men themselves, of course) talked mostly to men, and any women they did speak to were reluctant to divulge their secrets. This led the anthropologists to assume that women didn't possess any significant knowledge. In actual fact, "women's business" – their knowledge of sacred sites and ceremonies – was just as important as men's. However, this created an erroneous view of men as the religious leaders and "spokespeople" of tribes, and eventually gave rise to what the anthropologist Lesley Mearns calls "a practice by which men are charged with the responsibility for speaking publicly to non-Aboriginal Australians on matters of religious concern."[6]

NATIVE AMERICANS – THE ANOMALIES

The idea that the various tribes of Native Americans were generally matrist and peaceful might seem absurd. What about all those savage Indian warriors riding into battle with their war bonnets and battle cries and tomahawks, you might ask, intent on scalping their enemies? But it's important to remember that this image of Native Americans is only of one particular Indian culture: the Plains Indians of the eighteenth and nineteenth centuries, who included tribes like the Sioux, the Cheyenne and the Pawnee. They were most visible because they occupied the main heartland of America – which the Europeans were desperate to inhabit – and because of the massive resistance they offered to European domination. The Plains Indians certainly were violent: as well as fighting against the Europeans, the different tribes constantly fought against each other, so that for 100 years the Plains area was, as the anthropologist Elman R. Service writes, "one of the arenas of the most intense tribal conflict ever known."[7] At the same time, they had a high level of social stratification, with warriors acquiring different degrees of status according to how successful they were.

However, it's a big mistake to see the Plains Indians as typical of the Native Americans as a whole. Apart from being just one out of many different cultures, their culture was an artificial development which only came about as a result of European influence. As Service writes, "the famous Plains culture was not fully aboriginal, nor did it last long."[8] It only occurred after the Europeans had destroyed most other Indian cultures in both North and South America, and was mainly the result of cultural disruption and group migrations. Guns and horses were an important part of the culture, both of which came from the Europeans. In fact, it was because of these that the tribes couldn't stop fighting against each other, since the number of guns and horses they each had kept fluctuating so that they could never establish a balance of power. And even though they were intense, their tribal conflicts were still quite tame by European standards. The kind of extended battles with massive casualties which are common to European warfare were extremely rare. Tribes would usually only make short raids on each other, to try to steal horses or to take scalps. Often these didn't cause any fatalities at all, and if they did, it was usually only a small number.[9]

The three most famous civilisations of South America – the Incas, the Maya and the Aztecs – are all strikingly similar to the patrist cultures of Europe, the Middle East and Asia. This is true of the high level of technological development they reached, for instance. The Mayan civilisation covered parts of present-day Mexico, Honduras and Guatemala, and was the first to develop, becoming established during the early centuries of the first millennium CE. And in many ways it was the most advanced of the three. The Maya developed complex hieroglyphic writing, a high degree of mathematical and astronomical knowledge, and a calendar which was more accurate than the Gregorian calendar which most of the world uses today. They were the first people to use a zero, their artists and masons produced works as fine as those of any other ancient civilisation apart from perhaps Greece, they wore clothes woven from cotton and had elaborate jewellery. Meanwhile, the Incas – whose civilisation began to flourish around a thousand years later – built paved roads and suspension bridges, and hewed giant stone blocks, from which they made massive temples, fortresses and palaces. Like the Egyptians, they built large pyramids and elaborate tombs.

These peoples also showed the same facility for organisation and administration as the Saharasian peoples. The Aztec city of Tenochtitlan (which became present-day Mexico City), for instance, was divided into 20 different "boroughs," each with its own priests, schools, temples and elected officials. Each "borough" had three main officials, and all 60 together formed a council of state.

This council elected four of its members as chief officers of the city, each officer representing a different quarter of the city. The officers gave advice to the king, or "chief of men," as the Aztecs called him. The Aztecs – who were contemporaries of the Inca – even had a well-developed education system too. Schools taught children farming, warfare, history and religion, and special schools prepared both boys and girls for the priesthood. Similarly, the Incas divided their massive empire into four areas, which were in turn divided into provinces, which each had their own capital and were split into two or three "boroughs."

But as with the Saharasian peoples, this inventiveness and practicality was balanced by a dark side. The same psyche which produced it also gave rise to a high level of warfare, social stratification and (to a lesser extent) patriarchy. These peoples had the same lust for power and wealth as the "Old World" patrist peoples, and – consequently – the same empire-building instincts. The Aztec Empire included over 5 million conquered people, while the Inca Empire included over 7 million, and covered an area of 2,000 miles from north to south. Although the earlier Mayan peoples don't appear to have been particularly war-like, by 900 CE – in a manner which is strikingly reminiscent of Chinese history following the collapse of the Chou dynasty – they had divided into a number of small kingdoms, centred in walled fortress towns, which continually fought against one another.

The culture of the Aztecs, meanwhile, featured such a high level of savagery and cruelty that even the Spanish soldiers who conquered them (not exactly angels themselves) were shocked by some of their practices. Like the Plains Indians, the Aztecs rarely fought long pitched battles, and their fights rarely involved a large number of casualties. For them the main purpose of warfare was to collect the massive number of victims they needed for their sacrificial rituals. There were numerous religious festivals through the Aztec year of 260 days, each dedicated to one of their gods, and at most of them thousands of human beings would be sacrificed at the same time, to feed the gods' massive appetite for energy and strength. On one occasion, for example, Aztec soldiers captured 20,000 members of one of their subject peoples, the Huaxtecs, and brought them back to Tenochtitlan. There they were all forced to walk up the steps of one of the Aztec pyramids to a temple at the top, where they had their hearts cut out and their heads impaled. At one of the four main religious festivals of the year, named the Feast of the Flaying of Men, individual victims were tied up and made to fight against four expert warriors on stone platforms. The warriors showed their prowess by using delicate blades to tear off the victim's skin in strips, until he collapsed in agony. Then his heart would be torn out, and the strips of skin would be worn by the soldier who had originally captured him or by priests.

A high level of warfare generally goes with a high level of social stratification, and these civilisations were no exception. As well as being ruled by massively wealthy and powerful kings, they each had classes of privileged nobles and priests, and also – at the bottom of the hierarchy – large classes of landless labourers and slaves. As Alvin M. Josephy writes of the Incas, for instance, "The noble class...lived in pomp and splendour. Their homes and personal possessions were incredibly luxurious, and food, services and a wealth of goods were supplied to them by artisans and commoners."[10] These cultures don't seem to have been as oppressive to women as most Saharasian cultures, and there are even some signs of female equality – Aztec women could become priestesses, for example. On the other hand, there are some clear signs of male domination, particularly with the Incas. Inca noblemen could have several wives, as well as concubines, who would be strangled and buried with them when they died.

But why did these peoples become so similar to the Saharasian peoples of Europe and Asia? One possibility is that they belong to the first case I mentioned above, and environmental factors were responsible. The region where Inca civilisation developed, for example, is a coastal desert called the Atacama, with almost no vegetation or animal life. Temperatures are low – only 10C during the day and much colder at night – and the altitude is high. As Service writes of the area, "Such an environment would seem to present insuperable handicaps for the development of a civilisation."[11] However, it may be that the Inca civilisation developed *because of* these handicaps, in the same way that, indirectly, the civilisations of Egypt and Mesopotamia (and the later civilisations of China, India, Europe and so on) developed as a result of the desertification of Saharasia. As DeMeo notes, geographical evidence shows that the Atacama region was wetter and more fertile at earlier times. A process of desiccation did occur, and caused a great deal of population movement.[12] It's possible, therefore, that this environmental change had the same effect as the desiccation of Saharasia, transforming the psyche of the area's inhabitants and bringing about a switch from a matrist to a patrist way of life (and at the same time giving them new powers of practicality and inventiveness).

The patrism of the Maya – and their descendants the Aztecs – might seem more difficult to explain, since the area where their civilisation developed was largely a rain forest. However, as DeMeo notes, the archaeological record shows that "many Mesoamerican groups, particularly the Aztecs, were originally migratory within a desert environment at least once in their history."[13] It's possible, therefore, that the people who became the Maya and later the Aztecs – originally known as the Olmecs – were refugees from a desert area.

This is the explanation I prefer, but another possibility is that these "spots" of patrism were the result of the migrations of Saharasian peoples into America in the pre-Columbian era. This is the approach which James DeMeo favours. He notes that there were three main patrist areas of the Americas: Caribbean Mesoamerica (that is, where the Aztecs and Maya lived), Peru (where the Incas lived) and also the north-west Pacific (or the north-west coast of Canada, including present-day British Columbia). He speculates that Saharasian peoples may have arrived in the north-west Pacific first – possibly from Japan or China – and migrated southwards, displacing matrist cultures and painting further spots of patrism over the general background of matrism, until they reached middle America and then Peru. Evidence for this includes cultural similarities between Indians of the Pacific north-west and dynastic Chinese culture (such as artwork, clothing, drums and diet) and linguistic similarities. At the same time, there are cultural and linguistic similarities between the three patrist areas of the Americas, suggesting that the peoples are related.[14]

This theory is controversial, but it has gained some support from the Chinese archaeologist H.M. Xu. In his book *The Origin of the Olmec Civilisation* Xu suggests that, rather than being refugees from a desert area, the Olmecs were migrants from China. The Olmec culture flourished in Mexico from around 1200 to 400 BCE and is usually seen as the "mother culture" of all the middle American civilisations. The Olmecs built the first temples and religious centres in the region, and developed a rudimentary kind of state, in which an elite group ruled over a mass of peasant labourers. Xu argues that the Olmecs sailed to Mexico from China after the fall of the Shang Dynasty in 1122 BCE. He notes that around this time about 250,000 people disappeared, and suggests that at least some of these travelled to America. This explains the presence of what appear to be Chinese symbols in Olmec written records, and strong similarities in art, architecture, religion and astronomical knowledge.[15]

There are also some peoples of the Amazon rainforest who have strong patrist characteristics. As Service writes of the Jivaro of Peru, for instance, "They have long been considered one of the most bellicose peoples in South America. The normal form of warfare is a never-ending cycle of blood-revenge feuds between unrelated groups of Jivaro."[16] The Jivaro have the same obsession with status as the Plains Indians. Every man's greatest ambition is to be respected as a warrior, and his status increases with the head of every enemy which he brings back from battle. Another people, the Caribs (of Trinidad and Venezuela), were almost as cruel and violent as the Aztecs. They were cannibals who prepared for raids by eating preserved human flesh and drinking blood. When they took captives some were cut up and eaten at once, while others were taken home to be roasted and boiled. Their raids were partly motivated by the desire to increase prestige too, and they were also harshly patriarchal. Carib men often had several wives, who, as Josephy writes, "generally occupied a slave-like status."[17] The Yanomamo of southern Venezulua and northern Brazil are another patrist people. Their villages wage almost constant war against each other and polygamy is common for men, especially for successful warriors, who are "rewarded" with multiple wives.[18]

This patrism could be the result of cultural disruption from contact with Europeans or other patrist peoples. The Jivaro were constantly under attack for centuries, first by the Incas and then the Spanish, and probably became more aggressive as a result. Similarly, as Ferguson points out, the Yanomamo have been dealing with European intrusion since the 1700s, and their wars have been closely linked to this European presence. Even in recent times their wars have been mostly fought over access to goods, such as steel tools, left by Westerners.[19] On the other hand, archaeologists have now established that many Amazonian peoples are descended from settled peoples who reached a high level of technology, and who may have been related to the Incas or even Mesoamerican peoples. The remains of many large settlements have been found in the central Amazon, together with pottery shards, remains of artwork, and massive amounts of extremely fertile man-made soil, called *terra preta*. Archaeologists now believe that a civilisation existed there for 1,000 years, and was still flourishing during the sixteenth century when the Spanish arrived. In fact, it's likely that the conquistador Francisco de Orellana's legendary description of El Dorado is a genuine description of the Amazonian towns he saw. But like other Americans, the Amazonians had no resistance to European diseases. Smallpox, flu and measles decimated them and brought their civilisation to ruins in a matter of decades. However, it seems that the descendants of their population are today living as hunter-gathering tribes, and have retained some of their patrist characteristics.[20]

Before we leave these areas of patrism, it's important to note that in general – despite some incredibly barbaric practices – none of these peoples ever reached quite as high a level of patrism as the peoples of the Saharasian heartland of the Middle East and central Asia. Despite their constant conflict and their concern with status, the Plains Indians were still largely matrilocal and matrilinear. As we've noted, the Aztecs were non-patriarchal enough to allow women to become priests, and their political organisation was democratic to some degree, even though the "chief of men" had ultimate authority. And even the Incas, with their heavily stratified society and inequalities of wealth, had a well-developed welfare system, the like of which wouldn't be seen in Europe or colonial America until the twentieth century. In every Inca province there were a large number of public storehouses, full of food and other goods – mainly clothes – which were shared out amongst the poor, widows and the old and disabled.[21]

Another major difference between fallen and unfallen peoples – which we'll look at in detail later on – is their concept of religion. Whereas "fallen" religion is based around the worship of anthropomorphic gods who overlook and control the world, "unfallen" religion is based around an awareness of a spirit-force, which pervades the world and everything in it, and also a sense that the world is filled with a massive number of individual spirits, usually associated with natural phenomena. And the less extreme patrism of these American peoples is also clear from their religious practices. The religion of the Plains Indians, for example, was basically "unfallen." They believed that there was a Great Spirit, or Life Master, which pervaded all things, and that natural phenomena were controlled by spirits (rather than by otherworldly gods). The religion of the Inca is typically "fallen" in that they believed in an all powerful creator God, *Viracocha*, and other lesser gods, who they prayed to and made offerings to. But at the same time, their religion was "hylotheistic" – that is, they believed that god was present in all things. In Ronald Wright's words, to the Inca, "The world was alive with numinous rocks, springs and peaks, known collectively as *wak'a*. These were regarded as shrines to the creator."[22]

NATIVE AMERICANS – THE GENERAL PATTERN

I've given a disproportionate amount of space to these special cases, but it's important to remember that they were only isolated instances of patrism amongst a general pattern of matrism. As DeMeo puts it, "each of these regions acted as a locus of relative militant patrism amid a background of generally peaceful matristic culture."[23] The great majority of the Indian tribes were originally peaceful, democratic and non-patriarchal. Certain peoples such as the Californian Indians and the Pueblos of New Mexico (a large group of different tribes speaking many different languages) were, as Alvin M. Josephy puts it, "among the most peaceful on earth."[24] There is no archaeological evidence of any warfare in the Californian region in all of the thousands of years that Native Americans lived there, even though many different groups migrated into the area. Some Native American groups live in extremely inhospitable environments, and yet are peaceful and egalitarian. The Eskimo peoples of the Arctic regions have a very low incidence of warfare, for example – as we noted earlier, they are more likely to ritualise conflicts, as with their famous singing contests. Similarly, the Yahgan Indians of the barren islands of Tierra del Fuego have, as Service writes, "no organised warfare of any kind."[25] Outside the few spots of patrism, Indian villages are never fortified or built in inaccessible areas. As the anthropologist A.E. Hoebel wrote of North American Indians in general, "They release aggressions harmlessly: they provide exercise, sport and amusement without destruction; and only mildly is there any imposition of desires by one party on the other."[26]

Again, I'm not trying to say that these peoples were completely peaceful. Conflicts with neighbouring tribes certainly occurred from time to time and led to skirmishes and raids. But these were nothing like the constant conflicts of the Plains Indians, and probably involved even less bloodshed and hardly any casualties. In fact, it's doubtful whether the kind of conflicts which the Indians had with each other qualify for the term warfare. Even if we do use the term, we should at least accept that Indian "warfare" was of a completely different type to that practised by the Saharasian peoples (and peoples like the Incas and Aztecs). The whole concept of two sets of soldiers standing opposite each other and attacking and firing weapons until one side suffered so many casualties that they were forced to surrender was completely absent from Indian conflicts. The idea of war as a means of conquering and subjugating other peoples didn't figure either. There were no long battles, no sieges, no wars of conquest and no high casualty figures. Even when it was frequent (as with the Plains Indians) Indian "warfare" was on a much lower level, and almost never went beyond short raids.[27]

Whether they lived as hunter-gatherers or had a settled lifestyle, the great majority of Native American societies were also strikingly egalitarian. Inequality stems from the desire of individuals to possess wealth and power or status. There's a constant battle for these – manifesting itself in the competitiveness which is so common in capitalist Saharasian societies – and some people end up possessing more than others. But Native Americans don't seem to have this desire for wealth and power. Land and property are usually communally held and used. The community takes complete precedence over the individual, and charity and sharing are paramount. There are also no strongmen authoritarian rulers who impose their desires on the rest of the population against their will. Instead, there's an even distribution of power, with all individuals participating in decision-making. As Josephy writes of the Hopi Indians, for example, "In none of the towns were there social classes or differences in wealth; everyone, even members of the theocracies, worked and shared as equals."[28] Or, as one British officer wrote disapprovingly of the Cherokee Indians in the eighteenth century, "There is no law nor subjection amongst them...The very lowest of them thinks himself as great and as high as any of the rest...Every one is his own master."[29]

As with other egalitarian societies, generosity was a moral imperative, and any expression of greed or selfishness was seen as a crime. Indian chiefs were often expected to work as "social security" organisers, and to provide for the sick and needy from their own resources, or else to arrange contributions from others.[30] Because of this, chiefs were usually no more wealthy than anybody else – and even expected to be poorer. The Assiniboin Indians, for example, judged how able their chiefs were by their generosity, and any who displayed meanness were likely to be deposed.[31]

In many cases, egalitarianism was well developed as an *ideology* too. Many Native American societies were extremely conscious of what we would call the "rights of the individual." As Colin Taylor writes, one of the central principles of the Iroquois and the Algonquian Indians "emphasised and defined the rights of the individual such that all actions of individuals were based on their own decisions and all group actions on the consensus of the participants."[32] Or, as Jean Briggs wrote of the Utku, an Eskimo group:

The Utku, like other Eskimo bands, have no formal leaders whose authority transcends that of the separate householders. Moreover, cherishing independence of thought and action as a natural prerogative, people tend to look askance at anyone who seems to aspire to tell them what to do.[33]

Many people believe that the concept of democracy comes from ancient Greece. But aside from the fact that the Greeks had a very "special" idea of democracy – including slavery and the brutal oppression of women – there's a much stronger case for the view that Western democracy comes from the Native Americans. The American constitution's concept of a non-hierarchical society in which everybody had equal rights – which was, after all, completely alien to Europe at that time – was to a large extent inspired by Native American societies. The founding fathers of America – in particular Thomas Jefferson and Benjamin Franklin – admitted in their memoirs that they were influenced by the Iroquois model of democratic government, with its system of checks and balances and elected representatives. [34] The idea of a union of different states was adopted from the Native Nations League of the Iroquois – in fact, the idea was actually recommended to the Europeans by a leader of the Six Nations at a treaty signing in 1744, at which Benjamin Franklin was present.[35] The League had its own carefully worked out constitution and laws, which leaders learned by heart and passed on orally from generation to generation, and the founding fathers borrowed liberally from all of them. (Although, as M.A. Jaimes Guerrero points out, the one important part they left out was the authority and leadership of the clan mothers.[36] In fact, the original American idea of democracy was quite a "special" one too. Equality and freedom for "all men" was only limited to white, male landowners – women, African American slaves, Native Americans and landless white men were excluded).

In this way, it's possible to say that the Native Americans were partly responsible for the French revolution too, since the French revolutionaries were inspired by American democratic ideas (and, of course, Jean-Jacques Rousseau's *The Social Contract* – which massively influenced the French revolutionaries – was itself influenced by reports that Rousseau read of the natives of America and the South Pacific).[37] And it's ironic that, as well as being the originators of modern capitalist democracy, the Iroquois were also partly responsible for the creation of

Communist states. In 1851, Lewis Henry Morgan's book *League of the Iroquois* was published. Both Karl Marx and Friedrich Engels read the book, and were also inspired by what they saw as an example of a Utopian socialist society. As Engels wrote to Marx, "This gentle constitution is wonderful! There can be no poor and needy...All are free and equal - including the women."[38]

The great majority of Native American societies were clearly non-patriarchal too. Matrilinear and matrilocal societies were common, and women often had a large degree of authority. In fact, in many cases they had more control over political matters than men. Women often had the job of nominating new chiefs, and when agreements were made between Native Americans and Europeans documents often had to be signed by women, since the marks of men didn't carry any authority. Women were not seen as inferior to men, and as a result were not dominated or abused. As Service writes of the Yahgan of Tierra del Fuego, for example:

> Women enjoy particularly high status...In theory the husband is in command, but witnesses record many cases of husbands being contradicted by their wives. In their wider social relationships, women are not expected to keep quiet or to be more demure than men.[39]

The Copper Eskimos of northern Canada accept the equal status of women to such an extent that men's and women's roles are interchangeable, so that men sometimes do women's work and vice-versa.[40] And in contrast to many male-dominated Saharasian societies – where men were often entitled to throw out their wives and leave them to starve if they so desired, while women had no divorce rights at all – Native American women were usually free to end their marriages at any time. A woman of the Pueblo culture, for example, could divorce her husband simply by placing his possessions outside her door, at which point he would return to his mother's house.

THE AFRICANS

In the case of Africa, it's important to make a distinction between North Africa and Africa south of the Sahara desert. North Africa has been a strongly patrist area throughout recorded history. As we've seen, Saharasian peoples – including the founders of Egyptian civilisation – migrated there when Arabia began to dry up at around 4000 BCE. At that time North Africa was still fertile, but at around 3000 BCE it started to dry up too, and the Sahara desert formed. New peoples continued to arrive, though. At around 800 BCE one of the most savage peoples of the ancient world, the Phoenicians – a Semitic people from Syria and Palestine – began to dominate the area. After this the Assyrians, the Persians, the Greeks, and then the Romans in turn took control. When the Roman Empire began to fade the region fell under Christian influence, until Muslim armies invaded during the seventh century CE, and established the Islamic cultures which still flourish today.

But south of the Sahara it was a different story. The desert acted as a barrier, halting the movement of the Saharasian peoples, so that the peoples of central and southern Africa were never conquered in the same way that the indigenous North Africans were. The situation is complex, though, because even though Saharasian peoples didn't overrun the continent, they did have a great deal of contact with its people at various times, and did influence their cultural development. In sub-Saharan Africa we see the same basic background of matrism that we see in Australia and the Americas – only in Africa's case the spots of patrism are spread a little thicker, and there are fewer areas of pure matrism, since in many cases it was diluted by the influence of patrist peoples. However, despite this there's still an orientation towards matrism in sub-Saharan Africa.

One major patrist influence on sub-Saharan Africa was the movement of a people called the Bantu, who emerged from Nigeria and Cameroon (just south of the Sahara desert) during the second millennium BCE, and began a slow southwards migration which continued for many centuries. The Bantu had many Saharasian characteristics, such as polygamy, bride-price, strongman rulers and slavery. They were, however, only a mildly patrist people – for example, they weren't particularly militaristic, and had a matrilineal kinship system. Since they came from the Sahara region, it's possible that they were affected by the desiccation of the desert and underwent the same psychic transformation as other Saharasian peoples, albeit in a slightly milder form. The other possibility is that they were originally from north of the Sahara desert and had some contact with the Saharasian peoples who lived there, and picked up their patrist characteristics second-hand from them. In any case, by the fifth century CE, the Bantu had spread over large areas of Africa south of the equator, and in the present-day most southern African peoples speak Bantu languages. They didn't actually conquer these areas, though. As John Lamphear and Toyin Falola note, Bantu expansions were "a subtle cultural intrusion and integration, involving the diffusion and assimilation of various social and economic institutions, as well as languages."[41] In other words, rather than dominating them, the Bantu mixed and merged with the indigenous inhabitants of southern Africa. As a result, both their patrism and the original inhabitants' matrism were diluted.

However, since the Bantu were only interested in areas which were suited to intensive agriculture, there were large areas which they didn't migrate into, particularly arid or forest areas. The peoples in these areas remained in a pure state of matrism. Other groups appear to have migrated into the areas in flight from the Bantus, and also retained their pure matrism. The different Pygmy groups, for example, retreated into the central African rainforest, while the San (sometimes called the Bushmen of the Kalahari) moved to the arid southern tip of the continent.[42]

The Saharasian peoples who occupied North Africa had some contact with sub-Saharan peoples too, of course. By the end of the fourth century CE, Christianity had spread down the Nile from North Africa to Nubia and Ethiopia. Islam spread to some areas directly south of the Sahara desert too – such as Ghana, Mali and Sudan – partly as a result of the activity of merchants and traders, and partly due to military conquest. But here, again, the strong patrism of Islam was mixed with the area's original matrism, so that hard-line Muslims were often shocked when they visited the region. As one Muslim theologian wrote of his visit to Mali, for instance:

> The women there have "friends" and "companions" amongst the men outside their own families and the men in the same way have their "companions" amongst the women of other families. One day at Walata I went into the judge's house, after asking his permission and found him with a young woman of remarkable beauty. I was shocked and turned to go out, but...the judge said to me, "Why are you going out? She is my companion." I was amazed...for he was a theologian and a pilgrim to boot.[43]

Early African States

The biggest distortions of the basic matrist character of Africa, however, are the strongly centralised states which developed there at different times. The first of these was the state of Ghana, which probably began at around 700 CE. By the time of the European "scramble for Africa" towards the end of nineteenth century there were a large number of them, including the states of the Congo, the Zulu and the Ashanti. All of them were ruled by powerful and wealthy kings, and were usually militaristic and socially stratified. Social status was so important to the Zulus, for example, that they had a strict etiquette of seating arrangements at mealtimes, with places allocated according to sex and age. The Zulus were fierce warriors with strong empire-building instincts too. They caused a massive amount of devastation across southern Africa in the first decades of the nineteeenth century as they conquered and displaced neighbouring tribes.

However, none of these states was strictly indigenous to Africa; to a greater or lesser extent they were all the result of external influences. Ghana and all the states which followed it on the southern edge of the Sahara, were, as DeMeo notes, "partly stimulated by migrating tribes of Berber immigrants, forced south by invasions occurring across North Africa."[44] The states of west Africa, meanwhile, such as the Ahsanti and the Dahomey, were largely the result of the trading activities and the conflicts of the Arabs and Europeans – in particular, the slave trade. As Service writes of the Ashanti, for instance:

> Some of the militaristic features of the state were directly related to the wars and dislocations caused by the Europeans, who avidly sought the famous gold deposits which gave that portion of the coast its name, and later by the competitors involved in the slave trade.[45]

This was also true of the states of central and southern Africa, which were developed by Bantu-speaking peoples (who, as we've seen, weren't strictly indigenous themselves anyway.) As DeMeo summarises:

> The African kingly states of the sub-Saharan region formed partly in response to overland or sea trade with, or invasion from North

Africa, the Mediterranean, or Arabia. Not only did dominant males come to power through the stimulus of invasion and warfare, but the philosophies of the foreign groups dictated, more or less, the subordination of women and children. In more recent times, the Arab and European slave trade exacerbated these tendencies by stimulating tribal/ethnic groups.[46]

The Zulus in particular were an anomalous development, the result of a sudden and a dramatic cultural shift which occurred at the beginning of the nineteenth century. They were originally a peaceful pastoral people called the Nguni who only practised a highly ritualised form of conflict. However, as with the Plains Indians, a process of cultural disruption transformed them. Towards the end of the nineteenth century, the Nguni were subject to population pressures, partly because of the introduction of maize from America (which increased their numbers) and because Dutch settlers were pressing into their territory and shrinking their living space. And at this point, by an accident of history, one of the tribes of the Nguni came under the rule of a strongly militaristic chief named Shaka, a Sargon-like (or Hitler-like) figure who formed an army of strongly disciplined units and single-handedly established the Zulu as a fierce conquering nation.[47]

However, it's important to remember that, as with the patrist Native Americans, these peoples never reached the high level of patrism of Saharasian peoples, and always retained strong elements of matrism. The centralised states were nowhere near as male-dominated as those of Europe, the Middle East or China. Some were ruled by queens and even when kings ruled the queen mother had a great deal of authority. Matrilinearity was common too, and far from being excluded from their societies, women could become priestesses, healers and diviners, and often did traditionally European male jobs such as house-building or brewing beer.[48] Among the Ashanti – as with many Native American tribes – senior women were given the task of nominating chiefs.

And despite their social stratification, the states retained many democratic elements too. As Lamphear and Falalo note, the Sudanic states just below the Sahara desert, for example, had "powerful systems of checks and balances...to limit the authority of the kings."[49] Although kings collected taxes and tributes from the population, this was "routinely redistributed...as a means of maintaining the loyalty of their followers and ensuring the well-being of all parts of the state."[50] Similarly, among the Ashanti, although the chief has complete power in theory, he has to pay heed to the advice of his council of elders. The king's power is not really his own anyway, since he is seen as only the representative of the Ashanti's ancestors. In practice, as Service writes, he can't "indulge in any act of arbitrary power not agreed upon by the people."[51] The Ashanti's system of electing chiefs is also extremely democratic. Once the senior women have nominated someone, the council of elders (which may include both males and females) discuss it and then, if they accept it, present it to an assembly of the people. If the people don't approve it the whole process begins again.

MATRISM IN AFRICA

In a sense, all these cases are anomalous, though. Outside them there is a general pattern of cultures whose matrism either became only slightly diluted due to contact with the Bantus or remained completely pure. Outside the centralised states, African communities are strongly egalitarian, with no classes or castes. Even now the common system of government in villages throughout Africa is still rule by the elders of the community – sometimes called gerontocracy. As in Aboriginal society, however, the elders don't have absolute authority but are merely, in the words of John C. McCall – in his essay "Social Organisation in Africa" – "one voice of authority among the many which are continually negotiating the shape of community life."[52]

Like other unfallen peoples, traditional Africans appear to lack the inequality-creating drive to accumulate wealth and status. As with the Native Americans, land doesn't belong to individuals, but to the whole community. In fact, it's impossible for any one person to gain ownership of land or property, since it is inherited collectively by all people who are connected to the ancestors who owned it before them. As a result, everybody has an exactly equal claim to it. Or, as the African theologian Laurenti Magesa notes:

> One of the basic traditional African beliefs is that the earth is given
> to human beings as a gift, and all human beings possess an equal

claim to it and all the resources it offers…Water sources, mineral resources, forests and so on are in principle public property…In the strict sense, African morality does not and cannot sanction private ownership of land.[53]

And as with matrist Native American cultures, traditional African culture has strong moral principles which emphasise generosity and guard against any expression of greed. To hoard possessions or goods for yourself instead of sharing them is seen as a crime. As Magesa writes, "Greed constitutes the most grievous wrong. Indeed, if there is one word that describes the demands of the ethics of African Religion, sociability (in the sense of hospitality, open-hearted sharing) is that word."[54]

As we'd expect, women have high status in these societies too. This may not be so evident nowadays, since, as Sheldon Gellar notes, "The status of women throughout much of Africa declined under colonialism, as colonial policies often reinforced patriarchal authority."[55] Before European contact women were frequently chiefs and village leaders, and councils often included female officials. But the European colonists only recognised the authority of men, and refused to deal with women in positions of power, with the result that women began to lose these positions. Similarly, the important role which women played in producing goods began to decline. Before colonialism the idea of female domesticity didn't exist in Africa; women were just as economically active as men. As Lamphear and Falola write, "women dominated important areas of the economy, controlling many facets of agricultural production, the flow of commerce, and a wide variety of industries and crafts."[56] However, the colonists – accustomed as they were to female domesticity – generally wouldn't deal with women when they arranged for local products to be exported. As a result, men began to take control of cash crops and the rest of the economy.

For an example of a purely matrist African people, we can turn to the Nuer people of the Sudan, who were investigated by the anthropologist E.E. Evans-Pritchard during the 1940s. Evans-Pritchard found that the Nuer were so unselfish and community-oriented that whole groups shared the same common stock of food.[57] Even when food was scarce they shared everything equally. Similarly, their society contained no inequality or subjugation of any kind. The only kind of higher status was given to older people, who – as elsewhere in Africa – were respected for their wisdom and experience. Women had equal rights and equal influence. As Service notes of the Nuer, "They [women] take an active part in the daily life of the community, mixing freely with men and delivering opinions with an easy assurance."[58] The Nuer also had their own concept – or, more strictly, their own awareness – of spirit-force, which they called *kwoth*. As Evans-Pritchard puts it, *kwoth* "is in the sky, falls in the rain, shines in the sun and moon, and blows in the wind."[59] But at the same time *kwoth* is the essence of reality, which exists above and beyond the manifest world.

The Pygmy groups of the central African rainforest, such as the Mbuti and the Biaka, are also purely matrist. Before the Bantu expansion the pgymies were widespread throughout central Africa – as we've noted, they appear to have retreated to the rainforest in flight from the Bantus. (Although it's also possible that they were there already and the Bantu simply left them alone, since their forest environment would've had little use for them.) Colin Turnbull describes the Mbuti as an "exceptionally non-violent people" who wanted "nothing more than to live in peace with each other and the world around them."[60] Their social organisation was, in the words of Marion McCreedy, "lacking of any significant inequality in political status or authority between individual, men and women, or between generations, the old, the adult and the young."[61] The equality of men and women is so complete that, as with the Yahgan, their roles were interchangeable. As Turnbull noted:

> She [the Pygmy woman] has a full and important role to play, and there is little specialisation according to sex. Even the hunt is a joint effort. A man is not ashamed to pick mushrooms and nuts if he finds them, or to wash and clean a baby. A woman is free to take part in the discussions of men, if she has something relevant to say.[62]

Similarly, anthropologists have noted of the Biaka that "women have a great deal of autonomy and influence" and that "a woman is in no way the social inferior of a man."[63] And like the Native Americans, both the Mbuti and the Biaka have a kind of ideology of egalitarianism, which underpins their societies. As Marion McCreedy notes: "Individual autonomy is valued above all else…No one has the right or means to direct, order, or coerce another individual to do anything against his or her wishes." [64]

We've already seen that purely matrist peoples can inhabit extremely inhospitable environments, and this is also true of the hunter-gatherer peoples of the Kalahari desert in southern Africa, such as the !Kung, the G/wi and the Nharo (collectively known as the San). Like the pygmies, the San were much more widespread before the Bantu expansion, as is suggested by the similarities between them and the Hazda of Tanzania, who – although much further north – clearly once belonged to same cultural group. As with the Hazda (whose egalitarian practices we looked at briefly in Chapter 2), the !Kung have an extremely non-materialistic and egalitarian philosophy. Possessions – especially valuable ones – are seen as undesirable, because of the danger of their creating envy or conflict.[65] They also take various measures to ensure that no individuals can become too prominent or arrogant, so that their egalitarianism isn't disturbed by status differences. As we have seen, before they go hunting, men swap arrows, and when an animal is killed the credit doesn't go to the person who shot the arrow, but to the person it belongs to. And when the meat is brought home neither the person who killed it nor the person whose arrow it is are allowed a bigger share of it than anybody else; it has to be divided equally.[66] Similarly, observers of the G/wi people have noted how little conflict there is between individuals. According to the anthropologist George Silberbauer – who lived with them for several years – sharing was so central to G/wi culture that "good fortune, pleasure and contentment were referred to in terms of being shared. To experience them on one's own was a contradiction."[67]

OTHER "UNFALLEN" PEOPLES

Aside from these three continents, there are many smaller areas in the world where matrist cultures survived more or less intact until recent times. The area of Oceania, for example – to the north-east of Australia – shows a general pattern of matrism mixed with some "spots" of mild patrism. Consisting of thousands of islands, the area is traditionally divided into Micronesia, Melanesia and Polynesia. Some of the islands were completely cut off from the influence of Saharasian peoples, while on others there was only had a long-distance, indirect influence.

Some Polynesian peoples have mild patrist characteristics. The Tahitians, for instance, are as obsessed by rank as the Zulus, and have the same "dinner table" ranking, with taboos against lower ranks eating with higher. Men eat separately from women and children, suggesting a degree of patriarchy, and there are occasional (although quite rare) instances of aggressive warfare between islands.[68] The probable reason for this is that many of the peoples of Oceania (including the Fiji and Samoan islanders, the Maoris of New Zealand and the Hawaians as well as the Tahitians) were part of what archaeologists call the "Austronesian expansion." From the 4th millennium BCE onwards, peoples from southern China migrated into south-east Asia – for example, Malaysia, Indonesia and the Philippines – and from there into Oceania[69]. The original "Austronesians" could not have been Saharasian peoples – since the latter didn't reach China until around 2000 BCE – but they must have had some contact with them at later stages. It's clear that the early Malayan and Indonesian peoples had a great deal of contact with the Indo-Europeans of India, for example, from the large number of Sanskrit words in their languages. As a result they must have absorbed some mild patrist characteristics, which migrating groups then carried to Polynesia. Anthropologists have also noted that peoples in some parts of Oceania – including Polynesia – have Semitic words in their languages, including names for parts of boats, religious words and words associated with status and slavery.[70] This obviously suggests that Semitic peoples sailed to the region at some point and passed on patrist characteristics (or else caused mild cultural disruption which resulted in a degree of patrism).

However, as we would expect from this indirect influence, patrism in Polynesia was quite diluted. Apart from the Maoris, no Polynesian peoples had fortified villages, and chiefs practised the same kind of redistribution of goods as the African kings. A concept of spirit-force, *mana*, was common throughout the islands as well. As Ernst Cassirer describes it, *mana* "is conceived as a mysterious stuff that permeates all things…it is to be found in all things whatsoever, regardless of their special nature and their generic distinction."[71] And the Tahitians themselves also had some strong matrist characteristics. Although women had to eat separately, in almost every other respect they were the equals of men. They could become chiefs, were free to play sports with men, and had a great deal of sexual freedom.[72] Anthropologists have also noted that the Tahitians don't seem to have a "gender schema" – that is, they don't have the kind of strict gender differences and roles which characterise Saharasian peoples. The anthropologist Robert Levy, for example, found that "men in Tahiti were no more aggressive than women, nor were women gentler or more maternal than men."[73] At the same time, the Tahitian language doesn't seem to take account of gender. There are no male and female pronouns and most traditional names can be used for both men and women.

There were some parts of Oceania which peoples from South-East Asia or Semitic peoples apparently didn't reach, and where the matrism of indigenous peoples was relatively pure. This was particularly the case in Micronesia. It was true of the Trobriand Islands – close to Papua New Guinea – for instance, whose inhabitants were famously studied by the British anthropologist Branislaw Malinowski in the 1930s. Whereas the low status of women in Saharasian cultures means that baby girls are often seen as undesirable (leading to the practice of female infanticide), Malinowski found that to the Trobrianders "girls are quite as welcome as boys, and no difference is made between them by the parents in interest, enthusiasm or affection. It is needless to add that the idea of female infanticide would be as absurd as abhorrent to the natives."[74] As with the Tahitians and many other native peoples, there was also a lack of sex specialisation. Men frequently helped out with domestic chores and played a large part in childcare. They regularly fed, washed and cleaned their babies, and it was their special role to hug and pet them. Children of unmarried mothers were thought of as unfortunate; although not because they were "bastards" who were "born in sin," but rather because they were denied the hugging and cuddling that a father would give them. Another sign of sexual equality was the private "clubs" which women had at water holes, where they would come together to chat or discuss matters of importance to the community. These were important because, in Malinowski's words, "there is a distinct woman's public opinion and point of view in a Trobriand village, and they have their secrets from the male, just as the male has from the female."[75]

Malinowski was also struck by the affectionate and tolerant attitude of the Trobrianders to their children. As we'll see, this is another characteristic of all unfallen or primal peoples in general. The general pattern amongst fallen Saharasian peoples is to have a stern, controlling attitude to children, who aren't allowed much freedom or autonomy, are punished for "misbehaving" and are expected to be subservient. Again and again, however, anthropologists have noted the much more gentle and tolerant attitude of primal peoples to children, and the large degree of freedom given to them. As Malinowski writes of the Trobrianders:

Children enjoy considerable freedom and independence. They soon become emancipated from a parental tutelage which has never been very strict. Some of them obey their parents willingly, but this is entirely a matter of the personal character of both parties; there is no idea of a regular discipline, no system of domestic coercion. A simple command, implying the expectation of natural obedience, is never heard from parent to child in the Trobriands.[76]

The majority of the early anthropologists and missionaries who visited Oceania – and the neighbouring Papua New Guinea – were struck by the peacefulness of the "savages" they encountered there. The German anthropologist Maximillian Krieger noted that the Papuans "have no offensive weapons at all, but live without disturbance from neighbours and without care for the future."[77] In fact, many of these early visitors were so indoctrinated with the war ideology of their own cultures that they often interpreted this peacefulness as cowardice. Writing in 1911, for example, William Graham Sumner describes the people of German Melanesia as "cowardly and mean" because while they are prepared to make raids on each other occasionally, "they will not join battle." He notes that "on some of the small islands war is entirely unknown."[78]

The key to the long-surviving matrism of these peoples is their remoteness. Most of them lived on small islands far away from large landmasses – and in particular, thousands of miles away from the Saharasian landmass. And there are many other examples of matrist peoples on remote islands elsewhere in the world. Early visitors to the Chatham Islands, for example, hundreds of miles east of New Zealand, noted that although the islanders might sometimes quarrel over hunting, serious fights never occurred, since there was a law that they had to end with the first drop of blood.[79]

Probably the most famous surviving island matrists, however, are the peoples of the Andaman Islands, in the Bay of Bengal between Burma and India. Like all hunter-gatherers, they are effectively communists. They hold all their territory and natural resources in common, and everybody has equal rights to them. There is no form of government, and as Service notes, "No families are in a higher or more powerful social or economic position than others."[80]

But even on the Saharasian landmass there were remote and inhospitable areas where matrist cultures survived until modern times. The indigenous peoples of Siberia were also peaceful, egalitarian and non-patriarchal. As another example of role swapping between sexes, amongst the Reindeer Tungus it was common for older men who could no longer hunt to become "housewives," and take over a woman's domestic duties. As Service notes, the Tungus had "no preference for one sex over the other," and women "cannot be said to occupy a degraded status."[81] Similarly, the Tofa people of the Sayan mountains (north of Mongolia) are so peaceful that even play fighting was seen as shameful. They perceive that all things – including rocks and stones – have their own consciousness and being, and believe that any show of disrespect to animals or plants will be punished by natural forces.[82]

Even in the forests and hills of Indo-European India, many matrist peoples survived in a relatively pure state until recent times. Probably the most well-known of them are the Muria, a Dravidian-speaking people who were investigated by the anthropologist V. Elwin in the 1930s. He found that they were characterised by a "non-violent innocence" and that their children had an amazing degree of independence. Rather than in the houses of their parents, children of both sexes slept in a communal dormitory called a *Ghotul*. Adults had no role at all in running the *Ghotul*, and often weren't even allowed to enter it.[83] I've mentioned in passing that another characteristic of unfallen peoples is their extremely open attitude to sex and the human body. This is something which we'll look at in more detail later on, but we can note in passing that the *Ghotul* gave Muria children the opportunity to – with the full knowledge of their parents – experiment with different sexual partners.

In the nineteenth century the English colonists of India were shocked to encounter tribal peoples like the Khonds in Madras and the Rengmahs of the Assam hills, who showed no signs of aggression and didn't even seem to have any experience of warfare. As Sumner writes of the Mru people of the Chittagong hills (again showing how his own culture's war ideology had infected him): "[They] are peaceable, timid and simple. In a quarrel they do not fight, but call in an exorcist to take the sense of the spirits on the matter."[84] Even today there are many surviving tribal peoples in India, like the Hill Kharia of west Bengal, the Chenchu of Andhra Pradesh, and the Yanadi of Sriharukota Island.[85]

One of the most unlikely survival stories of an ancient matrist people, however, is that of the Mosuo people of southern China, whose isolated mountain home region enabled them to escape the fate of other pre-Saharasian peoples of China. In complete contrast to the severely patrist culture which has surrounded them for over 4,000 years, the Mosuo have a healthy, open attitude to sex and the body, and high status for women. Both men and women are free to have as many lovers as they like before marriage, and a woman has the right to initiate divorce if she isn't satisfied with her husband.[86]

ATTITUDE TO NATURE

So far we've mainly been looking at evidence for these peoples' unfallen state in terms of their lack of warfare, patriarchy and inequality. However, another major difference between unfallen – both primal and pre-historical – peoples and fallen Saharasian peoples is their attitude to nature. We've already seen that Neolithic peoples such as the Old Europeans seem to have worshipped nature – for example, that they decorated their houses, shrines and other buildings with a massive number of images of natural phenomena. And as we'd expect, this reverential attitude to nature is shared by the world's primal peoples.

Earlier I suggested that our modern-day environmental problems stem from our domineering attitude to nature, our assumption that the earth was put there for our own use and so we're entitled to abuse and exploit it. More precisely, though, I believe that this attitude itself can be traced back to a more fundamental problem, which is our lack of a sense of the alive-ness of natural phenomena. To most of us, natural phenomena like trees, rocks, mountains and streams are inanimate objects; we don't see them as beings, with a soul or an inner life of their own. However, primal peoples have a completely different relationship to nature. To them all natural things *are* alive, with their own kind of consciousness or inner life.

As with our pre-historic ancestors, it's impossible to separate this attitude to nature from the religious life of primal peoples. What makes trees, rocks and mountains alive is the spirit-force – the Life Master or Great Spirit – which flows through them. All native peoples appear to have a term for this spirit-force. In America, the Hopi called it *maasauu*, the Lakota called it *wakan-tanka*, the Pawnee called it *tirawa*, and the Ufaina (of the Amazon rainforest) call it *fufaka*.[87] We've just seen that in Polynesia it was called *mana*, while in parts of New Guinea it was called *imunu*. In Africa the Nuer of Africa call it *kwoth* and the Mbuti call it *pepo*.[88] This force isn't a personal being, a deity who watches over the world and who human beings can appeal to for help and worship. It has no personality and no gender. In Richard Heinberg's words, it is "not a concept but an immanent power and intelligence emanating from a non-physical but thoroughly real source."[89] *Wakan-tanka* (or *wakataka* to the Plains Indians) literally means "the force which moves all things."[90] Here a member of the Pawnee tribe describes it:

> We do not think of Tirawa as a person. We think of Tirawa as [a power which is] in everything and…moves upon the darkness, the night, and causes her to bring forth the dawn. It is the breath of the newborn dawn.[91]

Primal peoples therefore respect nature because they see it as the manifestation of Spirit. And since they see themselves as manifestations of Spirit too, they feel a sense of kinship and connection with nature, a sense of sharing identity with it, which contrasts with the sense of "otherness" to the natural world which we normally experience. According to the African theologian Harvey Sindima, for example, to traditional African people, "All life – that of people, plants and animals, and the earth – originates and therefore shares an intimate relationship with divine life; all life is divine life."[92] Similarly, the Australian Aborigines perceive that all things have their own "dreaming" – that is, their own inner life, or subjectivity. Because of this, as Robert Lawlor notes, Aborigines often talk aloud to rocks, rivers and vegetation "as if they have an intelligence deserving of respect."[93] They can't conceive of themselves as being separate from nature since to them, in the words of another anthropologist, Lynne Hume, "Everything is interconnected in a vast web of sacredness."[94]

This is perhaps the main reason primal peoples never see themselves as owning land. Even as communities they rarely see themselves as owning land or natural resources in the sense that we understand the term. As the anthropologist Colin Scott notes, to the Cree Indians, "no one, not even the Creator, owns land."[95] At the most, primal peoples might see themselves as custodians of the land, looking after it on behalf of the Great Spirit. Ownership implies a position of superiority and dominance. Since European peoples know that they're conscious and alive themselves, and perceive natural phenomena as *not* being alive and conscious, they feel that they're superior to nature, as a master is to a slave, and so feel entitled to dominate it. But primal peoples' sense of the sacredness and alive-ness of nature means that they could never take this attitude. (Although, as we'll see later, there is another reason for unfallen peoples' lack of desire for ownership: the simple fact that they don't have the psychological *need* to possess goods and territory.)

There are other characteristics of unfallen native peoples which make them distinct from fallen peoples, but since we'll be looking at them all later in this book, there's no need to investigate them here. We've already mentioned some of these in passing anyway: native peoples' tolerant attitude to children, their free and open attitude to sex and the body, their hospitality, and their different religious attitudes. Later we'll also look at their attitude to time and history and their views of the afterlife. As far as we can tell, all of these characteristics were shared by our prehistoric ancestors, and by all the world's matrist native peoples (at least until recent times).

PSYCHIC HARMONY?

All of this make it fairly clear that, like our hunter-gatherer and Neolithic horticultural ancestors, most native peoples were free from the kind of social suffering which has made life so unpleasant for countless human beings over the last few thousand years.

I pointed out in Chapter 1 that this was just the external aspect of the problem, though, and examined another kind of suffering which human beings are prey to: namely, the inner, psychic suffering, which makes it impossible for us to do nothing and leads us to become neurotic, depressed and even physically ill when we've got too much unstructured free time on our hands.

Since primal peoples are free from social suffering, we'd expect them to be free of this psychic suffering too. And apart from the fact that they *appear* to be generally serene and content, there are some aspects of their life which suggest this. The very fact that primal peoples – like their prehistoric counterparts – feel no need to accumulate wealth or to gain status and power suggests that there's no psychological discord inside them which they're trying to override or find compensation for. The fact that, unlike us, primal peoples appear to be able to do nothing suggests this too. One assumption the European colonists made when they went to America was that Indians were lazy because they only worked as much as they needed to, and often worked for six months and then rested for the next six. But the likelihood, of course, is that this was nothing to do with laziness – it was probably simply that the Indians didn't have the same psychological need for activity as the Europeans. It was possible for them to be inactive without becoming bored or discontent because they didn't have the same constantly chattering isolated egos as the Europeans. The fact that both ancient and present-day hunter-gatherers spend so little time (12 to 20 hours a week) searching for food – and so much time on leisure activities – suggests this too. Even if we were able to financially, most of us would find it very difficult to work as little as this, since we tend to suffer from boredom, anxiety and general psychological discord when our attention isn't focused on external things.

The author Edward T. Hall recalls how, when he worked on Indian reservations in the 1930s, the Indians seemed to possess an amazing quality of patience. In contrast to the Europeans, who fidgeted impatiently and become irritable, the Indians he saw waiting at trading posts and hospitals never showed any sign of irritation whatsoever, even if they had to wait for hours. As he writes:

> An Indian might come into the agency in the morning and still be sitting patiently outside the superintendent's office in the afternoon. Nothing in his bearing or demeanour would change in the intervening hours...We whites squirmed, got up, sat down, went outside and looked toward the fields where our friends were working, yawned and stretched our legs...The Indians simply sat there, occasionally passing a word to one another.[96]

We don't like waiting because it means doing nothing, and – although we might read magazines or daydream or chat to the person next to us – we find it difficult to keep our attention occupied with external things. As a result, we experience the basic psychological discord inside us. And since the inactivity of waiting didn't bother the Indians, we can presume that this disharmony wasn't there inside them.

THE COLONIAL ERA

It's strange to think that for thousands of years, while all manner of upheavals and atrocities were taking place over the Eurasian landmass – while its indigenous cultures were being destroyed by waves of Saharasian invaders, and while the Saharasian peoples were fighting savagely against one another and brutally oppressing the less powerful members of their own groups – peoples such as the Australian Aborigines and the Native Americans continued to live their matrist ways of life. Eurasia saw the rise and fall of the empires of the Sumerians, the Egyptians, the Romans and many others, the spread of Christianity and Islam, the trails of mayhem left by warmongers such as Sargon, Alexander the Great and Genghis Khan – and all the while, in Australia, the Americas, Oceania and large parts of Africa, nothing changed. Right until very recent times, the unfallen way of life these peoples had lived since time immemorial remained undisturbed.

They were always living on borrowed time, though. When the Saharasian peoples had covered the whole of the Eurasian landmass, their drive for new territory had to be put on hold. For centuries they had to be content with attempting to prise new territory and new wealth and power from each other. But their conquering and empire-building instincts were so strong that it was inevitable that, as soon as they had developed the right kind of technology, they would turn their attention to the rest of the world. And towards the end of the fifteenth century this is what happened. Improvements in shipbuilding, seafaring and food storage meant that long sea voyages became possible. The maritime age began, and sailors from a select few European countries plotted courses into the "New World." After a pause of 1,200 years (since the Yayoi had crossed into Japan from Korea), the migrations and conquests of the Saharasian peoples resumed.

In America, the Europeans destroyed the cultures of the Native Americans in exactly the same way that their ancestors had destroyed the peaceful Neolithic cultures of Europe and the Near East. Filled with the same "insatiable desire for possession and property" as the original Indo-Europeans, and aided by the Indians' lack of resistance to European diseases like smallpox, they stole the earth's second largest single connected landmass from its inhabitants. Some people have compared the Europeans' conquest of the Native Americans with the Nazi Holocaust of the Jews, but in some ways it was even more severe. Nobody knows for sure how many people there were in North and South America before

Columbus' arrival in 1492. Estimates range from 20 million to 100 million, and the true figure probably lies midway between. But after European contact the figure declined with amazing rapidity, and by 1860 there were only 340,000 Indians left in North America. By 1920 there were only 220,000.[97] (Fortunately, since then the figure has increased.) Admittedly, much of this wasn't the result of actual murder, but of the spread of disease and the loss of food sources. But even this was intentional in a lot of cases. Europeans purposely killed buffalo and burned crops and fruit trees so that Indians would starve, and gave spoiled food to Indians who agreed to move to reservations. There are even stories of Europeans purposely spreading disease to the Indians by giving them infected blankets and food, or sending infected people to live with them. And as populations disappeared, so did their cultures. Dozens of distinct cultures were completely lost to history, all of them thousands of years old. Just as in Old Europe thousands of years earlier, these largely peaceful, democratic, non-patriarchal and nature-worshipping cultures were swept away and replaced by Indo-European cultures based around violence and oppression.

In Australia, the Aborigines suffered the same fate. Estimates of their population at the time of Captain Cook's "discovery" of the country in 1788 range from 300,000 to one million. By the 1920s, however, there were fewer than 50,000 Aborigines.[98] They had no tradition of resisting foreign invaders with military force, and their lack of weapons, defences, and their peaceful nature meant that the Europeans had as easy a time conquering them as their ancestors must have had conquering the Neolithic peoples. The land which was so sacred to them became another treasure house for the Europeans to ransack, and their culture was suppressed and destroyed.

In Africa, the colonial process wasn't as direct or as intense. To Europeans, African people were sub-human in the same way that the Native Americans and Aborigines were, and so they felt entitled to use them as slaves to help them in their efforts to become wealthy in the New World. By the 1780s, when the slave trade reached its peak, an average of 80,000 Africans per year were being transported to North and South America, to work on sugar plantations.[99] Some observers have suggested that as well as being grossly immoral, the slave trade was irrational because it would surely have been easier for the Europeans to just start their plantations in Africa, since that was where their labour force was. But African land wasn't suited to sugar, and Europeans who went to Africa had a very low chance of survival because of their vulnerability to disease. (Africans who went to America, on the other hand, had a natural immunity to many diseases.) This also partly explains why the Europeans didn't attempt to directly conquer Africa as they had America and Australia.

By the end of the nineteenth century, however, with practically every other available part of the world already colonised (and also with medical advances giving them some immunity to African diseases), the major European countries did finally begin to consider colonising Africa as a way of gaining new national glory. A conference was held in Berlin in 1884 at which the "scramble for Africa" was legitimised. Like a giant birthday cake, the continent was divided up and allocated to the different European powers. But despite this, the Europeans never stole the Africans' land, decimated their population or destroyed their culture to the same extent that they did in America and Australia.

In more isolated and inaccessible areas, unfallen peoples survived for longer. In fact, some of them have even managed to survive till the present-day. Despite pressures from the Malaysian government and the incursions of tourism, for example, the tribal peoples of Borneo – such as the Murut, the Ibans and the Dayaks – still live something close to a traditional way of life. All in all, though, the picture looks very gloomy. The forces of globalisation – and the governments who pander to them – seem to be invincible. The Andaman Islanders are clinging precariously to survival, after decades of encroachment (and deforestation) by British colonists and the Indian government. In the 1950s, the population of the Onge people of Little Andaman was around 500, for instance, but in 1990 it was only 99.[100] The rainforest of the Pygmies is being chopped down by European and Japanese lumber firms, and the government of Zaire has forced many of them to leave the "primitive" hunter-gatherer way of life and become farmers or city-dwellers. In southern Africa, the Kalahari Bushmen (or San) have been forced off their ancestral lands and put into government-run reserves. Exactly the same thing is happening to the Amazonian Indians of Brazil and Columbia. The Trobriand Islanders have converted to Christianity, and lost their sexual freedom and openness. They have become so distanced from their native traditions that anthropologists from the University of Papua New Guinea have organised projects to help them relearn them. The Muria still live a tribal way of life, and still even have their *Ghotul*, but over half of them are now Hindus, and they are also under assault from Christian missionaries who see it as their mission to spread the gospel to all the world's remaining "unreached" peoples. Other tribal peoples of India, such as the Hill Kharia and the Chenchu, are close to extinction as a result of the destruction of their forest habitats.[101]

After 6,000 years of conquest and colonisation, the Saharasian peoples' domination of the planet is more or less complete. The peoples who migrated away from central Asia and the Near East when the area started to turn to desert at around 4000 BCE have spread their dominator value system to every corner of the earth. The most "successful" have been the Indo-Europeans, who now largely occupy three whole continents (Europe, American and Australasia), as well as parts of the Middle East and western Asia. Around half of the world's population speak Indo-European languages alone. And if you add to this the populations of the other Saharasian peoples – close to half a billion Semitic Arabic and Jewish peoples, one and a half billion East-Asian Saharasian peoples (the Chinese, Japanese and Koreans) plus other smaller peoples who originated from the region, such as the Turks and the Finno-Ugric speaking peoples – this constitutes a huge proportion of the human race.

On the other hand, the world's primal peoples – who even 500 years ago still constituted a large part of the world's population, and covered at least half of its surface – are a tiny minority, a barely visible reminder of a distant past.

THE ORIGINAL PEOPLE

One anthropologist who studied the Pygmies, J.P. Hallet, was so struck by their lack of jealousy and violence, and their gentle and harmonious way of life, that he believed they represented a kind of pure human state, the way that all human beings lived in the distant past.[102] Elwin also believed that the non-violent innocence of the Muria represented an ancient, original condition.[103] And to a greater or lesser extent (depending on whether, or to what degree, they were affected by patrist influences) this applies to all primal peoples.

There are some people who believe it's inaccurate to speak of all these peoples under general umbrella terms like "primal peoples" or "indigenous peoples." After all, there are hundreds – if not thousands – of different peoples, living in radically different climates and environments, with different cultures and different means of subsistence. But after the examination we've made it should be clear that there's nothing wrong with terms like these. Despite their differences – and despite the patrist influences which acted on some of them over time – there is a basic core of commonness between all of these peoples. They all shared the same basic social characteristics, the same basic relationship to the natural world, the same (or similar) religious concepts, and even the same kind of psyche.

In fact, it's not merely justifiable to speak of all of these peoples as one basic type, it's justifiable to extend the umbrella even farther, so to speak, deep into the human race's past. The primal peoples who have existed over recent centuries have a basic core of commonness with the hunter-gatherer and horticultural peoples who made up the world's population before 4000 BCE. The similarities between them are so great that it's possible to say that together they represent a kind of original or even natural human type. Or, as we would say, they were all unfallen peoples.

It's us – those of us who are descended from the Indo-Europeans, the Semites and other Saharasian groups – who are the different ones. The fallen psyche which our Saharasian ancestors developed, and the fallen cultures that it gave rise to, was (and is) really a kind of aberration.

What we need to do now, though, after this long examination of *what* happened, is to look at the reasons behind it all. What was it that made the Saharasian peoples so different from prehistoric and primal peoples? Why did their psyche change in such a way that they were the first ever human groups to wage war, to oppress women, to hanker after power and wealth, and so on? We've already seen that this was something to do with the desiccation of their homelands. Now we need to look more closely at this transformation, at what it consisted of and how this environmental change caused it.

In other words, we need to investigate why the Fall occurred.

5

THE EGO EXPLOSION

IT'S NOT SURPRISING that, living amidst so much suffering and oppression, people in the post-Fall era looked back to earlier times with nostalgia and longing. Memories of the pre-Fall era were probably passed down from generation to generation until eventually – after embellishments over time – they became folk stories, or myths. These stories, which we now know as the stories of a Fall, are common to all Saharasian peoples.

In themselves these myths are another piece of evidence for the fact that something "went wrong" at some point in human history. They tell us exactly the same thing as the archaeological evidence: that there was an ancient time when human beings lived in harmony with each other and with nature, when life was much easier and more pleasant, and when there was no war, and no selfishness or fear. But we fell away from this idyllic state. Human nature became corrupt, and life became full of suffering.

There are two types of Fall myths. One sees the Fall as a sudden dramatic event, and appears to refer to an environmental change of some kind which forces the original human beings to leave a lush, fertile environment. The Iranian myth of the Fall, for example, describes how the first man, Yima, lived in a walled garden – the old Iranian word *Paira-daeza*, from which the English word "paradise" comes – on a mountain where the water of life flowed and the tree of life grew. It was in a perfect country with a mild climate, and the people who lived with Yima knew "neither heat nor cold, neither old age or death, nor disease...Father and son walked together, each looking but fifteen years of age." However, this perfect age came to an abrupt end when an evil being called Airyana Vaejo intervened, and changed the mild climate to a harsh winter one. As a result, the garden became infertile and was destroyed by snow and ice.[1]

Despite its similarities, the famous Old Testament story of the Fall developed independently of this Iranian myth. The biblical Fall story tells how

God made the Garden of Eden for the first human beings to take care of. As with the Iranian *Parra-daeza*, there was a stream and beautiful fruit-producing trees. Adam and Eve lived there harmoniously, naked and unashamed, until the serpent tempted Eve to eat from the tree of knowledge, which God had forbidden them to do. God punished them by ejecting them from the garden, and at this point disease and death entered the world. God tells Eve that he will increase her labour pains and make her husband rule over her, suggesting the beginning of male domination.

Both of these stories appear to refer to the experience of the Saharasian peoples when their fertile homelands turned to desert and they were forced into exile. The fact that both stories developed independently supports this. Indeed, scholars have suggested that the Iranian myth was a part of original Indo-European folklore, and dates from around 4000 BCE. And if this is an original Indo-European story, then it's possible that the story of the Garden of Eden comes directly from the original Semitic peoples who were affected by the desiccation of Saharasia – a parallel myth describing their own experience of enforced migration.[2]

In other words, it's likely that this first type of Fall myth comes directly from the original Saharasian peoples. The second type of myth, on the other hand, appears to derive from the old Neolithic peoples who were conquered and enslaved by them. This doesn't refer to environmental factors, but sees the Fall mainly in terms of degeneration of the character and behaviour of human beings, a long, slow process which unfolds through different historical epochs. Greek and Roman myths tell of an ancient Golden Age when a "golden race" of human beings lived. The story – which seems to have been accepted as fact by most Greeks and Romans – was first put in writing by the Greek poet Hesiod at around 800 BCE, but probably originated much earlier. According to Hesiod:

> First of all the deathless gods having homes on Olympus made a golden race of mortal men…Like gods they lived with hearts free from sorrow and remote from toil or grief…And all good things were theirs. For the fruitful earth spontaneously bore them abundant fruit without stint. And they lived in ease and peace upon their lands with many good things.[3]

However, the Golden Age was followed by the Ages of Silver, Brass, Heroes and the present Age of Iron. Through each age human nature became more corrupt, and life became more difficult and full of suffering.

In India, there is a similar view of history. According to traditional Hindu folklore, time moves cyclically through four different *yugas* or ages. According to the ancient text, the Vaya Purana, during the first age, the *Krita Yuga* (or Perfect Age):

> Human beings appropriated food which was produced from the essence of the earth…They frequented the mountains and seas, and did not dwell in houses. The never sorrowed, were full of the quality of goodness, and supremely happy; they moved about at will and lived in continual delight…There existed among them no such things as gain or loss, friendship or enmity or like or dislike.[4]

Since then, however, history has moved through the three succeeding ages, through to the present *Kali Yuga* (Age of Darkness), in which human beings are materialistic, lawless and decadent. In fact, this age – as described in another religious text, the Vishnu Purana – sounds like a fairly accurate description of the way that many people live in the modern world: "Accumulated treasures will be spent on dwellings. The minds of men will be solely preoccupied with acquiring wealth; and wealth will be spent on selfish gratifications."[5]

Further east, meanwhile, in China, the Fall story appears in the form of the myth of the "Age of Perfect Virtue." During this time human beings followed the way of heaven rather than the way of men. They were naturally part of the Tao, the natural harmony or order of nature and the universe. As Chuang Tzu wrote in the fourth century BCE:

> In the Age of Perfect Virtue they were upright and correct, without knowing that to be so was righteousness; they loved one another, without knowing that to do so was benevolence… [They] did not rebel against want, did not grow proud in plenty. Being like this, he could commit an error and not regret it, could meet with success and not make it a show.[6]

Since then, however, human beings have become separated from the Tao. They have become selfish and calculating rather than spontaneous. They have begun to follow the way of men, and as a result, laws and rulers have become necessary, to keep their selfishness and greed in check.

These second kinds of Fall stories appear to refer to the peaceful, egalitarian and easy lives of the Neolithic peoples. There are clear references to a hunter-gatherer way of life – for example, Hesiod's statement that during the Golden Age "the fruitful earth bore them abundant fruit without stint," and the Vaya Purana's comment that "They frequented the mountains and seas, and did not dwell in houses" (that is, they lived a non-sedentary way of life). The Vaya Purana also comments that during the perfect age "the things which those people desired sprang up from the earth everywhere and always."[7] Similarly, Hesiod's phrase "remote from toil" hints at the leisure-filled lives of the hunter-gatherers, while the Vaya Purana's comment that during the Perfect Age there were "no such things as gain or loss" suggests a lack of property and materialism. However, perhaps the clearest mythical description of the unfallen hunter-gatherer way of life comes from the Greek philosopher, Decaearchus, of the fourth century BCE. According to his fellow philosopher Porphyry, he spoke of "men in the earliest age," who lived at a time when:

> all things grew spontaneously, since the men of that time themselves produced nothing, having invented neither agriculture nor any other art. It was for this reason that they lived a life of leisure, without care or toil, and also – if the doctrine of the most eminent medical men is to be accepted – without disease…And there were no wars or feuds between them; for there existed among them no objects of competition of such value as to give anyone a motive to seek to obtain them by those means.[8]

Clues from the Myths

Perhaps the most important thing about the myths from our point of view, however, is that they also give us some clues as to exactly *what* went wrong with human beings. We already know that the Fall was connected to an environmental disaster: the drying up of the Middle East and central Asia. In this chapter, however – with the aid of these myths – we're going to investigate exactly how the Eurasian peoples were affected by this disaster, how it altered their psyche in such a way that they became completely different from any human beings before them.

It's significant that the Bible tells us that the Fall occurred as a result of Eve eating from the tree of knowledge. This suggests that the Fall was connected to gaining a new intellectual power or awareness. We're told that now Adam and Eve were "given understanding" and, even more significantly, that now they "realised that they were naked; so they sewed fig leaves together and covered themselves."[9] This suggests that the Fall was linked to the development of a new self-awareness within human beings, which gave them a new ability to observe and judge themselves.

There are similar hints from other myths. The ancient Indian epic the Mahabharata says that the "holy men of old" were "self-subdued and free from envy," suggesting a lack of self-awareness and self-assertion.[10] While according to the Chinese myth of the Age of Perfect Virtue, when human beings fell out of the Tao they developed a new kind of individuality and self-sufficiency. They started to live by their own will rather than the will of nature. Chuang Tzu tells us that the "true man of ancient times...did not grow proud in plenty, and did not plan his affairs...He could commit an error and not regret it, could meet with success and not make a show."[11] In other words, these ancient men acted without analysing their behaviour, presumably because they were less self-aware, and so free from feelings of guilt and pride. Chuang Tzu also hints at how this new individuality led to a new kind of intellectual discrimination and an awareness of separateness. He states that early human beings "were not yet aware that there were things" but later human beings "were aware that there were distinctions."[12]

INDIVIDUALITY

This begins to make more sense when we examine exactly what it is which makes the psyche of prehistoric and primal unfallen peoples different from that of fallen peoples. We looked at many of the differences in the last chapter – as well as having a much lower level of violence and oppression, unfallen primal peoples are less materialistic and possessive, have a stronger sense of connection to nature, a more open attitude to sex and the body, and so on. However, it's possible to trace all of these differences back to one *fundamental* difference, which they are all the expression of.

It's a little known fact that the English novelist D.H. Lawrence was also, in effect, an anthropologist. In the 1920s he spent the best part of three years living on a ranch in New Mexico, and was in close contact with the south-western Native Americans, especially the Pueblo Indians. He describes his impressions of them in his book *Mornings in Mexico* – along with some other essays – in which he shows an amazing ability to step beyond the "objectivity" of observing the Indians from a European point of view (as most other anthropologists of his time did) and catch something of their experience of the world. (The critic Keith Sagar called this ability of Lawrence's "an almost occult penetration into the being of other creatures."[13]) What struck Lawrence most was how massively different the Indians' state of being was from that of Europeans. As he wrote, "The Indian way of consciousness is different from and fatal to our way of consciousness…The two ways, the two streams are never to be united. They are not even to be reconciled."[14] And one major reason for this difference, he sensed, was that the Indians don't experience the state of *separateness* to the cosmos which we do. Whereas we are "separated off," they live in a state of "oneness with all life…an ancient tribal unison in which the individual [is] hardly separated out."[15]

Similarly, the psychologist Heinz Werner compared the "perceptual and cognitive functioning" of European-Americans and native peoples, and also came to the conclusion that European peoples have a greater sense of individuality and separateness. He remarks that native peoples are "de-differentiated with respect to the distinctions between self and object and between objects."[16] In other words, they experience a strong sense of connection between themselves and other people, and between themselves and the world around them. And they can also sense a connection between objects, a way in which phenomena that we perceive as separate and distinct (for example, mountains, streams, trees, animals) are interdependent. But according to Werner, European/American peoples live in a world of separateness – between themselves and the world, themselves and other people, and between the different objects and phenomena they see around them.

Other anthropologists have come to similar conclusions. For the early twentieth-century anthropologist Lucien Levy-Bruhl, the essential characteristic of native peoples was their less "sharpened" sense of individuality. In his words, "To the primitive's mind, the limits of his individuality are variable and ill-defined."[17] He notes that rather than existing as self-sufficient individual entities – as we experience ourselves – native peoples' sense of identity is bound up with their community. He cites reports of primal peoples who "thought and acted in terms of the family group, clan or tribe – and not of the individual himself," and who use the word "I" when speaking of the activities of the tribe as a whole.[18] He also notes that native peoples' sense of individuality extends to objects they use and touch. A person's clothes, tools and even the remains of meals and their excrement are so closely linked to them that to burn or damage them is thought to lead to death or injury to the person. (This is one of the principles by which witchcraft works, or at least is believed to work.) As the early anthropologist Gill remarks of the people of Polynesia:

> The natives are absurdly sensitive to threats of burning anything
> belonging to themselves. There is no surer way of drawing down
> their anger than to hint at such a thing as the burning of a canoe,
> a hut, or even a garment. *To chop the property* of another is
> regarded as symbolical of an intention to *chop his person.*[19]

Similarly, George B. Silberbauer notes that to the G/wi of the Kalahari, "identity was more group-referenced than individual. That is, a person would identity herself or himself with reference to kin or some other group."[20] While the anthropologist Fred Myers, describing the sharing practices of the Pintupi Aborigines, suggested that at the root of their principle of "co-ownership" is their experience of "shared identity with others."[21]

In other words, primal peoples don't seem to exist as personal, self-sufficient egos to the same extent that we do. The naming practices of certain indigenous peoples suggest this too. For us, a name is a permanent label which defines our individuality. But for indigenous peoples this often isn't the case. The anthropologist Clifford Geertz found that among the Balinese, personal names and even kinship names, are rarely used. Instead, the Balinese commonly use tekonyms – that is, terms which describe the relationship between two people. As soon as a child is born, the mother is called "mother-of" and the father is "father-of …"; when a grandchild is born, they become "grandmother-of …" and "grandfather-of …"[22] As Gardiner et al note, this "denotes a very different understanding of the person, emphasising the connectedness of the individual with the family."[23] Similarly, Aborigines do not have fixed names which they keep throughout their lives. Their names regularly change, and include those of other members of their tribe.[24]

In general, American-European peoples appear to have what Markus and Kitayama refer to as "independent selves," whereas native peoples have "interdependent selves."[25] This is one of the reasons why native peoples have always had such problems adjusting to the European way of life, with its emphasis on private property and individual gain. The Native Americans, for example, found it almost impossible to work in the way that white people did, cultivating their own pieces of land or trading or running stores for profit. This conflicted with what Ronald Wright describes as the "ethic of reciprocity [which was] fundamental to most Amerindian societies."[26] Even now many Native Americans struggle to adapt to the highly individualistic and competitive nature of modern American life. As Alvin M. Josephy writes, "Many Indians still do not understand or cannot accept the concept of private ownership of land. Many find it difficult, if not impossible – to substitute individual competitiveness for group feeling."[27]

Some colonists actually became aware of the problem, and realised that they would never be able to fully "civilise" the natives unless they developed their sense of "self-ness." Senator Henry Dawes put his finger on it when he wrote of the Cherokees in 1887, "They have got as far as they can go [that is, they are not going to progress any further], because they hold their land in common. There is no selfishness, which is at the bottom of civilisation."[28] The English missionaries in Australia tried various measures to develop the Aborigines' sense of individuality. As the anthropologist Bain Atwood writes, "the missionaries sought to make each [aborigine] an integrated centre of consciousness, distinct from the natural world and from other aborigines."[29] To this end, they made them live in separate houses and tried to stop them going into each other's. They baptised them so that they would think of themselves in terms of permanent names, instead of the fluid Aboriginal names which could change and include the names of other tribe members. It didn't work, though – the Aborigines never developed a sense of personal ownership over their houses and the possessions inside them. They wandered in and out of each other's houses all the time, and continually swapped possessions.

Even today there is an apparently unbridgeable psychic gulf between white Australians and urban Aborigines. Whites sometimes complain that they can't understand why the Aborigines don't want to settle down in pretty little houses with lawns and hedges, and why they can't seem to settle into working 40 hours a week in factories or offices. Many urban Aborigines still live a communal, mobile lifestyle with few possessions, sharing houses (which they rarely own) with large numbers of relatives and moving back and forth between different towns.

Neither they, nor the Native Americans, nor any other primal peoples are ever likely to become fully paid-up members of European colonial societies, precisely because of their less "sharpened" sense of ego.

PRIMAL EMPATHY

This relative lack of self-ness is probably also the reason why, in general, primal peoples seem to have a more acute sense of empathy than European-Americans. Our highly developed sense of self means that, to a greater or lesser degree, we are "walled off" to the world, trapped inside ourselves with our own needs and desires. As a result, we often find it difficult to "put ourselves in other people's shoes" and "feel with" them. This makes us liable to put our desires before other people's – or other creatures' or the environment's – well-being, even if it causes suffering and damage. And it also means that we're sometimes capable of acts of appalling cruelty and inhumanity, since it's difficult for us to sense the pain and suffering which the person on the receiving end is experiencing.

Unfallen primal peoples, on the other hand, seem to be less "walled off" in this way. This is another major reason why they respect nature so much and are so reluctant to damage it. Not only do they see trees, rocks and rivers as alive, they also seem to have the ability to feel with natural phenomena, to enter into their being and potentially sense their suffering. In *The Dance of Life*, Edward T. Hall describes the difficulties a European-American agricultural agent had when he was sent to work with the Pueblo Indians of New Mexico. His work went well through the summer and winter, but when spring came around their attitude to him suddenly became hostile. The Indians refused to say what the problem was, just that "he just doesn't know certain things." Eventually, however, it emerged that the agent had tried to make them start "early spring plowing," which clashed with their empathic sense that in spring the earth is pregnant with new life and must be treated gently. In spring, Hall notes, the Indians remove steel shoes from their horses, and refuse to wear European shoes or to use wagons, for fear that they might damage the earth.[30]

It's true that all primal peoples get a small proportion of their food from hunting and killing animals, but this doesn't necessarily imply cruelty. They usually see hunting as an unfortunate necessity, and take little pleasure from killing. In fact, they often apologise to the spirits of animals before they set off hunting. In *The Forest People*, Colin Turnbull describes how, to the Mbuti Pygmy group, hunting is an "original sin" which occurred when a mythical ancestor killed an antelope and then ate it to conceal his act. Since then, all animals – including human beings – have been condemned to die. Partly because of this philosophy, the Pygmies are, in Turnbull's words, "gentle hunters" who never show "any expression of joy, nor even of pleasure" when they make a catch. They never kill more than they need for one day, since "To kill more than is absolutely necessary would be to heighten the consequences of that original sin and confirm even more firmly their own mortality."[31] Similarly, according to the anthropologist Melvin Konner, the San of the Kalahari desert are characterised by "a great respect for and fascination with the animals they prey upon."[32] In fact, hunting as primal peoples practise it has almost nothing in common with the barbaric forms, such as fox hunting or game hunting, that we're familiar with nowadays. As Rudgley notes, unlike "civilised" modern-day hunters, primal peoples have "a great degree of respect for their quarry and even a pang of regret at having to kill animals at all." There are, he states, "numerous cases of empathy and even reverence for animals among the hunting peoples of northern Canada and elsewhere."[33]

The quality of compassion is so central to Aboriginal culture that mothers "teach" it to their children. Often when a child grabs some food or another object and holds it to its mouth, the mother – or another female relative – pretends to be in need of it, to encourage a spirit of sharing. Similarly, whenever a weak or ill person or animal comes by, the mother makes a point of expressing sympathy for it, and offering it food. As Robert Lawlor notes, by these means "the child experiences a world in which compassion and pity are dramatically directed towards the temporarily less fortunate. The constant maternal dramatization of compassion in the early years orients a child's emotions toward empathy, support, warmth and generosity."[34]

Our strong sense of individuality develops slowly from birth to adulthood, as a part of our general psychic development. During the first year or so of our lives, we don't experience any degree of separation; we have no sense of anything "outside" us. As the philosopher Ken Wilber notes, for a newly born child, "there is no real space...in the sense that there is no gap, distance or separation between the self and the environment."[35] But after this our sense of "I-ness" grows, and we begin to feel a basic sense of aloneness. We try to subdue this by making use of what psychologists call "transitional objects" – teddy bears, dolls, toy soldiers or action men, for example. We treat them as living beings and they give us constant companionship, a feeling of never being alone. However, it's probably significant that, as Richard Heinberg notes, "This process does not occur in the same way in the case of primal child-rearing…The need for transitional objects seems to be minimised."[36] We can presume this is because the children of primal cultures don't *need* transitional objects since they don't develop a strong sense of separateness as they enter adulthood.

THE EGO

I'm not trying to say here that primal peoples don't possess any self-consciousness or sense of individuality. They do, of course – if they didn't perceive themselves as separate from the world, life would be impossible; and if they didn't perceive themselves as separate from each other, they wouldn't have individual names at all, or a word for "I" in their languages. It's a question of degree. The point I'm making is simply that our sense of self-consciousness and individuality is *more* developed than theirs.

The most simple way of putting this is to think in terms of the ego. Ego is simply the Latin word for "I am," and refers to the part of our psyche which thinks, the "I" inside our heads which makes decisions and plans, deliberates, worries and imagines, and which – most frequently – chatters away randomly to itself, sending an endless stream of memories, images and thoughts through our minds. The ego is also the part of our psyche which our powers of reason and logic stem from. Reason is the "I" inside our heads which talks to itself carefully and deliberately, in order to solve problems. And the basic difference between us and native peoples is that we have a *stronger* sense of ego than they have.

And this, finally, brings us to the point where we can suggest what the change which the idea of the Fall refers to actually was. We can assume that prehistoric unfallen peoples had the same less developed sense of individuality as primal peoples, and that this was the essential difference between them and the invading patrist peoples who conquered them from the fourth millennium onwards. These Eurasian peoples were the first human beings to develop a sharpened sense of ego – and since they are our ancestors, they've passed this down to us.

The Fall, then, refers to a change which occurred in the psyche of certain human groups around 6,000 years ago. It was the point in history when these peoples developed a strong and sharp sense of ego. The Fall was, and is, the intensification of the human sense of "I" or individuality.

The term "Brain Explosion" has been used for the extremely rapid growth of the human brain during our evolution, when it became a third larger in the space of half a million years. And here I'm going to introduce the parallel term the "Ego Explosion," to refer to this sudden and dramatic change within the human psyche.

HISTORICAL EVIDENCE

There is also some concrete archaeological evidence for this Ego Explosion. From around 4000 BCE – concurrent with the desertification of central Eurasia and the emergence of male domination, materialism, social inequality and intensive warfare – there are many signs of a new kind of sharpened individuality taking over.

We can see this in changes in burial practices. During the fourth millennium BCE, as the Saharasian peoples began their migrations, the old practice of communal burial started to be replaced by individual burial. The Old World peoples had been buried anonymously, with no markers and no possessions. But now people were buried with identity and property, as if their individuality mattered, and as if they thought it would continue after death. Chieftains were buried with their horses, weapons and wives, as if it was impossible to conceive of such powerful and important people ceasing to exist, as if they were bound to return to life at some point. As the Swedish archaeologist Mats Malmer has written, these new burial practices (and the new emphasis on private property linked to them) are part of a "surprising change [that] occurred in Europe, a new social system...giving greater freedom and rights of personal ownership to the individual." Referring specifically to the beginning of the third millennium BCE, he calls these new European peoples "the first individualists."[37]

Texts and inscriptions from the fourth millennium BCE also show a greater emphasis on individuality and personality. For the first time, people's names are mentioned and their speech and their activities are recorded. We learn about who did what, why kings built temples and went into battle, how goddesses and gods fell in love and fought with one another. As Baring and Cashford write, "We become aware not only of the personality of man and woman but also the individuality of goddesses and gods, whose characters are defined and whose creative acts are named."[38]

The new myths which appeared throughout Europe and the Near East during the third millennium BCE (as Saharasian peoples invaded and conquered these areas) also suggest a new sharpened sense of individuality. Whereas earlier myths had been based around the Goddess and nature (or symbols of them), now they became stories of individual heroes pitting their will and strength against fate. According to Joseph Campbell, these show "an unprecedented shift from the impersonal to the personal."[39] Many of these heroes actually battle against symbolic representations of the goddess of the earth, such as serpents or dragons, suggesting a new sense of separation and alienation from nature as the ego became more developed. In the Sumerian myth the *Enuma Elish*, for instance, the earth goddess Tiamat – represented as a serpent – is killed by the sky god Marduk. Marduk takes her place as the creator of life, and now gods and goddesses – and by extension human beings – are "outside" nature, detached from their creation rather than an organic part of it.[40] Whereas earlier human beings – and primal peoples – felt deeply interconnected with natural phenomena, now nature is something "other," to be tamed and exploited.

OTHER CONCEPTS OF THE FALL

I'm certainly not the first person to suggest that this Ego Explosion occurred, or to connect it with myths of the Fall or a Golden Age. In fact, the idea that our sharpened sense of individuality wasn't shared by earlier human beings, and developed at a particular historical point, has been put forward by many different scholars and philosophers.

In *The Masks of God*, Joseph Campbell refers to what I call the Fall as "the Great Reversal." This was when, in his words, "For many in the Orient as well as in the West, the sense of holiness departed from their experience both of the universe and of their own nature, and a yearning for release from what was felt to be an insufferable state of sin, exile or delusion supervened."[41] In other words, this was the point when human beings lost their natural state of contentment, and began to experience psychological discord. We lost our sense of the aliveness of natural phenomena and of our own connection with them, and as a result, the world became a dark and oppressive place. And as I do, Campbell links this "Great Reversal" to a new sense of individuality, which expressed itself in the new hero myths.

Similarly, in his book *The Next Development in Man* (published in 1950) the British physicist and philosopher Lancelot Law Whyte suggested that round about the beginning of the second millennium BCE, the "European disassociation," or the split between mind and body, began. Earlier peoples had minds too, of course, but theirs were integrated with their instincts. But now the mind underwent a massive surge of growth. What Whyte calls "rational self-consciousness" developed. Mind became a separate entity, apparently independent of the body, and people began to experience a sense of self-division, a conflict between thought and instinct. The completely spontaneous, natural behaviour of earlier peoples was no longer possible.[42] In Shakespeare's phrase (from Hamlet's "to be or not to be" speech), the "native hue of resolution" became "sicklied o'er with the pale cast of thought."[43]

Owen Barfield, Whyte's contemporary and compatriot, describes the same transformation as a "loss of participation." Earlier human beings experienced what he calls "original participation" – a sense of connection with natural phenomena. But with the beginning of what he calls "alpha thinking" – the logic and reason which gave rise to science – the human mind became "separated off" from nature. As Barfield notes, "when we think 'about' anything, we must necessarily be aware of ourselves (that is, of the self which is doing the thinking) as sharply and clearly detached from the thing thought about...It is in fact, the very nature and aim of pure alpha-thinking to exclude participation."[44] In other words, logical-theoretical thinking created a duality between human beings and nature which led to what Barfield refers to as "the individual, sharpened, spatially determined consciousness of today."[45]

The American psychologist Julian Jaynes put forward a similar – though more controversial – theory in his book *The Origin of Consciousness in the Breakdown of the Bicameral Mind.* Jaynes suggested that before the second millennium BCE, human beings had no sense of ego at all. They didn't think in the same way that we do because they had no "I" in their heads to think with. Instead of having thoughts, Jaynes believes, they heard voices inside their heads, stemming from the right hemisphere of their brains, telling them what to do. Thus, a person wouldn't suddenly "think" to herself that it was time to breast-feed the baby again, or that her husband might be home from his hunting expedition now so she'd better finish gathering food for the day and go home – instead, voices inside her head would command, "Breast-feed your baby again now," and, "Go home now because your husband should be back." During the second millennium BCE, however, this "bicameral" consciousness was replaced by a new ego-based consciousness. Human beings developed the sense of being an "I" inside their heads. They began to think, to talk to themselves mentally, and to be aware of themselves as finite individuals. According to Jaynes, "the great transilience in mentality had occurred. Man had become conscious of himself and his world...Subjective consciousness...was the great world result."[6]

Jaynes' position is a little extreme – as I've already pointed out, it's not a question of a sudden transition from no-ego to ego, but of a *more* developed sense of ego. And the dates which both he and Whyte suggest for the emergence of sharpened ego-consciousness are flawed. This is understandable, since they were writing before much of the archaeological evidence both for the existence of peaceful Old World cultures, and for the movements of the Indo-European and Semitic peoples across Europe and the Near East, became available. In many cases, what they see as evidence of a psychological transformation is simply a cultural change caused by the continued migrations of people who *had already undergone* a psychological transformation. What Whyte, for example, sees as the development of a new kind of consciousness amongst European peoples is simply the establishment of a new kind of culture by migrating peoples – the Indo-Europeans – with a different kind of consciousness from the Old Europeans. The "European disassociation" didn't take place in Europe at all, and involved many other peoples besides those who eventually became Europeans. It took place in central Asia and the Near East, 2,000 years earlier.

Both Whyte and Jaynes suggest interesting explanations for why this transformation occurred. According to Whyte, now that people were living in cities and trading with people in other areas, they were constantly being exposed to new situations and experiences. This meant that they could no longer rely on tradition and instinct. They suddenly had to "think on their feet," to react to each new situation on its own terms – and the ego developed as a way of enabling them to do this. In a similar way, Jaynes suggests that "subjective consciousness" developed mainly because life in big cities was becoming too complex for the old bicameral consciousness to deal with. It was also, he believes, connected to the invention of writing – which also made life more complex – and to the large number of natural disasters and wars of the second millennium BCE, which meant that people had to become more efficient and selfish in order to survive.

However, we've already seen that the Fall wasn't the result of living in cities, since the original central Eurasian peoples developed a fallen psyche centuries before they developed any urban centres, and many fallen peoples never developed any significant urban centres at all (at least, not for many centuries). And we also know of Neolithic peoples who lived in large towns without developing a fallen psyche. (Although it may be that, as we'll see in a moment, the factors Whyte and Jaynes identify contributed to a later intensification of the original Fall.)

Other authors have interpreted the Ego Explosion as an evolutionary development. This is the stance the American philosopher Ken Wilber takes in his book *Up From Eden*. According to Wilber, the development of the sharply defined sense of ego was a natural unfolding of what he calls *atman telos*, the evolutionary force which has pushed life forward to further levels of development since the first single-celled living creatures arose 4 billion years ago. It was a step forward from the simple, undivided consciousness of prehistoric peoples. Although it had some bad side effects – such as a painful sense of separateness from the cosmos – it gave rise to what Wilber calls "a logical and syntactical brilliance that would soon bring forth medicine, science and technology."[47] Or, in the words of another philosopher who takes this view, Ernest Becker:

> How can we say that evolution made a mistake with man, that the development of the forebrain, the power to symbolise, to delay experience, to bind time, was not 'intended' by nature?…The ego…represents the immense broadening of experience and potential control…a natural urge by the life force itself toward and expansion of experience, toward more life.[48]

I certainly don't deny that the Fall had these positive effects, and Wilber's view of evolution is actually very close to my own. I also believe that genetic mutations and natural selection can't account for the complexity and variety of living beings, and that evolution itself – or life itself – has an inherent propulsive force which moves life forward to higher levels of complexity and consciousness. But, at the same time, I don't believe it's possible to see the Ego Explosion as an evolutionary development. The problem is that the development was only a local one. If it had been an evolutionary development it would surely have happened to the *whole* human race, whereas it only happened to a relatively small proportion of the inhabitants of the earth, living in a particular area. (There is also a theoretical reason why the Fall shouldn't be seen as an evolutionary advance, which we'll look at later.)

SAHARASIA AND THE DEVELOPMENT OF THE EGO

In fact, we can already guess what the real cause of this Ego Explosion was. If the Fall is linked to the drying up of Saharasia (primarily the Middle East and central Asia) and the Ego Explosion *is* the Fall, then we can assume, logically, that the Ego Explosion was connected to this environmental change Saharasia. In other words, this catastrophe may have transformed the psyche of the Saharasian peoples. They may have developed their sharpened sense of ego in response to it.

There were perhaps two main ways in which this happened. Firstly, the new difficulties the groups faced as their environment changed must have brought a need for a new kind of intelligence, a practical and inventive problem-solving capacity. If they wanted to survive they had to deliberate, think ahead, find quick solutions, and develop new practical and organisational powers. For example, as their lands became more arid they might be forced to come up with new methods of hunting or farming to increase their yields, to find new water supplies or ways of making the ones they already had last longer. They might have to find ways of protecting themselves against the heat and dust of the desert or against invaders who might try to steal their supplies after their own had disappeared completely. In other words, the Saharasian peoples were forced to think more, to develop powers of self-reflection, to begin to reason and "talk" to themselves inside their heads. And they could only do this by developing a stronger sense of "I." After all, as we've seen, self-reflection is the "I" inside our heads talking away to itself. If you want to be inventive or to deliberate or plan ahead, you have to have an "I" to think with. In other words, this is how what Barfield calls "alpha-thinking" developed. And as he notes, this kind of thinking inevitably resulted in a sense of separation from the environment, and a "individual, sharpened, spatially determined consciousness."[49]

Secondly, the sheer hardship of these human groups' lives when their environment began to change – when their crops began to fail, when the animals they hunted began to die, when their water supplies began to fail, and so on – may have encouraged a new spirit of selfishness. In order to survive, people had to start thinking in terms of their own needs rather than those of the whole community, and to put the former before the latter. Sharing was no longer an option, since there weren't enough resources to support the community as a whole. It's true that, as we've seen, hunter-gatherer peoples generally don't react to shortage of resources by becoming more aggressive and competitive towards other groups; they simply move to a different area or merge with other groups. But the Saharasian peoples lived from agriculture. Shortage of arable land meant that the possibility of just moving to a new area wasn't open to them, and resources were so scarce that groups who couldn't even feed their own members were unlikely to accept new members. If a group wanted to gain access to resources, their only option was to use force.

As another more minor factor, the sheer physical pain and discomfort which people were now experiencing – as a result of famine and the heat and dust of the desert – may have encouraged the split between the mind and the body which Lancelot Law Whyte identified. This could have brought a tendency to withdraw from the body, to dis-identify with it and see it as something "other." In the same way, the new hostile environmental conditions probably encouraged a sense of separation between human beings and nature. Whereas to previous peoples nature had been a benevolent and nurturing mother, to the Saharasian peoples she had become tyrannical and harsh. She had become an adversary which they had to fight against to survive, an enemy to be conquered, and this must have helped to break the empathic connection between human beings and natural phenomena.

In other words, the difficult new environment encouraged separation: separation between the individual and the community, between the mind and the body, and between the individual and nature. And taken together with the need for greater powers of self-reflection and rationality, this created a new "separate, sharpened, spatially-determined" psyche.

Perhaps, however, the intensification of the ego wasn't the only cause of the dramatic shift from matrism to patrism. James DeMeo explains the transition in terms of Wilhelm Reich's concept of "armouring." In his view, the pain and suffering which the Saharasian peoples were confronted with made them "wall themselves off" from the world and from their own feelings. They covered over their natural pleasure-seeking impulses with secondary pleasure-denying instincts; and impulses such as the maternal-infant and the male-female bonds, connection to nature, the sexual instinct, trust and openness to other human beings were disrupted. And once this had happened to the first generation of Saharasians, it changed the way they treated their children. Children were given less attention and affection and treated harshly, which led to further armouring on their part. And once a generation of children had become armoured they would inevitably pass their armour on to their children by denying them affection and treating them harshly in turn.[50]

Reich's work has caused a great deal of controversy, but any open-minded person can hardly doubt that armouring is a real phenomenon. We do react to long-term pain and suffering – especially as children – by "shrinking in" on ourselves, and becoming emotionless and detached. The Saharasian peoples certainly would have become armoured, and as a result would have become more prone to violence and more indifferent to the sufferings of others.

All of these factors must have continued to act on the Saharasian peoples after their migrations began. Life would have still been extremely difficult for centuries after they left their homelands, still necessitating selfishness and self-reflection and creating armouring. In fact, in a way these factors would *always* act on the Saharasian peoples, no matter where they ended up, because their proclivity for warfare and oppression meant that life was always difficult, even if they were living in fertile lands.

However, probably the best way of thinking of the new fallen psyche isn't as a kind of tendency that was continually encouraged by external factors, but as a kind of "psychic template" which, once it had been reinforced to a certain point, became fixed and permanent. In other words, once a certain number of generations of the Saharasian peoples had lived with the new sharpened sense of ego, it became a fixed part of their being, the normal psyche which every individual naturally developed as an adult. This might have been a similar process to the way that we, as individuals, develop habits and instincts. After we've performed an act a certain number of times, it begins to take on a life of its own, and harden into a habit which we're forced to perform whether we like it or not. With smoking, for example, you might be able to have the occasional cigarette for months until the habit fixes into your psyche and you have to smoke regularly. There is a great deal of evidence showing that behavioural traits and personal characteristics can spread to whole groups of peoples in this way – even to whole species. As Rupert Sheldrake's theory of "Morphic Resonance" suggests, for example, animals develop new instincts when a certain critical number of them perform a new act (or show a new characteristic or trait). At this point it has built up the required resonance to become a permanent part of the group or species "blueprint" which every member develops in accordance with from birth.[51] Perhaps, then, the intensified ego became a part of the Saharasian peoples' developmental "blueprint" in a similar way.[52]

It's important to point out, however, that in a way the term Ego Explosion is a little misleading. Although there was a sudden and dramatic initial surge of ego development, the process was ongoing. This seems clear from the fact that the patrism of Saharasian peoples became more intense as time went by. We've seen that from around 2000 BCE traces of matrism fade away, oppression and inequality increase, and warfare becomes more intense. This may have been partly due to a natural diminishing of matrist influences from the conquered Old World peoples, but it could easily be evidence of a further intensification of ego-consciousness. Perhaps this was due to new social factors which developed around this time, such as those mentioned by Whyte and Jaynes above: the complexity of city life, the advent of writing, and natural disasters.

UNFALLEN PEOPLES IN HOSTILE ENVIRONMENTS

This is a good point to confront a potential problem with my argument, and with DeMeo's "Saharasia thesis." We've seen that the Saharasian peoples developed the fallen psyche in response to the desiccation (or drying up) of their homeland. But what about the native peoples who live in inhospitable arid areas, or other kinds of inhospitable environments? What about the Bushmen of the Kalahari desert, the Aborigines who live in desert areas, the Yahgan of Tierra Del Fuego (where temperatures are often below zero and there's hardly any vegetation), the Eskimos of North America or the tribal peoples of Siberia? Why should these peoples live in such inhospitable environments and retain their natural egalitarianaism and peacefulness without needing to change in the way that Saharasian peoples did?

But the point is that an arid environment with little vegetable or animal life isn't *necessarily* difficult to survive in. It depends on population. If the area only has a small population then its limited resources should be adequate. And this is the case with all of these peoples; they all live in very sparsely populated areas and manage to subsist fairly easily in them.

But in the deserts of Saharasia this wouldn't have been the case. Because the area had previously supported an agricultural way of life, its population would have been comparatively large – large enough to be supported by a fertile environment, but too large once the soil became arid, and especially when people were forced to leave their villages and farms and become nomads. As a result, in the Middle East and central Asia (and later in North Africa) there would have been a much greater struggle to survive, with a large number of people fighting over limited resources.

It's also important to point out that the Saharasian environmental catastrophe – and the cultural devastation which followed it – certainly wasn't the only event of its kind in history. We've seen that the patrism of the cultures of MesoAmerica and Peru was probably connected to episodes of desiccation, and that the early outbreaks of social violence during the fifth millennium BCE (in the Middle East and Anatolia) were linked to temporary episodes of drought and aridity. In addition, the violence at a few sites along the Nile valley around 12000 BCE took place "during an earlier phase of intense aridity."[53] Likewise, the second unequivocal instance of Paleolithic warfare, the social violence of south-east Australian Aborigines between 11000 and 7000 BCE, occurred "during an episode of unusually dry and possibly episodic famine conditions.[54] The only difference between these instances and the Saharasian environmental catastrophe is one of scale.

The Ego Explosion was the most momentous event in the history of the human race. The last 6,000 years of history can only be understood in terms of it. All of the different kinds of social and psychic pathology we've looked at – war, patriarchy, social stratification, materialism, the desire for status and power, sexual repression, environmental destruction, as well the inner discontent and disharmony which afflict us – all of these traits can be traced back to the intensified sense of ego which came into existence in the deserts of Middle East and central Asia 6,000 years ago.

So now it's time to try to understand how the Ego Explosion gave rise to, and still gives rise to, these social and psychological pathologies.

PART TWO

THE PSYCHOLOGY OF THE FALL

6

THE NEW PSYCHE

THERE WAS A positive side to the new kind of psyche which the Ego Explosion created. This book deals mainly with the negative side, but it wouldn't be right to ignore the other, especially when it has pushed the human race forward in ways which our pre-Fall ancestors could never have dreamed of – and is still, in fact, pushing us forward today.

It's important to remember that, despite all its disastrous consequences, in a way the Fall was also a "Leap." The new self-reflective ability which our ancestors developed in reaction to their harsh environment gave them – and us – new powers of invention, creativity and rationality.

THE TECHNOLOGICAL EXPLOSION

It's certainly no coincidence that the era following the Ego Explosion was one of striking intellectual advances. As we have seen, Anne Baring and Jules Cashford describe how the beginning of the Bronze Age saw "a tremendous explosion of knowledge took place as writing, mathematics and astronomy were discovered. It was as if the human mind had suddenly revealed a new dimension of itself."[2] This new dimension was, of course, the new "logical and syntactical brilliance" which Wilber describes. And this meant that the eruption of war and social oppression which occurred during the 4th millennium BCE was accompanied by an eruption of technology. Improved metal-working and building techniques, the wheel, the plough, the calendar, irrigation systems – all of these innovations were made by Saharasian peoples in Egypt and Mesopotamia in the space of a few centuries.

As well as technology, the new conceptualising and problem-solving ability which came with the Ego Explosion gave human beings a new talent for *organisation.* This is partly what made the civilisation of Egypt possible, since rulers and governments were now able to impose their authority over a wide area, and unite disparate groups of people under the same administrative regime. In a similar way, the complex administrative systems of the Aztecs and Incas could only have been developed by the highly practical post-Fall psyche. These civilisations were the result of their organisational ability combined with a desire for wealth and power combined with their organisational ability.

It's true, of course, that some pre-Fall peoples made technological innovations too. The Old Europeans built roads and drainage systems, were skilled artists and craftspeople, and even developed a form of writing. But the technology of the Egyptians and Mesopotamians went far beyond this. The form of writing apparently used by the Old Europeans, for example, was fairly simple and seems only to have been used for religious purposes. The writing systems developed by the Egyptians and Sumerians – and later the Chinese – however, were so complex that they could take years to learn properly. As Lenski notes:

> Even after a 2,000-year process of simplification, Mesopotamian cuneiform script still had between 600 and 1,000 distinct characters. Before a person could learn to read or write, he had to memorize this formidable list of symbols and learn the complex rules for combining them. The Egyptian hieroglyphic and hieratic scripts were equally complicated.[3]

The fact that unfallen peoples did have some expertise shows that we're not talking about the actual *birth* of ego-consciousness and the intellectual ability which comes with it – as Julian Jaynes believed – but about an *intensification* of it. I should point out too that I don't accept the old colonial assumption that the low level of technology of hunter-gatherer peoples like the Australian Aborigines or Native Americans is the result of a lack of intelligence. Hunter-gatherers' lives are so attuned to their environment and so free of difficulty that there's no reason for them to have advanced forms of technology. Why would they need metal tools, the plough or the wheel when they can survive from two to three hours' foraging or hunting per day, and spend the rest of their time singing, playing games and telling stories? Why would they need electricity or computers when they can live perfectly well without them? As the example of the Old Europeans shows, all unfallen peoples must have had the *potential* to reach a fairly high level of technological development – although not, I believe, the same level as Saharasian peoples.

And, of course, the new kind of intelligence which we gained from the Ego Explosion has never stopped giving rise to technological and intellectual advances – in fact, in recent times there has been another eruption of these advances. Some of them are so impressive that they can justifiably make us feel proud of ourselves as a species, even though the negative side of our fallen psyche means that they haven't always been put to good use. Air travel, space travel, quantum physics, genetic biology, computers, the Internet, the advances in hygiene and medicine which have improved (and lengthened) life for billions of people – all of these can be traced back to the capacity for innovation and invention which our ancestors developed 6,000 years ago.

THE ORIGINS OF CIVILISATION

In fact, we can go even further and say that the Ego Explosion was responsible for what archaeologists normally classify as "civilisation" – that is, the centralised and stratified post-Fall civilisations of ancient Egypt and Sumer and, later, those of India (the Indus valley civilisation), China, Mesoamerica and Peru.

Whether these were the first civilisations or not is extremely debatable, since we've seen that some pre-Fall peoples have many of the characteristics of what we normally think of as civilisation – large towns, arts, craft specialisation, trade, and so on. But as with their technology, the post-Fall civilisations reached a new level. Whereas the large towns of the pre-Fall era probably had no more than a few thousand inhabitants, for example, the post-Fall cities had populations of up to 100,000.

It all depends on how you define civilisation. Most archaeologists, however, have defined it in terms of what we would think of as positive and negative effects of the Fall. "Civilisation" usually means a high level of technology and social organisation – including strong centralised authority – a surplus of food and other goods, and also social stratification and warfare. But as I mentioned in Chapter 3, perhaps the best way we can think of the new cities of Egypt and Sumer is not as civilisation per se, but as a new kind of civilisation.

There are many different theories of how this new kind of civilisation arose. One is that it was the result of irrigation. Irrigation was used extensively by the Egyptians, the Sumerians and Mesoamericans, and, according to the theory, irrigation systems were so complex and time-consuming that these groups had to develop a centralised authority and a political elite to manage them properly. However, in some areas large-scale irrigation only developed after the civilisations themselves had formed, which takes away this theory's validity.

Another theory is that "civilisation" was the result of population pressure and competition. As populations grew there was bound to be conflict, especially in areas where space was limited. Groups would fight against each other for resources, and the victors would make the defeated people their subjects, and rule over them. Over time, one particular group might grow more and more powerful, until it dominated most of the other groups in the area. And in this way a ruling class would develop, and a centralised state with an administrative system. This theory seems reasonable, but the problem is that research has shown that not all of the new civilisations did follow a period of population growth. In Sumer, for example, the population was actually declining when civilisation began.[4]

And, finally, there is a theory that trade gave the impetus for "civilisation" to develop. According to Wright and Johnson, for example, the massive organisation that was needed to produce goods for export, to distribute imports and protect trade parties from attackers, wouldn't have been possible without a high level of administration and centralisation.[5]

However, there are some very good reasons for linking the development of post-Fall civilisation to the Ego Explosion. First of all, there is the chronological link – the first post-Fall civilisations of Egypt and Sumer developed only a few centuries after the Saharasian environmental disaster. Then there is the ethnographic link – the civilisations appear to have been founded by groups who migrated away from Saharasia. And since archaeologists see these civilisations as characterised by a mixture of positive and negative fallen characteristics, the connection seems indisputable.

A New Kind of Creativity

The Fall gave us other benefits too. It's possible to say that without the Ego Explosion there would have been no great philosophers like Plato or Kant, or psychologists like Freud or Jung. The insights of philosophers and psychologists come when rather than focusing outside at the phenomenal world (as with science), we turn our attention inside, and use our self-reflective ability to examine our own psyche and our predicament as human beings. In his *A Criminal History of Mankind*, Colin Wilson – using Julian Jaynes' terminology – refers to what we're calling "ego-consciousness" as "left-brain awareness," and notes that "above all, left-brain awareness has the power to contemplate itself, as if in a mirror."[6] We might also add that in a way philosophers and psychologists were much more necessary in the fallen era, just as doctors are needed in a time of suffering. Philosophers were needed to make sense of a "human condition" which seemed absurd and bewildering, and psychologists were needed to try to understand – and to try to heal – the deeply divided human psyche. And, ironically, in giving us these heightened powers of self-reflection, the Ego Explosion has actually offered us a kind of "get out clause," a way of transcending the difficulties it causes. It's given us the self-analysis and self-understanding to be able to transform ourselves in such a way that we no longer experience psychological discord. This is what the spiritual paths developed by teachers such as the Buddha, Patanjali, Plotinus and others show us. As we'll see later, spiritual paths can be seen as a solution to the problems of the Fall, escape routes from the suffering and misery of the "fallen" psyche.

In Chapter 1, I also listed the human race's amazing creative achievements – great novels, symphonies, poems and songs, for example – on the "positive" side of our balance sheet. However, it's a little problematic to say that these achievements are the result of the Ego Explosion. Ego-consciousness and creativity don't seem to be closely related – in fact, in some ways they seem to be opposed. The constant "thought chatter" of the fallen ego seems to block creativity. As every poet or painter knows, the best creative work comes from a state of total absorption, when your mind is completely quiet. If it's too full of worries and other chattering thoughts you're likely to suffer from writer's (or painter's) block.

This makes some sense in terms of split-brain psychology, that is, the study of the different hemispheres of the brain and their different functions. Ego-consciousness seems to be related to the left hemisphere of the brain. Our normal sense of self is, in the words of the psychologist Brian Lancaster, "bound up with…a language-based *interpreter* situated in the left hemisphere." On the other hand, creativity seems to come from the right hemisphere, which is typified by a "non-egocentric view of the world" and doesn't have the same urge to interpret and control the world as the left. The problem is that the two hemispheres seem, to some degree, to be mutually exclusive, so that the stronger a person's "right-brain" characteristics, the weaker the "left-brain" ones (or vice-versa).

Since, according to this terminology, unfallen peoples are more right-brain oriented than we are, you would expect them to be more creative and artistic. And in general this does seem to be true. The rich traditions of song, storytelling and painting of the Australian Aborigines attest to this. We've also seen that the Old Europeans covered their houses and other buildings with a vast number of depictions of natural phenomena. Archaeologists have been struck by what Nicolas Platon describes as the "delight in beauty, grace and movement" of their artwork.[8] Similarly, James DeMeo notes that the art of the pre-Fall inhabitants of the Sahara region of Africa shows "the smooth and steady hand of skilled and artistically sensitive individuals."[9]

After the Fall, the standard of artwork appears to decline. Riane Eisler notes that as the Indo-European Achaeans conquered Crete, art became "less spontaneous and free."[10] James DeMeo notes that as the Sahara turns to desert, rock art "lacks its former artistic flavour; it appears abstract and stickman-like, without the grace and sensitivity of earlier renderings."[11] In other words, at the same time as bringing about a change in the subject matter of art – from natural phenomena to images of war and violence – the Fall also seems to have brought about a decline in its quality. And if we interpret the psychic transformation of the Fall in terms of people becoming more left-brain oriented, this is what we would expect.

However, there are certain kinds of creativity which are particular to the post-Fall psyche. These are the great creative edifices such as novels and symphonies – and also, perhaps, philosophical systems – which don't just require creative inspiration but also a powerful intelligence to organise and structure them. These can only come when the two hemispheres of the brain work together, when the intellect organises creativity rather than opposes it. Poems, songs and paintings are a spontaneous expression of "right-brain creativity," and were probably a more important part of life for unfallen peoples than for us. However, without the Ego Explosion there would probably be no great novels such as *War and Peace* or *Crime and Punishment*, and none of the great symphonies of Mahler or Beethoven. These came from what Colin Wilson describes as the ability to "steer," which comes with "left-brain consciousness."[12] Whereas "right-brain awareness" (Wilson's term for what we would call the pre-Fall psyche) is essentially passive, "left-brain awareness" is active. As Wilson writes, "Right brain awareness is like a broad, gently flowing stream; left brain awareness is like a powerful jet of water."[13]

TRANSCENDING SUPERSTITIONS AND TABOOS

The final positive effect of the Ego Explosion was that our "logical and syntactical brilliance" helped us to develop a new understanding of how the world around us works.

I'm aware that I've been painting a very rosy picture of life in prehistoric and contemporary unfallen cultures. I'm not going to apologise for this, since there's no question that in many ways their lives were idyllic, especially compared with those of, say, the poor, oppressed and war-ravaged peasants of Europe, the Middle East and China throughout most of recorded history. In fact, it's clear that with their "original affluence," healthy diet and lack of disease, and their freedom from social oppression and warfare, their lives were idyllic compared with most of the world's present-day population.

But there was one negative aspect to unfallen cultures: their lack of understanding of cause and effect, and the large number of superstitions and taboos which filled their lives. For unfallen peoples there are no such things accidents or laws of nature which make natural phenomena happen (such as the wind blowing, a flood or an illness or death). They ascribe what we would think of as chance events to the actions of spirits, human witches or other forces. When a person gets ill or dies, it never just "happens," but is caused by an evil spirit entering the body, or by a magical spell. The Cherokees, for example, believed that illnesses were caused by the spirits of animals getting revenge for being hunted by humans. In general, unfallen peoples see supernatural forces at work whenever anything unusual or untoward happens, such as when a baby is born with a deformity, or even if a woman gives birth to twins, if crops are spoiled, if a house or hut burns down, or if a hunter is injured by an animal. In Africa, there used to be a common belief that human beings could take on the form of animals, and that when a hunter was bitten or maimed an enemy who had taken on an animal form was responsible. The Australian Aborigines believed that when a child was born very prematurely, it was an animal embryo (such as a kangaroo) which had somehow got inside the woman.[14]

You might wonder whether these beliefs are such a bad thing. We know that they're not true, but at least, you could argue, they emphasise the connections between things, and make the world a more meaningful and colourful place compared with the cold, mechanistic view of modern science. For example, the Plains Indians' beliefs that lightning and thunder were caused by giant thunderbirds flapping their wings, and that the changes of the seasons were caused by the spirits of the four winds, are probably more appealing than science's explanations. But surely truth is valuable for its own sake, whether it is appealing or not. And one problem with superstitions is that they lead to taboos – the association of certain kinds of behaviour with negative events. Unfallen people often have taboos against eating certain foods, eating with their hands, getting wet in the rain, having sex with a woman while she is on her period or breast-feeding, having sex during times of harvesting or hunting, or even – as with the Akamba of Africa – stepping on the blood of a girl's first period.[15] If taboos are broken it's assumed that massive calamities will occur, both to the person responsible and the community as a whole. Angry spirits might stop rain failing, cause the death of animals or crop failures, or cause lightning to strike and burn down houses.

You might argue that these taboos aren't particularly harmful either. After all, they're not really so different from some of the superstitions we have – the belief that bad things will happen if you walk under a ladder or forget to wave to a magpie, or a footballer believing that he has to kiss his right boot before a match otherwise he won't score. Taboos might sometimes seem to have a social or even biological purpose, as Marvin Harris' theory of cultural materialism suggests.[16] This might be true of taboos against incest, or against having sex while a woman is lactating (which might be to prevent her becoming pregnant again too early). Or they might have a kind of moral function, to symbolically preserve the harmony of the community, or even the universe. As Laurenti Magesa notes, for example, "taboos exist to make sure that the moral structure of the universe remains undisturbed for the good of humanity."[17] But I would argue that taboos are restrictive, and create an unnecessary sense of fear.

We should remember that taboos and superstitions are a part of the "fallen" world as well. The cultures of fallen peoples were, of course, dominated by irrational beliefs for thousands of years. But it seems that for fallen peoples these superstitions were mixed with *some* understanding of causal mechanisms, and some acceptance that chance events did happen. For example, if a child became sick and died people were likely to realise that the direct cause was an illness, even though the devil or an evil spirit might have infected her with it, and even though it was "God's will" that she didn't recover. In a similar way, fallen peoples' superstitions were more concerned with life-events rather than natural phenomena. That is, they were probably less inclined to explain natural processes such as the wind or the changes of seasons in supernatural terms because they could understand and accept that natural phenomena did "just happen" of their own accord.

I'm trying to say, then, that the new intellectual ability which came with the Ego Explosion gave people a greater understanding of causal mechanisms, and made them less superstitious. And if this may not have been so clear, say, three or four thousand years ago, we've begun to see its full consequences over the last two hundred years or so, as the superstitious religious view of the world has been superseded by science. Newton's laws, Darwin's theory of evolution, Einstein's theory of relativity, and our present-day age of science and rationality in general, have only been made possible by the "logical and syntactical brilliance" which the Ego Explosion gave us.

Again, you might argue that science and rationality haven't really been beneficial to us at all. Science has turned the universe into a drab, meaningless place. As poets have often complained – such as when Keats accused Newton of "unweaving" the rainbow – explaining phenomena scientifically seems to take away their wonder and beauty. But at least science and rationality have – if only in this sense – taken us closer to reality. Primal peoples are closer to reality than we are in the sense that they are aware of an all-pervading spirit-force and of the aliveness of all things, but at least we have a clearer and less confused understanding of the way the world works.[18]

THE ROOTS OF PSYCHOLOGICAL DISCORD

Now, however, it's time to turn our attention back to the negative aspects of the Ego Explosion. In the rest of this chapter we're going to stay within the new psyche which it created, but look at its flip side: psychological discord, or psychic suffering. It's especially important to examine this because all of the social problems which came after the Fall can only be explained in terms of it.

Psychic suffering only came into existence with the Fall. The Fall didn't just change the way human beings lived, it caused a radical change in the way that they experienced life, and in their relationship to the world. The Buddha's statement that "life is suffering" would simply not have been true in the pre-Fall world. But in the post-Fall world it was the most fundamental truth of all, and one which every human being was familiar with at the core of his or her being. Suddenly life is no longer a blessing but a terrible burden.

The question we now need to answer, then, is: How did the Ego Explosion give rise – and still give rise - to this psychological suffering? There are, I believe, four basic sources of this suffering.

ALONENESS

There is a poem called "To Marguerite" by the Victorian poet Matthew Arnold which expresses one of the reasons why the post-Fall "human condition" is one of suffering. The poem begins with the lines:

> Yes! in the sea of life enisled,
> With echoing straits between us thrown,
> Dotting the shoreless watery wild,
> We mortal millions live *alone*.

The problem is that our sharply developed sense of ego gives us a sense of being trapped inside our own heads, of being an "I" inside our skulls with the rest of the universe and all other human beings on the other side. As a result, we feel a basic sense of *aloneness*. Unfallen peoples' sense of kinship with nature and other living beings, on the other hand, means that they never experience this. They always feel a sense of connection to the world. In the words of a present-day Cherokee Indian, Jingme Darham, "We are taught from childhood that the animals and even the trees and plants...are our brothers and sisters. So when we speak of land, we are not speaking of property...we are speaking of something truly sacred."[19] But our sharpened sense of ego means that we're *dis*connected from the world around us, from other creatures and even other people. In a way, we live in solitary confinement. We can communicate with other people by speaking and writing, and we can perceive what's happening out there through our five senses, but we're always essentially alone, with an inner self which will never be truly known or understood by others, and thoughts and feelings which we're never able to truly share. We do our best to escape this sense of aloneness, but always have to return to it, and it generates an undercurrent of anxiety which is always there inside us. As Erich Fromm puts it, "[Man's] awareness of his aloneness and separateness...makes his separate, disunited existence an unbearable prison."[20]

This sense of aloneness is accompanied by a sense of *incompleteness*. Our ego-separation means that we're cut off. Whereas unfallen peoples are a part of the whole cosmos, we are isolated fragments, broken away from the whole. As a result, we have a fundamental sense of unfulfilment (in the literal sense), of not being sufficient as we are, a sense of something missing. We suffer from what Chellis Glendinning calls our "original trauma:"

> Because we are creatures who were born to live in vital participation with the natural world, the violation of this participation forms the basis of our *original trauma*...Original trauma is the disorientation we experience, however consciously or unconsciously, because we do not live in the natural world. It is the psychic displacement, the exile that is inherent in civilised life. It is our homelessness.[21]

The root of our "original trauma," however, isn't simply that we don't physically live in a natural environment any more, but that our ego-isolation means that we are always one step removed from the world, and can never fully participate in it.

EGO CHATTERING

The Ego Explosion gave us an ability to talk to ourselves inside our heads, to hold an inner dialogue with ourselves. This is what makes us able to reason and to deliberate. But it seems that at some point we lost control of this ability. The ego turned into a kind of wild animal, with a will of its own, which continually chatters away, filling our minds with an endless stream of random thoughts, images and memories.

This thought chatter takes place whenever our attention isn't occupied by external things. It's there when you're on the way to work on the bus and don't have a book or paper to read, when you drive to work and can't listen to the car radio because someone's snapped off your aerial, or when you're on your own in an empty bar waiting for a friend to turn up. Or, perhaps most frequently of all, it's there when you lie in bed at night trying to get to sleep. Here there's nothing external to occupy your attention at all, you're left completely alone with your own mind, and often your thought chatter becomes so powerful that it stops you getting to sleep. At the end of James Joyce's famous novel *Ulysses*, there's a 50-page-long passage which simply depicts the endless "thought chatter" running through his character Molly Bloom's mind when she's lying in bed. Her thoughts leap randomly and chaotically from one subject to the next:

> I saw him looking with his two old maids of sisters when I stood and asked the girl where it was what do I care with it dropping out of me and that black closed breeches he made me takes you half an hour to let them down...[22]

This thought chatter gives rise to psychic suffering for two reasons. On the one hand, its sheer *wildness* creates a sense of chaos and disturbance inside us, which gives rise to anxiety. We experience what Mihaly Csikszentmihalyi calls "psychic entropy" – a lack of control over our own minds.[23] On the other hand, because the atmosphere of our minds is charged with anxiety to begin with (as a result of our sense of aloneness), our thought chatter usually has a very negative bias, and often consists of negative thoughts such as worries and memories of bad experiences. And these negative thoughts trigger negative feelings: worries trigger feelings of fear, bad memories trigger feelings of guilt or bitterness, and daydreams where we imagine ourselves living different lives and achieving ambitions trigger feelings of dissatisfaction and failure. The chattering ego is like a depressed person who complains about everything and constantly talks about his troubles, so that when you come away from him you feel depressed and worried too; only this person is in our heads all the time, and inflicts negativity on us whenever we focus our attention on it. (Although this varies from person to person, of course. Some people are less prone to negative thought-patterns than others.)

PERCEPTUAL SLEEP

The third reason why our sharpened sense of ego gives rise to psychic suffering is a little more complicated. This stems from the different perception of the world which we developed as a result of the Fall.

To unfallen peoples the world is a fantastically *real* place. To them all things are alive, even so-called "inanimate" objects like rocks, rivers and mountains. To them, in D. H. Lawrence's words, "the wonder and fascination of creation shimmers in every leaf and stone, in every thorn and bud."[24] Or, as Stanley Diamond puts it, "Among primitives the sense of reality is heightened to the point where it sometimes seems to blaze."[25]

But for us fallen peoples the world is a more dreary place – so dreary, in fact, that we hardly pay any attention to it, but spend almost all our time focused on tasks or distractions, or else on the thought chatter in our heads. To us rocks, rivers and trees are just inert collections of atoms and molecules. We have lost awareness of their inner life, their "dreaming," as if we can only see them in two dimensions rather than three. In Lawrence's words, "we have lost almost entirely the great and intricately developed sensual awareness or sense-awareness, and sense-knowledge of the ancients."[26]

And in connection with this – since ultimately it's this which makes all things alive – we have lost awareness of the spirit-force which pervades the universe and everything in it. We've seen that all unfallen peoples have a different term for this spirit-force, but in fallen cultures the concept is conspicuously absent. If it appears at all, it's only as an esoteric, mystical concept known to a tiny number of adepts. It is the *Brahman* of Hindu philosophy, the *Tao* of Chinese philosophy, and the *Dharmakaya* of Mahayana Buddhism. What was an obvious, objective reality to primal peoples has for us become a rarefied concept associated with higher states of consciousness, which we can only attain awareness of through a long process of spiritual development.

But how did we lose this awareness of the aliveness of things and the presence of spirit-force in the world?

The best way to understand this is to think in terms of energy. We all have a certain amount of psychic energy (or consciousness-energy, to use my preferred term), which we expend in different ways. There are probably three main ways in which we expend it: through mental activity (that is, *thinking*), concentrative effort (that is, *doing*, including our jobs, and hobbies such as crosswords or playing musical instruments) and information processing (that is, absorbing perceptual information from our surroundings, verbal information from other people – *talking* – or information from other sources such as books and the Internet). Our unfallen ancestors probably didn't use up very much energy through mental activity or through concentrative effort, and as a result there was a lot available for them to devote to information processing – and, in particular, to perceiving the phenomenal world around them. But with the Ego Explosion this balance shifted dramatically. Now that the ego was so powerful and active, it used up much more consciousness-energy. At the same time, now that people's lives were so difficult, they needed to put more energy and attention into concentrative effort too, so that they could deal with the practicalities of keeping themselves alive. As a result, there was less consciousness-energy for them to give to the third function, information processing – and, in particular, to perceiving the phenomenal world around them. The act of perception was sacrificed to the ego and to the practical tasks of survival. People began to think and do more and to perceive less.

At a certain point our ancestors even developed a psychological mechanism especially for the purpose of stopping themselves putting energy into the act of perception, so that it could be redirected into thinking and doing. This is what I have called the "de-sensitising mechanism,"[27] which switches our attention off to our surroundings and experiences once we've been exposed to them for a while. This happens when we "get used" to things, or when what psychologists call "adaptation" takes place. When you go to live in a foreign country everything seems exhilaratingly real and each day is so full of new experiences that it seems to last many times longer than a day at home – but after a few months the de-sensitising mechanism begins to function, editing out the newness and realness from your perceptions. You get used to your new environment and in the end it seems as ordinary and uninteresting as if you were in your home country. The first time you do a particular train journey you spend most of the time looking out of the window and notice almost everything you pass – but once you've done the journey every day for a few weeks the de-sensitising mechanism operates, and you spend the whole journey either reading a newspaper or daydreaming.

Something similar happens when we learn new tasks. When we first try to drive a car or to type we have to put a tremendous amount of conscious effort into these activities. But gradually, through many hours of practice, a kind of "robot" – to use Colin Wilson's term – takes over these tasks, and we end up doing them automatically.[28] In the psychologists Norman and Shallice's terms, there is a shift from "deliberate" or conscious processing to "fully automatic processing."[29] The whole point is to conserve energy – the Robot does these things on our behalf so that we can put our energy and attention into other areas. And as Colin Wilson points out, exactly the same process of "automatisation" occurs with our perceptions too, presumably also as an energy-conserving measure. The de-sensitising mechanism turns our surroundings to familiarity so that we no longer pay attention to them, and no longer use up energy through perceiving them. And this makes sure that the ego always has the consciousness-energy it needs.

In this way, we can say that one of the effects of the Ego Explosion was to cause a *redistribution of energy* – consciousness-energy was diverted away from perception and redirected to the ego. And this explains why the world is a much less real place to us than to primal peoples. The de-sensitising mechanism doesn't appear to act on their perceptions, so that they always perceive their surroundings with the kind of bright "first-time" vision which we sometimes experience in unfamiliar surroundings, when we take certain drugs, or in spiritual states of being. But we see the world through a veil of familiarity, which makes us unable to perceive the aliveness of natural phenomena and the presence of the spirit-force in the world.

One reason why the de-sensitising mechanism adds to our psychological suffering is simply that it makes the world seem less exciting and interesting to us. It turns *all* the experiences we have in our lives, and *all* the surroundings we live our lives amongst, to familiarity, which means that we're liable to become bored and indifferent to the world, to feel that nothing interests or moves us, or even seems worth giving our attention to.

More importantly, however, this state of perceptual sleep cuts us off from the sense of *meaning* which primal peoples experience. This is something that is very difficult for us to grasp about primal peoples' relationship to the world. Because of their sense of connection to the world, and their awareness of spirit-force, they experience the world as a meaningful and benevolent place. Again, this is something which we occasionally experience in higher states of consciousness – an awareness of a kind of harmony in the world and a sense of the "rightness" of being alive in it. The Native American Thomas Yellowtail describes this in the following passage.

> I have spoken before about the sacred support that was always present for the traditional Indians. With this support, from the moment you arose and said your first prayer until the moment you went to sleep you could at least see what was necessary in order to lead a proper life. Even the dress that you wore every day had sacred meanings…and wherever you went and whatever you were doing, you were participating in sacred life and you knew who you were and carried a sense of the sacred within you. All of the forms had meaning, even the tipi and the sacred circle of the entire camp.[30]

Because of this, unfallen peoples probably have a powerful sense of being "at home" in the world. But without this sense of meaning – and with our sense of separation – we feel a sense of being somehow "out of place" in it. The world seems meaning*less* to us; it is a cold, inanimate place in which nothing is sacred, and which – because of its separateness – can seem alien or even hostile towards us. This sense of meaninglessness has been graphically described by the existentialist philosophers of the nineteenth and twentieth centuries. The Danish philosopher Kierkegaard called it "existential dread," while for Albert Camus it was what made human life "absurd." One of the forerunners of existentialism, the French scientist and philosopher Blaise Pascal, described it as follows:

> When I consider the brief span of my life absorbed into the eternity which comes before and after, the small space I occupy and which I see swallowed up in the infinite immensity of spaces

of which I know nothing and which know nothing of me, I take fright and am amazed to see myself here rather than there. Who put me here? By whose command were this time and place allotted to me?[31]

FEAR OF DEATH

When living beings develop self-consciousness and become aware of their own existence, they also become aware of their potential *non*-existence – that is, they become aware of death. Most animals – with a few exceptions, such as dolphins and chimpanzees – appear to have no self-consciousness, and as a result they don't appear to have any awareness of death. If pre-historic people had *no* self-consciousness, as Julian Jaynes suggests, they would also have had no awareness of death. But this wasn't the case, of course, as their funerals, graves and afterlife beliefs testify.

One major difference between us and unfallen peoples, however, is that they seem to be less afraid of death. Because their own particular individuality isn't so important to them – since they can't wholly separate their own existence from that of nature or that of the community or tribe they belong to – the prospect of no longer existing as an individual isn't so significant either. But when, with the Fall, individuals became more separate, their individual existence became the whole basis and axis of their lives, and so its end became a terrible prospect. It didn't matter that the community or the rest of the universe would continue to live after a person's death – all that mattered was that the person himself would no longer exist.

One of the ways in which fallen peoples have always tried to deal with this fear of death is through their concepts of an afterlife. Native peoples have concepts of an afterlife too, of course, but mostly they see life after death as a fairly humdrum affair, which isn't so different from this life. The Cheyenne Indians, for example, believe that after death people carry on living in the same way, but as insubstantial spirits, like shadows.[32] Similarly, members of the Lengua tribe of South America told the missionary W.B. Grubb that, "The *aphangak* or departed souls of men in the shade world…merely continue their present life, only of course in a disembodied state."[33] But it's important to note that for native peoples life after death doesn't involve the survival of the personality – or the ego – for the rest of eternity. For them life after death rarely means immortality. As Levy-Bruhl points out, "Everywhere primitives believe in survival, but nowhere do they regard it as unending." The Dyaks of Sarawak, for example, believe that everyone dies between three and seven times, until their souls become absorbed into the air.[34]

Other native peoples have a more purely "spiritual" conception of life after death, which doesn't feature the survival of the individual at all. The Nuer of Africa, for instance, believe that, in Evans-Pritchard's words, "When a man is dying the life slowly weakens and then it departs from him altogether, and Nuer say it has gone to God [or Spirit] from whom it came...Life comes from God [or Spirit] and to him it returns."[35] Similarly, the Keresan Pueblo Indians believe that when people die their souls go to *Shipap*, the "place of emergence," and return to the "fourfold womb of the earth" which bore them.[36] The Aborigines, meanwhile, believe that at death the soul divides into three parts. The "totemic soul" returns to the animals and plants which were the person's totems during his or her life, and the "ancestral soul" goes to join the tribe's ancestors who created the world during the Dreamtime. The third aspect of the soul is the "trickster," which is what we would call the ego, or personality. As with the ego-self of fallen peoples, the trickster hates the idea of dying and leaving behind all the people and things it's grown attached to, and as a result it may get stuck in the world. When people are unable to emotionally let go of an individual who's died, this is interpreted as meaning that the dead person's trickster has got inside their psyche and is refusing to leave. In other words, Aborigines' concept of life after death does feature the survival of the ego-self, but this is only the least significant and desirable aspect.[37]

But our ancestors' sharpened sense of ego led to very different concepts of life after death. These concepts had two main features. First of all, they did feature immortality – not strictly of the soul, but of the ego. People couldn't face the termination of the individuality which was so precious to them, and so convinced themselves that after death and for the rest of eternity they would exist as exactly the same persons they were in this life. And, secondly, their concepts of life after death were designed as a consolation for the terrible suffering which filled their lives. There was no way their egos could live on for ever in the same awful world as this – it had to be in a paradise which was free from war, oppression, poverty and disease, where they would live side by side with gods and angels. In other words, their idea of the afterlife became a kind of collective pipedream which made life more bearable. If they knew that this eternal paradise was waiting for them, then a few miserable decades of life on earth – of living as peasants who gave half of their income to their landlords and could be sent off to die on a battlefield at any moment, or as slaves, or as women who were beaten by their husbands and couldn't talk to other men or leave the house without permission – didn't seem so important.

In this respect, you could say that in the modern world – or at least in Europe – we're in a worse position than our ancestors. It's true that many of us are largely free of the kinds of social and physical suffering that filled our ancestors' lives, and which they developed their concepts of life after death in response to. But we still have the psychological suffering I'm describing in this chapter, and we still have to deal with the terrible prospect of the end of our individual existence. In theory, therefore, we still have the same (if perhaps slightly reduced) need for belief in an afterlife. The problem is that our rational, scientific view of the world (which ironically the Ego Explosion made possible) has made it difficult for us to believe in the old ideas of immortality and heaven. As a result, we have to face death without any kind of consolation, and are probably more afraid of it than earlier fallen peoples were.

We try to deal with this fear by thinking and talking about death as little as possible. If sex was the great taboo of the nineteenth century, death is the great one of the twentieth and twenty-first centuries. People who do bring up the subject are labelled as "morbid" and when we do have to confront it we usually dress it up in euphemisms like "when something happens" or "pass away." But no matter how much we try to avoid it, the prospect of death still haunts us. At the back of our minds we're always aware that, in Shakespeare's phrase, our "little life is rounded with a sleep," and that when that sleep comes the ego which has been the focus of everything we've ever done will be blotted out as if it had never existed in the first place. As the psychologist I.D. Yalom writes:

> The fear of death plays a major role in our internal experience;
> it haunts us like nothing else; it rumbles continuously under the
> surface; it is a dark, unsettling presence at the rim of
> consciousness.[38]

UNDERLYING UNHAPPINESS

These, then, are the four basic reasons why we've lost the natural contentment that native peoples seem to have, and why we live in a state of psychological discord. They are such fundamental features of our experience that they make true happiness impossible for us to find. Some of us think we can make ourselves happy by becoming rich and successful, by treating ourselves to endless pleasures and amusements, by finding an ideal partner, an ideal job, an ideal house, etc. But as is shown by the large number of studies of pools and lottery winners, of national levels of happiness over different decades, and levels of happiness in different countries,[39] none of these things really do make us happy. They can't satisfy us because they always leave our psychological discord completely untouched. No matter how rich or successful we become, it's always there inside us, ready to confront us the moment our attention is no longer occupied.

It's not surprising that so many of us feel that life is a kind of senseless riddle, and secretly suspect that the universe might be playing tricks on us. We look up at the stars, realise how vast and empty the universe is and how insignificant our lives are. We ask ourselves, "What's it all about?" but don't have any answers. Mostly we try not to ask ourselves these questions – so much so that there's a taboo against this kind of "serious" thinking. Sometimes when we hear about people who have nervous breakdowns or commit suicide we say that they were "too intelligent for their own good" or that they "thought too much." But in our heart of hearts most of us would probably agree with the existentialist philosophers that life is absurd and more or less pointless. As Albert Camus wrote, "The absurd is the essential concept, and the first truth."[40] In fact, this is the kind of philosophy which is at the core of the materialistic and hedonistic values of our culture: nothing really means anything and we're going to die at some point anyway so we've just got to enjoy ourselves as much as we can while we're here.

But even though we might not be aware of it, the desire to escape psychological discord is one of our deepest drives. To a large extent our lives are propelled by the effort to *find* the happiness which we're not born with, to overcome our psychological discord and attain a state of well-being and completeness – or at least to escape from our suffering into a neutral state.

7

ESCAPING FROM
PSYCHOLOGICAL DISCORD

ONE OF THE WAYS in which we try to deal with our psychological discord is simply to avoid confronting it. The activities and distractions we fill our lives with – our work, our hobbies, socialising, television and other kinds of entertainment – to some extent, we use all of these as methods of keeping our attention focused outside ourselves so that we don't have to face our psychological discord. In these moments of distraction we go *outside* ourselves; our consciousness is completely taken up by the job we're doing or the TV programme we're watching, and so there's no opportunity to experience the disharmony inside us. We're like a child whose parents argue all the time and who spends as much time as he can outdoors to avoid the terrible atmosphere that fills the house. As Trigant Burrow observed perceptively:

> The daily madness of these jobs is a repeated vaccination against the madness of the asylum. Look at the eagerness with which workers return from vacation to their compulsive madness. They plunge into their work with equanimity and lightheartedness because it drowns out something more ominous. Men have to be protected from reality.[1]

However, it isn't so much reality which men – and women too, of course – need to be protected from, so much as their own minds. The proof of this is that, as we've seen, when we do have to spend time inside our own psyche the effect can be devastating. Native peoples may be able to work happily for only ten or twelve hours a week, or wait for hours in a queue without becoming impatient or agitated, but for us inactivity is a curse. Even just a few hours of solitude and inactivity can open up a Pandora's box of boredom, anxiety and depression inside us. We've already noted – in Chapter 1 – the negative effects of unemployment and retirement, and this has also been shown dramatically by psychologists' experiments with sensory deprivation. In a series of experiments in the 1950s, for example, volunteers wore blindfolds, earmuffs and tubes fitted to their arms and legs (to deprive them of tactile contact). Almost all of them quickly began to experience great psychological discomfort, and couldn't endure the predicament for long.[2]

Another method we use to avoid psychological discord is drug-taking. Many unfallen peoples take drugs too, of course. Indians throughout South America inhaled powders made from hallucinogen plants, and even today many Amazonian Indians use this "psychedelic snuff." The Indians of Central America commonly took psychedelic mushrooms, while some North American Indians took peyote (which contains the drug mescaline). Similarly, "magic" mushrooms are taken by the primal peoples of Siberia and New Guinea – where cases of "mushroom madness" have been observed by anthropologists.[3]

However, primal peoples' attitude to drugs is completely different from ours. They never take drugs purely for recreational purposes, but only as a part of religious rites, initiation ceremonies and funerals, or for the purposes of shamanic journeys or medical diagnosis. For them the purpose of drugs is to intensify perception, to bring visions, or to melt away the divide between the seen and the unseen worlds and make contact with spirits. In other words, they use them to *expand* their vision of reality.

For the fallen psyche, however, the whole point of drugs is *escape*. We want to experience less reality, not more. Drugs – including alcohol – are often a last line of defence against the psychological discord we experience when our lives don't contain enough activity or structure to keep our attention focused outside us. This can happen as a result of unemployment or retirement (although there aren't many cases of old aged pensioners becoming heroin addicts, of course – they're more likely to start drinking heavily), or with musicians, actors and others whose professions include long periods of inactivity. Some drugs – such as tranquillisers and depressants – induce a feeling of numbness which immunises us to the discontent inside us, while others, such as cocaine or ecstasy, fill us with pleasurable sensations which *override* the inner discontent. (Of course, like primal peoples, some of us also use mind-expanding substances such as LSD or "magic" mushrooms, but even here there's usually still a big difference. Although some people do use them for what you could call "transcendental" reasons, most of us use psychedelics for recreational purposes, treating the few hours of crazy perceptions and visions they give us as an entertaining interlude from the dullness of ordinary consciousness.)

THE ROOTS OF MATERIALISM

The second way of dealing with psychological discord is to try to find alternative sources of happiness which will compensate for it, or cancel it out.

One of the most striking differences of all between fallen and unfallen peoples is a completely different attitude to material goods. Unfallen peoples generally have no desire to own property or land or to accumulate possessions. Amongst hunter-gatherer groups, personal ownership is usually seen as morally wrong. People are obliged to share everything apart from a few personal artefacts, such as cooking utensils and tools, which they use every day as individuals.[4] Everything else belongs to the group collectively. As we noted earlier of the Hazda of Tanzania, for instance, if for some reason a person comes into ownership of a second axe or a second shirt, this usually doesn't last for longer than a few hours, since the things are given or gambled away almost immediately.[5] In fact, the concept of personal ownership is so foreign to unfallen peoples that many of them don't even have words for "possession" or "property." As Colin Scott notes of the Cree Indian language, for example, "there is no substantive category either equivalent or similar to "property" in English, and no verb 'to own.'"[6] Similarly, as Robert Lawlor notes, none of hundreds of Australian Aboriginal languages have a word for "possession."[7]

The Aborigines' indifference to material goods confused early colonial visitors. As one of them wrote:

> In botanising today on the other side of the river we accidentally found the greatest part of the gifts and clothes which we had given to the Aborigines left all in a heap together, doubtless as lumber not worth carriage.[8]

The colonists of America were equally baffled by the Native Americans' lack of materialism. The Indians stopped work as soon as they had produced as much food as they needed, instead of building up a surplus which they might be able to sell or exchange for goods. They didn't bother digging for gold even though they knew where it was, and had little or no interest in objects which the Europeans considered beautiful and precious. As Alvin M. Josephy reports in *The Indian Heritage of America*, this attitude was so alien to the colonists that they saw it as evidence that the Indians were "not normal people but rather members of a subhuman or animal species, lacking souls."[9]

It's true that, as some observers have pointed out, the nomadic lifestyle of many primal peoples doesn't allow for the accumulation of possessions, since there are only a certain amount of things which they can carry from one site to the next. But many primal peoples do live a sedentary way of life, of course, and still show an indifference to material goods, and have strong moral principles which emphasise sharing.

Like their lack of warfare, the lack of materialism of native peoples shows how flawed and limited the view of human nature put forward by evolutionary psychologists and Neo-Darwinist biologists is. They tell us that human beings have a natural instinct to possess things to help improve their chances of survival. But as Lee and DeVore put it:

> All the assumptions economists make about economic man are absent in these [hunter-gatherer] societies. People in immediate-return societies are not acquisitive, self-centred cost-benefit calculators. In these societies, it can be most clearly seen that economic man as a universal type is a fiction.[10]

The need to possess land and material goods is, like war and patriarchy, a specifically fallen characteristic. In fact, some of the world's Fall myths explicitly state that the "love of possession" was one of the negative effects of the Fall. This is especially clear from the Roman poet Ovid's description of the human race's decline from the original Golden Age:

> There broke out...all manner of evil, and shame fled, and truth and faith. In place of these came deceits and trickery and

> treachery and force and the accursed love of possession…And
> the land, hitherto a common possession like the light of the sun
> and the breezes, the careful surveyor now marked out with long
> boundary line[s].[11]

Similarly, in Plato's description of the mythic island of Atlantis – which some scholars believe was a folk memory of the unfallen culture of ancient Crete – he states that the people "[bore] lightly the burden of gold and other property they possessed; neither were they intoxicated by luxury, nor did wealth deprive them of their self-control and thereby cause their downfall."[12]

The Aborigines and Native Americans, for their part, were baffled by the European disease of "love of possession." As we've seen, the Indians found the idea of owning land incomprehensible, and this was one of the main obstacles preventing them from adapting to the European way of life. Sometimes this worked in the colonists' favour, since the Indians thought that the concept of selling areas of land was an absurd joke, and let the Europeans buy them for ridiculously low prices. As one Seneca chief said, "A man cannot sell the land anymore than he can sell the sea or the air he breathes."[13]

The European obsession with gold seemed equally strange to the Indians. The colonists seemed to value it so highly and be prepared to go to such massive lengths to get hold of it, that some tribes reached the fairly logical – from their point of view – conclusion that it was a kind of deity with supernatural power. When one Indian chief in Cuba learned that the Spanish were about to invade his island, he decided to appeal to the gold spirit which he believed they worshipped to try to appease their wrath. He made prayers to a chestful of gold, but unfortunately it didn't make any difference. The Spanish still invaded the island, captured him and burned him alive.[14]

Since then the disease of possession has become even more rampant, of course. The modern world seems to have gone mad with materialism. The happiness paradigm of our culture – that is, the most socially accepted concept of what happiness is and how to find it – tells us that it comes from earning as much money as possible and using this to buy the "biggest and best" of everything (the biggest houses, the best car, the best food, best clothes, best furniture) and a whole host of other completely unnecessary luxury goods (jewellery, ornaments, cars and clothes which we have no use for), as well as spending money on hedonistic pleasures and amusements (holidays, socialising, going to concerts or restaurants or nightclubs, taking drugs, etc.). Ironically, in view of the fact that the Indians thought that gold was a deity, in the modern world materialism *has* become a kind of religion.

The only way we can understand materialism is in the terms I mentioned at the start of this section. Our desire to obtain and possess goods, property, land and money stems from a desire to find a source of well-being which will override – or alleviate – the psychological discord inside us. Unfallen peoples are not materialistic because they don't suffer from psychological discord.

Materialism does give us a kind of happiness. When we buy something new, an instinctive "pleasure button" is pressed inside us, giving us a temporary thrill of well-being. Possessions can also give us a sense of well-being in their function as status symbols. The big house and the big car, designer clothes, membership of exclusive clubs and so on – these give us the ego-thrill of feeling that we're superior or more important than other people who lack these things.

Perhaps most importantly of all, though, we hanker after possessions because they give us a sense of security. Probably because we experience the world as a fundamentally threatening place, and are aware deep down that our position as living beings is fragile and temporary, possessions give us a sense of permanence and protection. In the words of the psychologist Tim Kasser, materialistic values can be seen as "a symptom of underlying insecurity and a coping strategy (albeit a relatively ineffective one) some people use in an attempt to alleviate their anxieties."[15]

Closely related to this, we can also see materialism as an attempt to *complete* ourselves. We've noted that our strong sense of separation leaves us with a sense of lack, of not being sufficient as we are, like a child who has an emptiness and insecurity inside her as a result of not being given enough affection by her parents. Because of this we have a powerful need to complete ourselves, to fill the hole inside us – and perhaps accumulating money and material goods is a way of attempting to do this.

And, finally, our mania for material goods may also be related to the intensified fear of death which the Ego Explosion has left us with. At some level we may feel that by possessing goods and wealth we can somehow cheat death, or insulate ourselves against it. This interpretation is supported by the Terror Management theory of psychology, which sees a wide range of human behaviour as an attempt to deal with our deep, subconscious fear of death. Experiments by Tim Kasser and others, based on Terror Management theory, have shown that the more conscious people are of death, the more materialistic are their values.[16]

Hedonism is important here too. Although they're closely linked, hedonism – the effort to have as much fun and pleasure as possible – is really a separate way of trying to deal with our psychic suffering. We're all instinctively programmed to find certain things pleasurable – things such as food, drink, drugs, sex, and comfortable living conditions (a comfortable bed and furniture, soft, plush carpets, heating etc.). There are also the many instinctive thrills we get in certain situations, such as being surrounded by crowds of people and loud music and bright lights, driving, sailing or flying at high speeds, or being amongst pleasant climatic conditions. These are all "pleasure buttons" which give us a feeling of well-being when we press them. Some of them have been purposely placed there by nature to make sure that we will survive and reproduce – food, for example, is pleasurable so that we'll want to eat, and sex is pleasurable so that we'll reproduce. Others are more accidental buttons caused by chemical changes inside us, such as when speed or danger give us an adrenalin rush or produce endorphins.

The connection with materialism – apart from the fact that shopping is a pleasure button-pressing hedonistic activity – is that the more money we have, the more access we have to these pleasures. And as with materialism, the purpose of hedonism is to override our fundamental unhappiness with a sense of well-being.

It's probably not a coincidence that both hedonism and materialism have become so important to us at a time when the old religion of Christianity has begun to fade away. Since the consolation of religion is no longer available, we're more exposed to the suffering of the post-Fall psyche, and so have to look for well-being elsewhere. The sad thing is, though, that despite all our efforts this never completely works. Materialism or hedonism can never completely satisfy us because their pleasure-bringing thrills are so temporary. Whereas our psychological discord is ever present, the "buzz" which pleasure buttons give us always fades away after a short while, leaving us back where we started.

Psychologists' studies have repeatedly shown that wealth does not bring happiness. As we have seen, studies of lottery winners have found that after the first few months, these people are no happier than anybody else. They may, in fact, actually be *less* happy, since they no longer derive the same amount of pleasure from mundane everyday experiences.[17] Studies from individual countries have shown that although levels of income have increased many times over the last few decades, the population's level of happiness has remained almost constant.[18] And international studies have shown that the world's richest countries are not necessarily happier than poorer ones. In the words of Michael Argyle, these studies show that "international differences in happiness are very small, and almost unrelated to economic prosperity."[19]

STATUS

Another way in which we try to override our psychological discord is by chasing after what you could call "ego-based happiness." In fact, this is the other main part of our culture's happiness paradigm: we also believe that we can find happiness by "being someone," by becoming successful or famous, by gaining the respect and admiration of others.

There are basically two ways in which we can do this: through power or success. We can obtain the high status we crave by having power over other people, by dominating them, so that our authority and the deference with which they treat us "puffs up" our ego. (As we'll see in the next chapter, war, patriarchy and social stratification are all closely linked to this urge.) On the other hand, slightly more benevolently, we can obtain status through our achievements and talents, by doing things which make other people admire and respect us — in other words, by becoming successful and/or famous. Or, with a slightly different variation, we can become famous without being talented or successful, simply by grabbing the limelight and drawing attention to ourselves (by becoming a TV show contestant, for example, or by killing a celebrity.)

Unfallen peoples don't appear to have this need to be "someone." This is clear from the lack of stratification in their societies – since social stratification stems from the desire for power, together with the desire for wealth. It's also clear from the democratic nature of their societies, with their lack of authoritarian leader figures and their collective decision-making processes. If primal peoples did have a desire for status, then – as happened in the fallen world – individuals would not be satisfied with their equal share of power, but would be driven to try to accumulate more, and to take control of the decision-making process, in order to raise themselves above others.

One effect of this desire for ego-based happiness is that the societies of the fallen world are always very competitive. There's only a limited amount of power, success and wealth to go round, and since we all want it, we have to fight against other people to get it. This is true on an everyday level too: whatever we're doing, even if we're just playing football in the park or dancing or telling jokes, it's usually important for us to win, or at least to "do well" or be better than other people, in order to gain respect and status.

Unfallen societies completely lack this competitiveness. As Robert Lawlor notes, "The competitive spirit and the attitudes and drives associated with it have no place in the life of tribal Aborigines. None of their games or activities involve competition." [20] Similarly, the anthropologist L. Marshall notes that the children of the !Kung communities of south-west Africa do not have any competitive games. [21] Or as Jean Liedloff writes of the Yequana, a tribe of the Amazonian region of South America:

> They have no competitive games…There is wrestling, but there is no championship, only a series of matches between pairs of men. The constant practice of archery is always aimed at achieving excellence but never in competition with other boys, nor is hunting a competitive matter among men. [22]

As with personal property, competition goes against the communal principles of pre-Fall cultures. As soon as a person makes himself more important than everybody else, the balance and harmony of the community is disturbed. Even the great artists of unfallen cultures seem strangely ego-less from our point of view, and rarely state personal authorship of their work. As Eisler says of ancient Crete, for instance, "Even among the ruling classes personal ambition seems to have been unknown; nowhere do we find the name of an author attached to a work of art nor a record of the deeds of a ruler." [23]

In view of this, it's not surprising that things never went smoothly when European colonists tried to introduce their competitive sports to the natives. In New Guinea, boys were forced to play football in mission schools, but instead of going all out to win by as many goals as possible, they usually carried on until scores were level. [24] Football was also opposed to the communal sensibility of the Aborigines. They found the idea of "beating" members of their own community incomprehensible, and couldn't bring themselves to show the kind of aggression and confrontation that the game requires. [25] Similarly, in *Mornings in Mexico*, Lawrence describes watching Indian athletic races, and notes that their motivation is different from the European "racing to win" attitude. As he writes, "The youths and men whirl down the racing track in relays. They are not racing to win a race. They are not racing to win a prize. They are not racing to show their prowess." Instead, says Lawrence, their racing has a spiritual dimension. It's an attempt to make connection with the cosmos, and to gather new vitality from it. As he describes it:

> They are putting forth all their might, all their strength, in a tension that is half anguish, half ecstasy, in the effort to gather into their souls more and more of the creative fire, the creative energy, which shall carry their tribe through the year.[26]

In other words, like materialism, the desire for status – and the competitive drive that comes with it – is a specifically fallen characteristic. And perhaps, again as a reaction to the fading away of religion, in the modern world the desire for status is just as crazily endemic as the disease of possession. It's this (together with the material gains which success brings) which makes us determined to climb to the top of our career ladders, to "make it" as actors or singers or businessmen, to get on TV or have our names in the papers, or even just to own status symbols like BMW cars or Armani suits. We compete against each other to get better qualifications, better jobs, better promotion prospects, bigger houses, better cars, and more fashionable clothes. Many of us see life as a kind of race to attain as much money and success and status as we can; with every year which goes by we need to feel that we've moved a little farther forward, that we're at least keeping up with the others. And so we keep trying to gain new skills and qualifications, to improve our standard of living, to make our houses a little more luxurious.

For some people the desire for status goes much farther than this, though, and turns into a maniacal quest for power which often has appalling consequences. Perhaps because they were born with an even stronger sense of ego than normal and so had a higher level of psychological discord inside them, conquerors such as Alexander the Great, Napoleon and Hitler attempted to attain a kind of immortal god-like status by dominating the whole world. Modern-day politicians and "business conquerors" (like Rupert Murdoch) have the same kind of extreme hunger for power.

And it's true, again, that this ego-based happiness does work to a degree. In fact, in some ways it seems to work better than materialism or hedonism, since the glow of well-being it gives seems to last longer. The feeling of well-being you get from taking drugs or going shopping only lasts as long as the drugs or the shopping trip itself, but the positive feeling you get when you catch a stranger looking at you adoringly, or when an audience applauds your performances or your book is published, can last for hours or even days afterwards. It always fades away at some point, though, so that ego-based happiness can never completely satisfy us either. This is why we're never satisfied with any level of success or power we've achieved so far. Conquerors have to keep on invading new countries, business moguls have to keep on taking over companies, and pop stars have to sell more and more records and conquer more markets. We have to have new "hits" of ego-based happiness to replace the ones which have faded away.

Another problem here is that ego-based happiness is subject to the law of diminishing returns, so that each "hit" has to be more powerful than the last to provide the same glow of well-being. And at a certain point this is no longer possible. You run out of new countries or markets to conquer, or else you discover that the new levels of success or power you need are unattainable. And at this point you're stranded with your psychological discord, unable to resist it. This is the point that Alexander the Great reached when, according to legend, after building up the largest empire the world had known at that time, he was still dissatisfied and wept for new lands to conquer. Although this story is probably apocryphal, historians do now believe that Alexander died of alcoholism, which is exactly the kind of fate we would expect him to meet.[27]

The Roots of the Desire for Status

As with materialism, the only way to make sense of all this is to see it as a reaction to our inner disharmony. Unfallen peoples don't have this desire for status simply because they don't suffer from psychological discord. But we chase after success and power as alternative sources of happiness which we hope will override it, or cancel it out. Perhaps we're trying to complete ourselves with them in this way too, to fill the sense of lack we feel. We try so hard to become "someone" because we feel a basic sense of nothingness – or at least non-wholeness – inside us.

Fear of death may be a factor too. One of the basic desires of the over-developed ego is to live forever (which is why, as we saw in the last chapter, the religions of fallen peoples always feature the survival of the individual for eternity in "heaven"). But since many of us no longer accept the possibility of immortality in heaven, it has perhaps become more important for us to attain it on earth, by becoming so powerful that we attain immortal god-like status, or at least so powerful or famous that we transcend death in the sense that our memory – and the effects of our actions – will live on longer after us. ("Fame! I want to live for ever," as the song goes.) In other words, the desire for status is another facet of "Terror Management." As Solomon et al. note, "all power is ultimately bound to issues surrounding sustaining life and forestalling death, ideally permanently."[28]

Another way of looking at this is in terms of what Ken Wilber calls the *Atman Project*. According to Wilber, the true nature of human beings is pure spirit or *atman*. At the very core of our being we are one with the universe, infinite and eternal, beyond space and time and death. Although we have become alienated from this true nature, we still have an intuition of it, and our deepest drive is to regain the wholeness which we've lost. However, we go about this in completely the wrong way, and translate the characteristics of our true spiritual nature into the realm of the ego. In our deepest selves we are one with God, actually *are* God, but on the level of the ego this translates into a desire to *be* God, to be all powerful, to control and dominate other people – hence the desire for status, success and power.

Wilber explains materialism in this way too. In our deepest selves we *are* everything, but on the ego level this translates into wanting to *have* everything, hence the desire to possess things. Similarly, the spirit part of us is immortal, but on the ego level this translates into the desire to live forever as an individual, hence the fallen idea of the afterlife. This impulse to regain our lost wholeness – but in ways which paradoxically prevent this happening – is the *Atman Project*.[29]

In view of all this, it's not surprising that all fallen societies have been capitalist ones. The so-called "capitalist system" isn't something which was imposed on society by economists and politicians – as socialists sometimes say – but the inevitable result of the desire for wealth and status which is a part of the fallen psyche. Communism belongs to the pre-Fall era. As Marx and Engels themselves realised, all pre-Fall societies were effectively communist, with common ownership of property, no classes or castes and no exploitation – and this social system was simply the result of their lack of desire for what fallen peoples crave so strongly.

It's no wonder, then, that all of the attempts to impose Communism on societies in the last hundred years or so have failed. Communism is unnatural to fallen human beings; to ask the majority of people to give up private property, competition and power is as futile as asking them to give up sex or food. (However, as we'll see later, there has been a subtle emergence of a new kind of psyche over the last few hundred years – the "trans-Fall" psyche, as I call it – which has meant that societies in general have become gradually more egalitarian and democratic. The fact that these socialist philosophies emerged in the first place is a sign of this, as is their increasing popularity in recent times.)

We can say the same of the three characteristics of human society which we began this book by examining: war, social stratification and patriarchy. These are an inevitable result of the fallen psyche as well, and the emergence of the "trans-Fall" psyche has, it seems, caused a gradual de-intensification of them, especially over the last few decades.

And now that we've established how the Fall created psychological discord, and seen how this gave human beings a deep-rooted craving for wealth and status, we're in a good position to look at how it gave rise to war, social oppression and patriarchy.

8

THE ORIGINS OF SOCIAL CHAOS 1 - WAR

IF THE "SELFISH GENE" theory of human nature is correct, all kinds of pathological human behaviour are natural and inevitable. Some evolutionary psychologists have suggested that racism is inevitable, for example. To one group of human beings, other groups are potential competitors for the same sources of food, and so potentially dangerous to their survival. As a result, they are genetically programmed to be hostile towards them. People are only interested in the survival of their own genes – which are also carried by their relatives – and this is always threatened by members of other groups.[1] In a similar way, rape has been seen as inevitable. There will always be some men who can't find women to have a legitimate sexual relationship with; but their selfish genes are still desperate to replicate themselves, and so these men have little "choice" but to force women to have sex with them against their will.[2]

The human race's predilection for making war has been reduced to the same crude terms. According to the "selfish gene" theory, war is really only one step forward from racism. It happens when the survival interests of different groups collide. Nature only offers us limited resources – a limited number of fruit trees in a certain area, of animals for hunting, of streams for drinking water and washing, and so on. Our survival depends on our access to these, so when other groups either use them, or threaten to use them, our selfish genes impel us to fight and kill. In evolutionary psychological terms, groups become "forces of selection" which are permanently in conflict with one another.

Even more crudely, there are some attempts to explain war in chemical terms. We're often told that male aggression – which leads to both war and patriarchy – is the result of the large amount of testosterone which male human beings have inside them. The average man produces 5,100 micrograms of testosterone every day, whereas women produce just 100 micrograms. And testosterone chemically instructs us to - in Ken Wilber's phrase - "fuck it or kill it."[3] It means that, at heart, all men are Vikings who like to spend their time fighting and fucking.

Another theory is that male aggression – and by extension war – is caused by reduced levels of the brain chemical serotonin. Laboratory experiments have shown that when animals are injected with serotonin they become less aggressive, and studies have found that children who are impulsively aggressive tend to have low serotonin levels, as also do adults who commit violent crimes or suicide. Other studies have suggested that there's a link between violence and low levels of blood cholesterol or higher than usual levels of insulin.[4]

One problem with these chemical theories is that it's impossible to tell whether the chicken or the egg came first. It's perfectly possible that the chemical state in question (such as a lower level of serotonin or a high level of testosterone) might be the result of aggressive behaviour rather than its cause. And while you can imagine how a certain chemical state might make an individual prone to aggression at a particular time, it's difficult to see how this could explain the kind of collective, highly organised and long-term aggression which characterises war. A high level of testosterone might explain the desire to fight at a particular moment, but surely can't account for the motives of war which come before this – for example, the desire to conquer and enslave other groups and to increase a nation's wealth and power – or the kind of organisational requirements of war, such as manufacturing weapons and mobilising armies. As the anthropologists Clifton B. Kroeber and Bernard L. Fontana point out, "It is a large step from what may be biologically innate leanings toward individual aggression to ritualised, socially sanctioned, institutionalised group warfare."[5]

But the biggest problem with both the chemical and evolutionary psychological attempts to explain war is that, as we've seen, animal species and human beings are nowhere near as war-like as these theories would seem to suggest. If human beings are genetically and chemically programmed to be aggressive and to wage war, why was war almost completely absent from human history until only 6,000 years ago? Perhaps you could say that earlier pre-Fall human beings had a lower level of testosterone than later ones (or higher levels of serotonin), or that their genes weren't quite as selfish, but both of these suggestions seem very unlikely.

ENVIRONMENTAL EXPLANATIONS OF WAR

Other scholars accept that war is a relatively late historical development, and that it may not necessarily be innate to human beings. They suggest social and environmental reasons for its eruption. One popular theory, for example, is that war was the result of population pressure. There was no need for war when the earth was sparsely populated and tribes had vast areas to themselves, so this theory goes, but once the population increased and they began to encroach on each other's territory and food supplies, they had to start fighting to survive.

However, this "population pressure" theory is often used to explain the advent of agriculture too: the reason why human groups over the Middle East, central Asia and Europe gave up the hunting and gathering way of life was because population increases meant there were too many people in too small an area, too many to be supported by hunting and gathering. They had to turn to horticulture, which makes much more efficient use of space, and doesn't require a mobile lifestyle. If this was the case – and most scholars agree that it was – then we would expect the transition to agriculture to be accompanied by a great deal of conflict as the groups competed over dwindling resources. But as we've seen, there is almost no evidence of warfare in these areas until the fifth millennium BCE, more than 3,000 years after the advent of agriculture.

In any case, anthropological studies have shown that scarcity of resources does not necessarily lead to conflict between groups. Data collected by the anthropologists Carol and Melvin Ember establishes that "chronic, ordinary resource shortage is not a significant predicator of war."[6] Or, in the words of R. Brian Ferguson, "the data just does not support a direct association of increasing [population] density and increasing war."[7] In complete contrast to the selfish and competitive view of human nature put forward by evolutionary psychology, rather than turning to violence, hunter-gatherers are more likely to deal with a lack of food by moving to a different area, or – if land is scarce – merging with another group. The !Kung of Africa, for instance, consciously build friendly ties with neighbouring tribes by giving them gifts, so that they'll be able to share their resources if their own happen to fail.[8] In fact, this is true of most hunter-gatherer groups. In the words of the anthropologist Anderson, it is normal practice for foraging peoples to "keep a wide range of strategic social ties 'warm' as a security measure in the face of changing weather conditions and a changing population and supply of resources."[9]

Perhaps the fundamental factor here is that hunter-gatherers are generally not territorial – that is, they don't think of a particular area of land as belonging to them and them alone, and aggressively resist anybody who encroaches on it. As Burch and Ellanna put it, "both social and spatial boundaries among hunter-gatherers are extremely flexible with regard to membership and geographic extent."[10] Since they have no real concept of territory, they are obviously unlikely to fight wars to protect land or resources.

There is also the theory that war began with post-Fall "civilisation." But the problem with linking war to civilisation – or living in cities – is that peoples such as the early Indo-Europeans and Semites did not have any kind of civilisation – or even lead a settled lifestyle – and yet were extremely war-like. And as we noted in Chapter 2, there were many earlier peoples who were clearly "civilised," with a reasonably high level of technological development and large living communities (such as the ancient Cretans or the citizens of Catal Huyuk), who were extremely peaceful.

FURTHER THEORIES

In *The Origin of War,* J.M.G. van der Dennen puzzles over why the human race is so savagely war-like compared to the rest of the animal kingdom. The answer, he believes, lies in the different structure of the human brain. As he writes, "Is it not more logical to associate these specific forms of violence, not with the animal, but with the specific human brain, i.e. the neocortical acquisitions superimposed on the reptilian brain and limbic system?"[12] The problem here is to explain why earlier human beings weren't so violent, even though they had the same brain structure. Van der Dennen tries to do this by suggesting that the structure of our brains doesn't mean that we have to *continually* fight war, only that war is a possible option, which we choose under certain circumstances. And according to him, these circumstances didn't arise until a fairly late stage – until human beings started to settle down, from 8,000 BCE onwards. At this point they needed to develop what he calls a "male coalitional strategy" in order to defend their territory. However, the fact that human groups lived a settled agricultural lifestyle for thousands of years without resorting to war obviously argues against this theory. Van der Dennen's problem is that, like so many modern scientists, he assumes that human behaviour can only be explained in physical terms, and ignores the fact that the human mind or psyche is to some degree an independent entity, which can change or develop along its own lines, without necessarily altering physical structure (even though changes might have some physical correlates).

Gerhard Lenski's theory is that war came about because when people made the switch from the hunter-gatherer to the horticultural way of life, men no longer had the opportunity to go hunting. As a result, they began to wage war as a substitute, an alternative way of exercising their bravery and skill. But, again, the fact that human groups lived a peaceful, sedentary life for as long as 3,000 years following the transition to horticulture invalidates this view.[13]

There are even more attempts to explain war. As usual, Ken Wilber provides one of the most ingenious, and one which is in fact quite close to the explanation I'm going to put forward. He also links the origins of war to the development of the sharpened sense of ego. As he writes:

> Whatever natural aggression is innately present in humans, the important point is that it is amplified through the conceptual domains, and that amplification - itself not genetic - constitutes the specific, morbid, excessive aggression known only to man.[14]

Wilber suggests that the "conceptual domains" – which he elsewhere relates to the sharpened sense of ego – intensify aggression because human beings become more self-conscious and separate and therefore more afraid of death. As a result of this, they become, as he writes, "more joyously willing to deal in massive substitute sacrifices – The more you can rob others of immortality by killing them, the greater grows your own immortality account."[15] In other words, our terror of death makes us kill others so that they will die instead of us, and we won't have to die ourselves.

WAR AND THE FALL

Wilber's explanation may well be a factor, but I believe there are three, more fundamental, ways in which the fallen psyche was – and is – responsible for warfare.

We've seen that the Ego Explosion gave rise to a sense of inner discontent and incompleteness in human beings, and that this in turn gave rise to the desire for wealth and status. And to a large extent we can see war as the manifestation of this desire. After all, there are two main reasons why human groups have waged war on others throughout history: firstly, in order to steal their territory and property, and, secondly, in order to conquer and dominate them. All the "great" empires in history have had these two motivations. They usually go together, but in some cases nations have conquered other peoples purely as a matter of status even when there is no material gain to be had. In the same way that we try to gain status as individuals by impressing the people around us with expensive cars, fashionable clothes or big houses, governments have waged wars to gain colonies which have no real use to them except as a symbol of power. As Walt W. Rostow noted:

> Certain colonial powers came, as a matter of prestige and style,
> to desire colonial possessions as a symbol of their coming of
> age…The competition occurred essentially because competitive
> nationalism was the rule of the world arena and colonies were an
> accepted symbol of status and power within the arena.[16]

At the same time, the Ego Explosion created a lack of empathy between human beings, which is the second main reason for war. The question of empathy requires a little attention, since I see it – or the lack of it – as one of the most important effects of the Ego Explosion, and one of the most important causes of the devastation which followed it. In fact, when we bring the desire for wealth and power together with a lack of empathy, we have the basic source of most of the social pathology which makes up the last 6,000 years of human history.

Empathy is usually seen as an ability to read other people's feelings, or to use the imagination to "put yourself in someone else's shoes." According to Simon Baron-Cohen, empathy is about "reading the emotional atmosphere" and "tuning into the other person's thoughts and feelings."[17] However, while I don't for one moment dispute that this is a *form* of empathy – and the form that we most commonly experience – I believe that there is another, deeper kind. In a fundamental sense, all human beings share the same consciousness. This isn't the place for a discussion about what consciousness is, but in my view, rather than seeing consciousness as a product of the brain, it makes much more sense to see it as a kind of fundamental force which is beyond the brain, and pervades the whole universe. (This view has recently been put forward by physicists as well as philosophers such as Robert Forman and David Chalmers.[18]) As Robert Forman suggests, it may be that consciousness works through the brain to produce our own individual sense of being and personality. The brain acts as a "receiver" of consciousness, in the way that a radio receives radio waves. If this view is correct, then our shared consciousness transcends our individuality. And empathy, in this sense, works through this shared consciousness. It makes it possible for me to experience what you are experiencing, your pain, your fear or your joy. In essence your being is also mine, and so I can experience your feelings in my own being.

This spiritual sense of connection is often experienced by highly compassionate people. The psychologist Arthur Deikman recently interviewed a number of "service providers" – as he calls them – and found that almost all of them "experience a sense of connection to something greater than themselves." A doctor who founded an organisation giving support to cancer sufferers said that service gives her "a sense of connection to something beyond the moment. It's like seeing both of you as part of a much larger process that has no beginning and no end." A man who runs a hospice told him that when he takes care of other people, "I don't have such a feeling of separateness in this world." Some service providers spoke in terms of an energy which they can actually sense, a kind of electricity which flows between them and the people they serve. As one told Deikman, "The connection is at an energetic level – it's like food for the emotional or nervous system that really is a tangible energy exchange."[19]

This was the source of unfallen peoples' acute sense of empathy with other human beings, other creatures and with the natural in general. Because of their less developed sense of ego, they experienced this shared network of consciousness, and as a result they were (and are) "gentle hunters" who had a great deal of respect for their prey, and were reluctant to damage or abuse the natural world by mining the earth, chopping down trees or even ploughing the soil. But after the Ego Explosion this kind of empathy was no longer possible. When the ego is strongly developed, it breaks up this shared consciousness. Human beings become separated off into islands of individuality. And as a result we lose this ability to "feel with" other people.

This was partly responsible for the eruption of war after the Ego Explosion simply because not being able to sense the sufferings of others made people much more able to *inflict* suffering. They no longer found it a problem to kill women and children and raze whole cities to the ground because they were "walled off" from the shared consciousness which might have made them feel pity for their victims. Their lust for power and wealth filled them with a desire to gain other people's possessions and to exercise power over them, and their lack of empathy meant that they were able to torture and kill in service to these desires. Other human beings became one-dimensional objects who were just obstacles to the fulfilment of their desires or else had nothing more than a utilitarian value as slaves or concubines. As Simon Baron-Cohen remarks, "aggression, even in normal quantities, can only occur because of reduced empathising. You can't set out to hurt someone if you care about how they feel."[20]

The third of the fundamental causes of war is a little less obvious. One of the great puzzles about war is that people always seem to have enjoyed it so much, and seen it as a glorious and honourable pursuit. As Van Creveld writes in *Transformation of War*:

> Throughout history, for every person who has expressed his horror of war there is another who found in it the most marvellous of all the experiences that are vouchsafed to man, even to the point that he later spent a lifetime boring his descendants by recounting his exploits.[21]

But this makes some sense when we consider that one of the effects of the Fall was to make boredom a fundamental part of the human condition, and even to make us prey to a sense of *unreality*. Boredom is the result of the "de-sensitising mechanism" editing out the reality of our experience, so that the world is a shadowy, half-real place in which nothing really moves or interests us or seems worth giving our attention to. And the sense of unreality is the result of the constant thought chatter running through our minds. This thought chatter can be more immediate and powerful than – and seem *more real* than – the shadowy world outside us. We might feel that we're not really alive, not living in the world but in our own heads, swept away by the chaos of hallucinatory images and scenarios.

War may also have developed as a method of attempting to relieve this boredom and sense of unreality. In other words, it became important as a kind of entertainment, an activity to keep the terror of boredom and purposelessness at bay; and also as a way of making human beings feel alive. The American philosopher William James captured the essence of this when he wrote that war demands "such incredible efforts, depth beyond depth of exertion...[that] ranges of new energy are set free, and life seems cast upon a higher plane of power." (James goes on to suggest that human beings need a "moral equivalent of war," which has the same enlivening effect without the destruction and death).[22] And the French scientist and philosopher Pascal – who lived during an age of constant war 350 years ago – recognised the connection between boredom and war when, as we have seen, he wrote, "The sole cause of man's unhappiness is that he does not know how to stay quietly in his room." Pascal continues: "The only good thing for men is to be diverted from thinking what they are...that is why gaming and feminine society, war and high office are so popular."[23]

This is the reason why the outbreak of war has so often been a cause for celebration, particularly for the young men going to fight. In *Mein Kampf,* Hitler describes how the beginning of the First World War had exactly this enlivening effect on him, giving him a new sense of purpose and a "deliverance from the distress that had weighed down upon me during the days of my youth...I sank down on my knees to thank Heaven for the favour of having been permitted to live in such a time."[24] And, as historian Alan Bullock writes, speaking of the German people in general:

> The outbreak of war came...as a liberation from the monotony of their everyday – and in Hitler's case aimless – existence. The early days of August 1914 brought an unparalleled sense of national unity which those who experienced it never forgot, an exalted sense of patriotism.[25]

If these are the three main reasons for the eruption of warfare, there are perhaps two more minor ones. Warfare also served to give human groups a strong sense of collective identity, which helped them to overcome the sense of isolation which the Ego Explosion created. In his book *The Psychology of Nations*, the American psychologist G.E. Partridge noted that war creates a sense of "social intoxication, the feeling on the part of the individual of being a part of a body and the sense of being lost in a greater whole."[26] In this way, Partridge noted, war was "an attempt to meet the same psychological need otherwise fulfilled by love, religion, intoxication, art." [27]

Another possible factor is sexual repression. Wilhelm Reich argued that if you don't have a healthy sex life with regular orgasms, what he calls "undischarged bio-energetic tension" builds up inside you. This creates a sense of frustration and latent aggression, which has to have an outlet. And since Eurasian societies have always been – to a greater or lesser extent – sexual repressive, it's also possible that war has served as an outlet for this "undischarged bio-energetic tension."[28]

Reich's argument is supported by the research of the neuropsychologist James Prescott. He studied data from 400 different cultures and found a very strong correlation between sexual freedom and social violence. He found that societies characterised by "permissive premarital sexual behaviors" had a low level of adult physical violence, while societies which punished premarital (and extra-marital) sex were the most violent. As a result, he concluded that, "Premarital sexual freedom for young people can help reduce violence in a society."[29] Prescott also found a correlation between a society's level of violence and how much affection and bodily contact their children receive from their parents. As he writes:

> Those societies which give their infants the greatest amount of physical affection have less theft and violence among adults, thus supporting the theory that deprivation of bodily pleasure during infancy is significantly linked to a high rate of crime and violence.[30]

However, we shouldn't necessarily conclude from these correlations that sexual repression or a lack of childhood affection are the main causes of violence and war. The correlations are there because sexual repression and negative child-rearing practices were the effects of the Ego Explosion in the same way that war was. At the same time, these different characteristics must have affected each other *on a secondary level*. For example, although the primary cause of sexual repression and war is the fallen psyche, on a secondary level, the "undischarged bio-energetic tension" from sexual repression must have added to this, and caused a greater potential for violence.

THE FIRST AND SECOND WORLD WARS

All of this is very theoretical, so perhaps it's a good idea to look briefly at some real examples of war.

Germany wasn't the only nation to welcome the outbreak of the First World War. There was a general feeling of elation throughout the whole of Europe, suggesting that it came as a release from boredom and monotony – and provided a sense of collective unity – for everybody. As Barry McCarthy notes:

> Few populations in history can have been so eager to participate in battle as were the young men of Europe, cheered on so ecstatically by their womenfolk, in August 1914; their joy is preserved forever in grainy newspaper photos and on jerky, silent newsreels.[31]

In the first 18 months of war, two and a half million of Britain's young men enlisted voluntarily. After war was declared Buckingham Palace was surrounded by cheering crowds for days. When the United States joined the war in 1917, the audience at the New York Metropolitan Opera House cheered ecstatically.[32] Poets wrote paeans to the glories of warfare. Rupert Brooke, for example, wrote:

> Now God be thanked Who has matched us with this hour
> And caught our youth, and wakened us from sleeping.

Similarly W.N. Hodgson praised those who were "going to do the work of men."[33]

The First World War was related to intensified feelings of national pride which developed throughout Europe during the latter part of the nineteenth century. As Barry McCarthy notes, now that education was more widespread and more and more people could read, their governments took the opportunity to bombard them with "simplistic, exaggerated notions of national achievements and worth" through the popular press. The age of political propaganda had arrived. And at the same time as promoting national pride, of course, governments denigrated other nations, filling the press with "contrasting images of foreign nations and peoples that emphasised negative attributes: rivalry, cruelty, ignorance, godlessness, cowardice."[34] In other words, political propaganda led to an intensified sense of otherness between different countries, which led to reduced empathy and greater hostility. And the desire for status and wealth was obviously important here too. Now that nations were being encouraged to think of themselves as "great" they began to feel that they were entitled to rule over other peoples, and so felt an intensified drive to gain new territory and power.

The Treaty of Versailles at the end of the First World War punished Germany so severely that its economy was in ruin for years afterwards, with massive unemployment and terrible poverty. The allies believed this was the best way to ensure that the country would never be capable of warfare again, but it had exactly the opposite effect. It created a massive sense of national humiliation, and a desire for revenge – both of which led straight to the Second World War.

The devastation of the first war was so great that nobody – at least, nobody outside Germany – welcomed the outbreak of the second, so it's probably not possible to say that "war as a relief from monotony" was a factor here. Instead, we can see the Second World War as mainly the result of the German people's egotistical desire to regain the wealth and status which had been taken away from them, and to make themselves great again. As a reaction to their humiliation after the First World War, they began to believe that they were a chosen people who were racially superior and destined to dominate the world. Like other empire-builders before them, the Nazis attempted to complete themselves by dominating the rest of the human race, and to transcend death by building a thousand-year Reich. And, in addition, the propaganda of the Nazis, and the war itself, gave them an intoxicating sense of national unity, a sense of being one *Volk*, a powerful collective being which transcended the psychological discord of individual existence.

Their complete lack of empathy was a factor too, of course. They felt such a powerful sense of otherness to other ethnic groups – especially Jews, gypsies and Slavic peoples – that they saw them as sub-humans who didn't deserve to live. Their lack of empathy gave them a limitless capacity for violence and cruelty, which enabled them to terrorise and exterminate other human beings on a scale that the world had never seen before. (Admittedly this was mainly because of the twentieth-century science and technology available to them – if the ancient Assyrians or the Phoenicians had had access to this they would've been equally murderous, if not more so).

CRIMINALITY

Most of the points I've made above apply to the criminal behaviour of individuals too. We can be fairly certain that crimes like murder, rape and robbery, and human cruelty in general, were also at a much lower level during pre-Fall times, and that there was an explosion of them at the same time that as the explosion of war.

Crime seems to be largely absent from unfallen cultures. Anthropologists (such as Malinowski with the Trobriand Islanders, Elwin with the Muria, or Turnbull with the Mbuti) have repeatedly stressed their low levels of anti-social behaviour and inter-individual violence.[35] Because of their lack of possessiveness – and of possessions themselves – and the great importance they attach to sharing, crimes like theft and robbery are practically unknown. Some anthropologists have suggested that hunter-gatherer tribes maintain their equality through "tolerated theft,"[36] but this is really only a blindly Eurocentric way of looking at their practice of sharing and freely swapping possessions. The concept of "theft" doesn't apply at all, since there's no concept of ownership to begin with. Crimes such as rape, wife-beating and child abuse are also extremely rare. In fact, the most serious crimes to primal peoples are types of behaviour which we wouldn't think as of crimes at all. Apart from the breaking of taboos – which very rarely occurs – the most serious crime is the unbridled expression of egotism, when a person is greedy, shows off or tries to dominate others.

The Fall myths hint that criminality was a post-Fall development by telling us that earlier human beings were more "righteous" and had no need of laws of government. In his *Annals*, for example, the Roman historian Tacitus describes the earliest human beings as living "without guilt or crime, and therefore without penalties or compulsion...since by the prompting of their own nature they followed righteous ways."[37] On the other hand, historical records tell us how common crime became after the Fall. The danger of war wasn't the only reason why villages were situated inland rather than on the coast, and built on high ground with walls around them. There was also the danger of raids by gangs of bandits, or by pirates. Writing in the fifth century BCE, the Greek historian Thucydides tells us that piracy and banditry were a serious problem in the Mediterranean for over a thousand years, until the legendary King Minos of Crete took control of the sea at around 1600 BCE. As he writes:

> In ancient times, both Greeks and barbarians, the inhabitants of the coast as well of the islands, when they began to find their way to one another by sea, had recourse to piracy...They would fall upon the unwalled or straggling towns, or rather villages, which they plundered and maintained themselves by plundering them...The land too was infested by robbers; and there are parts of Hellas in which these old practices still continue...the fashion of wearing arms among these continental tribes is a relic of their old predatory habits. For in ancient times, all Greeks carried weapons because their homes were undefended and intercourse was unsafe.[38]

This suggests another reason why weapons became so common in the post-Fall era – not just because of the eruption of war, but also because people needed them to protect themselves (or, if they were bandits or pirates, as tools of their trade).

Crime was a part of daily life for the ancient Egyptians too. When the Old Kingdom collapsed at around 2180 BCE, the resultant chaos of crime and violence was described by the sage Ipuwer:

> The wrongdoer is everywhere. There is no man of yesterday. A man takes his shield when he goes to plow. A man smites his brother, his mother's son. Men sit in the bushes until the benighted traveller comes, in order to plunder his load.[39]

There are many social and economic causes of crime, of course, such as drug addiction, poverty, peer pressure and illiteracy.[40] But it's easy to see how crime might be related to the fallen psyche. The desire for wealth is certainly a motive of some crimes, as is – slightly less overtly – the desire for status. Criminologists have noted that many acts of violence (especially murder) stem from a sense of slight, as a retaliation for a perceived wrongdoing or lack of respect. Daly and Wilson found that two-thirds of all murders are the result of men feeling that they have been disrespected and acting to save face or regain lost status.[41] And in some cases crime may be a direct way of satisfying the isolated ego's need to be "someone." As John Archer notes in *Male Violence*, most violence committed by young men is related to status-seeking, especially when their social situation means that they can't get status in more benign, socially-sanctioned ways.[42] A desire for status might make a young man from a middle-class background strive to be a high-flying business executive; but with a young man from an underprivileged background – with no qualifications, a low level of literacy, and poor role models as parents – the same desire might lead to a career as a drug dealer.

This relationship between crime and self-esteem may be part of the reason why so many acts of violence are committed under the influence of alcohol. Alcohol has the effect of intensifying the ego, and generates an intense need for self-assertion. As John Archer notes, alcohol creates an "accentuated feeling of power and self importance which makes...one's own identity more easily threatened."[43] When a person is drunk he often feels more important, that his status is – or ought to be – higher, and so is more sensitive to slights or ridicule. And with chemical changes inside his body making him more prone to aggression, and fewer inhibitions to stop that aggression expressing itself, he is much more likely to respond with violence.

There is an obvious connection between crime and the inability to empathise too. Crime almost always means consciously abusing or mistreating other people, which is only possible – or at least becomes much easier – if you don't have a sense of empathy. Simon Baron-Cohen suggests, for example, that the reason why violent crime is much less common in women than men is because of women's greater capacity for empathy.[44] (We will look at this in more detail in the next chapter.) The early Greeks and barbarians wouldn't have been able to raid villages if they hadn't been walled off from the psyches of their victims to the point where they had no sense of the massive devastation and misery they were bringing. You could say exactly the same of a modern-day street robber who kicks an old lady to the ground and runs away with her handbag.

This is also true of rape. Evolutionary psychology's explanations for rape – one of which we looked at at the beginning of this chapter – are as crudely reductionist as they are offensive. Rape isn't caused by the genetic compulsion to reproduce, but by a pathological inability to empathise with other human beings. The normal sense of empathy men have with women – even if this might not be at a high level compared with native or prehistoric peoples – makes rape an impossibility, no matter how desperate their genes might be to be replicated. The defining characteristic of rapists is their psychic detachment and isolation, their psychopathic inability to empathise with the women they abuse. In fact, the main difference between murderers, rapists and paedophiles, and the rest of us may be that their state of ego-isolation is more severe than normal. They are walled off from other people to such an extent that they have completely lost the ability to feel with them. Their inability to sense suffering makes them capable of inflicting it.

The third factor I mentioned above – war as a reaction to boredom and unreality – is also significant for crime. In his *Criminal History of Mankind,* Colin Wilson puts forward an argument which is very close to mine in this book. He sees criminality as the dark side of human evolution, a terrible side-effect of the left-brain awareness which has made science and other amazing achievements of human creativity possible. The problem, according to Wilson, is that left-brain awareness often brings a sense of unreality. It creates a dangerous narrowness, traps us in our heads and alienates us from our instincts and our experience of the world. And criminality is a product of this loss of a sense of reality; it is an attempt to make yourself feel more alive and to reconnect with reality. This is especially true of sex crime, Wilson believes. The criminal is, he writes, "attempting to bring his mind to a focus it does not normally achieve. This element of sharpened perception explains the addictive element in crime."[45]

War and crime are two sides of the same coin, one of them collective and the other individual. They are products of the same pathology: the desire for status and wealth, and a desire to feel more *real,* combined with an inability to empathise.

9

THE ORIGINS OF SOCIAL CHAOS
2 – PATRIARCHY

TESTOSTERONE HAS GOT a lot to answer for. As if being responsible for thousands of years of war and murder isn't bad enough, it's also – apparently – to blame for thousands of years of male domination over women. In his book *Why Men Rule: A Theory of Male Dominance* (published previously as *The Inevitability of Patriarchy*), the sociologist Steven Goldberg suggests that men are inevitably "driven" to dominance because of their high level of testosterone. As he writes, "Because of the hormonal differences between males and females, it is inevitable that males will be socialised to aspire to the roles that have the highest status in a society."[1] Men's 50 times-higher level of testosterone makes them more aggressive and competitive, and enables them to snatch up the high-status roles. Women would like to have power and prestige too, but unfortunately their lack of testosterone means that they're always pushed to the back of the queue.

It's certainly true that men – at least, men in the post-Fall era – are more aggressive and competitive than women, but whether or not this is due to hormonal differences is another matter. Again, it could be that a high level of testosterone is just the *result* of aggressive or competitive behaviour. And anyway, there's a difference between taking the high-status roles and actually oppressing and mistreating women – and even actually *despising* women, as some fallen cultures have done. The practice of female infanticide, of ritual widow burning, the killing of millions of women as "witches," the denial of education and democratic rights to women, forcing women to cover their bodies and faces and to live in seclusion, and so on – it's difficult to see how a high level of testosterone could account for all this.

The typical Neo-Darwinian – or evolutionary psychological – explanation for male domination is that men are more driven to attain power and status than women because of the reproductive possibilities they bring. Women are attracted to powerful men because of the resources and the protection they can provide, and so, for a man, more power brings more reproductive possibilities. And since a man's selfish genes are only interested in getting themselves replicated, he has no choice but to seek power as an indirect route to sex. As Wrangham and Peterson write, "Males have evolved to possess strong appetites for power because with extraordinary power males can achieve extraordinary reproduction."[2] For a woman, however, more power does not bring more reproductive possibilities – since, after all, the best she can do to get her genes replicated is to have a baby every year or so.

Of course, the main argument against both Goldberg's and the Neo-Darwinian theories is that men haven't *always* dominated women. Patriarchy can't be inevitable because it's only a relatively recent historical development. And therefore it can't be the result of hormonal differences (unless you're going to say that pre-Fall human beings had a different hormonal make up). Goldberg devotes a large part of his book to attempting to prove that no matriarchal society has ever existed. But here he falls into the either/or trap of believing that societies have to be either patriarchal or matriarchal. An absence of patriarchy does not necessarily mean the presence of matriarchy. And in fact the evidence suggests that Goldberg is right – there has never been a society in which men were subservient to women and women had more power and status. But the point is that there *have* been many societies in which men and women had equal status, in which neither oppressed the other, in which there was no competition at all for high status or dominance. Some of these unfallen societies might show some superficial matriarchal characteristics – for example, they might be matrilineal or matriflocal, women might hold some positions of prestige or authority – but it's completely wrong to think of them as matriarchal, since the ethos of dominance and subservience was completely absent from them.

Like Goldberg, I believe that patriarchy is mainly the result of the fact that men have a greater drive for dominance than women. However, this drive for dominance isn't due to hormonal differences, but to the *psychic* differences between men and women. And these psychic differences only developed as a result of the Fall.

WHY MEN AND WOMEN
ARE FROM DIFFERENT PLANETS

It's usually accepted, both academically and as a matter of common sense, that there are certain general differences in personality between men and women. Ken Wilber summarises these as follows:

> Men tend toward hyperindividuality, stressing autonomy, rights, justice, and agency, and women tend toward a more relational awareness, with emphasis on communion, care, responsibility and relationship. Men tend to stress autonomy and fear relationship, women tend to stress relationship and fear autonomy.[3]

Women's "emphasis on communion" is one of the reasons why they gravitate towards caring professions like health, therapy, counselling and teaching. This also seems to make them more ready to form new relationships, even to make them more friendly. If a couple move into a new area it's usually the woman who becomes friendly with the neighbours first – usually with the other female neighbours – while the man remains a little aloof and reticent, until he's drawn into the relationships his wife has established. Men and women also seem to have different *kinds* of relationships. Research has shown that women's friendships tend to be based on mutual help and problem-sharing, whereas men develop friendships based on shared interests – for example, football, types of music – and involve a lesser degree of intimacy.[4] These differences also make men and women react to problems in different ways. If a woman has a problem, she usually needs to share it and talk it through; if a man has a problem, he's more likely to shut himself in his room and try to think it through on his own.[5]

Men also seem to have a stronger need than women to identify themselves with groups and align themselves with causes. They are, it seems, much more liable to become obsessive fans of football clubs or pop groups, or to espouse political or religious causes to an obsessive degree. This tendency often puzzles women, who can't understand why it should be a matter of life or death whether or not their husband's team gets through the qualifying rounds of the Champions' League, or why he spends so much time arguing in the pub with his friends about which Beatles' album is the best. Part of this may be due to what the psychologist Simon Baron-Cohen calls the male "systematising brain."[6] Football, with its results and league tables, satisfies the male need for systematising, as does music, with its sequences of songs and albums and release dates. But it's also as if men have a stronger need for a sense of belonging, to be a part of something greater than themselves.

Women also generally don't seem to have the same need as men for power and status. Research has shown that men and women have different speaking styles. Female speech is typically cooperative, reciprocal and collaborative. Women's conversations usually last longer, due to their use of more "back channel support"– verbal and non-verbal feedback like *mmm, uhuh, yeah*, and nodding, smiling and other kinds of body language such as gestures and body posture. If they disagree, they tend to express their opinion as a question rather than a statement (for example, "I see where you're coming from, but don't you think it would've been maybe better to…?" instead of, "That was the wrong thing to do. You should've done this"), which accepts differences of opinion and avoids humiliation.[7] On the other hand, men tend to be more blunt, rejecting ideas and suggestions with a seeming disregard for the speaker's feelings. Imperatives and orders are more common in men's speech, whereas women more frequently use empathic phrases such as, "I realise that…" or, "I know you feel…." Boys and men are also much more liable to brag, to threaten and to talk over or ignore others. In other words, for men language is to a large extent an instrument of their need to display status and to try to dominate others. As Simon Baron-Cohen puts it:

> Men spend more time using language to demonstrate their knowledge, skill and status. They are more likely to show off or try to impress. For women, language functions in a different way: it is used to develop and maintain intimate, reciprocal relationships, especially with other females.[8]

This male need for power and status shows itself very early. Studies of teenage boys' behaviour on summer camps have shown that from the moment they are together, they battle for status, and use ridicule and violence to establish dominance hierarchies. Girls in summer camps establish dominance hierarchies too, but theirs are established in a more "humane" way – by ridicule, gossip and flattery of dominant girls. And whereas boys' dominance hierarchies tend to last all summer, girls' break up quickly, as they split into groups of two or three and develop intimate relations with their new "best friends."[9]

According to Simon Baron-Cohen, however, the most fundamental difference between the male and female psyche – and the basic origin of many of the above differences – is their different capacity for empathy. In *The Essential Difference*, Baron-Cohen suggests that most men suffer from a mild form of autism. He defines autism as an "empathy disorder," a form of "mindblindness" in which you can't put yourself into someone else's shoes, can't tell what others might be thinking or feeling, and find it difficult to respond to them in an appropriate way. Autistic people – or those with the related Asperger's Syndrome – have poor social skills, obsessive interests and often appear emotionless and over-logical. And as Baron-Cohen sees it, this is merely an extreme version of the normal male brain. Men appear to suffer from "mindblindness" to a degree as well. This is shown by the fact that they are worse at reading people's emotions from their facial expressions or from their eyes than women, and that they make less eye contact when speaking. As Baron-Cohen summarises, "the female brain is predominantly hard-wired for empathy. The male brain is predominantly hard-wired for understanding and building systems."[10]

The male lack of empathy is also evident from an early age. When young children are given toys to share, the little boys commandeer them, and often push the girls away or steal the toys from them, showing a high degree of selfishness and a lesser degree of empathy. Girls are much more ready to share toys than boys. One study showed that girls permitted 20 times as much turn-taking in games as boys, while boys showed 50 times as much general competitiveness.[11] Another study, by the psychologist E.E. Macoby, has shown that girls' groups tend to have a more egalitarian structure than boys', and that girls are more likely to communicate by making polite suggestions, whereas boys are more likely to give orders and make demands.[12]

The question of *why* these general gender differences exist is also controversial. Physicalist scientists might say that they're just the result of hormonal differences. They might point to the fact that while testosterone makes men prone to aggression, women have a high level of a hormone called oxytocin, which is associated with caring and nurturing and induces strong feelings of attachment. Feminist scholars have argued that these differences aren't innate at all, but are just the result of social conditioning. Men are able to define social roles because they hold most of society's power and resources, and have created a "gender blueprint" which puts women into a subservient and subdominant role. Men are more goal-oriented and competitive and less empathic than women simply because they've been the dominant sex, and have always been conditioned to play this role.[13]

Alternatively, Simon Baron-Cohen believes that these different characteristics developed simply because they were "evolutionary advantageous" for men and women. Following the logic of evolutionary psychology, he suggests that the particular genes which give rise to them were selected because they gave our ancestors a better chance of survival. A talent for systematising was important for men because of their role as hunters and trackers, traders, and weapon and tool makers (and users). At the same time, a lack of empathy helped them to strive for social dominance, helped them to perfect their systematising skills (by making them able to endure long periods of solitude), and also facilitated aggression and violence. Meanwhile, a high level of empathy was advantageous to women because they needed to form communities of friends to help look after their children, because of their need to "read" their children's minds, and also because – according to Baron-Cohen – the ability to make friends meant that they spent lots of time gossiping, which gave them the chance to pick up information which might aid their survival.[14]

In my view, however, these differences are mainly a consequence of the Fall. The point is that the Fall did not affect men and women equally. In fact, this should be clear from the differences I've outlined above. The feminine characteristics – more relational, more feeling-based, less concerned with power and status, a greater sense of empathy, and so on – are exactly those we would associate with a less developed sense of ego, and a less "fallen" state of being. On the other hand, the male characteristics – autonomy, obsessiveness, lack of empathy, a high degree of systematising – are exactly those we would associate with a strongly developed sense of ego. This applies to the strong male need for belonging too – which probably derives from the fact that the male ego is more isolated than the female, more alone and less self-sufficient, and so has a greater need for external support.

In other words, what we think of as "masculine" behaviour is largely the result of the Ego Explosion.

An important piece of evidence for this view is that unfallen peoples don't appear to have these gender differences to the same degree. In the unfallen world, male and female personalities seem to be more similar, and men are more "feminine" in our sense of the term. Men have the same high degree of empathy as women and – as we've seen – don't possess the typically male drive for status and power. They are also more feminine in a practical sense, since they often take over of the roles of nursing children and doing housework. Presumably this role-swapping and the lack of sex specialisiation only exist because of the closeness of the male and female psyche. As we noted earlier, peoples such as the Tahitians and the Trobrianders do not seem to have a "gender schema" – that is, a concept of male and female "personalities" and different roles.

This is the real problem with Baron-Cohen's theory, of course. The present-day "non-empathic" male brain could not have been formed in the human race's ancient past simply because men in the ancient past didn't possess it. There's no question of a low level of empathy being "evolutionary advantageous" for them simply because they did not possess a low level of empathy. They didn't strive to gain status and power and weren't aggressive, and so it isn't possible to see the "non-empathic male brain" as an adaptation which helped them to replicate their genes.

The "male brain" is a relatively recent development. It was only with the Ego Explosion 6,000 years ago that men and women began to live on different planets. The Ego Explosion split them apart and created a profound gulf between the male and female psyches. Women were certainly affected by the Ego Explosion too, of course, but *not to the same high degree that men were*. In fact, it's probably possible to say that the "female psyche" (if there is such a thing) is a kind of midway point between the unfallen psyche of primal peoples, and the male fallen psyche. While the male ego intensified massively, the female ego lagged behind.

MALE CRIMINALITY

There's another piece of evidence for this: the fact that almost all of the social chaos which has blighted the last 6,000 years of history has been caused by men, from war to piracy and banditry to social oppression (a large part of which was inflicted *upon* women, of course). A deconstructionist might say that this is simply because women have never been in a position to organise wars and oppress lower classes, since they have never had any power. And it's true that when they do attain positions of power, women often behave in a traditionally "male" way, starting wars and oppressing social groups and other peoples (some British examples of this are Queen Elizabeth, Queen Victoria and Margaret Thatcher). But, of course, the reason why men have always occupied the dominant positions in the first place is *because of* their greater need for dominance and their greater capacity for cruelty, which resulted in the oppression of women. Even today the vast majority of all crimes are committed by men. Statistics from different countries show a surprisingly regular pattern – usually between 80 percent and 90 percent of all crimes during any given period are committed by men. However, these statistics are still slightly misleading since women usually show a relatively high level of non-confrontational crimes, such as fraud and shoplifting. When we focus on crimes like robbery, murder and sexual assaults individually, the percentage for males rise into the 90s.[15] As Daly and Wilson write, "There is no known human society in which the level of lethal violence among women even approaches that among men."[16] Their research showed that male on male homicide was 30 to 40 times more common than female on female.

There are certainly some other factors involved here. For example, although it's very unlikely that a high level of testosterone can account for war or male dominance, it's easy to see how it (or other hormonal/chemical factors) might make men more prone to commit sex crimes and acts of physical violence at a particular moment. But the differences between the male and female psyche are clearly very significant. Women's less pronounced need for power and status, and their greater capacity for empathy – both of which stem from their less sharpened sense of ego – mean that they are much less likely to be empire-builders, warmongers, terrorists, murderers, sex offenders or even street robbers. The less walled off you are to the psyche of other human beings, the more reluctant you are to inflict suffering on them.

THE DEVELOPMENT OF THE MALE AND FEMALE EGOS

I am suggesting, then, that the essential defining difference between men and women is not their different hormones, or even their different capacity for empathy, but *the fact that men have a sharper and stronger sense of ego than women.*

But *why* did the Fall affect the male psyche more strongly than the female?

One possible reason is that the female ego could never have become walled off to the same extent as the male because of women's need to empathise with their children. Being a mother is all about empathy – all about "feeling with" your baby so that you can recognise his or her needs and respond to them, and feeling closely bonded with them so that you can give them the love and protection they need. Caring for a baby generates a constant flow of empathy and a sense of bondedness which transcend ego-separateness.

In addition, the split between the ego and the body, and between the ego and the world, could never have become as severe for women due to the fact that women are more closely connected to nature – in terms of the biology of their own bodies – than men. Male biology is fairly inert, and makes few demands. Apart from sex, hunger, going to the toilet and periodic pain and injury, our bodily processes aren't obviously active. As a result, it's fairly easy for us to become disembodied egoic entities, to "rise above" our biology and experience a sharp sense of mind/body duality. On the other hand, female biology is more powerful and pronounced, with the monthly cycle of ovulation and menstruation and the processes of pregnancy and lactation. This may have checked the development of the female ego, and stopped a mind/body duality forming, so that women could never develop a state of fully-fledged ego-isolation.

Social and environmental factors may have been important too. I suggested that there were two main ways in which the drying up of Saharasia generated a sharpened sense of ego. Firstly, now that survival was much more difficult and there were no longer enough resources to go round, a new spirit of competition and selfishness developed. Individuals had to start thinking in terms of their own well-being rather than their whole community's, and to compete against others to satisfy their own needs. Secondly, the difficulties which now filled their lives forced them to develop a new kind of logical and self-reflective ability. A stronger sense of ego came with this, since logic and self-reflection require a sharply defined "I" to perform the thinking role.

Women must have been affected by both of these factors to some extent, but there are some good reasons for believing that they weren't *as* affected by them as men. Women's child-rearing role – pregnancy, breast-feeding and the lion's share of looking after children when they were older – probably meant that they were less involved with these survival problems. With their greater mobility, men would have been primarily responsible for trying to find new survival strategies – for example, ways of maximising water and food supplies through irrigation, finding different kinds of crops which would yield more, or scouting for new sources of water or new stretches of land. These tasks involved long-distance travel and danger, neither of which suited women. And once their land became so dry that migration was the Saharasian groups' only option, men would have been largely responsible for their safety and survival.

In other words, women's child-rearing responsibilities (especially when the groups switched to a nomadic way of life) would have made them less exposed to the pressures which created the sharpened male ego.

THE ROOTS OF PATRIARCHY

All of this deals with the differences between men and women. The question we need to answer now, however, is why did these differences give rise to the last 6,000 years of male domination, and the oppression of women?

As they do with war, many scholars accept that the earlier human societies were not patriarchal, and attempt to explain the emergence of male domination in terms of social and economic factors. One theory – put forward by Ken Wilber, for example – is that women's status is directly related to the contribution they make to the economy. A big contribution equals high status and a small one equals low status. In hunter-gatherer and horticultural societies women do a lot of the work and provide a lot of the food and so have high status. But advanced agricultural societies use heavy ploughs, which can be dangerous for pregnant women, and so women are largely excluded from the economy and therefore have low status.[17] However, the problem with this argument is that patriarchy is actually at least 1,000 years older than the horse-drawn plough. People started to use the plough at around 3000 BCE, whereas Saharasian groups like the Indo-Europeans and the Semites became patriarchal, socially stratified and war-like at around 4000 BCE. And these peoples were nomads. They didn't practise agriculture at all, and yet were still extremely patriarchal.

In *The Gardens of their Dreams*, Brian Griffith puts forward a similar argument. He suggests that as Saharasia began to turn to desert, "women's roles suffered more than those of men, because women's ways of raising and gathering food were rendered less productive."[18] As well as the advent of the plough, he notes that irrigation channels for water were now necessary, that fertile land would have to fiercely defended or else stolen from other groups, and that long-distance herding and trade became necessary. And because of the brute force, the danger and the travel which all of this involved, they became men's work. This argument is more persuasive than Wilber's, since Griffith mentions a number of different factors and is talking specifically about the people in the Saharasian region. But as Wilber's own "Four Quadrants" model tells us, economic life is not *all* life.[19] The fact that women began to be excluded from the economy doesn't explain why men began to oppress and exploit women so ruthlessly, and even to murder them. It seems logical that economic exclusion would lead to a degree of lower status for women, but not the kind of *extremely* low status – and the extreme hostility to the female – which gave rise to practices like *suttee* and *purdah*, large-scale female infanticide and the European witch murders.

To see how the stronger male ego led to patriarchy, we need to go back to Steven Goldberg's argument. Because of their stronger sense of ego – but not their higher level of testosterone – men have an innately greater need for status than women, which makes it inevitable that they "snatch up" the high status roles in a society. The same principle operates in any democracy: the people with the most ambition (that is, with the strongest desire for power, success and wealth) are the ones who rise highest in the social hierarchy, and become managing directors, politicians, pop stars, etc.[20] Particularly in previous eras, the most ambitious people were likely to be men.

But it's not just a question of women not craving status to the degree that men crave it, it is also a question of the male urge to dominate women, the fact that men made it impossible for women to have power or influence *at all*, and oppressed and maltreated them so brutally. It's easy to see how the strong male walled-off ego, with its need for status and its lack of capacity for empathy, was responsible for this. The same need which drove men to dominate other human groups and led to the formation of different castes and classes (which we're going to look at in a moment) drove them to dominate their wives and daughters, to make them subservient and rule over them. Lack of empathy meant that they were unable to "feel with" women, and sense the suffering they were causing.

But even this isn't enough to explain the full terrible saga of man's inhumanity to woman. There is also the basic antagonism towards women which has been a part of many fallen cultures, the view of women as impure and innately sinful creatures who have been sent by the devil to lead men astray. This view was at the heart of the European witch-killing mania of the fifteenth to eighteenth centuries, and has always been a feature of the three great Saharasian religions. As the Jewish Testament of Reuben states:

> Women are evil, my children…they use wiles and try to ensnare [man] by their charms…They lay plots in their hearts against men: by the way they adorn themselves they first lead their minds astray, and by a look they instil the poison, and then in the act itself they take them captive…So shun fornication, my children and command your wives and daughters not to adorn their heads and faces.[21]

This aspect of patriarchy is linked to the sense of separation from the body which the Ego Explosion created. People – especially men – began to see the body they lived inside as something lower than them. They saw their instincts and sensual desires as a part of their animalistic nature, and, as a result, as base and sinful. And since women are "closer" to their bodies and their biological processes are more pronounced, this attitude was extended to women. Men associated themselves with the "purity" of the mind, and women with the "corruption" of the body. As Marina Warner writes, "In this battle between the flesh and the spirit, the female sex was firmly placed on the side of the flesh."[22] Since menstruation, breast-feeding and even pregnancy disgusted the disembodied male ego, women disgusted them too. As Warner also comments:

> In the faeces and urine – in St. Augustine's phrase – of childbirth, the closeness of women to all that is vile, lowly, corruptible, and material was epitomised – in the "curse" of menstruation, she lay closer to the beast; the lure of her beauty was nothing but an aspect of the death brought about by her seduction of Adam in the garden.[23]

The sexual power that women have over men was probably a factor too. Since men felt that sex was sinful, and that sexual desires were base, they were bound to feel animosity towards the women who produced these desires. In addition, women's sexual power must have affronted men's need for control. It meant that they couldn't have the complete domination over women – and over their own bodies – that they craved. They might be able to force women to cover their bodies and faces and make them live like slaves, but any woman was capable of arousing powerful and uncontrollable sexual impulses inside them at any moment. The last 6,000 years of man's inhumanity to woman can partly be seen as a revenge for this.

10

THE ORIGINS OF SOCIAL CHAOS 3 – INEQUALITY AND CHILD OPPRESSION

YOU CAN PROBABLY already guess what evolutionary psychology has to say about social stratification. It's all about survival, of course. The more power and status we have, the more access we have to food and other resources, the more chance men have of attracting females, and therefore the more chance we have of surviving and reproducing. All human beings – although primarily men, of course – are therefore genetically programmed to try to get their hands on as much power and status as possible. As a result, all human societies are full of inequality, with different social classes and an uneven distribution of power and wealth.

Of course, anybody who puts forward these kinds of theories has to explain the complete *absence* of inequality and social stratification in primal societies. They have to explain why hunter-gatherer bands – and many settled horticultural peoples too – do not have authoritarian leaders, reach all their decisions by consensus, share their food, have no different classes or castes, and have strong ethical principles which work against any expression of greed or selfishness. The evolutionary psychologist Steven Pinker states glibly that "One of the fondest beliefs of many intellectuals is that there are cultures out there where everyone shares freely," and then goes on to say that this wouldn't have been possible since free sharing has no survival value, and so brains capable of it could never have evolved.[1] Similarly, E.O. Wilson states that equality is "based on an inaccurate interpretation of human nature."[2] But, as we've seen, there is such a wealth of indisputable evidence for the existence of egalitarian societies that it is clearly Wilson and Pinker's view of human nature that is inaccurate and needs to be revised.

To my knowledge, no evolutionary psychologist has attempted to deal with this problem, presumably because evolutionary psychologists aren't aware of the massive archaeological and ethnographic evidence against their views. Not surprisingly, however, some anthropologists have put forward explanations. One view – suggested by Elizabeth Cashdan, for instance – is that the egalitarianism of hunter-gatherer peoples is the simple result of the fact that they can't accumulate property because of their mobile lifestyle,[3] while according to Max Gluckman, the important factor is their lack of role specialisation.[4] The underlying assumption of both of these views is that social inequality is related to the settled agricultural lifestyle. Property creates inequality simply because different people own different amounts of it, and role specialisation results in the formation of different groups – craftsmen, bureaucrats, religious officials, soldiers, etc. – which eventually turn into fully-fledged classes, with different degrees of wealth and status.

Some scholars have also suggested that social inequality came about when villages developed a surplus of goods and services. People started competing against one another to get hold of this surplus, or to gain control of its distribution, and those who did became the wealthiest and most powerful members of the society.[5]

However, the major problem with these arguments is that there have been (and are) many societies – and even civilisations – which did practise agriculture and had economic specialisation, but were still egalitarian. Historically, social equality doesn't end with the transition to agriculture. Whereas the "agricultural revolution" began at around 8000 BCE, we don't see any signs of social inequality until 4000 BCE. And from an ethnographic perspective, there are many non-mobile agricultural tribes who follow the same egalitarian principles as hunter-gatherer bands. According to the anthropologist Christopher Boehm:

> Many other nonliterates [besides hunter-gatherers], people who live in permanent, settled groups that accumulate food surpluses through agriculture, are quite similar politically [to hunter-gatherers]…These tribesmen lack strong leadership and domination among adult males, they make their group decisions by consensus and they too exhibit an egalitarian ideology…[6]

We can't even connect inequality with civilisation, since we know of many large towns (for example, Catal Huyuk, the Jomon settlement of Aomori city) and whole civilisations (for example, ancient Crete and Old European civilisation in general) where craft specialisation and a high level of social organisation existed, but where there was an apparently even distribution of wealth and a lack of class differences. At the other end of the spectrum, we also know of many nomadic herding peoples – such as the Bedouin of North Africa – who have few possessions and little economic specialisation and yet are still extremely hierarchical.[7]

Christopher Boehm takes most of this into account and yet still tries to explain the egalitarianism of primal peoples in Neo-Darwinist (or evolutionary psychological) terms. He describes his basic theory as follows, writing in the past tense:

> The premise was that humans are innately disposed to form social dominance hierarchies…but that prehistoric hunter-gatherers, acting as moral communities, were largely able to neutralize such tendencies, just as present day foragers apply techniques of social control in suppressing both dominant leadership and undue competitiveness.[8]

We have already looked at some of these techniques. Many primal peoples make a habit of "putting down" or making fun of people who are boastful. The !Kung of Africa swap arrows before they go hunting, and when an animal is killed, the credit doesn't go to the person who fired the arrow, but to the person who the arrow belongs to. And in occasional instances, when a dominant male tries to take control of the group, primal peoples practise what Boehm calls "egalitarian sanctioning." They gang up against the domineering person, ostracise him, desert him, or even – in extreme circumstances, when they feel that their own lives may be in danger due to his tyrannical behaviour – assassinate him. In this way, Boehm says, primal societies are "reverse-dominance" societies in which, in his words, "the rank and file avoid being subordinated by vigilantly keeping alpha-type group members under their collective thumbs."[9]

One problem with this theory is that, as Boehm admits, "egalitarian sanctioning" occurs only very rarely. He says he "had to examine scores of forager ethnographies to find a few dozen usable reports of egalitarian sanctioning."[10] But surely if it was a question of suppressing an *innate* need for power and status in human beings then this would happen much more often, constantly even. In fact, if this need really were innate then it wouldn't be a question of a small number of alpha males breaking the egalitarian code; *everybody* would break it. It would be impossible to neutralise competitiveness and sustain egalitarianism because everybody would be competitive. After all, in later non-egalitarian societies, it isn't just a question of a few alpha males ruling over everybody else, but of a *general* desire for power and status, shared by almost everybody.

And if hunter-gatherer peoples managed, for the good of society as a whole, to neutralise their innate tendency to dominate, why couldn't later peoples manage to do this? Why were they so spectacularly bad at suppressing their domineering impulses?

The difference, I would argue, is that it's only possible to control potential dominators in primal societies because there are so few of them, since in them the need for status and power is not innate at all.

The Ego and the Need for Power and Status

Surely the easiest and most sensible way of explaining the egalitarianism of primal peoples is to say that they simply didn't have an innate need for status and power for the same reason that they didn't have an innate need to make war, or to oppress women: because they didn't have our over-developed sense of ego. The need for status and power – and the highly stratified and competitive societies which this resulted in – only became innate after the Ego Explosion.

We've already looked at the roots of this need for status (in Chapter 7). We crave it as an alternative source of happiness to override our psychological discord. Every time we achieve some success or experience a sense of power it gives us a glow of self-esteem, a fix of ego-based happiness. And the basic sense of lack and incompleteness we feel makes us crave to make our mark on the world, to become special and important people, to be someone, as if this will somehow make us complete. Fear of death may be connected to this as well, since status (especially when it means fame) can confer a kind of immortality on us.

Inequality is obviously connected to materialism too. One of the characteristics of egalitarian societies is a completely even distribution of wealth. Nobody possesses more goods and property than anybody else. In fact, as we've seen, the idea of possession itself has very little meaning to unfallen peoples. An uneven distribution of wealth could never occur because there is no individual ownership. But as soon as the need for personal ownership develops, inequality is inevitable. Psychological discord drives people to buy and possess as many goods and as much property as possible – and in order to do this, they have to make money. There's only a certain amount of wealth to go round, and either through social advantages or innate ability, some people take more of it than others.

The lack of empathy which goes with the over-developed sense of ego is certainly an important factor here as well. If the nobles and landowners of feudal societies, for instance, had been able to empathise with their starving peasants and serfs, they would never have been able to oppress them so brutally. But they were so walled off to them that they didn't even think of them as human beings, but as cattle.

THE OPPRESSION OF CHILDREN

We've looked quite extensively at the oppression of women by men, and the oppression of powerless social groups by powerful ones, but we haven't yet looked at another section of the population which has been cruelly dominated and oppressed over the last few thousand years: namely, children.

We have, however, already briefly noted that primal peoples have an extremely tolerant attitude to children, and treat them with great gentleness and affection. Service notes that the Copper Eskimos of northern Canada hardly ever punish children, but spend a lot of time "in teaching them what they *should* do."[11] He also notes of the Navaho: "To a white American, it appears that Navaho spoil their children. It seems to be true that a baby is indulged a good deal."[12] And as DeMeo says of matrist primal peoples in general: "They appear incapable of even conceptualising violent treatment of their children. They in fact never 'beat' them in a cold, calculated manner."[13] In fact, even showing anger to a child was seen as socially unacceptable. As Jean Briggs writes of the Qipisa Eskimos:

> To be angry with a child was demeaning; it demonstrated one's
> own childishness, and one older woman told me that, as an
> educational device, scolding was likely to backfire and cause a

child to rebel. When anger was expressed toward a child, the community strongly disapproved.[14]

The children of primal cultures also have a great deal of freedom. Not only do adults almost never punish children, they rarely bark orders and reprimands at them in the way that we do ("Stop that now!" "Don't do that!" "Come here!" "Get away from there!"). As Malinowski noted of the Trobriand Islanders, from a very young age children are allowed to think for themselves and moderate their own behaviour. And as Judith Kleinfeld writes of Eskimo culture in general: "Parents tended to be highly indulgent toward children and allow them to make their own decisions."[15] While as Jean Liedloff comments of the Yequana of South America:

> The Yequana do not feel that a child's inferior strength and dependence upon them imply that they should treat him or her with less respect than an adult. No orders are given to a child that run counter to his own inclinations as to how to play, how much to eat, when to sleep and so on.[16]

Other examples of this freedom are the children's dormitories of the Trobrianders and the Muria, which adults were forbidden to enter, and where children could choose sexual partners without any parental interference. In fact, primal peoples' lack of interference with their children's love lives is one of the most obvious signs of their non-domineering attitude. In contrast to Saharasian cultures, parents never arrange marriages for their children, or try to interfere with their relationships if they think a partner is "not right" or "not good enough" for them.

The way that fathers treat their children is especially striking. They are never the emotionally detached figures that the fathers of Saharasian cultures often are, who leave the basics of child-rearing to women and act as the family chief, dispensing punishment whenever the children "step out of line." As we've seen, the men of primal societies are greatly involved with childcare. They often wash, feed and clean babies, and allow women to lead an active social and economic life by taking over childcare for hours at a time. The anthropologist Barry Hewlett lived with the Aka Pygmies of the Congo, and calculated that fathers spent 20 percent of their time caring for babies, were never more than arm's length away from them for half of the day, and were only away from their sight 12 percent of the time.[17]

To make the contrast with Saharasian cultures even more stark, fathers often have a special role as providers of love and affection (rather than as disciplinarians). Hugging, nursing and petting children are primarily the father's job. As Malinowski wrote of the Trobriander men, "The father performs his duties with genuine natural fondness: he will carry an infant about for hours, looking at it with eyes full of such love and pride as seldom seen in those of a European father."[18] The men of primal cultures are, it seems, more like the "new men" we often hear about nowadays; the men who have rejected stereotypically masculine values and developed more feminine personality traits such as empathy, emotional openness and non-aggression. New men also reject the traditional gender schema of our culture, and are willing to take on traditional "feminine" roles such as child -rearing, cooking and housework.

All of this shouldn't surprise us, since this attitude to children is really only a part of the general pattern of democracy and egalitarianism which characterises primal societies. Adults don't dominate children just as men don't dominate women, and more powerful individuals don't dominate less powerful ones. And in societies where nobody has the right to give orders to anybody else – in which, as Jean Briggs wrote of the Utku Eskmos, "people tend to look askance at anyone who seems to aspire to tell them what to do"[19] – it seems only natural that children should be entitled to make their own decisions and to moderate their own behaviour.

CHILDREN IN THE POST-FALL ERA

But once again, with the Ego Explosion adults' attitude to – and their treatment of – children changed drastically. As DeMeo hints above, child-beating seems to be a specifically Saharasian phenomenon. Like wife-beating, the physical abuse of children was seen as essential, a way of teaching the child discipline, so that he might learn to control his naturally "sinful" and selfish nature.

Of course, there are still many people who believe this nowadays, and reserve the right to smack their children. But in previous centuries it went far beyond smacking; in fact, any parents who just hit their children with their bare hands would have been thought of as being far too lenient with them. As the historian L. DeMause writes, "A very large percentage of the children born prior to the 18th century were what would today be termed *battered children*."[20] Roman children were regularly beaten by parents and teachers, who used a special torture instrument made from the hard and sharp stalks of fennel plants. The early Christian church advised parents to regularly whip their children, and even made a special punishment day, Holy Innocents' Day, when children would be whipped to remind them of the massacre by Herod. Children who cried too much were thought of as evil "changelings" who the devil had swapped for the real baby; they were disciplined and punished extra severely as a result.[21]

The general Saharasian attitude to child-rearing is summed up by the following passage from a popular seventeenth-century Russian etiquette manual:

> Punish your son in his early years and he will comfort you in your old age and be the ornament of your soul. Do not spare you child any beating, for the stick will not kill him, but will do him good; when you strike the body, you save the soul from death…Raise your child in fear and you will find peace and blessing in him.[22]

Another, less direct, way of abusing children – or rather babies – was through the practice of swaddling: wrapping babies from head to toe in a tight bandage, or cotton sheet, making it impossible for them to move. In certain parts of the world – such as Russia and China – swaddling is still quite common today. In Europe and America it faded away in the nineteenth century, but is still sometimes recommended for newborn babies, as a way of supposedly making them feel secure. It has even been seen as a way of reducing the risk of sudden infant death syndrome, since it keeps babies sleeping on their backs.

In earlier centuries, however, swaddling was more severe. Children were swaddled at certain times long after their first few weeks, even until the age of three or four. Parents didn't change the wrappings very often, so that babies were often in contact with their own urine and faeces. The aim was partly to stop them hurting themselves, to save them from scratching their eyes or tearing their ears. There was also a belief that children's limbs would go out of shape if they were left free. But swaddling was also a convenience measure. It meant that parents could just leave children alone while they went out to work in the fields. It also made children more passive. Medical studies have shown that swaddling slows down children's hearts and makes them sleep more and cry less (hence the impression that babies actually like being swaddled), and makes them withdrawn and lifeless. As a result, parents didn't have to pay so much attention to them. They could treat their babies like "parcels" which could be put to one side for hours. There are historical reports of swaddled children being left behind a hot oven for hours, or being hung on pegs or left in tubs. We can only guess at the psychological damage this must have caused – and, in some parts of the world, still causes.[23]

In addition to this physical maltreatment, after the Fall adults – particularly men, we can assume – began to treat children as inferior beings with no rights, who were supposed to be unquestionably obedient. The relationship between children and their parents – particularly the father – became akin to the relationship between slaves and a master. Children were supposed to be "seen and not heard," or not to speak until they were spoken to. Any sign of autonomy – such as making suggestions or questioning why a parent wanted them to do something – was seen as an affront to the adult's authority, and punished.

This maltreatment of children probably arises from the same two main factors that we've looked at in relation to war, male domination and social stratification: the fallen psyche's need for domination and reduced capacity for empathy. People – particularly men – needed to have complete control over their children in the same way that they needed to have power over other individuals and social groups, over women and over nature. And surely the physical abuse of children – and treating them like slaves – would not have been possible without a weakening of the empathic bond between parents and children. Ego-separateness must have walled off parents to the full extent of the suffering they were causing, otherwise they would never have been able to whip their children or keep them swaddled.

But there was a slightly more complex cause too. Like women, children represented nature. With their complete instinctiveness and lack of ego, they represented the "corrupt" body which the over-developed ego despises. Children represented the biological force from which the ego had split itself off and was at war with. And so parents – and, again, especially men – were impelled to control and dominate their children in the same way that, as individuals, they tried to control and dominate their own biology.

ARE THE CHILDREN OF PRIMAL SOCIETIES DIFFERENT?

All of this may not be completely one-sided, though. Another important factor is that the children of unfallen cultures appear to be psychically different from the children of fallen cultures in the same way that adults are. It seems to be the case that parents in unfallen cultures don't actually *need* to control and discipline their children, because they are *innately* less unruly than children in fallen cultures.

To most modern-day parents, the idea of not giving children any kind of discipline at all and letting them do what they want all the time – as parents in primal cultures do – seems like a recipe for disaster. We may not want to smack our children, but we take it for granted that some kind of control and discipline is necessary. Children are often unreasonable, selfish and greedy, and we assume that if we don't punish them in some way they'll never learn to control their behaviour. We feel that we sometimes need to stand in the way of their desires, and refuse to give them what they want, or else they'll turn into "spoilt brats" who scream the house down if they don't get exactly what they want at the moment they want it.

There definitely is some truth in this. Children in our culture can, it seems, be "spoiled" by a lack of control and discipline, and have problems in later life as a result. They're liable to become selfish, to see themselves as the centre of the universe and to be unable to take the perspective of others. They might become excessively hedonistic or narcissistic, with a lack of self-discipline and a lack of control over their own desires.

But in primal societies the lack of discipline doesn't seem to affect children in this way. Allowing them autonomy and freedom doesn't turn them into "spoilt brats." Many anthropologists have been struck by how well-behaved, stable and cooperative the children of primal cultures are. Jean Liedloff described the children of the Tauripan Indians of the Amazon as "uniformly well-behaved: they never fought, [and] were never punished."[24] Service noted that the children of the !Kung of the Kalahari "are never harshly punished. On the other hand, they do not seem induced to do things that would require punishment."[25] While, in writing of the Jivaro of the Amazon, Service also notes that children "are rarely punished and have great liberty; yet like most children in the primitive world, they are well behaved and respectful towards adults."[26]

There is another possibility here, besides the idea that primal children are somehow innately less unruly. There might be something about the way that we bring up children, including how we treat them as babies, which *makes* them unruly and badly behaved.

This is the argument which Jean Liedloff puts forward in her well-known book *The Continuum Concept*. She suggests that a great deal of modern social and psychological disorders stem from what she calls "in-arms deprivation." In primal cultures, she notes, babies are never left alone. They are constantly carried, and sleep with their parents or other family members, so that they have constant skin to skin contact. At the same time, there is never any attempt to control their desires. Rather than imposing a routine on them – as modern parents do – children are allowed to feed and sleep whenever they want to. But in the modern world babies are deprived of this essential contact. They are left alone in prams and cots, even in their own rooms, and are often even deprived of the essential bonding of breast-feeding. It's therefore not surprising that our babies spend a great deal of time crying. We believe that it's natural for babies to cry, when in reality crying is only the expression of the baby's in-arms deprivation. The proof of this, says Liedloff, is that in societies such as the Yequana and Tauripan babies hardly cry at all.[27]

To extend Liedloff's argument a little further, we might say that the unruliness of our children is perhaps the result of "in-arms deprivation." If we had never denied our children their fundamental needs in the first place, then they would never have such powerful desires and be so unruly, and they wouldn't need to be controlled.

Leidloff's ideas are very important and there's no doubt that, as she suggests, a great deal of human suffering, and a great many social problems, could be alleviated if babies and children were given constant – or at least regular – "in-arms" contact.[28] However, it's also possible that children in our cultures need a degree of control because of the psychic difference between them and children in unfallen cultures. Our strong sense of ego doesn't suddenly emerge in adulthood; it develops slowly throughout childhood. And as it develops it manifests itself in certain – often unpleasant – ways. As psychologists such as Piaget have shown, young children can be very narcissistic and egocentric. Particularly at what Piaget calls the "concrete operational stage" – until the age of around six or seven – they are dominated by their own powerful desires.[29] They want anything and everything, get angry when they can't have it, and don't like sharing what they can have. This is the sharply defined ego beginning to express itself, perceiving itself as the centre of the universe and failing to see beyond its own perspective. And this is why children in our culture probably do need a certain degree of control. Their limitless desires need to be contained; they need to learn that they can't expect to have their every want satisfied. In Freudian terms, they need to develop an ego to control the impulses of their "id." But since children in primal societies don't have the same emerging powerful sense of ego, they don't develop this kind of selfishness and these kinds of powerful desires. (And they also – as we noted earlier – don't appear to need the transitional objects which American/European children need.) As a result, they are innately less unruly and their parents don't need to control them to the same extent.

This isn't at all to justify the way children have been abused and oppressed in Saharasian cultures. I'm only suggesting that they might need a small degree of discipline and control – and certainly not *physical* discipline; only the kind of control where a parent doesn't give in to their excessive desires, and teaches them a degree of *self*-discipline. To a massive extent, fallen cultures' treatment of children was pathological. In the same way as war, social oppression and male domination, it is a symptom of the insanity of the fallen psyche.

11

THE ORIGINS OF GOD

LIKE SO MANY of the characteristics of fallen cultures, we take the concept of "God" so much for granted that it's difficult for us to imagine how strange it really is. From the point of view of the alien observer who we've heard from intermittently in this book, the fact that human beings have always – or at least for the last 6,000 years – believed that all-powerful invisible entities were watching over them and manipulating the events of their lives would seem as puzzling as the endless wars which have filled human history, or the insatiable need for status and wealth which drives many of us. After all, have any of them actually *seen* these gods? Has anybody ever seen any real evidence for their existence?

Human beings have always been – and still are – convinced that gods can be influenced, and have used rituals, prayers and sacrifices to do this. For example, if we were going to war, we might pray or offer a sacrifice to try to make sure we were victorious; or if we were – to use more modern examples – going to have an operation or to play a vital sports match, we might pray to make sure everything goes according to plan. What would strike our alien observer as strange is that there has never been any evidence that gods actually do help us in these ways. In fact, there has never been any real evidence that he – or they – look after us at all. If God – or gods – are watching over us and helping, why does he let us have car crashes, die of diseases, or allow earthquakes to happen? Why does he let innocent young children die, and apparently allow evil people to prosper? But none of this, the alien observer would muse, has affected human beings' belief in gods at all. The conclusion he (or she) would probably reach is that there is a human *need* to feel that higher beings are watching over them and controlling their lives, a need which overrides the irrationality of the beliefs.

PRIMAL SPIRIT-RELIGION

Strangely, though, gods aren't as old as the human race in the same way that war isn't. Like war, belief in gods is a specifically fallen characteristic.

The religions of unfallen peoples are not theistic – that is, not based around the worship of gods. In fact, to them the concept of "God" or "gods" has very little significance. Some unfallen peoples do have a concept of a creator God, but such a God is always a very remote and detached figure who seems to have been developed purely as a way of explaining how the world came into being. After creating the world, this God steps aside and has very little to do with it. As Eliade wrote:

> Like many celestial supreme beings of "primitive" peoples, the High Gods of a great number of African ethnic groups are regarded as creators, all powerful and benevolent and so forth; but they play a rather insignificant part in the religious life. Being either too distant or too good to need a real cult, they are involved only in cases of great crisis.[1]

The Azande people of Africa, for example, have a concept of a supreme being called Mbori. However, the anthropologist Evans-Pritchard noted that there was only one rarely performed public ceremony associated with him, and that he had never heard anybody pray to him or even mention his name.[2] The Fang people of Cameroon believe that the natural world was created by a god called Mebeghe, and that the "cultural world" – of tools, houses, hunting, farming, etc. – was created by another god called Nzame. However, as Pascal Boyer notes, "these gods do not seem to matter that much. There are no cults or rituals specifically directed at Mebeghe or Nzame…they are in fact rarely mentioned."[3] Similarly, the Lenape Indians of Ontario and Oklahoma believe that a supreme being created the world and gave them everything they have. But this god is so far away, in the twelfth heaven (the highest), that they rarely give him any attention. They give most of their attention to the *Mani 'towak*, the "agents" of the supreme being who are present in every sunrise and thunderstorm, and every wind.[4] According to Lenski's statistics in *Human Societies*, only 4 percent of hunter-gatherer societies and only 10 percent of simple horticultural societies have a concept of a "creator god concerned with the moral conduct of humans."[5]

The religions of all unfallen peoples are strikingly similar – so much so that it's possible, I believe, to use the general term "primal religion" to cover all of them. There are two main aspects of "primal religion," neither of which involves gods in the sense that we think of them. We've mentioned one of these before: primal peoples' sense that the whole world – and everything in it – is pervaded with an animating force.

It's important to emphasise that this spirit-force is not God in the sense that we normally use the term. There's sometimes confusion here because occasionally anthropologists translate these terms as God. Evans-Pritchard did this with the Nuer term for spirit-force, *Kwoth*. At the same time, however, he makes it clear that *Kwoth* is not an anthropomorphic deity. As he writes, "The anthropomorphic features of the Nuer conception of God are very weak and, as will be seen, they do not act towards him as if he were a man...I have never heard the Nuer suggest that he has human form."[6] The translations of these terms by other anthropologists, however, make it clear that we aren't dealing with a deity. Early anthropologists used terms like "Lifepower," "Soulstuff" and *Potenz*,[7] while the early British anthropologist, J.H. Holmes, called it "soul" or "living principle." As he wrote of the natives of the Purari Delta in New Guinea:

> *Imunu*, or soul was associated with everything, nothing arrived apart from it...nothing animate or inanimate could exist apart from it. It was the soul of things...It was intangible, but like air, wind, it could manifest its presence. It permeated everything that made up life to the people of the Purari Delta...[It was] that which enables everything to exist as we know it, and distinct from other things which, too, exist by it.[8]

The second main aspect of primal religion is the concept of spirit*s* (in the plural). There are usually two types of spirits: the spirits of dead people and nature spirits who have always existed as spirits. They are everywhere; every object and every phenomenon is either inhabited by or connected to a particular spirit. As E.Bolaji Idowu writes of traditional African religion, "there is no area of the earth, no object or creature, which has not a spirit of its own or which cannot be inhabited by a spirit."[9] Like gods, spirits have control over natural processes – they can cause headaches, heal wounds, make arrows hit their target, change the direction of the wind, and make rain fall. But despite this similarity, it's a mistake to think of them as anthropomorphic beings with personalities, like gods. Spirits are not beings at all. As Idowu writes, "they are more often than not thought of as powers which are almost abstract, as shades or vapours."[10] They are also involved in the world in a way that gods are not. Whereas gods control human life from the outside, like puppeteers, spirits are always a part of the natural world, moving invisibly through the air or living inside rocks, trees, rivers and animals.

It seems common sense to assume that spirits don't really exist, and are purely a matter of superstition or illusion. The French religious scholar and philosopher Auguste Comte believed that since they themselves were conscious beings, our early ancestors simply assumed – in the absence of any other evidence – that all natural phenomena where alive too, with their own inner being.[11] Freud believed that spirits and demons were just the "projection of primitive man's emotional impulses."[12] But we should at least be open to the *possibility* that spirits exist. Buddhist philosophy accepts the existence of a whole host of beings which are invisible to the human eye (such as the *peta-yoni, asura-yoni* and *devas*), and which we only became aware of as our consciousness becomes more refined through spiritual practice.[13] And since we appear to have lost the ability to sense the presence of spirit-force around us, it's at least possible that we have lost the ability to sense the presence of spirit entities around us too.

But if spirits *are* illusory, then it's possible to see them as a kind of strategy that unfallen peoples used to try to explain the world around them. Since their whole world was pervaded with – and alive with – spirit-force, unfallen peoples saw all things as *individually* alive too. Every tree, rock or river was alive with spirit-force, and had its own soul or being. And perhaps, in order to explain natural processes, primal peoples came to believe that things weren't just alive in this general sense, but also in the sense of being active autonomous forces. Spirit became individuated into spirits, which had control over different natural processes. When the seasons changed, for example, this could be explained as the actions of the "the spirits of the four winds" (as the Plains Indians believed), and illness and death could be explained as the influence of "evil" spirits (as most primal peoples believe).

It's important to remember, however, that although they can act as individual forces, unfallen peoples see spirits as an expression of the Great Spirit itself. As Evans-Pritchard notes of the Nuer, "God is not a particular air-spirit but the spirit is a figure of God...The spirits are not each other but they are God in different figures."[14] (Note again that the term God here does not refer to the creator God but to God as spirit-force.)

GODDESS RELIGION?

Belief in God as spirit-force seems to have been the original religion of the whole human race, the "old religion" before gods, temples, priests and concepts of heaven and hell. As D.H. Lawrence described the "old religion" of the Indians of New Mexico:

> It was a vast and pure religion, without idols and images, even mental ones. It is the oldest religion, a cosmic religion the same for all peoples, not broken up into specific gods or saviours or systems. It is the religion which precedes the god-concept, and is therefore greater and deeper than any god-religion.[15]

A controversial issue here is the "Goddess religion" which, according to scholars like Marija Gimbutas and Riane Eisler, was practised by pre-historic human beings until around 3000 BCE.[16] As we've seen, Gimbutas believes that the "Old Europeans" whose civilisation flourished from 8000 BCE worshipped a Mother Goddess. However, the idea of a pre-historic "Goddess religion" is really little more than an assumption. Early human beings clearly revered the female form, and felt a great sense of awe at women's reproductive powers. Judging by the massive numbers which have been found, particularly throughout Europe and the Middle East, female figurines seem to have been their major art form. They also made a massive number of carvings and drawings of the vulva, had a custom of staining vulva-shaped cavities with red ochre (to represent menstrual blood) and another of placing vagina-shaped shells upon and around dead bodies. But to leap from this to say that our ancestors worshipped a Goddess – or goddesses – is hardly justified. As Morris Berman points out, "The goddess in these images is surely in the eye of the beholder; it is not in the images per se."[17] The archaeologist Timothy Taylor points out that very few of the figurines actually have any of the characteristics of a mother. In contrast to the Mother Goddess images of later cultures, there are hardly any figurines showing the "Goddess" giving birth or breast-feeding.[18] Goddesses certainly *were* worshipped by some peoples during the early part of the post-Fall era – for example, the Sumerian goddess Nammu, who gave birth to earth and heaven, the Egyptian goddess Nut, and Cretan goddess Ariadne. But we can see this later phase of obvious goddess worship as a transitional stage between primal spirit-religion and patriarchal theistic religion. As DeMeo writes, "Only for a brief period of history do we find 'goddesses' with temples, and these periods are transitional phases, when early matrism was being overrun by dominating patriarchal warrior cultures."[19]

In fairness to Gimbutas and Eisler – whose work I admire greatly – they do state that Goddess religion wasn't purely, or even mainly, anthropomorphic. They see the Goddess as representing spirit-force too. In fact, some descriptions of a Goddess religion sound exactly like primal peoples' spirit-religion. According to Eisler, Goddess religion "bespeaks of a view of the world in which everything is spiritual (inhabited by spirits) and the whole world is imbued with the sacred: plants, animals, the sun, the moon, our own human bodies."[20] While according to Anne Baring and Jules Cashford, in *The Myth of the Goddess*:

> The Mother Goddess, wherever she is found, is an image that inspires and focuses a perception of the universe as an organic, alive and sacred whole...Everything is woven together in one cosmic web, where all orders of manifest and unmanifest life are related, because all share in the sanctity of the original source.[21]

The idea of a prehistoric Goddess religion is, I believe, a similar kind of error to the belief that some prehistoric societies were matriarchal. Eisler points out that just because prehistoric societies weren't patriarchal, it doesn't mean they were matriarchal. In reality the whole ideology of domination was absent, and neither sex oppressed the other. And, in the same way, we can say that just because prehistoric societies – and primal peoples – didn't worship domineering male gods, it doesn't mean that they worshipped benevolent female goddesses. It's more likely that the concept of deities itself didn't exist.

THE BIRTH OF GODS

Early religious scholars like Auguste Comte and James Frazer also believed that early human societies did not have gods. Comte believed that "primitive" human beings were at what he called the "fetichist" stage, which comes before the polytheistic and monotheistic stages (and, later, the metaphysical and the positive stages).[22] While Frazer – author of one of the most famous ever books on primal religion, *The Golden Bough* – put early human beings at the "magical" stage, which comes before the religious (which is where gods enter the picture) and the scientific (when human beings transcend the need for gods).[23] Typically for their time, Comte and Frazer thought that "primitive" religion was at the bottom of the scale, and saw theistic religion as a step forward, part of the general progression which had taken human beings from savagery to "civilisation." This is very debatable – since theistic religion came with a loss of awareness of spirit-force and a new "de-sacralised" conception of the world – but the kind of transition they identify does seem to have taken place. In fact, the change took place at the same historical point as the other dramatic changes we've looked at, and involved the same peoples. The same peoples who, at around 4000 BCE, became warlike, socially stratified and patriarchal – the Indo-Europeans, the Semites, the Egyptians, the Sumerians and others – also developed theistic religions.

At first there were polytheistic religions. There were hundreds of different gods, presiding over different aspects of life – a god of love, of war, of agriculture, travel, and so on – as well as local gods looking after different towns, mountains, rivers and even different families. As Cassirer writes of the Roman gods, for instance, "They are, so to speak, administrative gods who have shared among themselves the different provinces of human life."[24] The earliest pantheon of gods that we know of is from ancient Sumer, where An was the supreme sky god, Utu was the god of the sun, Nannar of the moon, Nanshe was the goddess of fish and magic, Ninisina was the goddess of writing, and so on. The gods we're most familiar with, though, are those of ancient Greece, where Zeus was the king of the gods, Poseidon was the god of the sea, Ares was the god of war, Aphrodite the goddess of desire, and so on. Like many other peoples' gods, the Greek deities were almost laughably anthropomorphic figures, like comic book superheroes. They squabbled with each other, took each other to court, had headaches, and sometimes even had sex with humans (in which case, if they got pregnant, half-divine heroes like Hercules were born). This polytheistic tradition has even survived to the present day in India, where according to some estimates there are as many as 3 million different gods.

Initially, traces of the old spirit-religions blended with the new god-religions. As I've suggested above, the early goddesses may have been a kind of intermediary stage between spirits and male gods, since the female psyche was more closely linked to the nature, and possessed the same nurturing and caring characteristics. As Gimbutas and Eisler tell us, the Goddess was a symbol of the one-ness, the fecundity and the benevolence of nature. The idea of spirit-force wasn't completely forgotten by the early Egyptians, either. Their concept of *Akh* referred to a universal soul, while *Ba* referred to the animating force which flows from this and pervades the whole of nature. Even in Greece, there was a pre-theistic stage of religion, *Eue theia*, when there was, in Cassirer's words, "a natural kinship, a consanguinity that connects man with plants and animals."[25]

In time, however, these aspects faded away. By around 2000 BCE, all prominent deities were male, and spirit-force only existed as an esoteric concept. As Baring and Cashford write, "Towards the middle of the Bronze Age the Mother Goddess recedes into the background, as father gods begin to move to the centre of the stage."[26] The old sense of participation with nature had been replaced by a desire to dominate it, and the powerful new male gods reflected this. In Baring and Cashford's words, "God took the role of conquering or ordering nature from his counterpole of spirit."[27] This change was probably part of the overall intensification of fallen characteristics – and the disappearance of lingering traces of matrism – which took place until around 2000 BCE, possibly due to a further intensification of ego-consciousness.

Monotheism may have been the result of this too. The world's first ever monotheistic religion was founded by the Egyptian pharaoh Akhenaton in the fourteenth century BCE. Akhenaton proclaimed that the only God was Aton, the Sun God, and that all the old gods were obsolete. There's some evidence that Moses lived in Egypt at this time, where he was the son of a noble family (Moses is actually an Egyptian name), and that he assimilated this concept of one God and took it into the desert with him.[28] This may be how the Jewish religion, which eventually gave rise to Christianity, and – later still – to Islam, began.

These three religions – especially the latter two – became massively dominant amongst Saharasian-descended peoples. By 1000 CE only the Hindus and the far eastern side of the Saharasian world (that is, China, Korea and Japan) were untouched by them. Christianity had spread over the whole of Europe, from Ireland in the west to Russia in the east, and Islam had spread over the Middle East, North Africa and central Asia. Christians and Muslims sometimes claim that the fact that their religions have spread so widely and quickly is proof that they're divinely inspired, but in reality this was due to historical and psychological factors. Part of the reason why Christianity spread so quickly was the historical accident of the Roman Emperor Constantine converting to the religion, which meant that the whole of the Roman Empire suddenly became Christian (hence the addition of the adjective "Holy" to a revamped Roman Empire, and the fact that Rome is still the headquarters of the Catholic Church). Islam spread at a similar rapid speed because of the strength of the Islamic Arab armies, who forced their religion on the peoples they conquered.

However, perhaps the major reason for the conquest of so much of the world by these religions was the fact they were ideally suited to the post-Fall psyche. The notion that there is only one God – an omnipotent father figure who keeps a constant watch over us, controlling everything which happens, rewarding us for doing good and demanding complete subservience and devotion – obviously satisfied (and continues to satisfy) a deep-rooted psychological need of fallen human beings.

THE NEED FOR GODS

The question we need to answer now, then, is: How did the Ego Explosion bring an end to primal spirit-religion, and give rise to theism?

In fact, we've already answered the first part of the question. Spirit-religion ended because of the "redistribution of psychic energy" which came with the Ego Explosion. This meant that people could no longer perceive the presence of spirit-force in the world. As we saw in Chapter 5, the new ego monopolised such a large portion of people's psychic energy that there was very little left to devote to the act of perceiving present reality. In his essay "Meditation and the Consciousness of Time," the philosopher Phillip Novak describes how our minds are normally filled with "endless associational chatter and spasmodic imaginative-emotive elaborations of experience." Because of this, energy which could be "manifested as the delight of the open, receptive and present-centred awareness" (as it is with native peoples) is, in his words, "gobbled" away.[29] And the Ego Explosion was the historical point when we lost this "present-centred awareness" – and the awareness of spirit-force. And since awareness of spirit-force is the basis of the concept of individual spirits, this fell away too. The world became de-spiritualised. Rather than being alive with Spirit and spirits, the trees, rocks and rivers became inanimate objects, with no soul or inner being.

Fallen human beings needed gods partly in response to this loss of awareness of spirit-force – in particular, in response to the loss of the sense of meaning which spirit-force brings. Now the world was a cold, alien and even a hostile place, and their lives began to seem "absurd" and "unnecessary" (to use the terminology of existential philosophy). The concept of gods was a way of dealing with this, a way of making the world seem a more benign and less disorderly place. If gods were overlooking the world, protecting people and arranging everything that happened, then life wasn't absurd and the world wasn't completely indifferent. It's also easy to see how this feeling of protection and order would've been necessary in response to the warfare and social oppression which dominated people's lives after the Fall. People's lives were more insecure and dangerous than ever before, but if gods were watching over the world and looking after them, they could believe that ultimately everything was under control.

Perhaps even more importantly, though, gods were a reaction to the sense of separation and incompleteness which the Ego Explosion created. The belief that gods were always present, watching over them, was a defence mechanism against fallen human beings' sense of isolation, as transitional objects are to children. Here D.H. Lawrence describes how the idea of God arose from a sense of separation:

> The very ancient world was entirely religious and godless...The whole cosmos was alive and in contact with the flesh of man, there was no room for the god idea. It was not till the individual began to feel separated off, not till he fell into awareness of himself and into separateness...that the conception of a God arose, to intervene between man and the cosmos...God and gods enter when man has fallen into a sense of separateness and loneliness.[30]

This passage shows amazing insight, but it's not so much a question of God intervening between man and the cosmos, as of relieving this sense of aloneness. Fallen human beings needed to believe that there was an entity – or entities – who was always watching over them, who was always there, wherever they were and whatever they were doing (even if he wasn't actually in the world with them). If gods were there, people were never alone.

Gods – and God – had a secondary function too. Since they weren't aware of spirit-force, fallen human beings couldn't use the concept of spirits to explain natural events. But anthropomorphic gods took over this role, and became the explanation for everything. When a wind suddenly rose, for example, this wasn't because of the action of wind spirits any more, but because the god of wind was angry. When a person died of illness, it wasn't because an evil spirit had entered their body, but because God had decided they should die.

OTHER ASPECTS

Many of America's first European settlers assumed that, because the Native Americans didn't pray or have temples or churches, they were irreligious. But to the Native Americans there was no distinction between religion and everyday life. They didn't need to go to churches or temples to worship God because they felt that Spirit was everywhere around them at every moment. As Ronald Wright writes:

> Cherokees were so religious that there was no seam between holy and profane. The breath of the Life Master, the Great Spirit, was in all things: townhouse, field, forest and home were all temples to him and the earth. The Cherokees' daily worship was a ritual dip in the river...[31]

This illustrates another effect of the Fall in terms of religion: a new kind of separation between the sacred and the profane. As Service notes, in primal cultures "conceptions of the sacred, or supernatural, so permeate activities that it is difficult to separate religious activity from such activities as music and dance or even from play."[32] As well as not having special places of worship like churches or temples, primal peoples don't have special religious days of the week and other "holy days," nor do they have "religious specialists" like priests. The key to this, of course, is their awareness of spirit-force. There can't be any special places of worship because the whole world is sacred; every rock and every stream is full of spirit and therefore as sacred and special as any other place. And there's no need for religious specialists to act as intermediaries between human beings and God, because the divine is an obvious ever-present reality to everyone.

But with the loss of awareness of spirit-force, all this changed. Religion became a kind of hobby, something people practised in addition to their normal daily activities, and carried out at certain times and places and under the guidance of experts. Eating, dancing, singing and washing in the river weren't religious activities any more; now religion just meant the specific time that people spent praying, the rituals they performed and their visits to the temple. Communion with God was only possible in specially designated places, as if God was now an exclusive and elusive celebrity who had disappeared from everyday life. As one Orinoco Native American told a missionary, "Your god keeps himself shut up in a house, as if he were old and infirm; ours is in the forest, in the fields and on the mountains of Sipapu, whence the rains come."[33]

We've already looked at the Fall's other main effect in terms of religion: a new attitude to the afterlife. As we saw earlier, the survival of their individuality isn't so important for primal peoples. But the Fall brought an intensified fear of death, a sense of aloneness, anxiety and meaninglessness, and the social suffering of war and oppression – and as a result the Saharasian peoples *had to* believe that there was life after death, and that the next life would be a giant consolation for the sufferings of this one. The idea of heaven helped them to make sense of what would otherwise have seemed a cruel and absurd joke, and gave them a kind of pipedream to sustain them through the sufferings of their lives.

THE GOD-SHAPED HOLE

Both Marx and Freud were aware that religion has a compensatory function. Marx saw religion as a "consoling illusion" that people developed in response to the alienation of the capitalist state and the oppression and poverty which filled their lives.[34] Freud believed that religion was a compensation for the "privations" which civilisation causes. Being "civilised" means repressing our instincts and impulses, which makes us frustrated, and our repression makes us oppress and torment each other. And, as Freud writes, religion's task is "to even out the defects and evils of civilisation, to attend to the sufferings which men inflict on one another in their life together."[35]

Both Freud and Marx also believed that religion was only necessary at a certain stage of human development. Marx thought it would naturally fade away when the Communist state came into being, since the alienation and oppression which produced it would no longer exist. Freud saw religion as a sign of neurosis and immaturity, which was only necessary at what he calls the "object selection" stage. Beyond this there is what he calls "maturity," when we adapt to the world, develop a "rational" attitude to our problems and accept limitations to our desires without looking for compensation.[36]

Both of these views are naïve. Even if Marx's utopian state were somehow established, the fallen psyche would still be there, with its sense of separation from the cosmos and its lack of awareness of spirit-force. People would therefore still need religion, or at least some other way of compensating for their suffering (although, of course, the fallen psyche would prevent a Communist state from ever coming into being in the first place). The same goes for Freud's "maturity" level. The kind of rational outlook we're supposed to develop at this level might make it difficult for us to accept the illusion of religion any longer, but the psychological need for religion would still be there, and would just be directed into different areas.

In fact, this is the position many of us are in nowadays. Born-again Christians sometimes say that there's a "God-shaped hole" inside us. According to their philosophy, some of us try to fill it with money, fame, success or drugs, but none of these really satisfy us – in fact, we'll never be truly satisfied until we find God. And in a way they are right. The hole is the sense of separateness and incompleteness which goes with the fallen psyche. We've already seen how people try to compensate for this by accumulating material goods, living hedonistically or chasing after power and success. And it's probably true that becoming a Christian – or a Muslim or even a Scientologist or a Hare Krishna – is the most effective defence against the psychic suffering of the over-developed ego. As well as God's protective function and the compensation which the fallen concept of the afterlife brings, religions themselves provide a strong sense of belonging (which also mitigates our sense of separateness), and a sense of meaning, purpose and structure, which makes us less vulnerable to psychological discord.

But in the modern world the opium of religion isn't so readily available to us. It's ironic that the powerful reasoning abilities which the Ego Explosion gave us have meant that the consolation our ancestors developed to deal with its negative effects – that is, religion – is no longer so viable. Science has taken over religion's secondary function of explaining the world, and in the process negated its primary function. And as a result most of us are forced to turn to the other ways of filling the "God-shaped hole," such as materialism, status-seeking or hedonism.

Ultimately, though, religion doesn't really work either. It doesn't actually cure the disease, it just gives us some relief from the pain. That is, it doesn't actually take away our sense of separation and incompleteness, it just compensates for it.

There is another way of dealing with the problem: through spirituality, or spiritual development. It's important not to confuse spirituality with religion. In the purest sense of the term, spirituality doesn't have anything to do with prayer, holy books, heaven, priests or even with God (in the normal sense of the term). Spiritual traditions like Buddhism, Yoga and Sufism (amongst many others) are *transformational* systems. Their whole purpose is to heal our psychological discord, and to transcend our present state of suffering. They teach us how to overcome our sense of separation, how to be free of psychic entropy, and how to reconnect with spirit-force. In other words, they offer us a method of actually curing our psychological discord rather than just dealing with its symptoms. And as we'll see later, it's only through using these transformational systems that we can arrive at a point where religion – and other forms of compensation for our psychic suffering – is no longer necessary.

12

SEPARATION FROM THE BODY

The Bible tells us that before the Fall, Adam and Eve "were both naked, but they were not embarrassed." But after Eve ate from the tree of knowledge and they both became self-conscious, they became aware that they were naked. They felt ashamed, and "sewed fig leaves together and covered themselves."

This passage seems to refer to another massive transformation which came with the Fall: a completely new attitude to sex and the body. Like Adam and Eve before the Fall, many unfallen peoples – such as the Australian Aborigines – live their lives completely naked, and don't think of their genital areas as any more special or shameful than other parts of the body. Aborigine adults often playfully tickle and fondle young children's genitals in much the same way that, in our culture, we sometimes pinch children's noses and tickle their chins.[2] Even when unfallen peoples do cover their genitals, women generally go bare-breasted (climate allowing), and breast-feeding is done completely openly.

Primal peoples also generally have a completely open attitude to sex. Sex is seen as a healthy, natural source of pleasure and is never an uncomfortable subject. Adults talk about it freely, and don't try to shield their children from knowledge of it. As Robert Lawlor notes of the Aborigines, "The sex act itself is never hidden from children (although adult couples tend to prefer privacy). Children sleep in the same camp as their parents, and sex is an open topic of conversation."[3] Starting at a very young age – sometimes as young as five – Aborigine children play erotic games with each other, including mock lovemaking. They start having sex at what we would think of as a very young age too, sometimes even at the age of nine. In fact, this seems to be true of all primal peoples. As Malinowski wrote of the Trobriander Islanders, for example:

> The children initiate each other into the mysteries of sexual life
> in a directly practical manner at a very early age. A premature
> amorous existence begins among them long before they are

really able to carry out the act of sex. They indulge in plays and pastimes in which they satisfy their curiosity concerning the appearance and function of the organs of regeneration, and incidentally receive, it would seem, a certain amount of positive pleasure.[4]

And once their sex lives do begin, the children of unfallen cultures have a degree of sexual freedom which most of us would find shocking. The concept of virginity is of no importance whatsoever. According to the anthropologist Shostak, the !Kung don't even have a word for virginity.[5] Adolescence is seen as a time of sexual experimentation. As Service notes of the Nuer of Africa, "After puberty, boys and girls have a good deal of freedom in experimental love-making and usually find lovers without any particular interference from their respective families."[6] One reason why we don't condone sexual freedom for teenagers is the danger of pregnancy, of course, but unfallen peoples' use of plant contraceptives ensures that this almost never occurs. Details of these are still quite sketchy, because of women's reluctance to reveal their traditional secrets to anthropologists, but they seem to be at least as effective as modern contraceptives. Malinowski estimated that only 1 per cent of Trobriander children came from adolescent affairs, while Elwin estimated 4 per cent for the Muria of India.[7]

Sometimes children have their own communal dormitories, away from the adults, where they regularly have sex with different partners. The most famous of these (which we looked at briefly earlier) is the *Ghotul* of the Muria, a special children's house which adults were usually barred from entering. According to Elwin, boys would be fined if they slept with the same girl for more than three nights running.[8] The Trobrianders had a similar dormitory called the *bukumatula*. Youths from one village would go to the *bukumatula* of the next, to try to meet new sexual partners. Girls initiated sexual relations as often as boys, and were never thought of negatively for being sexually forward and uninhibited. This period of sexual experimentation is seen as one of the most special and joyous times of a person's life.[9]

Eventually, however, by the time of late adolescence, children do begin to "pair bond." In contrast to many Saharasian cultures, young people have complete freedom of choice over their partners, and their parents never force them to "marry" a particular person. (The term "bond with" is probably more accurate than "marry" because primal peoples often don't have special ceremonies to mark marriages, or have any marriage vows.) But even while bonded to a particular person, primal peoples have a great deal of sexual freedom. In some cases, extramarital sex even appears to be a moral imperative. For the Matis Indians of the Amazon Basin, for example:

> Extramarital sex is not only widely practised and usually tolerated; in many respects it also appears mandatory. Married or not, one has a moral duty to respond to the sexual advances of opposite-sex cross-cousins (real or classificatory) under pains of being labeled "stingy of one's genitals," a breach of Matis ethic far more serious than plain infidelity.[10]

Many primal peoples practise what we would today call "swinging" or "spouse-swapping." This was common amongst the Inuit Eskimos and the Qolla Indians of Peru, for example. The Qolla called their spouse-exchanges *Tawanku*. They were organised by men with their wives' consent, and any children who came from them were seen as legitimate, and brought up with the woman's children by her husband.[11] Some peoples, such as the Siriono of Bolivia and the Chickasaw Indians, also practise what we might call "sibling-swapping." When a man marries he assumes the right to sleep with any of his bride's sisters, while the bride can sleep with any of her brothers-in law.[12] We've already seen that affairs are commonplace in Australian Aboriginal cultures too, and tolerated as long as they don't break up marriages. For the Aborigines marriage is mainly a matter of economic and social convenience, and a husband never tries to deny his wife (or wives) the right to have sex with other men, particularly if he is old and can't satisfy her completely.[13]

In addition, many cultures have festivals or ceremonies at which people are free – or even duty-bound – to have sex with new partners. Many Indian groups of South America held tattooing ceremonies at which people were expected to have "extra-marital" sex, while the Warao (also of South America) have regular periods called *mamuse* at which normal pair-bonds are dissolved and everyone is free to have sex with whoever they like.[14] Even nowadays on the Trobriand Islands, during the yam harvest women wander around the islands "raping" men from other villages, and bite off the eyebrows of men who don't give them enough pleasure.[15]

Primal peoples also acknowledge – and cater for – the differences between male and female sexuality. The Aborigines accept that women sometimes need to have sex with multiple partners, since the lovemaking of one man can't always satisfy them. This is so acceptable that, just like European/American men, women sometimes boast about the number of men they've slept with. As James Cowan writes, quoting from a survey into the sexual behaviour of Aborigines:

> Gossip songs often address sexual prowess among women in the following manner: "How many men can you take before you get tired?" "Why, I had so many, one after the other, and I could have taken more. My thighs and vagina are strong – see, even after washing myself, I still drip juices."[16]

The Mangaia of the Cook Islands (close to New Zealand) take account of women's more rarefied sexual needs by giving boys aged 13 to14 "sex lessons." Older women teach them the different ways of giving pleasure to a woman, including oral sex, clitoral stimulation by finger, and different love-making techniques. At the end they're expected to be able to give women multiple orgasms, and if they don't reach the required standard word spreads around and they find it difficult to get sexual partners.[17] In the same way, women of the Trukese Islands in Micronesia see it as their right to have an orgasm every time they have sex. According to the anthropologist Goodenough, if a man ejaculates too soon and doesn't satisfy her, the woman tells her friends and the man soon has a reputation as an inadequate lover.[18]

As Christopher Ryan points out, this easy-going attitude to affairs, and the lack of jealousy and possessiveness towards partners, fits very closely with the other sharing practices of primal peoples.[19] They share food and don't allow themselves to individually possess anything but the most basic objects, so why would we expect them to be possessive when it comes to sex?

In contrast to later fallen cultures (with some exceptions such as Greece and Rome, where the segregation of the sexes and the unavailability of women led to socially accepted gay relations, usually between older men and adolescent boys), many unfallen peoples also had a very tolerant attitude to homosexuality. Until the late nineteenth century, transsexuals were accepted and even revered by many Native American groups. If any young person wanted to live the life of the opposite sex, people reacted sympathetically. The *bedarche* (or Two-Spirit person, as they have been called more recently) was thought to have special powers because of his/her male-female duality, and would often become a shaman.[20]

A form of ritualistic homosexuality is still practised by some of the peoples of Melanesia. Particularly amongst the tribes of Papua New Guinea, there is a traditional belief that sperm provides masculine energy, and that adolescent boys can only become men by ingesting large quantities of it. Semen is seen in the same light as breast milk and helps a boy to grow quickly. In order to get the semen they "need," boys have regular anal sex with older men, or give them oral sex and swallow the sperm. According to the anthropologist Gilbert Herdt, as many as 10 to 20 per cent of tribes in Melanesia have these "boy-inseminating" practices, although they are now quickly disappearing.[21]

Homosexual relationships between adolescent boys and older men were accepted by a number of African peoples as well. When the English anthropologist Evans-Pritchard studied the Azande people of Zaire in the 1920s, he found many cases of adolescents serving as "boy-wives" to older men. The boys would help them with their work and sleep with them at night, and they referred to each other as "my love" or "my lover."[22] In some traditional African cultures, homosexuality is discouraged amongst adults, but acceptable in adolescents. In his studies of the Fang people of present-day Gabon, another early anthropologist, Tessman, found that while homosexuality was unheard of in adults, adolescents frequently had gay relations with each other, in a playful, adventurous way.[23]

PREHISTORIC ATTITUDES TO SEX AND THE BODY

Everything we know about prehistoric peoples suggests that they had the same guilt-free attitude to sex and the body. As we've seen, the art of the Palaeolithic and the Neolithic Ages is dominated by sexual images. The female figurines with massive breasts, the engravings and carvings of vaginas, images of erect penises, sculptures of couples having sex, womb-like tombs with small "vaginal" openings – as well as showing a veneration of the female form, all of this shows a healthy, unselfconscious attitude to sex. We've already noted that ancient Crete was the "Old European" culture which survived the longest (until 1500 BCE, when Indo-European invaders finally overran it), and the culture which flourished there was notable for what the archaeologist Jaquetta Hawkes calls a "fearless and natural emphasis on sexual life that ran through all religious expression."[24] Ancient Cretan art is full of sexual symbols, and Hawkes believes that the Cretans held sexual rituals every spring to celebrate the marriage of the Goddess and the Bull God.

However, the Cretans' open attitude to sex is most evident from their paintings, which show both men and women wearing sexually provocative clothes. Women are shown bare-breasted, and wearing what we would today call short "sexy" dresses. Men wear codpieces, heavy metal belts to emphasise their narrow waists, and short garments which show off their thighs. According to Hawkes, this "free and well-balanced sex life" was one of the reasons why the Minoans were so free from aggression and war-like behaviour.[25] This makes sense in terms of Wilhelm Reich's argument that aggression is linked to the "undischarged bio-energetic tension" which builds up in sexually repressive societies.

MENSTRUATION

In complete contrast to later cultures, our prehistoric ancestors seem to have had a healthy attitude to menstruation too. In fact, they seem to have felt the same kind of awe towards the female reproductive cycle that they felt towards the female form in general. In Upper Palaeolithic art there are many representations of vulvae, which, as Richard Rudgley suggests, are "not depicted for [their] role in sexual pleasure but rather because of [their] associations with childbirth, pregnancy and menstruation."[26] When Palaeolithic peoples found caves with openings shaped like a vulva, they marked them with ochre, apparently to symbolise menstrual blood.[27] This suggests that menstrual blood had some ritual significance, and was perhaps even thought of as sacred. In 1980, archaeologists in the Urals in Russia discovered a female figure with 28 red dots between her legs, dating from the Upper Palaeolithic period (40,000 to 10,000 years ago). This seems an obvious reference to the menstrual cycle.[28]

The attitude of primal peoples to menstruation is a little more problematic, since some of them – though by no means all – do seem to have a negative attitude to it. Some Native American peoples, such as the Chickasaw, had menstrual huts for women to live in while they were on their periods, so that they wouldn't "defile" pots and tools with their touch.[29] Even the !Kung of the Kalahari desert – one of the most purely matrist peoples of Africa – don't let women touch hunting weapons while they're menstruating. And like many African peoples, the !Kung have a strict taboo against sex during menstruation.[30]

However, this attitude probably isn't due to a revulsion to the process of menstruation itself. If it were, we would expect these peoples to have a similar kind of revulsion to other bodily processes, such as breast-feeding, pregnancy or sex. This certainly *is* case with the fallen peoples, but since it isn't with unfallen peoples we might assume that another factor is involved. And this factor appears to be fear of blood. Many primal peoples see blood as a terrifyingly potent substance which is dangerous to have contact with under any circumstances. Its appearance is an evil omen, and as Colin Turnbull writes of the African villagers around the Congo forest, "menstrual blood is even more terrible because of its mysterious and constant recurrence."[31] As a result, girls of the villages who have their first periods are isolated and have to undergo purification rituals, while her tribe hold rituals to try to ward off the evil which they are sure is coming their way.

The problem here may be that these peoples don't recognise the connection between the menstrual cycle and reproduction. The Pygmies are afraid of blood too, but they don't have a negative attitude to menstruation. To them, menstrual blood is a special case because of its connection with reproduction. While normal blood symbolises death, menstrual blood symbolises life. A girl's first period means that she has been "blessed by the moon," and is an occasion of great joy. As Turnbull describes it:

> When blood comes to her the first time, it comes to her as a gift, received with gratitude and rejoicing; rejoicing that the girl is now a potential mother, that she can now proudly and rightfully take a husband. There is not a word of fear or superstition, and everyone is told the good news.[32]

The Aborigines also have a positive view of menstruation. In fact, they seem to have the same reverential attitude to menstrual blood as that of our prehistoric ancestors. Semen and menstrual blood are often used in religious ceremonies, and are the only sex-related topics which can't be talked about openly. Both substances are too weighted with religious significance to be treated in a trivial way. As Lawlor writes: "Menstrual blood is…highly revered and is the focal interest in much of Aboriginal religious life. Men do not react to menstruation with disgust or horror, nor are menstruating women labelled unclean."[33]

THE (FIRST) SEXUAL REVOLUTION

Although it was more subtle, the change in attitude to sex and the body which occurred from 4000 BCE onwards is just as clear an indication of the Fall as the advent of war, patriarchy, social inequality or theistic religion.

The Fall brought about the same kind of division between the ego and the body as that between human beings and nature. With their over-developed sense of ego, fallen human beings saw themselves as separate from their bodies. *They* were the thinking ego inside their heads, and looked out at their bodies with the same sense of separation they experienced when they looked out at their surroundings. Rather than actually *being* their bodies, they saw themselves as just inhabiting them, like a "ghost in a machine," or mind trapped inside a "mortal coil." The body - and all its processes and instincts - was "other" to them.

The Katha Upanishad famously states, "Where there is other, there is fear"[34] – and we could just as easily say, "Where there is other, there is hostility." When a sense of separation develops, conflict is always close at hand. It's possible to look at the effects of the Fall purely in terms of conflict: conflict between different human groups (war in the normal sense), conflict between different social classes and social groups (social inequality), conflict between men and women (patriarchy) and conflict between human beings and nature (environmental problems). And we can see the transition we're examining in this chapter as a conflict too: a conflict between the ego and the body. Following the Ego Explosion, the ego declared war on the body. In the same way that the over-developed male ego tried to dominate other human beings – especially women – and nature, it tried to dominate the body. Completely natural human instincts became "sinful" and completely natural bodily processes became "unclean." Even to mention sexual matters or other bodily processes became "obscene." As D.H. Lawrence wrote, "Obscenity only comes in when the mind despises and fears the body, and the body hates and resists the mind."[35]

SHAME OF SEX AND THE BODY

One of the most obvious of the effects of the Fall in any area is the transition from the complete nakedness of primal peoples like the Aborigines to the complete covering of the body which is still practised by the women of some Middle-Eastern cultures, such as Saudi Arabia and Iran. In these cultures women cannot expose any part of their body apart from their eyes and hands. Some more moderate Middle-Eastern countries allow them to show their faces – as long as they keep their hair covered – but in many countries they are required to cover their faces with the *hijab*, or veil.

It's often assumed that veiling is a specifically Muslim custom, but this isn't the case. There's no evidence that Mohammed advocated it, and no clear reference to it in the Qur'an. It seems that even the prophet's wives didn't wear the veil. Umar, who later became the second Caliph – or leader of Islam – after Mohammed's death, is on record as complaining to him: "Messenger of god, you receive all kinds of people at your house, moral as well as evil. Why do you not order the *hijab* for the Mothers of the Believers?"[36] The *hijab* actually predates Islam by many centuries. The first known historical reference to it is from 1500 BCE – in an Assyrian inscription which mentions veiling as a way of indicating which women were already in custody, so that raiding groups wouldn't try to capture them again.[37] This is the function it came to have in the Islamic world after Mohammed's death too. Muslim women had to wear veils as a kind of uniform, so that raiders and warriors would leave them alone when they searched for women to rape and abduct. But at the same time as having these origins, the *hijab* – and the covering of every other part of the body – clearly shows a neurotically repressive attitude to the female body, together with an impulse to dominate women and restrict their freedom.

After the Fall pre- and extra-marital sex were punishable by death. To guard against the possibility of adolescent sex, fallen cultures kept boys and girls separate, and crushed any romantic liaisons. (This was especially important because marriages became economic transactions arranged by parents, and all of the bride's "value" was based on her sexual "purity.") If these measures didn't work and a new wife was found to be "impure," in many Indo-European and Semitic cultures she would be stoned or burnt to death. Affairs between married men and women were punishable by death too – or, at least, the death of the woman. Men who had sex outside marriage were sometimes castrated, but rarely killed.[38]

In some cultures, "illicit" sex is still just as dangerous nowadays. In her book *The Veil of Shame*, Evelyne Accad describes how – in complete contrast to unfallen cultures, where the concept of virginity isn't important and may not even exist – many modern Middle-Eastern cultures suffer from what she calls a "virginity mania":

> From early childhood, a girl is brought up in constant fear of losing her virginity…In this culture a man is only convinced that he made a wise choice if his bride brings an intact hymen to the marriage bed; he considers it evidence of exclusive possession, proof that the merchandise is brand new…Virginity represents the "honor" of the girl, and, more importantly, of her family.[39]

This honour is so important for the family that a girl's father and brothers often see themselves as the "guardians" of her virginity. They chaperone her wherever she goes to make sure that she's never left alone with other men and never has the opportunity to cultivate male friendships. With this kind of social pressure, surely very few – if any – women would dream of having affairs even if they had the chance. But most men have such a distorted view of female sexuality – and so little trust – that they imagine girls will give in to lust the moment they get the chance.

But, again, if these measures somehow don't work and a girl does have sex before marriage, male members of the family may attempt to regain the family's "honor" by murdering her. In many cases, girls lose their virginity through rape, often by a family member, but this doesn't make any difference. The fact is that she is no longer a virgin, that nobody will ever marry her, and the family name will always be dishonoured. In 1998 a teenage girl in Pakistan was raped by her uncle and then murdered by her brother as a result. And in a tragic case of the value systems of two cultures clashing, in 2001 a middle-aged Pakistani man stabbed his English-born daughter to death after finding her in bed with her boyfriend. While in the same year in India – usually thought of as having a more open attitude to sex than Muslim countries – two teenagers from different castes who had a sexual relationship were killed by their respective families. In this case, the teenagers hadn't simply broken the taboo against sex before marriage, but also the taboo against relationships between different castes.

SEX AND RELIGION

This hostility to sex and the body became an integral part of the Saharasian peoples' religions. One of the earliest Saharasian religions was Zoroastrianism, founded by the Persian teacher Zoroaster during the sixth century BCE. The religion's central idea was that the whole material world, including the human body, was corrupt and evil, and only the soul was "good." (The heretical Christian sect of Gnosticism developed similar ideas a few centuries later.) For Zoroastrians, sex for non-procreative purposes was sinful. The Indian religion of Jainism, which also arose during the sixth century BCE, had the same hostile attitude to the body. Jains were forbidden to talk to or even look at a woman lest the desire to commit the "evil" act of sexual intercourse might arise.

The three great Saharasian religions of Judaism, Christianity and Islam had the same dualistic attitude, pitting the corruption of "the flesh" against the purity of "the spirit." Early Christian ascetics put themselves through appalling torments to try to tame their physical desires and make themselves more "spiritual." From a positive perspective, we can see asceticism as a spiritual technique aimed at trying to stop our lower, hedonistic and materialistic impulses monopolising our consciousness-energy. By learning to control our instincts and desires, we retain the energy they normally drain away and so become more spiritual inside ourselves. But some ascetics took this process to absurd and gruesome extremes. The early Christian saint Simeon Stylites only ate once a week, wore a rope of palm leaves twisted around his body, went completely without food and drink for the whole of Lent, and spent the last years of his life at the top of 67-foot-high pillar with an iron collar around his neck. Similarly, the fourteenth-century German mystic Henry de Suso spent years wearing a hair shirt and an iron chain, as well as a leather belt containing 150 inward-facing sharp brass nails. He didn't have a bath in 25 years, never sheltered from the cold in winter, and never touched or scratched any part of his body apart from his hands and feet.[40]

According to Christian teaching, human beings who let perfectly healthy and natural sexual desires express themselves – by having sex before or outside marriage – would be sent to hell to suffer for eternity. But it wasn't just sex out of marriage which was sinful. Christian teachers like St Clement of Alexandria and St Augustine believed that even married couples "corrupted" themselves by having sex, and that good Christians had to be celibate. No one would be pure enough to enter the kingdom of heaven unless they were celibate. In this spirit, Jesus' saying, "You must become as little children if you would enter the kingdom of heaven", was interpreted as meaning being completely free of knowledge of sex. Some Christian groups, such as the Syrian Church, even refused to baptise married couples and recommended castration as the only sure way of avoiding the sin of sex.[41] The early Christian theologians who put forward these views were influenced by the Jewish teacher Philo, who wrote:

> For since among all the passions that of intercourse between man and woman is greatest, the law givers have commended that that instrument, which serves this intercourse, be mutilated, pointing out, that these powerful passions must be bridled...[42]

Not surprisingly, female sexual pleasure was also taboo. Less extreme Christian teachers permitted sex between married couples, but only for procreative purposes. Neither partner – and especially the woman – was allowed to enjoy it. Good Christian women were supposed to hate sex. There was even a belief that sexual pleasure stopped women getting pregnant. As Barbara G. Walker points out, "The 'missionary position' was the only permitted sexual position, because it afforded the least pleasure, especially to the wife."[43] And in some cultures men even took – and still take – physical measures to make sure women didn't enjoy sex. Many Middle-Eastern and African cultures still practise forms of female genital mutilation, most usually clitoridectomy (removal of the clitoris). In contrast to male circumcision, which increases a boy's status and is seen as an occasion for rejoicing, female genital mutilations are, in Evelyne Accad's words, "largely an act of degradation," with the intent to "reduce or preclude the girl's sexual desires, in part to ensure that she will arrive at her marriage bed an intact virgin and in part to make her completely passive as a sex partner."[44]

BODILY PROCESSES

As we'd expect, fallen peoples' attitude to bodily processes was extremely negative too. The tribes of the Hebrews believed that women were unclean for seven days after the start of their periods, and that everything they touched or even looked at would be infected with their "uncleanness." Menstruating women were used as scapegoats for natural problems, and often took the blame when plants died, livestock miscarried and fruits went sour.[45]

According to traditional Hindu myths, menstruation began when the God Indra killed Vrita, a learned Brahman. As the story is told in the Vasistha Dharma Sastra, when Indra realised the terrible crime he had committed, he ran to the womenfolk and asked them to share his guilt. They agreed, in return for being able to have children during "the proper season," and now, according to the myth, "That guilt of Brahmana murder appears every month as the menstrual flow."[46] In the orthodox Brahmanical tradition, a woman is sinful and corrupt during the days of their period, and only becomes clean on the fourth day, when she performs her ablutions. The Vasistha Dharma Sastra has a long list of prohibitions for menstruating women, which are filled with a sadistic cruelty and a neurotic repulsion to bodily processes:

> During that period she shall not apply collyrium to her eyes, nor anoint [her body], nor bathe in water, she shall sleep on the ground; she shall not sleep in the daytime, not touch the fire, not make a rope, nor clean her teeth, nor eat meat, nor look at the planets, nor smile, nor busy herself with [household affairs], nor run...[47]

Any blood which came from the vagina was seen as dangerous, even poisonous. In ancient India and Japan new husbands employed priests and monks to have sex with their wives on their wedding nights. The belief was that if the husbands themselves did it, the blood would make them ill and possibly even kill them. Only these "holy men" could be exposed to the blood without being affected by it. As one Japanese Buddhist teacher wrote, "Blood flowing in the first intercourse of man and woman has in it a venomous poison, a root of all evils. Man can die on the spot."[48]

Even pregnancy had taboos attached to it, partly because of vaginal blood and partly because a pregnant woman had obviously committed the "evil" of sexual intercourse. Hebrew women had to be ritually purified three times after giving birth.[49] In Christian Europe, new mothers who went back to church without first being purified had to do penances. They would also be punished – together with their husbands – if they confessed to having sex in the weeks after birth.[50] As recently as the seventeenth century in Europe, pregnant women were thought of as "sick with sin" because they'd had sex. As if to emphasise this, they were often sent to have their babies in church-run sick houses. These were full of genuinely sick people who often infected the women with their diseases and killed them and their babies.[51]

Breastfeeding became taboo as well. As another illustration of the drastic change which came with the Ego Explosion, breast-feeding went from being a completely open and public practice to a shameful, clandestine one, performed behind closed doors, not even in the presence of the husband. Christian teachers called it a "swinish and filthy" habit and rich women hired wetnurses to do it for them.[52]

CAUSES OF HOSTILITY TO THE BODY

In some ways, the story of this transition from a positive, open attitude to the body to the repressive, guilt-laden attitude of fallen peoples is one of the most depressing in this book. After the healthy and free atmosphere of the pre-Fall era, the fallen era seems to stink of sickness, to be rancid with repression and guilt. If we need any more evidence that for the last 6,000 years human beings have suffered from a kind of psychosis, then this is surely it. How did human nature become so twisted and perverted that people could wage war on their own biology in this way? How did they become so alienated from their own biology that they could punish themselves so severely for doing exactly what nature wants them to do?

We know the answer to this question, of course: the Ego Explosion. The Ego Explosion caused what Lancelot Law Whyte called the European disassociation, the split between mind and body. And as soon as the body became separate from the ego, conflict was inevitable. The ego began to look on the body not just as something "other" but as something *lower* than it. To human beings after the Fall, the body was animal and instinctive, while they – the ego – were "spirit" or "mind."

It was a question of control too. More than anything else, the over-developed ego craves for power. We've already seen how this desire for power is one of the basic causes of war, social inequality and patriarchy. The ego wants to control the body too, of course, and we can see all the restrictions on – and taboos about – sex and other bodily processes as an attempt to do this, an attempt to suppress our biology and keep our instincts in check. But the problem is that the ego can't completely control the body. No matter how you try to check and suppress natural instincts, they're so powerful that they keep rising up and keep taking control over *you*. No matter how hard you try to keep your mind "pure" and to live a celibate life, sexual impulses keep stirring inside you. Gandhi was celibate from the age of 37, and after three decades felt that he had finally conquered his sex instincts. But one morning as an old man, he woke up and was devastated to find that he'd had a wet dream during the night. And this ultimate lack of control adds to the ego's enmity towards the body. In the same way that it craves for domination, the ego hates to *be* dominated. It furiously resents the body's control over it.

Body-hostility was linked to men's hostility to women, of course. As we noted earlier, this hostility was fuelled by the fact that most of the bodily process which revolted men – menstruation, pregnancy, breast-feeding – were a part of female biology, and also by the fact that women stimulated the sexual desires which men felt were base and resented being controlled by. And as we've also seen, body-hostility is connected to war. In societies where boys and girls aren't permitted to have sex for years after they're biologically ready, and where it's impossible to escape from an unsatisfactory sex life through extra-marital liaisons or even through divorce, there is bound to be a large build-up of what Reich called "bio-energetic tension," which will express itself in aggression and violence.

The possessive instinct which came with the Ego Explosion was probably a factor here too. Men began to feel that they "owned" women in the same way that they owned property, and so for a man to make love to another man's wife was an act of theft or trespass. The fallen instinct for competition and ownership meant the end of group-sharing practices. People no longer shared their food, their goods or their decisions – and they no longer shared their partners.

13

THE ORIGINS OF TIME

ANOTHER EFFECT OF the Ego Explosion was a change in the way we perceive time. It's possible to say that the Ego Explosion actually *created* time.

Our normal perception of time is linear. The past is behind us, the future is in front of us, and the present is a brief moment at the intersection of the two. It flashes for a tiny instant and then disappears. The past is a gigantic "trash box" of old present moments, none of which can ever be relived, and the future is an endless sequence of new moments waiting to happen, which are unknowable until they arrive.

The sense that time is always flowing in this way puts a constant pressure on us. We feel that it's continually slipping away, and struggle to keep up with it. We're always behind time, there never seems to be enough of it, and every time we let a few precious moments pass by without making use of them we feel like we've wasted it.

This flow of time can be a depressing phenomenon too. It means that nothing is permanent, that all the circumstances which give us happiness fade away after a short while. As the German philosopher Schopenhauer wrote, "In a world like this, where there is no kind of stability, no possibility of anything lasting, but where everything is thrown into a restless whirlpool of change...it is impossible to imagine happiness."[1] Time takes everything away from us. It eats away at our youth, beauty, health, optimism, and even our lives themselves. Every hour we live through takes us closer to death – "The hours are killing you, one by one," as the French saying goes.

This linear view of time seems self-evidently true to us, but in a sense it's just as much a product of the fallen psyche as male domination, theistic religion or body-hostility.

TIME AND UNFALLEN CULTURES

Unfallen peoples don't seem to experience a flow of time. In fact, it's debatable whether the concept of time has any meaning to them at all. Very few – if any – unfallen peoples appear to even have words for time, or for the future or the past. As Lawlor notes, for example, "None of the hundreds of Aboriginal languages contain a word for time, nor do the Aborigines have a concept of time."[2] And as Evans-Pritchard wrote of the Nuer:

> The time perspective of the Nuer is limited to a very short span – in a sense they are a timeless people, as are most primitive societies. They have no word for time in the European sense. They have no conception of time as an abstract thing which can be wasted, or saved, or which passes.[3]

After living with the Quiche Indians of Guatemala, the anthropologist Barbara Tedlock concluded that they don't experience a flow of time either. Whereas we isolate time into "moments" that come and go, to them, she writes, "at no given time, past, present, or future, is it possible to isolate that time from the events that led up to it and which flow from it."[4] Similarly, Edward T. Hall noted that as well as having no words for time, the languages of the Hopi and Navaho have no past or future tenses. They seem to live in an "eternal present." "To the Hopi," Hall writes, "the experience of time must be more natural – like breathing, a rhythmic part of life."[5] We've already noted that Hall was struck by the fact that the Native Americans didn't seem to be disturbed by *waiting*. Unlike the Europeans, the Indians that he saw waiting at trading posts and hospitals never showed any sign of irritation or impatience, but just sat quietly until it was their turn. I suggested that this was probably because unfallen peoples don't suffer from the psychological discord which makes it difficult for Europeans to spend any amount of time *inside* themselves, with their attention not focused on external things. But another factor here may be that the Native Americans didn't have the same acute sense of time passing as Europeans. Perhaps they weren't disturbed by waiting partly because they didn't have the sense that time was slipping away and that "precious" moments were being stolen from them. To them the period of time they spent waiting was somehow a static whole rather than a flow of time made up of isolated moments.

THE FUTURE AND THE PAST

Because unfallen peoples don't experience a flow of time, the future and past have very little meaning to them. Whereas our preoccupation with the future and the past alienates us from the present, to them the present is the only reality.

This was another reason why unfallen peoples found the European way of life so difficult to adjust to. European colonists tried to force native peoples to switch from hunting and gathering to an agricultural way of life. But often this wasn't successful because of their lack of awareness of – and interest in – the future. They didn't see the point of working hard to produce yields of food which wouldn't arrive for months, especially when sources of food – animals and plants – were all around them at every moment.

This also meant that native peoples found the European concepts of deadlines and timetables difficult to deal with. Edward T. Hall noted that the Navaho and the Hopi didn't have the European drive for "closure," and didn't feel that leaving a task unfinished was an embarrassing sign of incompetence and failure. Hopi villages were full of unfinished houses, with beautifully built walls and windows but without a roof. The wood for the roof might lie by the side of the house, needing just a few more weeks' work, and yet would still be there years later. Dams that should have been finished within three months were still incomplete after a year.[6] As Hall writes, "To the Navajo the future was uncertain as well as unreal, and they were neither interested in nor motivated by 'future' rewards."[7]

Part of the problem, Hall recognised, was that the European sense of linear time means that we are, in his phrase, "monochronic." This means that we usually do one thing at a time, that when we have a task to do we concentrate all our attention on it and try to complete it in the shortest possible time, before moving on to the next item on our list of things to do. But the Native Americans were "polychronic." Completing one particular task wasn't so important to them; they were happy to spread their attention more widely and have several different projects under way at the same time.[8]

The same holds true in the other direction: unfallen peoples also have a limited awareness of – and very little interest in – the past. As the anthropologist Maurice Bloch noted, unfallen African peoples such as the Hazda and Mbuti never talk about the past, and have no concept of "history."[9] This appears to be true of all unfallen cultures. They generally don't have a tradition of oral history which is passed down from one generation to the next, and seem to have very little concern for past events or important personalities from the past. Although they all have origin myths of one form or another, these aren't history in our sense of the term. They don't describe a process of one thing being created after another, and the creation of the world isn't necessarily seen as complete or as a past event. As Elman R. Service writes of the Trobriand Islanders:

> The Trobriander is distinctly unhistorical in his cosmogony. Agriculture, magic, law, the people themselves, islands – everything – came into being once, full-blown, and that is the way they *are*. The Trobriander, like so many primitive peoples, does not view phenomena as being in a process of change through time. A being is changeless; therefore, the Trobriand language has no word for *to be* or *to become*.[10]

The Aborigines don't make a clear distinction between the present and the past, either. According to their mythology, the world was created during the Dreamtime, when giant beings strode over the earth's surface, leaving their imprints as mountains, lakes and oceans and the rest of the earth's topography. But the Dreamtime isn't a historical period which happened long ago and is over and done with. In a sense, the Dreamtime is still happening now, and the world is still in the process of being created.

THE FALL INTO TIME

Just as I do, Ken Wilber – in *Up From Eden* – links the development of linear time to the advent of "fallen" self-consciousness. He explains it in terms of the greater awareness of death which self-consciousness brings. As we noted earlier, being more aware of your own existence also means being more aware of your potential *non*-existence. And greater awareness of death also means greater *fear* of death. And according to Wilber, the original fallen psyche dealt with this fear of death by convincing itself that it *wasn't* going to die, that after it cast off its body there was a future of eternal linear time waiting for it.

The development of a linear sense of time was, therefore, closely connected to the fallen concept of the afterlife. Our ancestors had to believe that they were going to live for ever, and in order to do this they had to conceive of time in a linear way. And in addition, says Wilber, the concept of an everlasting future gave us the opportunity to fulfil the limitless desires for power and wealth which the separate self-sense also gives rise to. As he writes:

> In its more intensified awareness of death, the ego needed more time...By cutting itself loose into a linear and progressive world of time...the ego's essentially unquenchable and unfulfilable desires had room to pitch forward everlastingly.[11]

Wilber's explanation is typically ingenious and may well have been a factor. But there is, I believe, a more fundamental and simple reason why the new ego gave rise to linear time. An important point we need to grasp is that the past and the future don't *really* exist. The only thing which exists is the present, and it's just that while we're in the present, we have *thoughts* about the future and the past. We remember what has happened to us before the present and we anticipate what is going to happen after it. As St Augustine wrote, "The past is only memory and the future is only anticipation, both being present facts."[12]

In other words, linear time is created by abstraction, by *thinking*. Unfallen peoples don't have a sense of linear time simply because their minds don't work abstractly in the way that ours do, because their minds don't chatter away incessantly, recalling the past and projecting the future. The future and the past have little relevance to them simply because they aren't continually reinforced as concepts by thought-chatter.

Historically, therefore, we can say that the linear sense of time developed when a high degree of abstraction – or incessant thought-chatter – became a feature of our psyche. And this was, of course, linked to the Ego Explosion. As we saw earlier, the hardship and complexity of our ancestors' lives after the desertification of Saharasia forced them to develop new powers of self-reflection. They had to deliberate more, to plan and to reason, in order to deal with the practical difficulties of their lives. The sharpened ego developed in response to this, as a way of *enabling* them to reflect and deliberate. (If you want to think, you have to have an "I" to think with.) The philosopher Erich Neumann made this connection between self-reflection and linear time when he wrote, "So long as an apperceptive ego consciousness is lacking there can be no history; for history requires a 'reflecting' consciousness, which by reflecting, constitutes it."[13] At some point, as we've seen, our self-reflective ability became a kind of automatic mechanism, an involuntary never-ending stream of thought-material running through our minds. And this was presumably when the past and the future became firmly established as concepts.

CYCLICAL AND LINEAR TIME

Initially, though, fallen human beings' sense of time was *cyclical* rather than strictly linear. Time did flow, but not for ever onwards. The Mayans believed that history goes through a cycle of only 260 years; the Greeks conceived of a cycle of 36,000, while the ancient Hindus believed that history moves through four *mahayugas* (or ages), lasting a total of four and a half million years, before returning to the beginning.[14]

We can see this cyclical view of time as a kind of intermediate step between the no-time of primal peoples and true linear time, a part of the general pattern of less intense patrism during the first phase of the Fall, like polytheism. True linear time belongs to the second, more intense phase of the Fall, after ego-consciousness intensified further. This presumably had the effect of intensifying human beings' thought-chatter, or their general self-reflective ability, and so gave them a more acute sense of the past and the future.

And, indeed, linear time does seem to have developed at roughly the same time as the other effects of the second phase of the Fall, such as monotheism and intensified warfare – that is, during the mid to late centuries of the second millennium BCE. This is when the strongly linear Judaic vision of the world developed: the belief that the world was created at a certain point in the past, that time was moving like an arrow from the past to the future, and would keep moving until – at a certain future point – the world came to an end. It also seems to have been the point when recorded history began. The cultures with a cyclical view of time must have had a sense of history too, of course. The creation myths of the Sumerians and Egyptians show that they also believed that the world was created at a particular point in the past. But midway through the second millennium BCE, we see the beginning of the first detailed historical records, showing a clear awareness of the linear flow of events and of the backward-looking gaze of future generations. At around 1300 BCE, we see significant changes in the inscriptions on royal buildings in Mesopotamia. Before then inscriptions had usually just mentioned the king's name and his gods, and perhaps when and how the building was constructed. But from 1300 BCE, inscriptions were packed with historical detail, mentioning events that took place before the building was started and listing the king's military exploits and achievements. And within just a few centuries, Assyrian kings were keeping detailed year-by-year records of their reigns.[15]

ALIENATION FROM THE PRESENT

Their acute sense of the past and the future gave our Saharasian ancestors huge survival benefits. To a large extent, the intellectual and practical abilities which the Ego Explosion gave rise to – and which led to the development of modern civilisation – are linked to the linear perception of time. A linear sense of time gives us the chance to learn from the past, to learn from the mistakes of previous generations, and to take account of their achievements and take them further. This must have fuelled the rapid technological growth that took place from 4000 BCE onwards, when every new invention or discovery was a stepping stone to the next.

The ability to project the future also enables us to anticipate events and prepare for them, and to "invent" the future by imagining possible scenarios and plotting sequences of events. And as well as this, our acute sense of the future gave us the "monochronic" awareness of deadlines that I mentioned above, a sense of the importance of "closure," which has great practical and organisational benefits.

But as with the Ego Explosion in general, the linear sense of time brought problems. I mentioned two of these at the beginning of this chapter: the passing of time pressurises us, and gives us a disturbing sense of the fleetingness of the present and of the inevitability of decay and death. This sense of the transitoriness of life is one aspect of the atmosphere of world-weariness and pessimism which characterises the post-Fall era. Right down to the Romantic poets of the nineteenth century and the Existentialist philosophy of the twentieth, the poets and philosophers of fallen cultures have constantly bemoaned the impermanence of all things. In the sixth century BCE, the Buddha stated that this was one of the reasons why human life is inevitably full of suffering. In the Old Testament book of Ecclesiastes, the Preacher – who can lay a claim to be the first ever existentialist philosopher – shows a painfully acute awareness of the passing of time. Throughout our lives, the spectre of our future death is always hanging over us, draining away the meaning from everything we do. As a result, life is "Vanity of vanities, all is vanity."[16] The same awareness runs through Shakespeare's plays. As Macbeth remarks, for example:

> To-morrow, and to-morrow and to-morrow
> Creeps in this petty pace from day to day
> To the last syllable of recorded time;
> And all our yesterdays have lighted fools
> The way to dusty death. Out, out, brief candle![17]

In the nineteenth century, the French poet Baudelaire complained of "the horrible burden of Time weighing on your shoulders and crushing you to the earth,"[18] while John Keats complained of a world in which "beauty cannot keep her lustrous eyes,/ or new love pine at them beyond to-morrow."[19]

Perhaps the biggest problem which our sense of linear time gives us, however, is our alienation from the present-tense reality of our lives. The fact that we spend so much of our time immersed in thoughts about the future and past means that we don't live fully – or even mainly – in the present. Rather than focusing our attention on the surroundings we're in at a particular moment or the things we're doing in the surroundings, we think about things we were doing – or surroundings we were in – at times in the past, or things we are planning to do in the future. This is slightly bizarre; the present is the only reality we have, we can *only* live in the present. The fact that we're largely alienated from it means that, to a large extent, we aren't actually living. As Blaise Pascal wrote, "We are so unwise that we wander about in times that do not belong to us, and do not think of the only one that does; so vain that we dream of times that are not and blindly flee the only one that is…Thus we never actually live, but hope to live."[20]

More strictly, though, this isn't specifically an effect of our awareness of the future and the past, but of our thought-chatter in general. It isn't so much that we think about the future and the past, but just that we *think*, that whenever our attention is free we become immersed in a world of abstraction in our heads. Rather than giving our attention to the present-tense reality of our lives, we give it to our thoughts – or, failing that, to distractions like television, computer games or newspapers. The only time we frequently come close to living in the moment is in moments of "active absorption" or "flow," when our attention is completely concentrated on an activity – for example, dancing, writing, painting or playing a musical instrument – and get so involved in it that we forget ourselves and our surroundings.[21] In these moments we do live in the present in the sense that we give our whole attention to something that we're doing in the present. However, this is a very limited kind of present-tense awareness, since it involves "blanking out" the whole of our surroundings and our experience apart from one small part of it.

And our inability to live in the present is connected to the de-sensitising mechanism too, which makes our present surroundings and the things we experience in them appear so drearily familiar to us that we don't feel the *need* to pay attention to them, just as we don't feel the need to watch an old film which has been on TV dozens of times before.

The ability to live fully in the present is one of the benefits that what I call the "trans-Fall" state of being brings us. In the words of D.H. Lawrence, there is a "marvellous rich world of contact and sheer fluid beauty/ and fearless face-to-face awareness of now-naked life"[22] waiting for us, if we can manage to subdue our constant thought-chatter and transfer some of the vitality we waste through it into our perceptions of the world around us.

14

THE END OF NATURE

AT THE BEGINNING of the twenty-first century, the human race's future hangs in the balance. Our alien observer might well have concluded that the whole human race has agreed to a collective suicide pact. Perhaps, he might surmise, human beings couldn't stand their psychological discord any longer, or the bleak vision of reality filtered through their fallen psyche was too much for them. As a result, they decided to put an end to their misery and make themselves extinct as a species. Their original plan seemed to be to obliterate themselves with nuclear weapons, but perhaps that was too drastic and violent. Now they've introduced a much less dramatic method, which is so gradual that many people don't even realise it's happening.

We're destroying the life-support systems of our planet in so many different ways that it *is* as if we're determined to make this suicide attempt work, as if we're using several different methods as an insurance policy, in case one or two of them aren't successful. The world's carbon dioxide levels are 25% higher than they have ever been at *any* time in the last 20 million years, which has already resulted in rising sea levels and is beginning to throw the earth's climatic systems into chaos. At the end of the Permian era, 251 million years ago, there was a mass extinction in which 95 percent of all the world's living species became extinct. Geologists believe that this catastrophe was caused by global warming – a worldwide temperature rise of 6°C, due to massive volcanic eruptions in Siberia. These may have triggered a runaway greenhouse effect, releasing enormous clouds of carbon dioxide, which triggered vast methane "burps" out of the oceans. And the frightening thing is that, according to scientists' most recent estimates, during this century the world is going to warm up even more than this, by *7 to 10° C.*[1]

The world's freshwater resources are being dangerously depleted too. Global consumption of water is doubling every 20 years – 26 countries had serious water shortages in 1990, and by 2020 the figure will rise to 65 countries, by which time two out of three people in the world will be living in areas of what the United Nations calls "severe water stress."[2] Massive numbers of species are becoming extinct due to human activity. The World Conservation Union estimates that as many of 20 per cent of all plant and animal species could become extinct in the next 30 years, and as many as half in the next 100 years. Since 1970, consumption of wood and paper has increased by two-thirds, and consumption of fish has doubled, so that now supplies are seriously declining.[3] And then there's over-population, pollution, increasing economic development, adding even more weight to the above problems...

The prediction which Chief Seattle made in a speech to President Franklin Pearce 150 years ago appears to be coming true. "One portion of the land is the same to [the white man] as the next," he complained. "He is a stranger who comes in the night and takes from the land whatever he needs...His appetite will devour the Earth and leave behind only a desert."[4]

How has this state of affairs come about? How can the most intelligent life form the world has ever known – supposedly the only animal with powers of reason and of foresight – be mismanaging its own existence on this planet in such a catastrophic way? And, moreover, why aren't those of us who are aware of the problems reacting to them with the kind of urgency we should be? Even though we know about it, we don't seem to be fully *aware* of the danger we're facing, and so aren't prepared to take the appropriate kind of action.

One of the main problems is the *narrowness* of our vision of the world. Our attention is usually taken up with the present and immediate realities of our lives – our day to day problems, our own needs and desires, the things we've got to do now or tomorrow or next week. Many of us are fairly indifferent to social and political problems until they affect us directly. The issue of nuclear power may not bother us until a power station is built a few miles away and the children in our town develop leukaemia. The issue of global warming may not bother us unless we happen to live on the coast, and our homes start to subside because of rising sea levels. Our awareness is usually confined to our everyday worlds. And this is the problem with environmental issues: they are too "wide" for us for grasp. Issues like global warming, the chopping down of the rain forests and the extinction of other species are too far away from our everyday worlds – too vague, intangible and impersonal for us to be clearly aware of.

The narrowness of our vision of the world causes another problem too: a lack of foresight. Human beings undoubtedly have a greater ability to plan and anticipate the future than any other animal, but our powers of foresight are still limited. Like our general awareness, they work well enough for the immediate future, but not for the long term. Anything beyond 15 or 20 years seems to be a vague, foggy reality to us, and so what happens then doesn't really concern us. As a result, we're not prepared to make sacrifices for the future; we're reluctant to endure inconvenience for the sake of future generations.[5]

A lack foresight and "wide angle" vision sometimes led to environmental problems for unfallen peoples too. Human beings' habit of making other species extinct may be thousands of years old. Prehistoric animals like the mammoth, the giant armadillo of South America and the pygmy hippopotamus of Cyprus may have disappeared as a result of over-hunting or changes to their environment caused by humans.[6] And prehistoric humans seem to have caused some major environmental changes by burning massive areas of forest or grassland. As Theodore Roszak has written:

> Tribal societies have abused and even ruined their habitat. In prehistoric times, the tribal and nomadic people of the Mediterranean basin over cut and overgrazed the land so severely that the scars of the resulting erosion can still be seen. Their sacramental sense of nature did not offset their ignorance of the long range damage they were doing to their habitat.[7]

PRIMAL ECOLOGICAL AWARENESS

Nevertheless, there are some good reasons why, even allowing for their much lower level of technology and population, unfallen peoples could never be anything like as environmentally destructive as modern human beings. Whereas the ideology of our culture promotes environmental destruction, the ideologies and moral systems of most primal cultures encourage respect for nature. Many of them see themselves as stewards or custodians of the earth. The Hopi Indians, for example, saw themselves as apprentices of *Maasauu* (spirit-force). According to their myths, when *Maasauu* left the earthly plane of existence long ago, it gave them the job of keeping the earth in balance, and taught them ceremonies to do this. The Hopi have meticulously performed these ever since, one for every single plant and animal, with a full ceremonial cycle sometimes lasting several weeks.[8]

Primal peoples are also careful to maintain harmony through their lifestyles, by showing respect to animals and plants. They have to kill animals to survive, of course, and sometimes have to chop down trees or destroy other kinds of vegetation. But this has to be done respectfully, by apologising to the spirits of the animals or plants, and honouring them in death. If they do not do this, harmony will be disrupted. Alvin M. Josephy writes that the Native Americans "strove to exist in balance with [nature]. If harmony with nature were disturbed, pain, illness, death or other misfortunes could result."[9]

The essence of primal peoples' attitude to nature is their desire to fit into *its* scheme of things, and live in harmony with *it*, rather than to see it as an enemy to tame, or as a supply of resources to be used for their own benefit. They could never set themselves apart from the rest of nature and think of themselves as its master. As the anthropologist M.A. Jaimes Guerrero writes of indigenous peoples in general, "The essence of Native Spirituality is that peoples lived in reciprocity with each other and with their environment in ecological balance (comparatively speaking) with other living entities."[10]

And, in any case, while some unfallen peoples may have lacked foresight in their treatment of the natural world, it seems that many of them *do* manage their resources a lot more sensibly than we do. Their empathic connection to nature generates an attitude of responsibility, and a concern for its long-term well-being. The Indian groups of northwest America and California fished for salmon using elaborate weirs or fish dams, under the auspices of special ceremonial directors. It was their job to conduct rituals and manage resources, and they took careful measures to ensure that overfishing never occurred. Fishing could only take place at certain times, to allow enough salmon to swim upstream for other groups to catch and to prevent the salmon population itself from being dangerously depleted. For the same reasons, traps could only be extended to two-thirds of the river.[11] However, when Europeans began to fish the same rivers, they behaved with a reckless lack of concern for the long-term future. They filled rivers with a massive number of nets, disregarding other fishermen upstream as well as their own future well-being. According to the Yurok Indian Lucy Thompson, speaking of the Klamath River in California at the end of the nineteenth century:

The whites set one net from one side two-thirds across, and then just a few steps up another net from the other side, and which extends two-thirds across in distance. And in a distance of sixty yards, there will be from eight to ten nets, making so complete a network that hardly a salmon can pass.[12]

It is, of course, exactly the same kind of short-term greed and recklessness which lies behind our chopping down of rainforests, killing of other species, global warming and our mismanagement of energy supplies and water resources.

Part of the reason for primal peoples' respect for nature is their ability to empathise with it. Like the Pueblo Indians in Edward T. Hall's story – who were reluctant to begin ploughing in spring while the earth was "pregnant with new life" – they have the ability to "feel with" natural phenomena, and so are reluctant to damage or destroy them, in the same way that they are reluctant to kill animals. And perhaps even more importantly, their sense that all things are alive with – and a manifestation of – spirit means that to damage or destroy natural phenomena would be a crime against spirit itself, and would disturb the harmony of the universe. In Chief Seattle's words, "to harm the Earth is to heap contempt on its creator."[13]

It's a question of *value* too. Since all things are a manifestation of spirit, they are all equally sacred and valuable, and no one being – such as a human being – has the right to exploit or abuse any other. Equal value means equal respect. As we've seen, primal peoples give children the same rights of autonomy as adults, and in a sense this egalitarian philosophy extends to the whole of the natural world. No human being has the right to dominate any *thing*, not just other human beings. Animals, trees, rocks, rivers and other natural phenomena also have the right to exist without being oppressed or exploited.

As a result of all this, the kind of abuse and exploitation of the natural world which has become second nature to us – mining the earth for metals and minerals, digging for oil, damming rivers, paving over the countryside, pumping chemicals into rivers – is unthinkable as far as most primal peoples are concerned. It's not surprising that they are often sickened by our environmental abuse. As one chief of the Native American Wanapum said of European-American attitudes to mining and agriculture: "Should a knife tear my mother's bosom? Shall I dig under her skin for bones? You ask me to cut grass and make hay and sell it, and be rich like white men. How dare I cut off my mother's hair!"[14] Or, as one contemporary Aborigine, Anne Pattel-Gray, has said, "My people became more and more distressed at the sight of the white men raping, murdering and abusing their Mother Earth through mining. We knew the price they would pay for abusing Mother Earth."[15] Even now there is frequent conflict between primal peoples and European-American companies who want to "develop" lands which they believe are sacred. Often Native American groups refuse to allow mining on their reservations, despite the massive financial benefits it would bring. In the Northern Cheyenne Reservation in Montana, it's estimated that there are around 50 billion tons of coal, but despite large-scale poverty and unemployment, the Indians' sense of the aliveness of the earth and their empathy with it means that they can't allow it to be raped and plundered by mining companies.[16]

THE IDEOLOGY OF ENVIRONMENTAL ABUSE

Our environmental problems are sometimes seen as the result of the anti-nature ideologies of our culture. In *The Myth of the Goddess*, Anne Baring and Jules Cashford suggest that myths are "the fundamental inspiration of the evolution of consciousness."[17] They trace our problems back to the beginning of the Iron Age, around 1500 BCE, when hero myths began to arise showing individuals triumphing over monsters and dragons. (The most familiar of these to us is St George slaying the dragon.) These symbolised man's conquest of wild nature, and helped to form a new, adversarial attitude to the natural world. And this new attitude was reinforced – and reflected – by new religious beliefs. The old goddesses were fading from prominence, and being taken over by new male sky gods, who were apart from the natural world.

A similar point is often made by ecologists or ecopsychologists. The ecologist and poet Gary Snyder, for example, has suggested that our problems began when we invented otherworldly gods. This was the point when nature became "de-sacralised." Early polytheistic gods were associated with natural phenomena, presiding over mountains, rivers and seas. But the monotheistic gods who came later were disassociated from nature. They were in heaven, on high, in a realm apart from the earth. And this meant that nature was no longer sacred, and that human beings were given licence to abuse it.[18]

This brings us to the Christian religion, which has also borne a large share of the blame for our environmental abuse. There's no doubt that Christianity does have a very hostile attitude to nature. Right at the beginning of the Bible God urges the human race to "fill the earth, and subdue it: and have dominion over the fish in the sea, the birds of the air, and every living thing that moves on earth."[19] Part of the reason why we are entitled to this dominion is because we are, according to Christian belief, the only living beings with souls. Animals and plants don't have souls, and as a result they have no value, for us or God, except as a supply of resources to help us live more easily. In the words of Michael Perry, the Archdeacon of Durham, this biblical view has given us licence to:

> take and take and never give back; to squander the fossil remains
> of forests which had taken a million years to build up, and burn
> them in a generation; to make dustbowls out of wheatfields and
> deserts out of fruitful ground; and to believe that, as lords of
> creation, we were not only allowed but divinely commanded to
> do so.[20]

From around 1600 CE, the ideology of materialistic science began to supersede Christianity, with an even more negative attitude to nature. Descartes declared that the whole of nature was a machine, and that phenomena which seemed to be "alive" were really just automata with no soul or mind. Later Newton showed that the "machine" of the universe operates according to a number of rigid laws, and that all things (including living beings) are just arrangements of inert elementary particles. The scientific revolution which Descartes and Newton initiated gave human beings a new sense of power over nature, which led some philosophers and scientists to extremes of megalomania. Descartes himself stated that human beings were destined to become "lords and masters of nature," while the philosopher Bacon declared that nature "should be hounded in her wandering, bound into service...and made a slave." [21] As the modern scientist Rupert Sheldrake writes, the seventeenth century saw "a vast inflation of the ambition to dominate and control nature, a way of treating the natural world as if it had no inherent value or life of its own, and an overthrow of traditional restraints on human knowledge and power."[22]

This ideology still dominates our culture at the beginning of the twenty-first century. Many of us still believe that natural phenomena like rocks, rivers and the sun and the moon are nothing more than inanimate collections of atoms, with no soul or being of their own. Modern science even tries to convince us that this is true of living beings too. It tells us that we are nothing more than inert physical matter. We're made up of chemicals and particles which are inanimate in themselves, but which work together in such an amazingly intricate and complex way that they create the *illusion* that we are "animate," and give us the ability to interact with our environment and to be conscious of the world around us. Even our own consciousness is just a product of the stodgy grey matter of our brain, a kind of illusion created by the buzzing of millions of neurons. In other words, as far as modern science is concerned, the universe and everything in it is just dead matter.

THE ROOTS OF ENVIRONMENTAL ABUSE

All of these factors have encouraged environmental abuse in the same way that primal peoples' ideologies help promote a respectful attitude to nature. However, none of them should be seen as a cause of ecological destruction in themselves. The myths which symbolise the conquest of nature, the religions which feature a separation between gods and the earth and which promote a hostile attitude to nature, and the scientific ideology we've just examined, are really only secondary effects of the different relationship to – and perception of – the natural world which came with the Fall.

Aside from the narrowness of vision I mentioned earlier, the environmental crisis has three root causes. These are really just the inverse of the reasons for primal peoples' respectful attitude to nature. Firstly, there is our lack of a sense of connection to nature. The same "walled-off-ness" which makes it difficult for us to empathise with other people makes it difficult for us to feel any kinship with nature. We don't feel any qualms about chopping down trees or mining into the earth because the natural world is "other" to us, in the same way as the body. In the words of geneticist David Suzuki, our sense of separation from nature enables us to "act on it, abstract from it, use it, take it apart; we can wreck it, because it is *another*, it is *alien*."[23]

This sense of separation from nature is very closely linked to separation from the body. In both cases, the ego has become disassociated from the biological – or material – world. In this respect, as Ken Wilber has pointed out, the ecological crisis can be seen as a giant neurosis. As he writes, "Every neurosis...is a miniature ecological crisis (repression of the biosphere by the noosphere), and the worldwide ecological crisis is in fact a worldwide psychoneurosis."[24] And as with the body, this sense of otherness creates an attitude of hostility to nature. The natural world consists of the same base, mindless matter as the body, and we believe that, like the body, it should bow down before the superior human ego. As a result, in the words of Chief Seattle, "The earth is not [white man's] brother, but his enemy."[25]

The second cause is the fact that the fallen psyche can't sense the aliveness of natural phenomena – or, more accurately, it can't sense the presence of spirit-force in all things (since this is what *makes* them alive). With the de-sensitising mechanism acting on our perceptions, the phenomenal world is a shadowy, one-dimensional place to us. Natural things are just objects, with no depth or inner being. As one Aboriginal elder commented, the white man doesn't have the ability to "enter the dreaming of the countryside, the plants, and animals before he uses or eats them," as a result of which "he will become sick and insane and destroy himself."[26] If trees, plants, rocks, rivers and the whole earth itself are just inanimate objects, there is absolutely no reason for us *not* to damage and abuse them. Objects have no value apart from the use we can make of them, and they don't have any inner being to be hurt or damaged.

Thirdly, the fallen psyche's need for dominance was also a factor. In the same way that it craves for power over other human groups, over other people in its own group, over women, children and its own body, the fallen psyche craves for power over the natural world. It craves to conquer its wildness, to harness its resources, and to turn its chaos into order. It craves to understand its workings so it can get control of them and use them for its own devices. This was what drove scientists such as Descartes and Bacon, and even now many scientists have the same attitude, viewing nature as a territory on which to stamp their authority and to gain control over. Modern science is carried away with a desire to manipulate all natural and biological phenomena, to completely understand the world and construct a complete explanation for everything, which will give it a satisfying sense of control and conquest. (As Francis Bacon noted, knowledge is power.) In this regard, it's not surprising that most scientists are men, since the male ego craves for this kind of dominance much more than the female.

IS OUR EXTINCTION INEVITABLE?

The human race's predicament seems bleak enough now that environmental problems have already become so far advanced that they may be difficult to correct, even if we had the will to. But when you consider that the fundamental problem is our psyche, our 6,000-year-old fallen state of being, then the situation seems even more hopeless. If the problem is our psyche, it makes sense to assume that the only sure way in which we might overcome our environmental problems would be for this psyche to *change*, for us to somehow transcend the fallen psyche, and regain the sense of connection to nature and the sense of the aliveness of natural phenomena, and lose our desire to dominate nature. And how could a change like this take place? After 6,000 years, why should we change now?

In fact, it's possible to make a good case for the idea that this ecological catastrophe was inevitable right from the beginning, that as soon as the Ego Explosion happened the human race's days were numbered. There's another surface cause of our environmental problems which we haven't looked at so far: overpopulation. If the world's population were only, say, half a billion, our abusive attitude to nature wouldn't be a serious problem. There would be no shortage of water and other resources, we would only be causing minimal damage to the habitats of other species, and the world's ecosystems would easily be able to handle the amount of carbon dioxide and other pollutants we send their way. But the pollution and consumption of over five billion people is a different matter altogether, and is too large a strain for the environment to cope with. And, ultimately, the earth's over-population can be traced back to the positive side of the Ego Explosion, the new intelligence and inventiveness which it gave us. This intelligence gave us the technological means to support larger populations. It gave us mechanised, highly efficient ways of producing food, as well as transport systems to bring it from distant places. A country the size of Great Britain might only be able to support a few hundred thousand people living a hunter-gatherer lifestyle, and possibly a few million living a simple horticultural lifestyle. But due to the technological innovations of the fallen psyche's sharpened intellect, it's able to support a population of 60 million. At the same time, the world's population could only have risen to such a high level through another important contribution of the fallen psyche: the advances in medicine, hygiene and sanitation – particularly those of the nineteenth and twentieth centuries – which drastically reduced the infant mortality rate and increased longevity.

In theory, over-population isn't enough in itself to take the human race to catastrophe. The earth probably could support five billion people who were forward-thinking and sensible, and who respected nature. Our abusive attitude to nature has to be thrown into the mix too, of course. As soon as the Ego Explosion happened, over-population was inevitable. And since the majority of the world's over-large population can't help but exploit and abuse nature, ecological catastrophe was inevitable too.

Fortunately, though, the situation may not be quite as bleak as this. In the final section of this book, we're going to look at evidence which suggests that a change actually *is* taking place, that in some way the human race as a whole may be moving beyond the separate sense of ego, and transcending the fallen psyche.

Before we move into this section, though, we need to conclude the first two parts of the book by looking at some general issues which my examination of the Fall raises.

THE EGO EXPLOSION AND CULTURAL CHANGE

Over the last few chapters we've looked at many different aspects of the cultural transformation that were caused by the Ego Explosion. And one point I would like to emphasise is the *interdependence* of all these changes. Anthropologists have always noted that particular social traits are linked. For example, cross-cultural studies have shown that low female status is usually associated with social stratification, private property and use of the plough, and also that social stratification appears to be linked to a lack of sexual freedom.[27] A cross-cultural study by the anthropologist Martin Whyte found that societies with a high level of warfare almost always have low female status,[28] while a study of 50 different societies by Guy Swanson found that societies with a hierarchical structure (consisting of three or more decision-making groups) were likely to have a belief in an all-powerful "high god."[29] And as we noted earlier, the cross-cultural studies of James Prescott found a very strong correlation between negative child-rearing practices, sexual repression and social violence. In fact, Prescott noted that these correlations went further, and that societies with these three characteristics were also likely to have class stratification, bride price, slavery and high gods concerned with human morality.[30]

Perhaps inevitably, anthropologists have attempted to explain these correlations in terms of each other. For example, Ember and Ember suggest that the correlation between sexual restrictiveness and social stratification is due to the fact that "as social inequality increases and various groups of peoples have differential wealth, parents become more concerned with preventing their children from marrying 'beneath them.'"[31] Swanson, meanwhile, suggests that the correlation between social stratification and high gods exists because religion is a "conceptualisation" of the structure of a society, so that to conceive of an "almighty" God is natural in a society where power is concentrated into a small number of people's hands, and there is a "hierarchical structure of superordinate and subordinate groups."[32] There are also theories that the low status of women in many societies is due to a high level of warfare in those societies, or to the existence of centralised political hierarchies – the reasoning being that since men dominate both war and political hierarchy, societies where they are especially important will place a low value on women.[33]

None of these theories is satisfactory. They are only really "pass the buck" answers. Explaining male domination in terms of war only begs the question of why these societies have a high level of warfare – and explaining the existence of high gods in terms of social stratification only begs the question of why the social stratification exists.

It's true that some of these factors may affect each other on a secondary level, so that, for example, sexual repression creates "undischarged bio-energetic tension" which leads to a heightened propensity for violence. But, ultimately, the reason why these characteristics can't be explained in terms of one another is the same reason why they all exist in the first place: because they are all effects of the same event, the Fall.

A similar point I would like to emphasise is the *co-incidence* of all of these changes. There's probably no clearer piece of evidence for the reality of the Fall than the fact that all of the cultural changes we've looked at occurred *at exactly the same time in history*, and – initially at least – *to exactly the same human groups*. New levels of technology and civilisation, intense warfare, patriarchy, social inequality (manifesting itself as "capitalist" social systems), the oppression of children, theistic religion (including a new concept of the afterlife), hostility to sex, to the body and to nature, and a linear sense of time – all of these happened at the same time to the same peoples from the same area of central Asia and the Middle East. And, of course, these social and cultural changes coincided with changes to the way that human beings existed as individuals – a new materialism and possessiveness, a new drive for status, a desire for distractions to avoid facing their psychological discord, and an inability to empathise with other people, other creatures and the natural world. These changes aren't as obvious as the social and cultural ones, since they aren't as visible from archaeological and historical records, but strictly speaking they were the most fundamental, since they gave rise to the social and cultural effects of the Fall.

AFTER THE FALL

Another area we've touched on but not gone into in any real detail is psychic development after the Fall. If you look at the world today, there are clearly some Saharasian peoples who are more patrist – and therefore more "egoic" – than others. James DeMeo's "World Behaviour Map" in *Saharasia* shows a large heartland of what he calls "extreme patrist armored culture," covering North Africa, the Middle East and central Asia. The characteristics of these areas are a high level of patriarchy, a high level of hostility to sex and the body, strong monotheistic religion, and highly disciplined and relatively non-affectionate child-rearing. Outside this "heartland" there are large areas of what DeMeo calls "intermediate, moderate patrism," including parts of central and southern Africa, eastern Europe, eastern and northern Asia, and small areas of the American continent. And then there are some areas of what DeMeo calls "Extreme matrist unarmored culture," including western Europe, parts of South-East Asia and most of Australia and America.[34]

The question is: Why did some Saharasian peoples end up more or less patrist than others? Why do the Saharasian peoples of the Middle East still have an extremely hostile attitude to sex and the body and a high level of patriarchy, while the Saharasian peoples of western Europe have more liberal attitudes to sex, are more democratic and have a higher status for women? (Although whether countries like England, Australia or America can really be classed as matrist is questionable, since they're obviously still far away from the respect for nature, the positive attitude for sex, the natural democracy and absence of oppression of unfallen peoples.) There are probably two reasons for this. One is that the Saharasian heartland of the Middle East, central Asia and North Africa has continued to be dry and infertile right down to the present day. All through history the people who lived there have faced the kind of problems which beset the original Saharasian peoples. Because of this, the strong sense of ego that the original Saharasian peoples developed has presumably been continually reinforced. But other Saharasian peoples migrated to more fertile areas, such as western Europe and east Asia, where life was easier. As a result, these peoples' strong sense of ego wouldn't be reinforced to the same degree. Over time, their sense of ego might actually have become weaker, with the result that they developed a more mild kind of patrism.

The other reason – and probably the more important one – is to do with distance. The farther away you go from the Saharasia heartland, to the western edges of Europe and the eastern edges of Asia, the more mild patrism becomes. Britain, for example, only developed patrist characteristics at a fairly late stage. Until the Norman invasion of the eleventh century, as DeMeo notes, "British people lived under much freer conditions than existed on the mainland."[35] Women could own land, sex before marriage was common, peasants had rights, and there was only limited slavery. But after 1066 the Normans established themselves as a brutal, despotic ruling class, and the level of patrism dramatically increased. (Although, as DeMeo notes, "Still, such traits never developed in Britain to the extent seen on the continent itself.")[36] Similarly, Thailand – on the edge of South-East Asia – is another place where even now, according to DeMeo, "extreme unarmored matrist culture" exists.

In other words, patrism diluted over distance, presumably because fewer Saharasian people would actually reach more distant areas, resulting in a larger cultural influence from the indigenous matrist peoples. In these places, the indigenous cultures were more likely to survive and mix with the invaders' new culture, and to soften their patrism.

THE EGO EXPLOSION AS EVOLUTIONARY ADVANCE

In Chapter 5, we looked briefly at the possibility that the Ego Explosion was actually an *evolutionary* development – as suggested by authors such as Ken Wilber, Jean Gebser and Ernest Becker. I pointed out then that the fact that the Ego Explosion was such a localised phenomenon – that is, that it just happened to people in the Middle East and central Asia – works against this theory. Surely, if it were an evolutionary development it would have involved the whole human race. However, I also mentioned that there is another, more theoretical, reason why this probably isn't true.

In order to understand this, we first need to look at the question of how evolutionary developments actually occur. Neo-Darwinists usually see evolution purely as a process by which living beings change *physically*. But there's an internal aspect to evolution as well; it also involves a development of *consciousness*. The French priest and philosopher Teilhard de Chardin pointed out that as living beings become more complex physically – as their brain size increases, for example, together with the number of brain cells and the complexity of the interactions between the cells – they also become more conscious.[37] That is, they become more aware of their surroundings, more capable of interacting with their environment, and more aware of their condition as living beings in the world.

In other words, evolution occurs on a *psychic* as well as a physical level, and both levels develop in parallel. The most simple living beings are amoebae – unicellular organisms with no organs. The question of whether they are "conscious" in any way is controversial, but since they react to their environment – by, for example, moving towards sources of food and reacting to light – they must also be *aware* of their environment to a degree. They have, we might say, a tiny flicker of consciousness, which gives them a tiny amount of awareness of reality. And as evolution progresses from the beginnings of life through to bacteria, plants, insects, reptiles, birds, and so on, at the same time as becoming more complex physically, that tiny flicker of consciousness grows gradually more powerful. A few hundred thousand years ago, this process led to the development of human beings, the most complex and the most conscious life forms the world has yet seen. These human beings were more intensely aware of the phenomenal world around them than any animal before them, as shown by the complex language they developed to describe this world. They were also aware of their own mortality, and perhaps most importantly of all, they were *self*-conscious. Not only were they conscious, they were aware of themselves *being* conscious. (It's true that some animals, like chimpanzees or dolphins, do seem to have some self-consciousness and to be aware of death, but even they don't seem to be as *intensely* aware of death or of themselves as human beings.) What was once a tiny flicker of consciousness has now, with the human race, become a powerful spotlight.

All of this begs the questions: What exactly *is* consciousness? Where does it come from? Modern materialistic science assumes that it's just a product of the brain. In some mysterious way, our brain cells are wired up to produce self-awareness in the same way that the circuits of a television set are wired up to produce images and voices on a screen. Scientists talk about the "circuitry of consciousness" as if it really were as simple as this.[38] But after decades of intensive research in neurobiology, it's becoming apparent that consciousness is much more strange and complex. Although neuroscientists have been able to solve some of the "easy problems" of how the brain processes environmental stimulation, or how it integrates information, no progress at all has made on the "hard problem" of how its physical processes supposedly give rise to subjective experience.[39]

Some more open-minded scientists and philosophers are beginning to doubt whether it's at all possible to explain consciousness in these terms. The problem is that no matter how much you investigate the brain, there will always be an unbridgeable gulf between physical processes and the subjective experience of consciousness. The brain is just matter, but consciousness is something wholly other, an entirely different level of reality. As the philosopher Colin McGinn puts it, "you might as well assert that numbers emerge from biscuits or ethics from rhubarb" as suggest that the "soggy clump of matter" which is the brain produces consciousness.[40] Contemporary philosophers and physicists have suggested a radically different theory, which is that consciousness doesn't come from inside the brain, but *outside* it, that it is, in fact, a fundamental force of the universe, which pervades all reality. As the Australian philosopher David Chalmers suggests, for example, consciousness – or "experience," in his terminology – should be seen as a "fundamental feature of the world, alongside mass, change, and space-time."[41] Unfallen peoples have always known this, of course. They were aware of this universal field of consciousness as the Great Spirit, or Life Master – the animating force which pervades all reality and of which all things are the manifestation.

This doesn't mean that the brain has no role in consciousness. It may be that rather than actually *producing* consciousness itself, the human brain – or the brain of any other living being – acts as a kind of receiver of it, in the same way that a radio set receives radio waves. It translates the raw essence of universal consciousness into an *individuated* consciousness. As the American philosopher Robert Forman puts it:

> Consciousness is more like a field than a localized point, a field which transcends the body and yet somehow interacts with it…Brain cells may receive, guide, arbitrate, or canalise an awareness which is somehow transcendental to them. The brain may be more like a receiver or transformer for the field of awareness than its generator.[42]

This theory gives us an interesting way of looking at the difference between living and non-living things. In a sense, *all* things are alive, as primal peoples believe, since they are all pervaded by consciousness, or spirit-force. But there is a difference in the way that rocks and rivers are alive and the way that an insect or even an amoeba is alive. Rocks and rivers do not have their own psyche, and are therefore not *individually* conscious. Consciousness goes through them, but they aren't conscious themselves. They can't be, because they don't have any cells – let alone brains or nervous systems – to "canalise" consciousness. It's only when cells begin to form that this is possible. A cell acts as a "receiver" of consciousness, so that even an amoeba has its own very rudimentary kind of psyche, and is therefore individually alive. And as living beings become more complex – as their cells increase in number and become more intricately organised – they become capable of "receiving" more consciousness. The raw essence of consciousness is channelled more powerfully through them, and they become more alive, with more autonomy, more freedom and more intense awareness of reality. In Teilhard de Chardin's phrase, their "spiritual energy" increases.

But to come back to our main argument, the point is that if an evolutionary development occurs there has to be an intensification of consciousness. There has to be a greater influx of spiritual energy, so that the living being can become more conscious and more alive. And the important thing is that the Ego Explosion didn't involve this. In some ways the Ego Explosion certainly has the *appearance* of giving us more spiritual energy. Our ancestors certainly became more conscious of themselves, and more free to organise their own lives and to change their environment. But this wasn't due to an intensification of consciousness-energy, but to a redistribution of it. We saw earlier that with the Ego Explosion, the consciousness-energy which people had previously channelled into the act of perceiving the phenomenal world was swallowed up by the powerful new ego, which needed it to fuel its constant thought-chatter. We saw that our ancestors developed a "de-sensitising mechanism" especially for the purpose of diverting consciousness-energy away from the act of perception – and towards the ego. As a result, the phenomenal world became a dreary, half-real place, and we lost the awareness of spirit-force.

This was the redistribution: consciousness-energy was diverted away from immediate perception and towards the ego. Human beings' self-consciousness didn't increase because of a new influx of spiritual energy, but because of a kind of internal shake up, a reallocation of resources. If there really had been an intensification of consciousness, then human beings would have retained their intense awareness of the phenomenal world *at the same time as* developing their new sharpened sense of ego. There would have been no reason for them to take energy away from one to give to the other.

In my view, therefore, there has been no genuine evolution of consciousness throughout pre-history and history. There has been cultural evolution, of course, and a dramatic psychic change caused by an environmental disaster 6,000 years ago – the Ego Explosion. But, fundamentally, the human race has remained at the same level of evolution. Our consciousness has remained at the same level of intensity, but has just been distributed in a different way.

But this doesn't mean that an evolutionary development can *never* take place. In fact, in the final section of this book we're going to look at evidence that the first real evolutionary development in the history of the human race is taking place *now*, and has been over recent centuries.

PART THREE

THE
TRANS-FALL ERA

15

THE FIRST WAVE

EARLY IN THE first millennium BCE, small groups of people in the fallen world began to make an amazing discovery. Human beings' main reaction to psychological discord has always been to try to escape it, or to try to find consolation for it. We've always tried to escape it by chasing after alternative sources of happiness such as wealth and power, or, increasingly, by occupying our attention with constant activity, distractions and entertainments. On the other hand, we've consoled ourselves against it – and against our bleak existential condition and our social suffering – by believing in an idyllic afterlife.

However, a tiny number of people realised that there was another, much more satisfactory possibility – that they could actually *heal* their psychological discord rather than just try to escape its symptoms. They realised that by following certain practices and adopting a certain lifestyle, they could transform their own state of being. They discovered that they could transcend the separate sense of ego – and in the process, transcend the suffering it brings.

As far as we know, this realisation was first made in India. At around 800 BCE, certain people there began to follow a new way of life. They left their families and communities and went to live alone in the forests, practising what we now call meditation. Their solitary, detached lifestyle and their long periods of meditation apparently transformed their vision of the world, and gave them profound insights into the nature of reality and human consciousness. Groups of students began to gather around them in the forest, and revered them as *rishis*, or sages. The students learned their teachings and passed them on to others, until eventually they were written down and collected. These became known as the Upanishads.

The view of the world which the Upanishads put forward is something completely new in the fallen world. They bring into question one of our most basic assumptions as human beings: that the world as we see it is the world *as it is*. According to the ancient Indian sages, our normal vision of reality is not true.

We're like people who are partially blind without knowing it, and assume that they're seeing the world as it is, when in reality they're only seeing a pale shadow of it. In particular, the separation and duality which we see everywhere around us – separation between ourselves and the world, and between different objects and phenomena – is an illusion. The truth, so the Upanishads tell us, is that the whole universe and everything in it is pervaded with *Brahman,* or Spirit. *Brahman* is the ultimate reality of the universe, which transcends all things of space and time, but at the same time emanates through them. The Chandogya Upanishad describes it as "an invisible and subtle essence [which] is the Spirit of the universe,"[1] while the Mundaka Upanishad states:

> Shining, yet hidden, Spirit lives in the cavern. Everything that sways, breathes, opens, closes, lives in Spirit...
> Spirit is everywhere, upon the right, upon the left, above, below, behind, in front. What is the world but Spirit?[2]

Since *Brahman* pervades everything, there can be no separation. All things are one, folded into unity in its all-pervading embrace. And this includes human beings. The Upanishads also speak of *Atman,* the human spirit. *Atman* is our own personal consciousness, the essence of our being, which makes us able to think, see, hear, feel and act. As the Maitri Upanishad puts it, *Atman* is the "perceiver, thinker, goer, evacuator, begetter, doer, speaker, taster, smeller, seer, hearer."[3] And the important point is that *Brahman* and *Atman* are one and the same. Our personal consciousness is also the consciousness of the universe itself, so that we *are* the universe. After describing *Brahman* as "an invisible and subtle essence" the Chandogya Upanishad goes on to say, "That is Reality. That is Atman. THOU ART THAT." Or, as the Brihad-Aranyaka Upanishad describes it:

> He who, dwelling in the moon and stars, yet is other than the moon and stars, whom the moon and stars do not know, whose body the moon and stars are, who controls the moon and stars from within – He is your Soul, the Inner Controller, the Immortal.[4]

But all of this wasn't completely new, of course. It was a rediscovery of what earlier unfallen peoples had always known. The sages of the Upanishads had found a method of transforming their state of being in such a way that they could reverse one of the major psychological consequences of the Ego Explosion: the loss of awareness of spirit-force. *Brahman* is one and the same as *Maasauu, Wakan-Tanka, Tirawa* or *Kwoth*. The above description of *Brahman* closely echoes the description of spirit-force by a member of the Pawnee tribe, which I quoted in Chapter 10:

> We do not think of Tirawa as a person. We think of Tirawa as [a power which is] in everything and moves upon the darkness, the night, and causes her to bring forth the dawn. It is the breath of the newborn dawn.[5]

The *rishis* were unpicking the "lie" of the fallen psyche. The terrible sense of ego-isolation, of being trapped inside your head with the rest of the universe out there, the sense of living in an indifferent alien world – a vast sigh of relief should have swept through the whole fallen world, as the *rishis* discovered that this wasn't the truth about human life after all. (It didn't, of course, because so few people heard their teachings, and even fewer understood them.) But their deconstruction of the fallen psyche was even more direct. They also realised that the sharpened sense of ego is a kind of impostor, which gives us a false sense of who we are. We suffer from a case of mistaken identity. We believe that we *are* these egos, but we only become our true nature when they fade away. We have two different selves, the Upanishads tell us: the false, superficial ego-self (which some translations of the Upanishads refer to as "spirit" with a lower case "s") and *Atman*, our true self (which is sometimes translated as Spirit with a capital "S").

BUDDHISM AND JAINISM

This was the beginning of the first wave of a movement beyond the Fall, a rebellion against it and an attempt to undo its effects. And at around 600 BCE – at the beginning of what the philosopher Karl Jaspers called The Axial Age – this rebellion became much more powerful, as the Buddha began to teach his method of transcending the fallen psyche. The Upanishads are more descriptive than analytical. They're like a giant wake-up call which shouts, "*This* is the reality of things. This is the way the world really is, and this is the true state of human beings." Buddhism, on the other hand – at least in its original form – is completely the opposite. It rarely discusses the ultimate reality of things at all. Whenever his disciples asked him philosophical questions – such as, "Does an enlightened man exist after death?" – the Buddha usually refused to answer, believing these kinds of discussions were a waste of time and energy. As far as he was concerned, the only important issue was to free human beings from suffering – the suffering which had become part of human experience since the Fall.

The Buddha developed a profound understanding of how the fallen psyche gives rise to this suffering, and a very detailed and systematic method of transcending it. The foundation of his teachings is the statement – which we've referred to before – that "Life is suffering." According to Buddhism, this suffering can be both physical and mental. Physical suffering comes from the decay of our bodies as we get older, and from disease and death. Mental suffering comes when our desires are frustrated, when we're separated from things we love, and when we have to face things we despise or fear. And all of this suffering has one cause: craving. As the Dhammapada states, "From craving arises sorrow and from craving arises fear. If a man is free from craving, he is free from fear and sorrow."[6] Craving keeps us chained to the wheel of rebirth. At the most fundamental level, the very fact that we are *attached* to the world, that we crave for life and the pleasures it can give us, means that we keep being reborn, and continue to be subject to suffering.

Suffering can only be overcome by overcoming craving. And the way to do this is to follow the Eightfold Path, which consists of various lifestyle guidelines such as Right Thoughts or Understanding, Right Speech, Right Livelihood, Right Effort and Right Concentration. According to Buddhist philosophy, we're all becoming a little more enlightened through every reincarnation, and will all be freed from suffering eventually, even if it takes thousands of lifetimes. But we can speed up our progress by following the Eightfold Path, and have a chance of attaining enlightenment in *this* lifetime, through our own conscious efforts. And if we do this, and manage to reach the point where all craving is extinguished, we will attain Nirvana. We will go beyond name and form and experience pure blissfulness. And this time, when we die that will be the end; we won't need to come back. We will remain in oneness with absolute reality for all eternity.

There's one sense in which Buddhism – at least in its original form – isn't completely a "trans-Fall" movement: it doesn't have a sense of the sacredness of this world. It doesn't have a concept of spirit-force pervading all reality; and as far as it is concerned, life on earth will *always* be suffering. Freedom only comes when we go beyond the material world. But in all its other aspects, Buddhism makes complete sense in terms of the Fall. The craving which the Buddha speaks of is the desire for power, wealth, possessions and hedonistic pleasures which the Ego Explosion gave rise to. There's a slight difference in that Buddhism tells us that craving itself is the source of suffering, whereas I'm suggesting that the over-developed sense of ego was the fundamental cause, and this created the craving for power and wealth as alternative sources of happiness and fulfilment. But the end effect is the same. As long as the separate sense of self exists, craving will always exist; and so overcoming craving also means overcoming the separate sense of self. And this is exactly what happens when we attain Nirvana. Our ego-identity disappears "as a flame blown out by the wind."[7]

At roughly the same time as the Buddha, another Indian teacher called Vardhamana Mahavira emerged. He formulated a different – although similar – method of transcending psychological discord, which became known as Jainism. Like the Upanishads, Jainism tells us that our limited ego-self isn't our true self, and that our sense of separation from the world is an illusion. We're essentially free and one with the universe, but the karma of our actions and desires "binds" us to our bodies, and sustains the illusion of ego-separateness. Jainism sees karma as an actual substance which continually flows into the body-mind. Liberation depends on stopping this flow of karma, which can be done through meditation, renunciation and following a moral lifestyle, including the non-harming of any other living beings. If these practices are successful and the flow of karma is halted, the separateness and suffering of the fallen psyche is transcended. The adept reaches a state in which, according to one ancient Jain text, "The Self is free from punishment, without opposites, without me-sense…free from defects, free from delusion, and fearless."[8]

OUTSIDE INDIA

India was certainly the main centre of this trans-Fall movement, but similar kinds of rebellions took place all over the fallen world. In China, for example, we know that during the lifetime of Confucius – the sixth century BCE – there were people who lived as hermits, and spent their time contemplating life. Completely independently of India, it seems, these hermits discovered the practice of meditation. They referred to the state of *tso-wang* – "sitting with a blank mind" – and used breath-control exercises as a way of inducing this. By the fourth century BCE, there were many teachers throughout China who taught mental stillness and claimed that the practice could bring knowledge of the ultimate reality of things.[9]

These teachers made the same (re)discovery as the sages of India: that the apparent separateness of things was an illusion, since the whole universe was pervaded with Spirit, or consciousness. Their name for *Brahman* – or *Wakan-Tanka* or *Kwoth* – was the *Tao*, and the philosophy which they developed became known as Taoism. Both of the major early Taoist teachers we know of, Chuang Tzu and Lao Tzu, were aware that there had been a historical Fall away from a more harmonious age, and saw their teachings as methods of regaining the "pure" state of being which earlier peoples had experienced. We've already heard, in Chapter 5, Chuang Tzu telling us that there was once an Age of Perfect Virtue when people followed the "way of heaven" and were "upright and correct" and "did not grow proud in plenty" and "were not aware that there are things."[10] But at a certain point human beings began to follow the "way of man" instead. They became aware of distinctions, aware of right and wrong, and became proud and selfish. As a result, they fell out of harmony with the *Tao*. But the Taoist teachings tell us that by practising *tso-wang* and living a life of detachment, it's possible to transcend separateness and return to a state of harmony with the *Tao*. In the words of Chuang Tzu, "To a mind that is still the whole universe surrenders."[11]

In ancient Greece, starting at around the seventh century BCE, the initiates of the "mystery" cults discovered a more crude and direct way of transcending the fallen psyche. Rather than trying to do this through meditation, they chose a method of violently disrupting their normal state of being by fasting, taking drugs, dancing frenziedly and beating themselves. This certainly didn't give them the same profound sense of one-ness with Spirit which the Indian and Chinese sages experienced, but it did allow them to transcend the normal fallen world of separation and familiarity. In the words of a later observer of the mysteries, the Greek philosopher Proclus, the initiates became "filled with divine awe" and could "assimilate themselves to the holy symbols, leave their own identity, become at home with the gods, and experience divine possession."[12]

We can also see the philosophy of Plato – who was born in 427 BCE – as inspired by a trans-Fall vision of the world. Like the sages of India, Plato believed that the world which we normally see and take for granted as "real" is only a kind of grey, shadow-reality. In *The Republic* he illustrates this with his famous cave metaphor. Most of us see the world as if we're imprisoned in a dark cave, says Plato. All phenomena pass by behind us, and all we see are their shadows as they're projected on to the wall in front of us by the light of a fire. If we turned and looked at things as they really are we would blinded by their incandescence. But by using our reason it's possible for us to purify ourselves and gradually grow accustomed to the light of the Real.[13] What Plato may be referring to here is the intense "blazing" reality which fallen peoples are aware of, but which we lost when our consciousness-energy was redistributed after the Fall.

A little more than a century after Plato's birth, another group of Greek philosophers, the Stoics, developed a vision of the world which harked back to the pre-Fall era. They believed that the whole world was pervaded with a force called *Pneuma* – their equivalent of *Brahman, Wakan-tanka* or *Kwoth. Pneuma* was the soul of the universe, an invisible essence which filled all space and all things. The Stoics used this concept to solve some philosophical problems too. They saw *Pneuma* as the "sustaining cause" which guides the growth of living beings and holds them together. It was the reason why some beings are more intelligent and conscious than others – for example, why human beings were more alive than animals. All living beings had varying concentrations of *Pneuma* inside them, with "higher" life forms having larger concentrations than lower.[14]

MEDITATION

The essential discovery that all these groups made was that it was possible for them to change their own state of being. They discovered that it was possible to cure themselves of the psychic turmoil which came with the Fall, and return to a pre-Fall state of being.

The basic tool which they used to accomplish this was, as we have seen, meditation. It's possible to say that the whole purpose of meditation is to undo the effects of the Ego Explosion. When the philosopher Philip Novak describes how the strongly developed ego monopolises our psychic energy – gobbling away energy that could be "manifested as the delight of the open, receptive and present-centred awareness" – he also notes how the practice of meditation reverses this process. The normal structures of consciousness need to be constantly fed with attention. But when we focus our attention on the present, as we do when we meditate, they are deprived of their attention-food, and begin to weaken and fade away. As a result, says Novak, "the mind acquires a new habit of spending less energy on the imaginative elaboration of desire and anxiety" (that is, thinking) and more on perceiving present reality.[15]

In other words, the practice of meditation results in a redistribution of energy – exactly the reverse of the redistribution which occurred with the Fall. In that redistribution, the consciousness-energy which used to be put into perceiving the phenomenal world (including spirit-force) was redirected to the ego. But if a meditation practice is successful, the ego dies down, and stops eating up so much energy. And that energy naturally returns to perception – with the result that you become able to sense consciousness-force in the world, and become aware of the intense is-ness and beauty which primal peoples are aware of.

We can also look at this in terms of the de-sensitising mechanism, the part of our psyche which turns our perceptions to familiarity in order to conserve energy for the ego. Since the ego is quiet, it's not using up nearly as much energy, and so there's no reason for the de-sensitising mechanism to function. It naturally falls away, and we see the world with the same intense vision of unfallen peoples.

Another way in which meditation "undoes" the effects of the Ego Explosion is by blunting our sense of separateness to our surroundings. To a large extent, our sense of ego is sustained by its thought-chatter. When the ego quietens down, its boundaries become less defined. And if it becomes *completely* quiet, all sense of boundary fades away, and we experience the sense of one-ness with the cosmos which the Upanishads describe.

It's important to note, however, that all of this wasn't just about re-experiencing unfallen peoples' view of the world. The kind of consciousness which is normal for unfallen people exists for us as a *higher* state of consciousness. But there are different degrees of higher states of consciousness, including levels beyond the normal "unfallen" one. In fact, we can probably think of the typical unfallen state only as a "medium level" higher state of consciousness. Unfallen peoples do have egos, of course – it's just that they are less strongly developed than ours. The activity of their egos is still, therefore, taking up some of their consciousness-energy, even if it's not enough to stop them being aware of spirit-force. But in meditation, when the ego is *completely* quiet, it's possible to generate an even higher level of consciousness-energy than the normal unfallen level. The outflow of consciousness-energy may be halted completely. As a result, you may experience an even greater sense of unity with the cosmos, a more intense awareness of spirit-force, and an even greater sense of inner peace. (Unfallen peoples presumably experience these higher levels too, in situations where their level of consciousness-energy become even more concentrated than normal.)

As examples of this, we can look at some modern reports of mystical states of consciousness induced by meditation (or other spiritual practices), which appear to be more intense than the typical unfallen state of consciousness. As the philosopher of mysticism W.T. Stace pointed out, there are two basic types of mystical experience: extravertive and intravertive.[16] The first type is closest to the unfallen state of consciousness. In this you become aware of the presence of God or *Brahman* (spirit-force, in other words) in all things, and see the whole world as its manifestation. In the following example, the person had just been initiated into Transcendental Meditation, and had an extravertive mystical experience after an evening meditation session:

> This was a perception of oneness, all was a manifestation of Being. Through all the objects in the room glowed a radiance. All problems dissolved, or rather, there were no problems, there was no death and no "I-ness"; it was a feeling of absolute bliss. This was followed, as I gradually "came back into the world", by a feeling of intoxication, so great was the happiness.[17]

We can see that this experience has all the characteristics of the normal unfallen state of being – an awareness of spirit-force as the ultimate reality of the world, pervading all things and making them one; an awareness of the is-ness and beauty of the world and a sense of inner well-being. But all of these characteristics are pushed up a level, to a slightly higher intensity.

The intravertive mystical experience is different from the unfallen state of consciousness since it isn't about a new way of experiencing the world, but a new experience of our inner selves. It occurs in very deep states of meditation, when the sense of ego disappears completely and all form and substance and all sense of boundary fade away as well. We experience a "void" which appears to be the fundamental reality of the universe from which all things arise. The Zen Buddhist D.T. Suzuki, for example, describes a typical intravertive mystical experience as follows:

> The individual shell in which my personality is so solidly encased explodes at the moment of *satori*. Not necessarily that I get united with a greater being than myself or absorbed in it, but my individuality which I found rigidly held together and definitely separate from other individual existences…melts away into something indescribable, something which is of a quite different order from what I am accustomed to.[18]

Some philosophers of mysticism – such as Stace himself – believe that intravertive experiences are superior to extravertive, because they're about going beyond the whole world of form and experiencing the ultimate spiritual reality in its pure state, rather than experiencing it *through* the world of form. This may or may not be true, but we can certainly see them as a more intense state of consciousness than the normal unfallen state.

RENUNCIATION AND ASCETICISM

The spiritual traditions of the post-Fall era weren't just about the practice of meditation. The simple, solitary lives the sages and mystics led, with a minimum of distractions and responsibilities, were also a part of their effort to transcend the fallen psyche. This is the spiritual tradition of renunciation, of giving up the concerns of everyday life, such as families, business, socialising, money and possessions. All of these things drain away our attention and energy, and the sages realised that if they wanted to build up a permanently high concentration of consciousness-energy, they had to conserve the energy they normally gave away to them. According to one of the most profound scholars of mysticism, Evelyn Underhill, the purpose of this detachment from ordinary life was to remove "those superfluous, unreal, and harmful things which dissipate the precious energies of the self."[19] She notes that possessions in particular "are a drain upon the energy of the self, preventing her from attaining that intenser life for which she was made."[20]

The sages attempted to conserve consciousness-energy by taming their physical desires as well. They realised that our energies are also drained away through the constant desires we feel – sexual desire, the desire for good food and drink, for comforts and luxuries, and so on. Many hermits and saints went to great lengths to try to tame these desires, forcing themselves to be celibate, to live without possessions, and without any kind of comforts or pleasures. Some, like the Christian desert fathers of the third to fifth centuries CE (who lived as hermits in the deserts of Egypt and the Middle East), even took this to the extreme of torturing themselves. One of them, Dorotheus, lived naked in a cave for 60 years, never allowed himself to lie down (even when sleeping) and forced himself to go out and gather heavy stones in the midday sun.[21] When asceticism reaches this extreme there clearly is a masochistic element to it. It's also easy to see it as an expression of the hostility to the body (and to the material world in general) which was a part of some early spiritual traditions – the idea that only the spirit was pure and divine, and all physical matter was corrupt. But in a more moderate form, asceticism was also an attempt to stop consciousness-energy being drained away by desires and instincts. Together with meditation and renunciation, it was part of the mystics' struggle to build up a high concentration of consciousness-energy inside them, which would enable them to transcend the fallen psyche.

MORALITY

We've spent a large part of this book looking at how the intensified sense of ego naturally gives rise to social pathologies such as war, male domination, inequality and oppression. We've also seen that all of these are strongly connected to (although not completely the result of) the reduced level of empathy which goes with the fallen psyche. If these early spiritual adepts and traditions discovered ways of "undoing" the effects of the Ego Explosion, then we would also expect them to change in these ways. We would expect them to show a much greater ability to empathise with other people, other living beings and the natural world in general, and we'd expect them to transcend these social pathologies.

And this does seem to have been the case. This first wave of the trans-Fall movement gave birth to a new kind of morality. The essence of the Buddha's teachings, for example, was a kind of compassion which was completely new in the fallen world. It was his compassion for the suffering of human beings which made the Buddha determined to find a path to freedom, and all Buddhists are expected to feel the same deep desire to alleviate the sufferings of others. In Mahayana Buddhism, compassion – *karuna* – is one of the two supreme virtues, alongside wisdom. And this sense of compassion isn't limited to human beings. Buddhists are expected to extend "loving-kindness" (*metta*) throughout the whole universe, to all living beings, even insects. As the Metta Sutta proclaims, "May all beings be happy and secure! May their hearts be wholesome!" It exhorts us to "Let thoughts of boundless love pervade the whole world – above, below, across – without any obstruction, without any hatred, without any enmity."[22]

This empathy expressed itself in every aspect of the Buddha's teachings and views. He opposed discrimination against women, and founded what seems to have been the world's second ever female religious order, the order of Bikkhunis (Buddhist nuns). He was against slavery, banned the sacrifice of animals, and also rejected the caste system. As he declared, "By Birth is not one an outcast, by birth is not one a brahman; by deeds is one an outcast, by deeds is one a Brahmin."[23] The Buddha showed the same egalitarian attitude in his dealings with his followers. He was the complete opposite of the domineering leaders of religious sects we're familiar with nowadays. He never tried to attract followers just to increase his power and influence, and never forced anybody to accept his teachings without questioning them. Again and again in his teachings, he tells his followers that they shouldn't just take his word for what he's saying, but *find out* for themselves whether it is true.

In Jainism, Mahavira also preached against the caste system, and showed the same compassion for all living beings. The Jain vow of *ahimsa* – non-violence to all living beings – is so strict that Jains have to filter water before drinking and wear a gauze over their mouths to stop them swallowing insects. Mahavira also opposed the oppression of women, and founded the world's *first* ever female religious order, possibly around two decades before the Buddha.

In ancient Greece, the Stoics developed a similar trans-Fall morality. Alone amongst the Greek philosophers – even Plato thought it was inevitable – they opposed slavery as an affront to the dignity of the individual. They advocated an egalitarianism which was as opposed to the hierarchical Greek society of their time as the egalitarianism of Buddhism and Jainism was to the Indian caste system. As they saw it, nobody was superior to anybody else; Greeks and Barbarians, men and women, and citizens and slaves were all equal. The Stoics envisaged an ideal city, the City of Zeus, in which the needs of the community took precedence over individuals' needs, and everything was decided for the good of the majority. This anticipated the political philosophy of Communism – or, if you like, it harked back to egalitarian communities of the pre-Fall era.

This new kind of morality can only emerge from what we could call a "trans-egoic" state of being – that is, a state in which the painful ego-separation of the fallen psyche is transcended.

There are some early spiritual or religious groups who were clearly a part of the trans-Fall movement in terms of their morality, even though we can't say clearly whether they were aware of the same higher realities as the Indian or Chinese groups. The Essenes, for example, were a Jewish community who lived on the western shores of the Dead Sea from around 150 BCE to the first century CE. They were ascetics who believed that the end of the world was nigh, and that they had to purify themselves in readiness for it. They spent most of their time in prayer, study and manual work, and avoided contact with people outside their community except when absolutely necessary. Some scholars believe that the Dead Sea Scrolls were written by an Essene community, and the Scrolls do clearly show the kind of spiritual vision of reality which you would expect from people who lived an ascetic, contemplative lifestyle. "My eye has gazed upon eternal Being," says the author of *The Manual of Discipline*, while *The Revelation of Dositheus* proclaims, "We have seen That which truly was at the beginning, That which truly was, That which was the first Eternal, the Unbegotten."[24] But in any case, we can be fairly certain that the Essences did attain a "trains-egoic" state of being from the morality of their views and their lifestyle. The Essenes put into practice the "communist" ideals of the Stoics. All property was shared, all meals were cooked and eaten communally, and each person was given according to his own needs. Like the Stoics and the Jains and Buddhists, they opposed slavery and – according to the philospher Philo, who is one of the main sources of information about them – they didn't practise the sacrifice of animals.[25]

There is a belief that John the Baptist and even Jesus himself may have been Essenes, and although this is dubious, it seems clear that Essene beliefs influenced Jesus' teachings, and early Christianity in general. We can see Jesus' teachings as an excellent example of the trans-egoic state of being at work, transcending the selfishness and separateness of the fallen psyche. There are some hints from the Gospels that Jesus experienced the pre/trans-Fall sense of oneness and spiritual presence. The phrase, "The Kingdom of heaven is within you" suggests this, as does the phrase, "I am in my Father and my Father in me," hinting at a state of oneness with the Spirit of the universe (the Father). And outside the official Gospels, these hints are stronger. For instance, in the so-called "Oxyrhynchus" sayings of Jesus, discovered in Egypt around a century ago, Jesus describes the same state of oneness with God as that described by later Christian mystics. He is recorded as saying, "You shall know yourselves that you are in God and God in you. And you are the City of God."[26]

But, again, it is clear enough that Jesus experienced a "trans-egoic" state when we look at his lifestyle and his teachings on morality. As with the Buddha, the essence of Jesus' teaching is the kind of intense compassion which can only come through transcending the separate sense of self. Jesus identified himself with his followers to the extent that there was no separation of identity between him and them; he *was* them. As he is quoted as saying in the Gospel of Matthew: "Inasmuch as you did it to one of the least of these my brethren, you did it to me," and, "He who receives you receives me, and he who receives me receives him who sent me."[27] Jesus taught love and compassion for the poor and the sick, and opposed any kind of violence. He even advised his followers to feel a sense of compassion for their enemies, and to "turn the other cheek" to them. He also opposed the practice of stoning women for adultery, and scandalised his community by accepting women as his equals and even consorting with a prostitute. (Although admittedly Jesus was by no means a "feminist" – he preached against divorce, and said that marrying a widow was the same as sleeping with a married woman.)

All of this is itself evidence for the idea that social pathologies such as war, male domination and social inequality are the result of the intensified sense of ego. As soon as the separate sense of ego is transcended – or even just "blunted" – these pathologies fade away.

It's important to note that this applies to the concept of gods as well. I've suggested that the belief that anthropomorphic gods are watching over the world and intervening in its affairs is a product of the separate sense of ego. And this view is supported by the fact that the concept of gods is generally absent from these trans-Fall movements. Neither the Vedanta philosophy of the Upanishads, nor Jainism, Buddhism or Chinese Taoism (at least in their original forms) has any concepts of gods. As with unfallen peoples, the "highest power" in the universe is not God but Spirit, which is not a being but an impersonal force. This is inevitable, since if the members of these groups transcended ego-separateness and experienced a sense of oneness with the cosmos, they would have no *need* for God or gods. The Stoics did have a concept of God, but not as a personal being. To them God was the *logos* or eternal reason, the force which directs the development of life, and the seed or "living heat" which gives birth to all things.[28] Even the God which Jesus speaks of in the Oxyrhynchus sayings isn't the same separate, anthropomorphic entity which Christians traditionally worship. God is a spirit which is in human beings, and Jesus himself – as the manifestation of God – is a spirit which is in all creation: "Raise the stone and there thou shalt find me; cleave the wood and there I am."[29]

WORLD-REJECTION

The only part of the fallen psyche which isn't convincingly transcended right from the start of the first wave of the trans-Fall movement is the negative attitude to the body and to nature. The Vedanta philosophy of the Upanishads and Taoist philosophy do see nature as divine. All nature is seen as being pervaded with *Brahman* or the *Tao*. But other early trans-Fall movements thought in terms of a duality between spirit and matter. Like Theravada Buddhism (the original form of Buddhism), Jainism doesn't have a concept of spirit-force. As these traditions see it, the world is not pervaded with spirit; it's made of unconscious matter, and spirit belongs to another realm. Life on earth is *samsara*, illusion, and will always be unsatisfactory and full of suffering. In Buddhism, we can only transcend suffering by offloading all of our karma so that we don't have to be born here again. In Jainism, we can only find freedom by conquering the "base" needs and desires of the body, which halts the flow of karma.

Plato has a similar world-negating attitude. In his view, the ordinary world will always be a pale and unsatisfactory imitation of the perfect world of ideas. The Essenes were clearly "anti-material" too, as were other early mystical sects around the Middle East, such as the Gnostics and the Manichaeans. The Gnostics believed that the material world – including the human body – was evil, and that only a tiny divine spark in human beings gave them the possibility of freedom. And even the massively influential Yoga of the Indian mystic-philosopher Patanjali – who lived during the second century CE – treats matter and spirit as opposites. Patanjali's system of transcending the separateness and suffering of the fallen psyche was as detailed as the Buddha's. It involves following a different eightfold path, beginning with moral disciplines, moving to postures and breath control and different degrees of meditation and concentration, and culminating in ecstasy or *samadhi*. And as with Buddhism, in Patanjali's view *samadhi* means going beyond the material world, "dropping" the finite body-mind and entering a transcendental realm.[30]

This attitude expressed itself in the ascetic practices of some of these groups. We've seen that asceticism can be a genuine technique of intensifying consciousness-energy by controlling the instincts and desires which monopolise a large amount of it. But when asceticism develops in the context of anti-material traditions such as Jainism, Gnosticism or Christianity, it's easy to see how it might go beyond this, and become a system of punishing the body for its corruption and baseness.

In other words, all of these traditions are otherworldly, or dualist. They don't hark back to the pre-Fall vision of the world in a complete way because they don't see the whole of the material world as the manifestation of spirit-force. They focus mainly on overcoming the disharmony of the fallen psyche. One possible reason for this is simply that the people in these groups may only have *partially* transcended the fallen psyche. They may only have created a *partial* redistribution of consciousness-energy within their own psyche. This enabled them to experience a sense of inner peace and a freedom from psychological discord, but there was not – apparently – a high enough concentration of consciousness-energy to give them awareness of all-pervading Spirit or a sense of their oneness with it. This admittedly doesn't seem to make much sense for Buddhism and Jainism, which deal with states of consciousness in which the ego disappears completely, and in which there would be an extremely high concentration of consciousness-energy. But it could apply to groups such as the Essenes, the Gnostics and the Desert Fathers, who don't appear to have reached the same spiritual heights as people in the Indian traditions. At the same time, perhaps these groups' discovery that their needs and instincts were a major channel through which their consciousness-energy drained away – and that they could make themselves more "spiritual" by controlling them – gave them a negative attitude to the body. They began to think of it – and by extension the rest of the material world – as an enemy. (This was the fallen view of the body too, of course, but for different reasons.)

In the case of Buddhism, Jainism and the Yoga of Patanjali, their negative attitude to the material world is related to their *inwardness.* The Buddhist state of nirvana, or the *samadhi* of Jainism or Patanjali's yoga, are intravertive mystical states, whereas the mysticism of Vedanta or Taoism is both extravertive *and* intravertive. The world-rejecting traditions completely ignored the extravertive dimension; they jumped above it, straight into union with the Void (or *Brahman*) in its pure state. Perhaps, again, the discovery that on a basic level of economy the instincts and desires associated with the body *do* stand in the way of enlightenment, made them see the whole of the "gross" realm of matter as opposed to spirit and turn away from the possibility of extravertive mystical experience.

THE NON-DUAL TRADITIONS

However, from around the second century CE, new extravertive spiritual traditions began to arise which did fully return to the pre-Fall vision of the world – and go beyond it. Like the earlier Vedanta and Taoism, they saw all reality as the manifestation of Spirit, and treated the human body and the whole of the gross physical realm as divine.

At this time Mahayana Buddhism began to emerge from the old Theravada tradition, with a radical new vision of nirvana and *samsara* as one and the same. According to one of the central texts of Mahayana Buddhism, the Heart Sutra, "Emptiness does not differ from form, and the very emptiness is form."[31] In other words, Spirit is matter and matter is Spirit. The supreme reality of the universe is *Dharmakaya*, or Buddha-nature, which underlies and pervades everything. And in line with this, nirvana doesn't mean leaving the body behind and transcending the physical realm; it's possible to experience it in the world and in the body, because nirvana *is* the essential reality of the world. In the words of one early Mahayana philosopher, Ashvaghosha, nirvana means "the annihilation of the ego-conception, freedom from subjectivity, insight into the essence of Suchness, the recognition of the oneness of existence."[32]

At the same time – the second century CE – the Neo-Platonic tradition began to establish itself in the West. This sprang mainly from the teachings of the Greek mystic philosopher Plotinus, whose philosophy was strikingly similar to that of the Upanishads. Plotinus famously attacked the Gnostics for "despising the world and all the beauties that are in it." He knew that the world of matter is infused with the essential spiritual reality which he called the One, or the Good. As he wrote, "How can *this world* be separated from the *spiritual* world?" Spirit pours itself into the world, "penetrates and illumines it" so that the world becomes "a living and blessed being." And in the same way, says Plotinus, Spirit is the essential nature of human beings. It's up to us whether we become one with this higher part of our nature or allow ourselves to be dominated by our lower, animal selves.[33]

Back in India, both Mahayana Buddhism and Hinduism were affected by a new tradition called Tantra, which developed two or three centuries after Mahayana. Tantra became massively influential: it spread around Asia, flowering into different Buddhist traditions such as Ch'an (Chinese Buddhism), Zen (Japanese Buddhism) and Tibetan Buddhism, all of which emphasise the divine nature of all reality. Tantra went further than any other tradition in emphasising the sacredness of the human body. It's often seen as being all about sex, but its main insight is the same as Mayahana Buddhism: all the world, and all living things, are infused with Spirit, including the human body. All parts of the body and all physical processes are sacred, and sexual union is a mystical union of the active and passive principles of the universe, Shiva and Shakti. In an exact reversal of the typical fallen attitude to bodily processes, and a complete return to the positive attitude to menstruation shown by the Aborigines or the Mbuti, one Tantric text, the Jnanarnava Tantra, states:

> The menstruation of women
> Emanates from the body.
> How can it be impure?
> It is a substance through which (the devotee)
> Attains the supreme state.
> Faeces, urine, menstruation, nails and

Bones – all these are,
O beloved, considered to be pure by
The Master of mantras.[34]

Nothing could be further away from the disgust and revulsion to bodily processes shown by fallen religions.

LATER MYSTICISM

The first wave of the trans-Fall movement continued over the centuries, giving rise to many more spiritual teachers and mystical traditions. In every culture and in every period a very small minority of people discovered that it was possible to transcend the fallen psyche by using methods of redistributing their consciousness-energy.

One of the paradoxes of these trans-Fall traditions is that they often developed in the framework of – and became allied to – religions whose beliefs were radically opposed to theirs. Throughout most of their history, the three great Saharasian religions of Judaism, Christianity and Islam played host to mystical traditions which argued against their basic views of the world. Judaism included the mysticism of Hasidism and the Kabbalah; Islam included the mysticism of the Sufis; and from the beginning of the second millennium onwards, a long and illustrious sequence of mystics appeared in the Christian tradition, including Meister Eckhart, Thomas a Kempis, St Teresa of Avila, St John of the Cross and Jakob Boehme. These mystics sometimes used the term God – for example, they spoke of "union with God" or "surrender to God." But their concept of God was vastly different from the conventional religious view. Their God wasn't an anthropomorphic being who watched over the world; their God was effectively *Brahman*, spirit-force. To them the whole world was filled with the radiance of God. As one Christian mystic of the fourteenth century, Angela de Foligno, wrote, describing a mystical experience: "I beheld naught save the divine power in a manner assuredly indescribable, so that through excess of marvelling the soul with a loud voice, saying: 'This world is full of God!'"[35]

One of the cornerstones of Jewish, Christian and Islamic belief is that

God is separate to human beings. He's up there, we're down here, and our relationship with him is like an unapproachable master to a slave. But the mystics knew that "God" is within our own being. They knew that in a sense they *were* God, because the divine essence of their being was the same divine essence which pervades the universe. And their goal was to be united with God, so that, in the words of the Sufi mystic Dhu al-Nun, "Their words are the words of God which roll upon their tongues, and their sight is the sight of God which has entered their eyes."[36]

These views were completely heretical as far as conventional religion was concerned, and it's not surprising that many mystics had a very uneasy relationship with religious authorities. In India and other parts of Asia, the trans-Fall traditions of Yoga and Buddhism were respected and allowed to prosper. But in the West and the Middle East the fallen outlook of Christianity and Islam formed into a rigid orthodoxy. In 922 the Islamic mystic Mansur al-Hallaj was crucified in Baghdad for claiming that he was one with God, while great Christian mystics such as Meister Eckhart and Jakob Boehme were tried for heresy and excommunicated from the church for similar views.

Since the first wave shows the first stirrings of a movement beyond the post-Fall state of being, beyond the painful separateness of the sharpened sense of self and the social pathology which it generates, it might be tempting to see it as an evolutionary development. After all, if we see evolution as a process of intensifying consciousness, these mystics probably did reach higher levels of consciousness than any human beings before them. (Although it's possible that earlier unfallen peoples reached these levels too.)

However, we can't see the first wave as an evolutionary development for exactly the same reason that we can't see the Ego Explosion as one: because it didn't come from an intensification of consciousness-energy but from a *redistribution* of it. These trans-Fall traditions were based on a discovery made by individual human beings, a discovery which was repeated millions of times over, and which – ironically, using the sharpened intellectual powers that the Ego Explosion gave – became the basis of the systematic methods of transcending the fallen psyche devised by philosopher-mystics such as Patanjali and the Buddha. Evolution *is* part of this: in a sense someone who redistributes their consciousness-energy and makes themselves more conscious is taking evolution into their own hands, pushing the process of evolution forward as an individual. But this isn't the same as a collective evolutionary development which unfolds naturally.

This kind of evolutionary development didn't happen until later, when the second wave of the trans-Fall movement began.

16

THE SECOND WAVE

If any of us were transported back to eighteenth-century England, we would be horrified by the complete lack of compassion people showed for one another. We might cringe now when we see films showing crowds of Roman citizens cheering while gladiators hack each other to pieces, but 300 years ago executions were spectator sports in England; "hanging day" was a bank holiday. People could be hung for offences which would bring little more than a fine nowadays, offences such as burglary, pickpocketing, shoplifting, stealing linen and even cutting down trees or destroying fishponds. Another popular form of punishment – both in terms of its frequency and in terms of entertainment value – was the pillory. This was like the stocks, with holes for offenders to place their heads and arms in, and was used for offences such as blasphemy, card-cheating, fortune-telling, bestiality and homosexual offences. The difference with the stocks was that members of the public were encouraged to throw stones or any other projectiles at the criminal, who would often die from head injuries as a result. For less "serious" crimes, people could be punished by branding with a hot iron on the hand or the cheek. Vagrants could be branded with V, beggars with S for slave, while people who started fights could be branded with F as well as having their ears cut off.[1]

Cruelty to children occurred on a massive scale as well. Unwanted babies were thrown into dung heaps or open drains. The poorest parents sent their children out to be pickpockets or prostitutes, while others forced them to beg and even purposely scarred and crippled them to excite more pity. Thousands of homeless children walked the streets, and were routinely arrested for vagrancy and sent to prison. There was also incredible cruelty to animals. The most popular sports were forms of animal torture, such as cat-dropping, cockfighting and ratting – which was when people betted on how many rats a terrier dog could kill in a minute. Other popular sports were bear-baiting or bull-baiting, in which the animal would be put in a ring with two or more dogs to see who would win the fight. These animal fights often took place in pubs, and were advertised in local newspapers, like present-day karaoke sessions and pub quizzes.

Almost as little compassion was shown in the treatment of people with disabilities, which were seen as the result of possession by evil spirits. Women who gave birth to disabled children were sometimes exiled or killed. Children with disabilities often didn't survive, and if they did they were subject to appalling prejudices and restrictions. They were seen as evil and threatening and banned from entering churches, exiled from towns and even murdered.[2]

England at the beginning of the eighteenth century was, we might say, a typically "fallen" society. Practices like bear-baiting, cruelty to children and to people with disabilities were an expression of the separation and lack of empathy of the fallen psyche. As the historian Christopher Hibbert remarks of this period, "Pity was still a strange and valuable emotion."[3]

But now, at the beginning of the twenty-first century, things are different. There are still many cases of cruelty to children or animals, of course, and the treatment of people with disabilities is by no means perfect, but in general practices like these are much more rare. In modern Europe and parts of America – and certain other parts of the world – we seem to have a much higher level of compassion, a much greater capacity to "enter into" the mind-space of other people and sense their pain and suffering. Most of us wouldn't be able to treat children or animals with so much brutality because we're able to "feel with" them. We've gone from cat-dropping and ratting to vegetarianism and animal rights movements, from hanging children for stealing to laws protecting them against physical punishment at school and at home, and charities like the NSPCC or the NSPCA to protect them against cruelty. We've gone from hanging poor people for minor crimes to recognising that most people become criminals because of factors beyond their own control, and thinking in terms of rehabilitating prisoners rather than just punishing them.

The whole idea of charity would have struck an eighteenth-century person – even a rich person – as absurd. But now most of us feel some degree of pity for people less fortunate than ourselves, whether they are children, earthquake or famine victims or homeless people, and feel conscience-bound to give to charities. Our societies as a whole – especially in Europe – also go some way to ensuring that everyone's basic survival needs are met. Until recent times people who were unemployed, old or long-term sick were likely to starve or become homeless if they couldn't be cared for by their families, but now we have social security systems to make sure this rarely happens.

And along with this sense of compassion there is an emphasis on *rights*. With our ability to enter into the mind-space of others and see the world from their perspective, we realise that people who might be superficially different from us are essentially the same, and entitled to exactly the same rights as us. Many of us realise that people with disabilities have the right to do the same jobs and use the same facilities as the able-bodied, that female workers have the right to be as well-paid as men, that ethnic minorities should have exactly the same rights as the majority, and so on. The popularity of vegetarianism stems partly from an awareness that animals should have the right to live out their lives in peace in a natural environment. And although unfortunately homophobia is still common (especially in parts of the United States), many people now realise that gay people should have exactly the same rights as heterosexuals, and be able to marry if they want to.

I don't want to exaggerate our compassion and benevolence – there's no doubt that we've still got a long way to go in some of these areas. But when you compare our society with English society 300 years ago, it's clear that we've already made some real progress.

Where has this new spirit of compassion come from? You might argue that it's just the result of increasing prosperity. Our ancestors 300 years ago were too busy fighting to survive as individuals to think about other people, you might say, but now our bellies are full of food and our bank accounts are full of money so it's easy for us to widen our circle of concern. This might be a factor, but in my view this new spirit of compassion is a sign of something deeper.

Compassion is sometimes seen as the use of imagination. You "put yourself in someone else's shoes," imagine what they feel or what the world looks like through their eyes, and as a result you feel sympathy for them. Or, as we noted earlier, the psychologist Simon Baron-Cohen sees it as a matter of "reading the emotional atmosphere" and "picking up" hints of how someone is feeling by looking at their expressions and general behaviour.[4] But, as I suggested, in its true sense compassion is more than this. Compassion means transcending ego-isolation. As with the Buddha, Jesus and the first wave in general, it means going beyond the separateness of the fallen psyche and experiencing a shared sense of identity with other beings. This doesn't mean that we are all Buddhas and Christs, of course – there are different degrees of this, and it may be that your ego-separateness is only *slightly* blunted, so that you can feel a *slight* degree of compassion. But even a slight blunting of ego-separateness allows you to make some contact with the spiritual essence of your own being – and since all other beings have this same spiritual essence, it makes you part of them, and able to feel with them.

In other words, this new spirit of compassion can be seen as the expression of a collective psychic change that seems to be taking place within human beings: a gradual movement beyond ego-separateness. The first wave was something that individual human beings made happen, but this – the second wave – is something that seems to be happening to us.

The effects of the second wave are everywhere around us. Like the first wave, the second wave has affected all the social pathologies which the fallen psyche gave rise to. In a way, the first wave had a more powerful effect, because its mystics and spiritual seekers reached a much higher level of ego-transcendence. On the other hand, the effect of the second wave has been much more pronounced, because changes have happened on a much bigger scale. Whereas the first wave was a tiny undercurrent, the second wave is a mass movement, involving a sizeable proportion of the human race.

THE SECOND WAVE ERUPTS

Although it had been building up slowly for many decades before then, the second wave first became a powerful visible force in the world in the second half of the eighteenth century. This short period saw some of the most significant changes in human history. In a way, these changes were almost as momentous – if not as drastic – as the giant transition which occurred at 4000 BCE, especially since they began a process of *undoing* that transition.

The second half of the eighteenth century was an amazing time to be alive. For almost 6,000 years people – at least those in the fallen world – had taken the institution of slavery for granted. It was seen as inevitable, even ordained by the gods. What else could you do with captive soldiers – it would've been a waste to kill them – and how would society survive without slaves to do the degrading jobs that no one else wanted to do? Some of the early popes used slaves on their estates, and in eighteenth-century Britain slave traders were mayors and members of Parliament. It was only in the last decades of the eighteenth century that a widespread movement against slavery began to build up. In 1765, the anti-slavery society was formed in England, and seven years later the Lord Chief Justice Mansfield outlawed slavery in England, freeing 15,000 African slaves. This paved the way for other, more widespread changes. Anti-slavery societies formed all over the colonies, and in 1807, the British Parliament ruled that slavery was illegal for British citizens anywhere in the world. Within ten years, the United States, France, Denmark and Holland had made it illegal too.

In the same way, it had always been taken for granted that some human beings were born superior to others, and entitled to special rights and privileges. Members of the aristocracy saw peasants as little more than animals, and kings believed that they had a divine right to rule over their subjects. But towards the end of the eighteenth century a new concept of democracy began to spread, based on the idea that all human beings were born equal and entitled to the same rights. And alongside this, there was a realisation that if the great majority of people did not have the equal rights they were entitled to, it was because they were being oppressed by an unfair social system. The first powerful statement of these ideas was Jean-Jacques Rousseau's *The Social Contract* in 1762, with its famous statement that "Man is born free, but everywhere is in chains." Rousseau was very influenced by the accounts he had read of early European people's encounters with unfallen peoples of the Americas and the South Pacific. *The Social Contract* in turn influenced the founders of America, who were also greatly influenced by their own observations of the "natural democracy" of Native American societies.[6] As a result, in 1776 the world's first modern democracy came into being, with its egalitarian principles set down in the constitution of 1791 – even though, as with the "democracies" of ancient Greece and Rome (although not to the same extent), the American ideas of equal participation and freedom were limited. They only applied to white male landowners, and excluded women, African Americans or Native Americans. In France, the spread of democratic ideals, together with the pressure of poverty and the abhorrence of a corrupt ruling class, led straight to the Revolution of 1789.

For almost 6,000 years people in the fallen world had also taken it for granted that women were inferior to men. Women were childish, non-rational creatures who weren't fit to decide their own destinies, to contribute anything to the cultural, economic and political life of their societies, or to own their own property – but who *were* fit to be beaten. Towards the end of the nineteenth century these views were widely questioned for the first time ever. When the French Revolution broke out in 1789 the revolutionaries presented a list of their grievances to the Estates General, 33 of which were demands by women for more rights. In the same year, the American constitution was ratified, and its use of the terms "people" and "electors" rather than "men" implied the recognition of women's rights as well as men's. Under the influence of these changes, the world's first ever major feminist tracts appeared. In 1792, Mary Wollstonecraft's *Vindication of the Rights of Women* was published in England, while two years later Theodore Gottlieb von Hippel's *On the Civil Improvement of Women* appeared in Germany.

All of this is the first major evidence of a collective movement beyond the separation of the fallen psyche. The walls of the isolated fallen ego were, it seems, being blunted; as a result, an intense wave of empathy was building up, a new ability to enter the "mind-space" of other beings and feel with them.

Another major consequence of this was a movement to end the kind of socially accepted cruelty and brutality which I described at the beginning of this chapter. The animal rights movement – which we sometimes think of a very modern phenomenon – effectively began in the second half of the eighteenth century. There was a growing revulsion to sports such as bull-baiting and cock-fighting; newspapers and journals carried many essays and letters protesting against them, and clergymen began to give sermons on the theme of the humane treatment of animals. In 1776, a clergyman named Humphrey Primatt published *A Dissertation on the Duty of Mercy and Sin of Cruelty to Brute Animals*, which argued that cruelty to animals is even more immoral than cruelty to people, since animals can't defend themselves or plead their cause. Similar works appeared, such as John Lawrence's self-explanatory *On the Moral Duties of Man towards Brute Creation* (1798), and even education manuals which taught children how to treat animals properly.[7] This new spirit of empathy led to the setting-up of several reform societies to campaign against cruelty to animals, including, in 1824, the SPCA (later the RSPCA). And a decade later came the passing of the first act against cruelty to animals, outlawing blood sports that used cattle or domestic animals.

The same spirit of empathy brought major changes to the punishment of criminals. In Britain, there was a growing protest against the free use of the death penalty, and transportation – to America or Australia – began to be used for child felons and for less serious capital offences, such as sheep stealing or petty theft. Until the end of the eighteenth century, imprisonment was rarely used as a long-term punishment – most long-term prisoners were debtors who were held until they could pay their fines. But as revulsion grew to brutal public punishments such as whipping or hanging, imprisonment was used much more frequently. Branding was abolished in 1799, followed by the stocks and the pillory in 1821 and 1837 respectively. Elsewhere in Europe, the rack and flogging were abolished in France, torture was banned in Italy, and Frederick II of Prussia – one of the so-called "enlightened" monarchs of this period – also banned torture.

There were similar changes in the treatment of children and disabled people. All over Western Europe the practice of swaddling started to be abandoned, and there were protests against the corporal punishment of schoolchildren. A sense of empathy grew for the vast number of babies, many of them disabled, who were left to die by their parents. England's first Foundling Hospital was opened in London in 1741, and was quickly followed by others. There was a growing realisation that it was society's duty to care for old and disabled people rather than this just being the responsibility of the person's family, and in the late eighteenth century the first almshouses – state institutions for the community's "unfortunates" – were opened in America.

Again, I certainly don't want to over-emphasise the effect of these changes, and paint the second half of the eighteenth century as a utopian age. In some ways, the changes were admittedly superficial. Cruelty and oppression were still rife. The egalitarian ideals of the French Revolution rapidly gave way to massive violence and another form of state oppression. After the industrial revolution, the factory workers of nineteenth-century Europe were just as poor and oppressed – if not more so – than the peasants of the seventeenth century. The egalitarian principles of the United States didn't stop them systematically exterminating the culture – and the population – of the Native Americans. But this was the point where the process began, where the first signs of a collective trans-Fall psyche emerged, even if the traits of the fallen psyche were still dominant.

THE ROMANTICS AND THE NOVEL

Another way in which the second wave manifested itself towards the end of the eighteenth century – and in the first decades of the nineteenth – was in literature. The great poets of the late seventeenth to mid eighteenth centuries were imposing, rationalistic figures like Dryden, Pope and Johnson. To us nowadays their poetry has an air of coldness and cleverness. Their poems – which are normally extremely long – deal with political and moral issues and are often satirical and whimsical. But at the end of the nineteenth century a new kind of poetry emerged, the so-called Romantic movement. This gave rise to the idea – which we now take for granted – that poetry should be *subjective*, an expression of the inner life of the author, or a lyrical description of the beauty of the natural world. In England, the major Romantic figures were Blake, Wordsworth, Coleridge, Byron, Shelley and Keats, and similar movements arose all over Europe. In Germany, poets like Goethe and Schiller represented the Romantic movement, while France had writers such as Chateaubriand, Lamartine and Victor Hugo. In the United States, meanwhile, the Transcendentalist movement – featuring figures such as Thoreau, Emerson and Whitman – was roughly equivalent to the Romantic, although it didn't begin until the 1840s.

All of these poets have a powerful immediacy which earlier poets lack. Rather than discussing ideas or satirising politicians or fellow poets, they are preoccupied with their own inner worlds, their own sufferings and joys and hope and despair. They also have a strong political and social idealism. Wordsworth and Coleridge's *Lyrical Ballads* aimed to be a new "democratic" poetry which ordinary people could understand, a poetry stripped of high literary devices and arcane vocabulary. Blake wrote poems describing the terrible plight of the working classes, and Shelley's revolutionary socialist ideals are clear from poems such as "The Mask of Anarchy" – in which he urges the working classes to revolt – and "England in 1819," in which he describes the king as "old, mad, blind, despised."[8]

Most of all, though, what set the Romantics apart from earlier poets was their new attitude to *nature*. The Romantics were awestruck by nature's beauty and power, and felt a strong sense of connection to it. They addressed poems to the wind, to clouds, mountains, birds, flowers, the seasons and the stars. To them, nature was a refuge and an inspiration. As Shelley wrote:

Away, away from men and towns
To the wild wood and the downs
Where the soul need not repress its music.[9]

At times, their awareness of nature's beauty and aliveness crosses over into the "blazing" mystical reality which unfallen peoples perceive, and which the spiritual seekers of the first wave were aware of. Both Shelley and Wordsworth were aware of the presence of spirit-force in the world, pervading all things. Shelley describes it as "The awful shadow of some unseen Power/ [that] Floats though unseen among us."[10] Wordsworth describes it in many passages, the best known of which is probably the following from *Tintern Abbey*. These lines are very reminiscent of descriptions of *Brahman* in the Upanishads; although this perhaps isn't surprising since they are describing the same thing:

And I have felt
A presence that disturbs me with the joy
Of elevated thoughts; a sense sublime
Of something far more deeply interfused,
Whose dwelling is the light of setting suns,
And the round ocean and the living air,
And the blue sky, and in the mind of man:
A motion and a spirit, that impels
All thinking things, all objects of all thought,
And rolls through all things.[11]

In other words, with the Romantics the new spirit of empathy didn't just extend to other human beings and animals, but to all nature. They *participated* in the world, rather than just being detached dualistic observers of it. The transcendence of the fallen psyche in the second wave was bringing about a return to unfallen peoples' reverential attitude to – and sense of connection to – nature. Or as the philosopher Jay Earley puts it:

The Romantic movement in Europe was also a strong and vital protest against the hegemony of reflexive consciousness [his term for the sharpened sense of ego]. Emanating primarily from the arts and humanities, especially poetry, this movement celebrated participatory consciousness. The romantics reminded us that there was another side to life, different from the mechanistic, dehumanised worldview that ruled the day. They wrote of love, spirituality and passion; they told of the virtues of aliveness and feeling.[12]

There was another major development in literature in the eighteenth century too: the advent of the modern novel. There were novels before the eighteenth century, of course, such as *Don Quixote* or *Robinson Crusoe*. But these were adventure yarns without any real introspective dimension. They didn't give the reader a real insight into the reality of other people's lives, or a glimpse into their minds. As Colin Wilson has pointed out, the novel as we understand it now came into being with the publication of Samuel Richardson's *Pamela* in 1740.[13] This quickly became the best-selling book in Europe, mainly because the heroine's inner world was so vividly portrayed that it enabled readers to enter into her mind and empathise with her. Many similar books followed. In 1761 Rousseau – surely the single most influential person in the eighteenth century – published his similarly sentimental novel *Julie, or the New Heloise*, which was even more successful than *Pamela*. While in Germany in 1774 Goethe published his novel *The Sufferings of Young Werther*, which had a similar effect. Readers empathised with the plight of Werther – the jilted lover who kills himself – to such a degree that there was a wave of copycat suicides throughout Europe. It was as if a great tidal wave of feeling swept across the continent, as these novels – and many others like them – allowed people to share the mind-space of fictional characters. As Colin Wilson puts it, the novels allowed people to step outside their own lives: "It was as startling as if human beings had learned to leave their bodies and float around in space. The novel taught human beings to dream."[14]

From the point of view of the second wave, however, the massive popularity of these novels shows that people had a powerful *desire* to enter the mind-space of others. The fact that they responded so powerfully to them is evidence of the same sense of empathy which gave rise to democracy and the women's movement and to protests against cruelty to animals and children.

A new surge of feeling ran through the art and music of this period as well. There was a transition from the neo-classical and representational art of the eighteenth century to works which were more personal and charged with emotion, which aimed to express the artist's own sensibility rather than to be "objective." Art historians actually refer to this period as Romanticism, with European artists such as Goya, Caspar David Friedrich, Turner, Constable and Delacroix – all of whom worked during the latter part of the eighteenth and early part of the nineteenth centuries – showing a similar heightened sensitivity and sense of connection to nature as the Romantic poets. Romanticism led to the Impressionist movement of the second half of the nineteenth century, and – in the United States – to the Hudson River School, with its dramatic depictions of America's wilderness.

In music, the eighteenth century was dominated by the same neo-classical ideals as art. Composers were inspired by the art of ancient Greece and Rome, and tried to make their works well-proportioned and disciplined, with distinct melodies. But in the first half of the nineteenth century, with Beethoven bridging the gulf between the old era and the new, music became more expressive and dramatic. Composers like Schubert, Berlioz, Chopin and Liszt rejected formality and restraint and filled their music with a new intensity.

THE RISE OF SOCIALISM

After this initial burst, the second wave of the trans-Fall movement continued through the nineteenth century. The women's liberation movement made steady ground. Women gained the right to hold their own property independently of their husbands, to earn their own wages, to sit on juries, to enter professions like law and medicine and to go into higher education. In 1893, New Zealand became the first country to give women full voting rights, with Australia following suit in 1902. Women in America and Great Britain had to suffer for longer, but were finally given these rights in 1928 and 1920 respectively.

The new ability to take the perspective of other people (and the resulting awareness that everyone is equal and entitled to the same rights) gave rise to the socialist movement of the nineteenth century. Early socialists like Robert Owen and Saint-Simon put forward visions of ideal societies in which there was no central government, no material incentives and everyone cooperated for the common good. These ideas seemed particularly urgent after the industrial revolution, when factory workers became even poorer and more oppressed than the generations of peasants before them. In 1848, Marx and Engels published the *Manifesto of the Communist Party* and developed a vision of history as a process leading inevitably to complete equality between people, with a collective ownership of property, collective decision-making, and self-government by the working class. As I noted earlier, like Rousseau and the founding fathers of America, Marx and Engels were influenced by reports they read of egalitarian Native American societies – in particular, Lewis Henry Morgan's book *The League of the Iroquois*.[15] And the ideal society they advocated – and predicted – is very close to the egalitarian societies of unfallen peoples.

By the late nineteenth century, socialism was a real political force throughout Europe, with most socialist groups trying to achieve change gradually by parliamentary means. In Russia there was no parliament, however, and the only way forward seemed to be to overthrow the government, which occurred with the Communist Revolution of 1917. But the radical socialism of Communism was always doomed to fail, simply because it was too great a leap for the fallen psyche to make. When and wherever Communism has been established, the fallen psyche's desire for status and wealth and its lack of empathy have become dominant again, and the societies have become as riddled with inequality and oppression as any feudal capitalist society. A new hierarchy of rich and privileged party officials and party members has taken over the role of the middle and upper classes, and their desire to hang on to their power has resulted in a complete absence of democracy. The problem, we might say, was that although the second wave was spreading, it was still nowhere near powerful enough to sustain the complete return to egalitarianism that Communism advocated. The pathology of the fallen psyche was still too strong.

But if Communism was far too ambitious, the second wave manifested itself in a more effective way in the orthodox socialist parties, which worked through the system. After the Second World War, many of these gained power in Europe, and established greater equality and individual rights. All over Europe social security systems were introduced, ensuring that the old, the sick and the unemployed wouldn't want for the basic necessities of life, and government grants meant that higher education (and therefore the highest professions) were accessible to working class people. As a result, over the last few decades in Europe, class boundaries have faded away and something close to equality of opportunity prevails, if not actual equality of status.

And as socialism thrived, so did democracy. In 1790, there were just three countries in the world whose governments were democratically elected and whose constitutions declared that all men (if not women) were entitled to equal rights: the United States, Switzerland and France. By the end of the nineteenth century there were 13 democracies – including Canada, Great Britain, Greece, Chile, Argentina and Denmark – and by 1919 there were 25. And now, at the beginning of the 21st century, there are 119.[16] In principle, the political systems of all these democracies are strikingly similar to those of unfallen societies. They all have group decision-making processes, checks to make sure that no individual can obtain too much power, and any unpopular leader can be relieved of his duties by the electorate. It's clear, however, that we haven't yet reached the same level of democracy as unfallen peoples. Some hunter-gatherer groups don't have any leaders at all, and if they do have them, they aren't entitled to "hold office" for a certain period of time, but can be replaced at any moment if the rest of the group aren't satisfied with them. And our democracies are also, of course, corrupted by media bias and the massive propaganda campaigns that political parties can stage.

THE TWENTIETH CENTURY

The second half of the twentieth century was similar to the second half of the eighteenth, a period in which the second wave moved forward with great intensity.

While real progress was made against the pathologies of male domination and social inequality in the eighteenth and nineteenth centuries, there wasn't much progress against warfare. Military conflict did become less frequent in the nineteenth century, but new kinds of weapons meant that more people died in wars. It was only really in the twentieth century, and particularly in its second half, that the second wave manifested itself in this area. The First World War was the last European war to be welcomed by all its participants. After it proved to be such a disaster there was a realisation that nothing like it should ever be allowed to happen again. The League of Nations was set up to try to ensure that it didn't, with the aim of promoting international cooperation and security and peace. There was a new sense of empathy between different nations, an eroding away of the sense of otherness which fuels warfare. As a result, there was peace in Europe for the longest period in recorded history up to then: 21 years. It didn't last, of course – but the Second World War was one which nobody apart from its perpetrators wanted, and which everyone else tried to avoid until it was too late. The lust for power and wealth and the sense of otherness which give rise to war weren't spread everywhere – as they had been before – but only came from the German side (and later the Italians and Japanese). And there is a good case for the view that if the punitive measures against them after the First World War hadn't been so harsh, the Second World War would never have taken place anyway.

There have been many wars in the world since then, of course, but particularly in Europe, there has been a general trend towards reconciliation and peace – caused, we can say, by the same spirit of increasing empathy which led to the abolition of slavery, to women's rights and democracy and socialism. The European nations – such as Spain, France, Great Britain, Germany (or Prussia) – which fought against one another ceaselessly for centuries have now been at peace for almost 60 years.[17]

On a worldwide basis, the United Nations is a giant step beyond the old sense of otherness between different nations and the blind lust for material gain and power that give rise to warfare. The UN is at the spearhead of the second wave, in its mission to overcome the pathologies of the fallen psyche, with its stated aims to "maintain international peace and security," to "harmonize the actions of nations" and to "promote respect for human rights."[18] And the UN is also a clear expression of the second wave in its highly democratic nature, with 191 member states making collective decisions by consensus. Significantly, the anthropologist Christopher Boehm notes that "In many ways [the United Nations] behaves very much like a hunter-gatherer band."[19]

Another major area where there wasn't much progress in the nineteenth century was in attitudes to sex and the body. But here all the progress which might've been made earlier occurred in a very short space of time in the second half of the twentieth century. Attitudes to sex and the body changed so quickly that if a young man from the 1940s walked through a city centre in the year 2004 – with girls wearing short skirts and shoulderless tops and half-naked women on the covers of magazines and newspapers – he'd probably have a heart attack from sexual excitement. His shock would intensify if he sat down in a café and saw a mother openly breast-feeding or heard women at another table talking about pre-menstrual tension.

Although these new attitudes have had some bad side effects, such as an increasing perception of women as sex objects and sexual over-stimulation by the media, in some ways this is one of the most welcome transformations of the second wave. After centuries of being told that sex is sinful and of treating completely natural bodily functions like menstruation and masturbation as taboo, we've begun to treat them as the natural and healthy processes they are, and begun to lose the sense of shame which was associated with them. Most progress was made in this area in the 1960s, with the introduction of the pill, the lifting of bans on books like *Lady Chatterley's Lover* and *Tropic of Cancer*, the advent of modern pop music (with its overtly sexual connotations), and a shift to more revealing and sensual fashions. National surveys in the US have shown that since the 1940s pre-marital sex has become much more socially acceptable and much more frequent. We haven't completely returned to the open and positive attitude of unfallen peoples – for example, we're still less accepting of adolescent sex and extra-marital affairs and it's certainly not acceptable to walk the streets naked, or for women to go bare-breasted in daily life. But there has certainly been a growing acceptance of our own biology, an eroding away of the mind-body duality which L.L. Whyte called the "European Disassociation."

The 1960s was a hotbed of second wave progress. The hippie movement of the late 1960s expressed all of the different facets of the trans-Fall movement: a more open attitude to sex and the body, a blurring of gender distinctions, men who were increasingly feminine (in appearance and in attitude), egalitarian ideals, non-violence, connection to nature, an interest in Eastern mystical philosophies of the first wave, and so on. As Riane Eisler points out, the sensual fashion styles of the ancient Cretans, the long hair of Cretan men and the unisex clothes they sometimes wore, are strikingly similar to fashions of the 1960s, which she describes as a time when "women and men frontally challenged restrictive gender stereotypes of male dominance and female subservience."[20] The hippie movement was a brave attempt to create something close to a modern-day unfallen culture, and its clashes with "straight" society were in some ways reminiscent of the clashes between indigenous peoples and fallen colonial cultures. Just as European colonists were perplexed by the Native Americans or Australian Aborigines, ordinary people were perplexed and offended by the hippies' lack of interest in possessions, success and power and their lack of competitiveness. And just as the indigenous peoples were appalled by the behaviour of the colonists, the hippies were appalled by the greed, injustice and militarism of "straight" society. Even if it often didn't live up to its own ideals, and even though it faded away quickly in the 1970s, the hippie movement was a powerful expression of the collective psychic change which had been building up since the eighteenth century.

The blurring of gender boundaries which began in the 1960s has now taken us somewhere close to the interchangeable gender roles of unfallen cultures. At the beginning of the twenty-first century, we have the popular notions of the "new man," who helps out with childcare and domestic chores, and the "househusband" who is happy to take care of domestic duties while his wife follows a career. And at the same time, of course, more and more women are rejecting their old "gender schema" and taking on traditionally "male" roles. And to some degree these changes in role have, it seems, been accompanied by a change in *character*. The strong distinction between the male and female psyche which the Fall created also appears to be fading away. The "new man" is closer to the less "fallen" feminine psyche – he is more sensitive and empathic, less aggressive and self-assertive. In other words, it seems that he doesn't have the same isolated non-empathic ego of the typical "fallen" male psyche.

There are a few other expressions of the trans-Fall movement in the twentieth century that we should mention briefly as well. One of them is a more empathic attitude to nature. This seems to have begun in the late eighteenth century – as shown by the Romantics – but has really expressed itself in the environmental and ecological movements of the last few decades. These movements show a return to the respectful attitude to nature of unfallen cultures, an awareness of a shared sense of being with nature and a sense that natural phenomena possess their own being or subjective dimension (their own dreaming, in Aboriginal terms) – and also an increasing awareness that by abusing the natural world we are endangering our own survival as a species. This has gone hand in hand with an increasing respect for animals, as shown by the growing popularity of vegetarianism and veganism. People choose not to eat meat for a variety of reasons, but perhaps the main one is a simple moral aversion to eating the flesh of creatures who we respect and empathise with, who we don't see as objects but as sentient living beings.

We saw earlier how theistic religions were a product of the fallen psyche, and another sign of the emergence of a new "trans-Fall" psyche may be the rejection of these religions over the past 150 years or so. Of course, there are many cultural and social reasons for the decline of religion, such as the rise of science and increasing material prosperity. But it's also feasible that theistic religions are no longer so important to us simply because the fallen psyche – which needs so desperately to feel that an all-powerful entity is watching over the world and that all its sufferings will be justified in the afterlife – is no longer as strong. There is further evidence for this in the new *kinds* of beliefs and practices which replaced theistic religion. Since the end of the nineteenth century, the obscure esoteric traditions of the first wave have entered into the mainstream. By the late 1800s, ancient Eastern spiritual masters were commonly "passing on" secret wisdom in séances, and movements like the Theosophical Society and the Order of the Golden Dawn were formed, based on Eastern mystical beliefs and practices. Interest in first wave traditions such as Buddhism, Yoga and Taoism grew steadily until it exploded in the 1960s. These ancient methods of transcending the fallen psyche – or at least elements of them – were suddenly available to massive numbers of people. And since then interest in spirituality or self-development has been increasing at an exponential rate. The increasing popularity of meditation is particularly significant, since the practice is expressly designed to "soften" our sense of ego-separateness. Nowadays people's spiritual lives have become less centred on the consoling effects of theistic religions, and more on the transformative effect of spiritual practices.

It's also significant that in the second half of the twentieth century attitudes to indigenous peoples began to change. After centuries of seeing them as sub-humans who could be abused and even killed without any qualms, a new sense of respect for unfallen peoples began to emerge. Many people began to feel a sense of shame at the way that previous generations had treated them, a desire to try to give them back the rights which had been taken away, and also a respect for their spiritual traditions and their vision of nature as sacred and alive. As well as the result of the new spirit of empathy, this is probably because, now that we've begun to transcend the fallen psyche ourselves, we feel more of a kinship with indigenous peoples' ways of life and their worldviews.

We saw earlier in this book that one of the main effects of the fallen psyche is an intense desire for wealth and status, and that this is one of the main causes of pathologies such as war and social oppression. The fallen psyche believes that wealth and status can provide it with the sense of well-being and wholeness which it lacks. It thinks it can complete itself with possessions, and overcome its sense of insufficiency by becoming important and powerful. And a further sign of the second wave may be that the effort to attain wealth and status appears to be becoming less important to many people. Many people are now voluntarily choosing to "downsize" or "downshift" – that is, to have fewer possessions and less wealth and responsibility in return for a less stressful life. The Trends Research Institute of New York has identified the "voluntary simplicity" movement as one of the top ten social trends throughout the world, growing faster than any other trend they have ever recorded.[21] As the social scientist Duane Elgin puts it, "masses of people are beginning to embrace the belief that they can enhance the quality of their lives by cutting back on the quantity of products they consume."[22]

THE SECOND WAVE AS AN EVOLUTIONARY LEAP

Once again, I don't want to over-emphasise the effect of these changes, and paint the twentieth century as a utopian age. After all, this century has seen some of the worst atrocities in human history. While the socialist movement was bringing equality to countries like Great Britain and France, in Russia, Stalin – supposedly a socialist himself – was killing millions of his own citizens. And 150 years after the new spirit of empathy led to the first real progress against slavery and male domination, the Nazis treated people of other ethnic groups as inanimate objects, and murdered 6 million Jews. And even in the "enlightened" Europe of the 1990s, ethnic conflict in the former Yugoslavia eclipsed the empathic bonds between people and led to mass genocide.

In other areas, any progress which has been made by the second wave seems to be offset by trends in the opposite direction. Although there is a movement against materialism and status, the late twentieth century was probably the most materialistic and status-obsessed period in history, when many people were prepared to sacrifice anything and everything to get rich or famous or powerful. And although the environmental movement is getting stronger, the last half of the twentieth century probably saw more damage to the environment than all of the rest of human history put together, due to increases in population and per capita consumption, and powerful multinational companies who abuse the earth on a gigantic systematic scale.

I'm not trying to say that the fallen psyche is fading away – it's still strong, of course. The majority of people have probably been only been affected by the second wave in a very small way. And it seems that the potential is always there for our bonds of empathy to fade away and for us to regress to the extreme aggression and the lust for power and wealth of the fallen psyche. But the point is that, for the first time in history, there is a growing movement against the pathologies of the fallen psyche, even if it's still only a minority movement. According to the massive "World Values Survey" coordinated by Ronald Inglehart (which covers 43 societies and 70 per cent of the world's population):

> We are seeing deep rooted changes in mass world views [that] are reshaping economic, political and social life. An empirically demonstrable shift is taking place. The great religious and ideological metanarratives are losing their authority among the masses. The uniformity and hierarchy which shaped modernity are giving way to an increasing acceptance of diversity. [There is a] greater tolerance for ethnic, cultural and sexual diversity and individual choice concerning the kind of life one wants to lead.[23]

We appear to be moving towards what Riane Eisler describes as a "new world of social and psychological rebirth," a shift from what she calls a "dominator" to a "partnership" society, in which "we will live free of the fear of war" and in which there will be "more equal and balanced relations between women and men and the reinforcement of gentler, more pro-human behavior in children of both sexes."[24]

There are certainly some sociological and economic reasons for these changes, but taken all in all, they are a clear indication that human beings are changing *inside* – or, more specifically, that there is a collective movement towards transcending the fallen psyche. If most of the changes I've described are due to an increasing spirit of empathy, this means that the walls of separateness which the Ego Explosion created are fading away. And perhaps, to a smaller extent, the changes have also been caused by the very fact that since the fallen ego has become weaker, people have felt a less pronounced lust for wealth and status. The movement towards equality for women and lower classes may not have happened unless there had been some willingness by men and the higher classes to give up some of their power. In the same way, the decline of wars of conquest – and war in general – may be partly due to a less pronounced desire of nations to dominate others and steal their wealth.

The question we need to ask now is: *Why* is this change occurring? Why does this movement to transcend the fallen psyche seem to be taking place?

As we've noted, this isn't something that human beings are making happen, but which is happening *to* us. It's not coming about through a redistribution of consciousness-energy, like the first wave. This new spirit of empathy isn't the result of using techniques of quietening and weakening the ego so that we can redirect the consciousness-energy it normally uses up into perception, or simply retain it inside ourselves. There is no redirection of consciousness-energy away from the ego. In theory, the ego is using up just as much consciousness-energy as it did before.

But at the same time it's likely that the new perception of the world which is developing *is* the result of a higher level of consciousness-energy. The fundamental difference between us and our ancestors 300 years ago may be that we are *more alive* than they were. There may be a higher level of consciousness-energy inside us, which is enabling us to develop a new spirit of empathy and a new respect for nature without redirecting energy away from the ego. And if this new consciousness-energy didn't come from inside us, as a result of redistribution, it must be *coming into* us.

This suggests that the second wave is a genuine evolutionary movement. If we see evolution as a progressive intensification of consciousness-energy in living beings – as they become physically more complex they become capable of receiving and "transmitting" more consciousness – it begins to look as though a further step in that process of intensification is taking place now. An intensification of consciousness-energy may be taking place *in human beings*, a new influx of "spiritual energy" (in Teilhard de Chardin's terms) may be entering into us, which is offsetting the effects of the Ego Explosion and taking us beyond the pathologies of the fallen psyche. The human race may be literally becoming more alive.

This evolutionary movement may be happening now because it *has* to, because if it doesn't the human race will destroy itself and most of the other species on earth. In other words, it may be a kind of natural check, a move on the part of life itself – or nature – to protect its investments. As Eisler puts it, "the modern gylanic thrust [that is, the movement towards equality and partnership] may be seen as an adaptive process impelled by the survival impulse of our species."[25]

On the other hand, the change may simply be happening as a natural part of the unfolding evolution of life. The conventional Neo-Darwinist view of evolution sees it as a slow progressive process, in which random mutations very occasionally have beneficial effects and are "selected for" until they become a part of the collective gene pool of a species. But there are some serious problems with this view, especially when we think about how mutations might be responsible for new species, rather than just variations within a species. Biologists have estimated that mutations only occur at a rate of about one per several million cells in every generation. However, since only a miniscule number create beneficial traits which give a survival advantage, some scientists have doubted that, in the words of Fritjof Capra, "This frequency [is] sufficient to explain the evolution of the great diversity of life forms."[26] It's true that these changes have had millions of years to take place, but biologists have doubted that such a negative and blind process could have such staggeringly creative and positive consequences, no matter how much time it is given. One problem is that the mutations don't just have to be beneficial, they also have to be *cumulative*. As the French anti-Neo-Darwinist biologist Andree Tetry puts it, each mutation has to "adjust itself to the preceding mutation, and occur at precisely the right place and time."[27]

Imagine the thousands of separate genetic mutations which would be needed to produce birds' wings, for example. Each one would have to be exactly the right kind of mutation in terms of the previous one, to create the next step along the line of development to wings, and each time the odds against these occurring accidentally would increase massively. There also appear to be invisible boundaries between species which mutations cannot cross. They can create variation *within* a species, but to actually create *new* species may be asking too much of them.

It may be that evolution is not accidental, but propelled by a kind of force within living beings which makes them develop along predetermined lines. In other words, evolution might follow a pattern, a process of unfolding, like the development of a human being from conception through to birth and then adult maturity. After all, the development of an individual human being (ontogeny, to use the technical term) closely parallels the evolution of life: in both cases, the being(s) becomes progressively more complex physically (with more cells and more interactions between them) and, at the same time, more conscious.

This leads us to what might seem to be a problem with my argument. If I'm saying that an intensification of consciousness always goes together with an increase in complexity, where is the increase in complexity which goes with *this* intensification of consciousness? Am I saying that present-day human beings are more physically complex than the people of, say, 400 years ago, with bigger brains and more nerve cells?

That would be nonsense, of course. But if you look farther afield, at the human race as a collective rather than as individuals, it's clear that this intensification of consciousness *has* coincided with a new complexity. Over the past 250 years, the human race has become increasingly interlinked, like – in the analogy used by Peter Russell in his book *The Awakening Earth* – individual cells which are organising themselves into a "global brain." As Russell points out, in the last 50 years or so this process has moved – and is moving – at an amazing rate, as the world's population increases rapidly, as transport networks cut distances down, as the interactions between people increase, and as we become increasingly interlinked through improved technologies.[28] Similarly, Teilhard de Chardin believed that this increasing complexity was leading to the formation of the *noosphere*, when our whole species unites into a single interthinking group.[29]

Another possible problem with seeing these changes as an evolutionary development is the question of why they don't seem to be happening to *all* the human race. They have been mainly been occurring in Europe, or in areas which European peoples have migrated to, such as North and South America and Australia. To a lesser extent, and in more recent times, they have been occurring in East Asia, in countries like Japan and North Korea. But large parts of the world seem to have been untouched by them, particularly the Middle East and many parts of Africa. Surely, you would argue, an evolutionary development would affect the *whole* human race. After all, this was one of the arguments I used against seeing the Ego Explosion as an evolutionary advance: it only happened to peoples in central Asia and the Middle East.

Africa seems to be a special case. Throughout this book we've seen examples of peoples who were once peaceful but became war-like and socially oppressive as a result of cultural disruption. This is what happened to the Plains Indians, the Nguni (who became the Zulus), the !Kung and perhaps also the Jivaro and Yanamomo of South America. This isn't just a human phenomenon either –

it also happened to the chimpanzees at Gombe in Tanzania, who were peaceful and egalitarian until their feeding patterns (and later their actual habitat) were disrupted by human beings, when they became aggressive, hierarchical and ridden with social disorders (such as rape and cruelty to children). And modern-day African countries such as Liberia, Sierra Leone, Sudan and Nigeria – with their corrupt governments, frequent civil wars, high level of robbery and rape – can also be seen as tragic examples of the effects of cultural disruption. Centuries of Arabic and European influences – in particular, the colonial periods of the twentieth century – have disrupted African culture so massively that there seems to be almost nothing left of the matrist values which were once common throughout the continent.

The fact that these changes have been affecting European peoples (and peoples in east Asia to a lesser extent) but not Middle-Eastern cultures may be significant. The fallen psyche was never as strong in Europe, particularly western Europe. As we noted in Chapter 14, the effects of the Fall diminished over distance: the farther the distance from the Middle East and central Asia, the smaller the number of Saharasian peoples who migrated there, and the greater the lingering influence of the indigenous matrist cultures. As a result, if an evolutionary movement is taking place, it seems logical that people in Europe will be more susceptible to it, and that it will manifest itself there more rapidly. It will be easier for them to transcend the fallen psyche because it never had such a powerful hold on them to begin with.

But the Middle East was the epicentre of the Fall. The fallen psyche and the pathologies which go with it have always been stronger there. So we would expect the trans-Fall movement to meet with some resistance in that part of the world, and to proceed more slowly. It's important to note, however, that there are signs that change is taking place there as well, and in other parts of the world where the fallen psyche was always stronger than in Europe. In the Middle East, the status of women seems to be slowly increasing, for instance. Over the last five years Qatar and Bahrain have given women the right to vote and to stand for election, and the Kuwaiti parliament has recently passed a new law giving women the same political rights as men. Three times as many Arabic women are literate compared with 1970, and twice as many go to primary and secondary school.[30] There are still major problems, of course, but there is now an increasing debate about women's rights throughout the Arabic world, which is starting to bring changes. In India, there are signs that the caste system is beginning to weaken, and that women are gaining greater respect and equality. In China, a long overdue process of democratisation seems to be beginning, and the gulf between the oppressed workers and the aristocracy of party officials seems to be closing.

There is good reason to expect that this process will begin to pick up speed in these countries, just as it did in Europe and America in the second half of the eighteenth century, as evolution continues to infuse human beings with new consciousness-energy and as the spirit of empathy continues to spread.

17

A QUESTION OF TIME

WE ARE TURNING a full circle. Thousands of years after falling out of the Tao, we may be coming back into harmony with it, and returning to the Age of Perfect Virtue. After beginning in a state of "original participation" – in Owen Barfield's terms – and then losing our sense of connection to the cosmos, we are reaching "final participation."[1] Or, to put it another way, after 6,000 years of psychosis, we may finally be regaining our sanity.

In a sense, however, we aren't truly going back, but going forward to a wholly new state of being. Transcending ego-separation doesn't necessarily mean sacrificing the *positive* effects of the Fall. Although we've spent most of this book looking at the problems that the strong sense of ego has caused over the last 6,000 years, it's important to realise that this strong sense of ego isn't the problem *in itself.* The real problem is not the sharpness of our sense of ego but its *separateness,* and the fact that it's become too dominant within our psyche, and that its thought-chatter has become too wild and chaotic. As many spiritual teachers have pointed out, the ego doesn't have to be destroyed – in fact, this would be disastrous, since we need a sense of ego to function in the world. Instead it needs to be *tamed,* and its walls of separateness need to be melted away. It needs to become an integrated part of our psyche, performing an important function when it's required to, instead of monopolising our psychic energy and attention.

This is what happens in a trans-Fall – or spiritual – state of being. Our sense of ego is still there, but it's no longer as separate, no longer as powerful, and it no longer monopolises our consciousness-energy. And, most importantly, the heightened intellectual powers which the Ego Explosion gave us are still there – the "logical and syntactical brilliance"[2] which gave rise to the scientific and technological wonders of the modern world. Transcending the fallen psyche doesn't mean going back to the magical vision of the world of unfallen peoples, where every natural event has a supernatural cause and evil spirits and witches are constantly working to find ways of doing us harm. It means keeping our rational understanding of the way the world works, and our amazing capacity to invent and create. In this way, we might say, the trans-Fall psyche is a combination of the positive aspects of both the unfallen and the fallen psyches.

This is looking too far into the future, though. A more pressing issue is the question of whether there is actually *time* for us to reach a new age of sanity. Time is running out. It's true that the second wave is a powerful force in the world – especially compared with the first wave – but it still hasn't brought about the kind of sweeping changes that we need. The fallen psyche still holds sway, and is still pushing the human race towards self-destruction.

By far the biggest problem is our ecological devastation of the planet, and global warming in particular. Most scientists now agree that unless we take very prompt and very serious action against global warming – such as reducing our carbon emissions by 60 per cent – it will be too late. And even if this threat is averted, there are problems like species extinction, over-population and resource depletion, which are also potentially fatal to us. As we saw in Chapter 13, our environmental problems are a direct result of the fallen psyche, and can only be solved by transcending it. The planet Earth will always be under threat until all – or at least the majority – of human beings experience an empathic sense of respect towards nature and other species, a sense of the aliveness and sacredness of nature, and a sense of responsibility to the world as a whole. Averting this catastrophe will involve other trans-Fall characteristics too – a political shift to a less domineering and materialistic attitude, as governments realise that economic power or military domination and ever-increasing economic growth have to take second place (and might even have to be sacrificed) to environmental concerns; increased cooperation between nations and an end to international hostilities and oppression as we realise that this is the a crisis which can only be transcended by collective decisions and actions; and, on an individual level, a less selfish outlook which will make us willing to put up with a little inconvenience (such as more expensive cars and less air travel, compulsory recycling or having to use non-disposable nappies) for the collective well-being of our species.

Whether or not our species survives depends, therefore, on how rapidly the trans-Fall movement grows. And unfortunately the present rate of change seems to be too slow. The problems are so vast, and the fallen psyche is still too strong. We may be evolving, but we seem to be evolving too slowly. Biologists such as Steven Jay Gould have suggested that under the right circumstances evolutionary leaps can occur in as little as 1,000 years.[3] This is a tick of the clock in evolutionary terms, but if we apply it to the evolutionary leap that is taking place now – which has been clearly visible for around 300 years – it still means that, at the very least, we may have to wait several more centuries for a real transformation to occur. And when we look ahead at the ground we still have to cover this kind of timescale seems realistic. It seems sensible to think in terms of centuries rather than decades.

If this is true, the human race's future looks very bleak indeed, since it's clear that we don't have anything like that much time to play with. But this is where we come in. There's an important difference between human beings and other forms of life, which means that this evolutionary development could happen much faster than any previous one. In human beings the process of evolution has, in the biologist Julian Huxley's famous phrase "become conscious of itself."[4] For us evolution doesn't have to be just an unfolding natural process. If we're actually aware of the process of evolution it's possible for us, if we so desire, to consciously aid or direct the process. We've seen that one of the beliefs of Buddhism is that all beings are naturally evolving towards enlightenment but that it's possible to consciously speed up your own progress by following the Eightfold Path. In the same way, it's possible for us to add our own conscious efforts to the collective transformation which is already occurring naturally, and so speed up the rate of change.

We can do this by bringing the first wave and the second wave together. The mystics of the first wave discovered what we might call *self*-evolution. They made themselves more conscious and more alive, and attained a slightly premature glimpse of the next level of evolution. And by using the spiritual technologies they developed – and other more modern variants – we can also take evolution into our own hands. By consciously working on ourselves, by practising meditation and other first-wave methods of intensifying consciousness-energy, we can push the evolutionary process forward. We can melt away the walls of ego-separateness and reach a trans-Fall state of being ourselves, and in the process help our species as a whole to do the same.

This is possible because all human beings are psychically interconnected. In Chapter 5, I suggested that the fallen psyche was a kind of "psychic template" which became fixed and permanent. Patrist characteristics didn't have to be handed down from one generation to the next because at a certain point the fallen psyche became a part of "developmental blueprint" which all individuals follow from birth to adulthood. This may have worked through Rupert Sheldrake's theory of morphic resonance, which suggests that once a large enough number of a group or species show a particular trait or characteristic, it is naturally taken on by *all* members of the species, as an instinct or innate characteristic. From that point on all members of the species are born with the trait, or at least with the "programming" to develop it in later life.[5] And something similar may happen with the trans-Fall psyche. If we apply Sheldrake's theory – which has now been validated by a massive number of experiments – to our predicament, it suggests that if we make a conscious effort to move towards a trans-Fall psyche, it will become easier for other people to do the same, as the "morphic resonance" for the psyche builds up. All around the world, people will feel more naturally impelled to evolve as individuals, to follow the ancient paths of Buddhism, Vedanta, Yoga and other spiritual technologies, and to live more selflessly and compassionately – until, at a certain critical threshold, the trans-Fall psyche will become a part of our "species blueprint," will spread to every single member of the human race. Every new person will naturally develop the psyche as they grow up.

Spiritual paths and practices are beneficial enough in themselves. They are psychotherapy for the fallen psyche. Meditation melts away the walls of ego-separation, quietens our chaotic thought-chatter, and redistributes our consciousness-energy so that we can perceive beauty and Spirit in the world. None of us *have to* endure the fundamental isolation and psychological discord of the fallen psyche. We all have the opportunity to heal ourselves, to transform the psyche which we're born with. But it's no longer just an individual matter, as it was for people in the first wave. Now spiritual practice is an evolutionary imperative. Every time you sit down to meditate, every time you do yoga or tai chi, or any other activity which has the effect of intensifying your consciousness-energy, you are – in however small a way – working on behalf our species as a whole, adding a little more momentum to the evolutionary movement which may save us.

But spiritual practice isn't all that's needed, of course. Change can also come from how we choose to live our lives. We can also 'blunt' the separateness of the ego by making sure that we devote at least part of our lives to *service*. Rather than spending all our time trying to follow our own desires and interests, we should try to serve other people (and other beings and even the world itself), helping them to realise their potential and to reduce their suffering. Service and compassion take us beyond our own thoughts and desires, create a bond with others, and so help us to become less egocentric.

We need to make a conscious effort to live lightly too, to limit our consumption of material goods and the damage we do to the environment. And we need to make a conscious effort to *remember* – to remember that that we are a part of the universe, that the whole world is the manifestation of spirit-force (including us), to remember that the purpose of life isn't to 'get on' in the world or to have as much fun as we can, but to realise our true spiritual potential and contribute as much as we can to the well-being of the world.

And we need social change too, of course – organisations and popular movements which fight against the worst expressions of the fallen psyche, against the corporations which cause ecological destruction, the governments with skewed priorities which ignore the dangers we're facing, and any institution which promotes the old fallen values of warfare, inequality, hostility to nature and sexual repression. Environmental groups, human rights groups, women's rights and animal rights groups and many others – they are all at the spearhead of the trans-Fall movement, and need as much support as we can give them.

There are two scenarios, two different paths we can choose to take. The first future is no future – or, at least, only a very short term one. The details are difficult to predict exactly, but perhaps if global warming isn't halted, nations will struggle against one another to protect and procure dwindling food, water and energy supplies. There will be more climatic disasters, more devastation from storms and floods, and more arid lands and failing crops. The world will be filled with a chaos of war and social turmoil and the human race will spiral inevitably towards self-destruction. Countries may develop nuclear arsenals to protect their interests, and the spectre of nuclear catastrophe which haunted the world during the 1980s could finally occur a few decades later. In this way the last 6,000 years of human insanity will reach their logical conclusion.

The second scenario is the victory of the trans-Fall psyche. This leads to a bright future which rekindles the Golden Age of our past. In this future there will be no (or at least a much lower level of) war, male domination and social inequality, no shame of sex or the body, and no domination of other species and the natural world. As we move beyond the separateness of the fallen psyche, all of this will naturally fade away, like the symptoms of a disease which has been cured. A shared sense of being will unite all human beings, an open network of empathy and identity which will end cruelty and oppression. Exploitation and competition will be replaced with respect and cooperation. A new spirit of harmony will fill the world.

Once a disease is cured there is no longer any need for medicine. When we transcend ego-separateness we no longer have any need for consolations and alternative sources of happiness. Marx said that religion would be unnecessary once the Communist state was founded, but in the trans-Fall era religion is just one of the things that will no longer be necessary. Just as it will no longer be necessary for us to believe that a higher being is watching over us and organising the events of our lives (and to believe that an eternal paradise is waiting for us when we die), we will no longer need to spend our lives chasing after wealth and status, or obsessively use shopping, fast cars, drinking and other kinds of hedonism to press our instinctive "pleasure buttons." We will no longer have to work, or watch endless television, or invent unnecessary tasks, to divert our attention from the disharmony inside our minds, or take drugs to numb ourselves to our discontent. None of this will be necessary because our psychological discord will no longer be there. With our ego-separateness transcended, we will no longer feel a fundamental sense of isolation and aloneness. Instead, there will be a new sense of inner wholeness and contentment – exactly the same inner well-being which the mystics of the first wave have described to us time and again over the centuries.

We will also have a new relationship to the cosmos. The world will no longer be a dreary, unreal place which is "out there," and whose alien-ness and apparent indifference makes us feel threatened. Instead, we'll look at the world with fresh, non-automatic perception (caused by a higher level of consciousness-energy) and see it as a radiant, beautiful, benevolent and meaningful place. We will see the presence of spirit-force in everything, in all things and in the spaces between things, and be aware of it as the source of all things, the ultimate reality of the universe. We will be aware that spirit-force is the essence of our own beings as well, and feel a sense of communion with the world, a sense of belonging and participating in it rather than being outside it looking in.

We will no longer be separate, and so we will no longer be afraid – afraid of death, afraid of the world, afraid of God, afraid of our own selves, afraid of other people. The disharmony of the human psyche will be healed, and the insanity which it gave rise to will fade away.

The choice is yours.

NOTES

1. What's Wrong with Human Beings?

1   In Wilson, 1985, p.4.
2   Wrangham and Peterson, 1996.
3   Power, 1991.
4   Sussman, 1997; Boesch &
    Boesch-Achermann, 2000;
    Morgan & Sanz, 2003.
5   Fromm, 1974, p.103.
6   van der Dennen, 1995, p.54.
7   Weisfeld, G., 1991,
8   Fromm, 1974.
9   van der Dennen, 1995, p.595.
10 Ferguson, 2000, p.160.
11 Ehrenreich, 1996.
12 Lenski & Nolan, 1995.
13 Goldberg, 1973.
14 Eisler, 1987; Gimbutas, 1991;
    DeMeo, 1998; Griffith, 2001.
15 Schopenhauer, 1930, p.65.
16 DeMeo, 1998.
17 Stacey, 1983, p.40.
18 DeMeo, 1998.
19 Lenksi, 1995.
20 Eisler, 1987; Gimbutas, 1991;
    DeMeo, 1998; Griffith, 2001.
21 Crawford, 1991, p.24.
22 Lenski, 1995.
23 ibid.
24 ibid.
25 ibid.
26 ibid.
27 Whitman, 1980, p.73.
28 Service, 1978, p.83.
29 Turnbull, 1993, p.29.
30 Leidloff, 1989, p.24.
31 Pascal, 1966, p.67.
32 Argyle, 1989; Raphael, 1984.
33 Argyle, 1989; Atchley, 1985.
34 Csikszentmihalyi, 1992.
35 ibid.
36 In Wright, 1992, p.304.
37 Dr. Johnson, 1905, p.206.
38 The Dhammapada, p.9, verse 42.
39 Pascal, 1966, p.48.

2. The Pre-Fall Era

1   Lee and DeVore, 1968.
2   Turnbull, 1972.
3   Lenski, 1995; Lee and DeVore, 1968.
4   Sahlins, 1972, p.13.
5   Ryan, 2003, p.55.
6   Lawlor, 1991.
7   Rudgley, 2000, p.36.
8   Diamond, 1992.
9   Ryan, 2003.
10 Rudgley, 2000.
11 DeMeo, 2002.
12 Ferguson, 2000, p.159. Another
    scholar who believes there is early
    evidence of warfare is the English
    archaeologist Nick Thorpe (e.g.,
    1999, 2000). He believes there is
    evidence of warfare as far back as
    the Mesolithic (ninth millennum
    BCE). He suggests three different
    types of evidence that show signs of
    conflict: weapons, depictions of
    fighting, and skeletal remains
    However, as he admits himself, no
    matter how many daggers and axes
    we find, we can't be sure that these
    were actually used as weapons,
    rather than just as tools or for
    hunting. He points to
    Levantine Spanish rock art as
    evidence of conflict from the
    Mesolithic (or Neolithic, since he
    suggests that the traditional dating
    may be erroneous), but again
    undermines his own argument by
    admitting that "there are many who
    question the straightforward
    approach to interpreting rock art"
    (Thorpe, 1999).
        The most reliable pieces of
    evidence, he suggests, are skeletal
    remains, particularly those showing
    wounds from projectiles. He cites
    evidence of "a couple of Upper

Palaeolithic bodies with flint points lodged in the bones, both from Italy," (ibid.) and other scattered individual cases from Sweden, Zealand, Brittany and Romania. He also cites evidence of cranial injuries in Denmark and California. However, the fact that these cases are so scattered makes it dubious that they are evidence of warfare. Surely if they were the result of warfare, they would occur in groups. As individual cases, it makes more sense to see them as the result of accidents – hunting accidents in particular. And even if they were the result of violence, they would only suggest a small level of inter-individual violence, rather than actual warfare. Again, Thorpe admits this possibility by stating that "we need to stress the importance of care in interpretation" (ibid.). He points out that there are cases of "parry fractures" in Mesolithic Europe, which have been interpreted as the result of fending off blows to the head or upper body. But recent research has shown that "there are actually a large number of accidents which can result in parry fractures" (ibid.).

The only clear evidence of anything resembling warfare which Thorpe puts forward is from the mid to late Neolithic. There is a cave at Ofnet in Bavaria with two pits containing the skulls and vertebrae of 38 people, all of whom had been wounded before death. At Dyrholmen in Denmark, the bones of 9 people were discovered, with signs of scalping. At Talheim in Germany, there is a mass grave from 5000 BCE, with 34 people killed by blows to the head.

In other words, the evidence for warfare before the Neolithic is – apart from the two cases I mentioned in the main text – unconvincing. And even in the Neolithic there are very few clear instances. But perhaps in the end it doesn't matter whether we question the conclusions of archaeologists like Keeley and Thorpe: even if we accept their dubious claims, we would still have a picture of *extremely limited* warfare until around 4000 BCE, and then a sudden and dramatic intensification of it.

13 Chapman, 1999; Dolkhanov, 1999; Vencl, 1999.
14 Ferguson, 1997, p.333.
15 Keck, 2000, p.xxi.
16 In Heinberg, 1989, p.169.
17 Gabriel, 1990, p.21.
18 Lawlor, 1991, p.9.
19 Lenski, 1978, p.137.
20 Wrangham and Peterson, 1996.
21 Ferguson, 2003.
22 Lenksi, 1978, p.422.
23 Service, 1978, p.27.
24 Sumner, 1964, p.205.
25 Malinowski, 1964, p.251.
26 Service, 1978; Sumner, 1964; Malinowski, 1978.
27 Divale, 1973.
28 ibid., p.xxi.
29 Burch & Ellanna, 1994, p.61.
30 Power, 1991, p.44.
31 Haas, 1999, p.14.
32 Knauft, 1991, p.391.
33 Jaimes Guerrero, 2000, p.37.
34 Barnard and Woodburn, 1988.
35 Woodburn, 1982, p.432.
36 Lenski, 1978.
37 Barnard and Woodburn, 1988, p.16.
38 Woodburn, 1981/1998.
39 Power, 1991, p.47.
40 Lenski, 1978, p.125.
41 Briggs, 1970, p.42.
42 Boehm, 1999.
43 ibid., p.69.
44 DeMeo, 1998.
45 Ryan, 2003, p.78.

46 Diamond, 1992.
47 Diamond, 1987, p.64.
48 In Lawlor, 1991, p.55.
49 Eisler, 1995, p.62.
50 Lenski, 1978; Gimbutas, 1991.
51 Lenski & Nolan, 1995, p.151.
52 Boehm, 1999, p.38.
53 Gimbutas, 1991; Eisler, 1987;
   Mellaart, 1975.
54 ibid.
55 Gimbutas, 1982, 1991.
56 ibid., 1980, p.17.
57 In Rudgley, 1998, p.23,
58 Platon, 1966.
59 Eisler, 1987, p.32.
60 Griffith, 2001, p.167.
61 Gimbutas, 1982, p.24.
62 DeMeo, 1998, p.225.
63 Davidson, 1996, p.51.
64 In Lenski & Nolan, 1995, p.146.
65 DeMeo, 1998, p.347.
66 Griffith, 2001.
67 ibid., p.168.
68 Rudgley, 1998.
69 In Rudgley, 1998, p.32.
70 In Eisler, 1987, p.32.
71 ibid.
72 Eisler, 1987, p.18.
73 Taylor, 1996; Rudgley, 1998.
74 Hawkes, 1968, p.156.
75 Eisler, 1987, p.39.
76 DeMeo, 1998, p.4.
77 ibid.
78 ibid., p.8.

3. The Fall

1 Eisler, 1987, p.43.
2 DeMeo, 2002, p.21.
3 ibid.
4 DeMeo, 1998, p.8.
5 DeMeo, 2000, p.10.
6 Griffith, 2001, p.18.
7 DeMeo, 1998; Griffith, 2001.
8 In Mallory, 1989, p.266.
9 ibid., p.238.
10 Gimbutas, 1973, pp.202-3.
11 Eisler, 1987, p.50.
12 Eisler, 1995, p.90.
13 DeMeo, 1998, p.231.
14 Mallory, 1989.
15 Gimbutas, 1977, p.281.
16 Stern, 1969, p.230.
17 DeMeo, 1998, p.286.
18 Gimbutas, 1991, p.352.
19 Eisler, 1987, p.58.
20 Lenski, 1978.
21 ibid., p.147.
22 Lenksi's use of the term "advanced
   horticultural" for these societies is
   also a little problematic, since it
   suggests a basic sameness with
   "simple horticultural" societies. In
   reality, the fact that they both lived
   by horticulture is just an incidental
   similarity amongst a mass of giant
   differences. This is suggested by
   Lenski's own statistics for
   contemporary simple and advanced
   horticultural peoples. These
   indicate the same momentous
   transition as the archaeological
   record, with a massive increase in
   warfare, class stratification,
   inequality and slavery. For example,
   warfare is perpetual in 34% of
   advanced horticultural societies,
   compared with just 5% of simple.
   There is class stratification in 54%
   of advanced horticultural societies,
   compared with 17% of simple.
   Even this doesn't tell the whole
   story, however, since class
   stratification is just one aspect of
   inequality, and it's possible to
   have social classes *with* equality.
   This may well have been the case
   with these 17% of simple
   horticultural societies. As Lenski
   notes, "The class systems of
   [advanced horticultural societies]
   are generally more complex, involve
   greater degrees of inequality and are
   more often hereditary" (1978, p.170).
23 Childe, 1964, p.77.
24 Baring & Cashford, 1991, p.150.
25 Gimbutas, 1982, p.17.
26 Griffith, 2001, p.104.

27 DeMeo, 1998, p.231.
28 Baring & Cashford, 1991; Crawford, 1991.
29 Baring & Cashford, 1991.
30 DeMeo, 1998.
31 DeMeo, 2000, p.12.
32 Kramer, 1969, p.16.
33 Crawford, 1991.
34 Oates, 1986, p.68.
35 ibid., pp.30-31.
36 In Wilber, 1981, p.165.
37 Eisler, 1987.
38 In Eisler, 1987, p.64.
39 Griffith, 2001.
40 DeMeo, 1998, p.231.
41 DeMeo, 1998.
42 ibid.
43 Rice, 1990.
44 DeMeo, 1998.
45 ibid, p.233.
46 Eisler, 1987, p.54.
47 Bewley, 1994.
48 DeMeo, 1998.
49 Ibid., p.348.
50 ibid., p.350.
51 Baring & Cashford, 1991; Eisler, 1987.
52 Hawkes, 1973, p.xxv.
53 Stone, 1976.
54 Eisler, 1995, p.116.
55 Baring & Cashford, 1991, p.162.
56 In Baring & Cashford, 1991, p.289.
57 ibid., p.286.
58 Griffith, 2001.
59 DeMeo, 1998.
60 Griffith, 2001.
61 ibid.
62 ibid.
63 Taylor, 1953.

4. Unfallen Peoples

1 DeMeo, 2002.
2 Lawlor, 1991, p.247.
3 ibid., p.251.
4 Cowan, 1992.
5 Lawlor, 1991, p.202.
6 Mearns, 1994, p.279.
7 Service, 1978, p.134.
8 ibid., p.133.
9 The anthropologist W.W. Newcomb (1950) suggested three main reasons for the Plains Indians' high level of warfare. First, Indian tribes were forced to flee their homelands when European invaders arrived. They inevitably encroached on the territory of other tribes, and this caused conflict.

    Secondly, now that the Indians had lost their livelihoods, they began to depend on the horse for survival. This was partly because the bison they hunted were fewer in number and farther away. As a result, there was intense "horse competition" between the tribes.

    Thirdly, there was the influence of the European colonists. European weapons (which were traded with Europeans for furs and hides) made their warfare much more violent. The colonists – especially traders – also consciously exploited the Indians' desperation by pitting tribes against one another, as well as against colonial powers.
10 Josephy, 1975, p.251
11 Service, 1978, p.326.
12 DeMeo, 1998.
13 ibid, p.378.
14 DeMeo, 1998.
15 Xu, 1996.
16 Service, 1978, p.208.
17 Josephy, 1975, p.268.
18 Wrangham & Peterson, 1996.
19 Ferguson, 2003.
20 Mann, 2002; "The Secret of El Dorado," 2002.
21 Wright, 1992; Josephy, 1975.
22 Wright, 1992, p.69.
23 DeMeo, 1998, p.375.
24 Josephy, 1975, p.37.
25 Service, 1978, p.42.
26 In Fromm, 1974, p.151.
27 Josephy, 1975.

28 ibid., p.166.
29 In Wright, 1992, p.74.
30 Boehm, 1999.
31 ibid.
32 Taylor, 1991, p.227.
33 Briggs, 1970, p.42.
34 Jaimes Guerrero, 2000; Wright, 1992.
35 Wright, 1992.
36 Jaimes Guerrero, 2000.
37 Ryan, 2003.
38 In Wright, 1992, p.276.
39 Service, 1978, p.41.
40 Service, 1978.
41 Lamphear & Falola, 1995, p.92.
42 DeMeo, 1998.
43 In DeMeo, 1998, p.243.
44 ibid., p.243.
45 Service, 1978, p.353.
46 DeMeo, 1998, p.243.
47 Keegan, 1993.
48 Lamphear & Falola, 1995.
49 ibid., p.94.
50 ibid.
51 Service, 1978, p.360.
52 McCall, 1995, p.183.
53 Magesa, 1997, p.61.
54 ibid., p.62.
55 Gellar, 1995, p.139.
56 Lamphear & Falola, 1995, p.95.
57 Evans-Pritchard, 1967.
58 Service, 1978, p.170.
59 Evans-Pritchard, 1967, p.2.
60 Turnbull, 1993, p.7.
61 McCreedy, 1994, p.17.
62 Turnbull, 1993, p.140.
63 McCreedy, 1994, p.19.
64 ibid.
65 Ember & Ember, 1981.
66 Boehm, 1999; Barnard & Woodburn, 1988.
67 Silberbauer, 1994, p.130.
68 Service, 1978.
69 Diamond, 1997.
70 DeMeo, 1998.
71 Cassirer, 1970, p.96.
72 Service, 1978.
73 In Wade & Tavris, 1994, p.124.
74 Malinowski, 1932, p.25.
75 ibid., p.15.
76 ibid., p.44.
77 In Sumner, 1911/1964, p.205.
78 ibid., p.207.
79 ibid.
80 Service, 1978, p.64.
81 ibid., p.123.
82 Sorin, 1992.
83 Elwin, 1968.
84 Sumner, 1911/1964, p.207.
85 Reddy, 1994.
86 DeMeo, 2002.
87 Heinberg, 1989; Hildebrand, 1988; Eliade, 1967.
88 Cassirer, 1970; Levy-Bruhl, 1965; Berman, 2000; Evans-Pritchard, 1967.
89 Heinberg, 1989, p.37.
90 DeMeo, 1998, p.168.
91 In Eliade, 1967, p.13.
92 Sindima, 1990, p.144.
93 Lawlor, 1991, p.166.
94 Hume, 2000, p.127.
95 Scott, 1997, p.40.
96 Hall, 1984, pp.132-33.
97 Wright, 1992; Josephy, 1975.
98 Lawlor, 1991.
99 Keim, 1995.
100 Reddy, 1994.
101 ibid.
102 Hallett & Relle, 1973.
103 Elwin, 1968.

5. The Ego Explosion

1 Heinberg, 1989, pp.43-44.
2 The fact that the Iranian story refers to snow and ice might seem strange, but it's important to remember that the drying up of Saharasia wasn't caused by an increase in temperature, but by a decrease in moisture due to the eventual melting away of the glaciers (whose gradual melting had made the area fertile in the first place). In some areas the dessication of Saharasia may have occurred in a period of falling temperatures. For example, the archaeologist J. P. Mallory (1989)

locates the homeland of the Indo-Europeans as the Pontic-Caspian area of southern Russia. Nowadays the area is a semi-desert with harsh winters and between 40 to 80 days of snowfall per year. Mallory notes that the area was probably both colder and drier in the past, but that before 4000 BCE conditions were milder.

3   In Heinberg, 1989, p.47.
4   ibid., pp.50-51.
5   In Cross, 1994, p.43.
6   In Heinberg, 1989, p.95.
7   ibid, p.51. The biblical myth of the Fall clearly refers to a transition from a hunter-gatherer to an agricultural way of life as well. In the beginning Adam and Eve lived off the fruit of the trees in the Garden of Eden, but after Eve ate from the tree of knowledge God punished them by making them farm the soil for food. He tells Adam, "You will have to work hard and sweat to make the soil produce anything."
8   ibid., p.48.
9   Genesis 3.
10 In Heinberg, 1989, p.68.
11 ibid., p.69.
12 ibid., p.95.
13 In Lawrence, 1990.
14 Lawrence, 1971, p.63.
15 ibid., p.84.
16 Werner, 1957, p.152.
17 Levy-Bruhl, 1965, p.127.
18 ibid., p.68.
19 Ibid., p.121.
20 Silberbauer, 1994, p.131.
21 Myers, 1997, p.54.
22 Geertz, 1973.
23 Gardiner et al., 1998, p.113.
24 Atwood, 1989.
25 Markus & Kitayama, 1991.
26 Wright, 1992, p.304.
27 Josephy, 1975, p.37.
28 In Wright, 1992, p.363.
29 Atwood, 1989, p.103.

30 Hall, 1984.
31 Turnbull, 1993, p.7.
32 In Keck, 2000, p.29.
33 Rudgley, 1998, p.113.
34 Lawlor, 1991, p.247.
35 Wilber, 1980, p.7.
36 Heinberg, 1995.
37 In Keck, 2000, pp.47-48.
38 Baring & Cashford, 1991, p.154.
39 ibid., p.154.
40 ibid.
41 In Wilber, 1981, p.305.
42 Whyte, 1950.
43 Hamlet, Act 3, Sc.1.
44 Barfield, 1957, p.43.
45 In Wilber, 1981, p.28.
46 Jaynes, 1976, p.247. Other philosophers who have put forward similar views are Jean Gebser and Ernst Cassirer. Cassirer (1954-7) believed that early human beings lived in a state of "cosmic continuity," in which there was no sharp distinction between the individual and the environment. But later human beings "wrestled [their] subjectivity out of the world…by polarising that world gradually into a duality. And this is the duality of the subjective-objective, or outer-inner."
47 Wilber, 1981, p.303.
48 Becker, 1973, p.262.
49 In Wilber, 1981, p.28.
50 DeMeo, 1998. According to DeMeo, the actual desert atmosphere itself, with its humidity, heat and dust, may have affected the way parents treated children too. He cites scientific studies showing that when air particles (or ions) are negatively charged (as they are in lush vegetation or waterfalls) this has an invigorating and stimulating effect, making human beings feel more alive and alert. In desert regions, however, air particles are positively charged, which has the opposite effect, and creates

feelings of irritability, restlessness, and malaise.

51 Sheldrake, 1991.

52 In terms of the conventional Neo Darwinist view of evolution, this is impossible, of course, since one of its main principles is that characteristics which people develop in their own lifetime can't be passed down to their children (that is, the inheritance of acquired characteristics). The only possible Neo-Darwinist explanation of the Ego Explosion would be that mutations created a few individuals with a new sharpened sense of ego. Social conditions and the environment would have favoured them, their children would have survived, and so their genes would become more and more dominant. But this would obviously be a very a long process, whereas we know that the Ego Explosion happened quite suddenly. However, there is a growing consensus that the Neo-Darwinist view is too narrow and reductive to fully account for evolution, and that other – possibly as yet unknown – factors must be involved in it. See, for example, Sheldrake, 1991; Capra, 1997; Harman & Sahtouris, 1998; Rose & Rose, 2000.

53 DeMeo, 2002, p.36.

54 ibid.

6. The New Psyche

1 Wilber, 1981, p.303.
2 Baring & Cashford, 1991, p.150.
3 Lenksi & Nolan, 1995, p.181.
4 Ember & Ember, 1981.
5 Wright & Johnson, 1975.
6 Wilson, 1985, p.148.
7 Lancaster, 1991, p.84.
8 Platon, 1966, p.148.
9 DeMeo, 1998, p.225.
10 Eisler, 1987, p.54.
11 DeMeo, 1998, p.227.

12 Wilson, 1985.
13 ibid., p.144.
14 Levy-Bruhl, 1965.
15 Mbuta, 1975, p.76.
16 Harris, 1977, 1980.
17 Magesa, 1997, p.76.
18 The problem is that modern science has gone too far in this direction, and reduced the world to a purely physical, one-dimensional plane. The basic assumption of modern science is that everything has a rational physical explanation and there are no phenomena or forces apart from those which we can perceive or detect. Any phenomena or forces which are potentially unexplainable (such as telepathy, near death experiences or mystical experiences) are illusions or else can be explained away in physicalist terms. This gives scientists a satisfying sense of being "in control" of the world, and a sense of power through possessing "complete" knowledge.
19 In Wright, 1992, p.311.
20 Fromm, 1957/1995, p.311.
21 In Keck, 2000, pp.50-51.
22 Joyce, 1992, p.742.
23 Csikszentmihalyi, 1992.
24 Lawrence, 1971, p.72.
25 Diamond, 1974, p.170.
26 Lawrence, 1979, p.42.
27 Taylor, S., 2003.
28 Wilson, 1985, 2004.
29 Norman & Shallice, 1980.
30 In Versluis, 1994, p.34.
31 Pascal, 1966, p.47.
32 Service, 1978.
33 In Levy-Bruhl, 1965, p.314.
34 ibid., p.313.
35 Evans-Pritchard, 1967, p.154.
36 White, 1969, p.88.
37 Lawlor, 1991.
38 Yalom, 1980, p.103.
39 Kasser, 2002; Kasser & Kanner, 2004; Argyle, 1987.
40 In Bartlett, 1968, p.1068.

7. Escaping from Psychological Discord
1   In Becker, 1973, p.186.
2   Gross, 1996.
3   Rudgley, 1993.
4   Barnard & Woodburn, 1988.
5   ibid.
6   Scott, 1997, p.37.
7   Lawlor, 1991.
8   ibid., p.61.
9   Josephy, 1975, p.165.
10 Lee & DeVore, 1968, pp.xx-xxi.
11 In Heinberg, 1995, p.100.
12 ibid., p.76.
13 In Wright, 1992, p.361.
14 Josephy, 1975.
15 Kasser, 2002, p.29.
16 ibid.
17 Brickman et al., 1978.
18 Kasser, 2002.
19 Argyle, 1987, p.97.
20 Lawlor, 1991, p.173.
21 Marshall, 1976.
22 Liedloff, 1989, p.118.
23 Eisler, 1987, p.36.
24 Lawlor, 1991.
25 ibid.
26 Lawrence, 1971, p.98.
27 Worthington, 2004.
28 Soloman et al., 2004.
29 Wilber, 1980.

8. The Origins of Social Chaos 1 – War
1   Boyer, 2002.
2   Shields & Shields, 1983; Thornhill & Thornhill, 1983.
3   Wilber, 1996, p.6.
4   Archer, 1991.
5   Kroeber & Fontana, 1986.
6   In Ferguson, 2000, p.160.
7   ibid.
8   Barnard & Woodburn, 1988.
9   Anderson, 1968.
10 Burch & Ellanna, 1994, p.61.
11 Haas, 1999, p.14.
12 van der Dennen, 2001, p.2.
13 Lenski, 1978.
14 Wilber, 1981, p.161.
15 ibid.
16 Rostow, 1960, pp.110-11.
17 Baron-Cohen, 2003, p.23.
18 Forman, 1998; Chalmers, 1996; McTaggart, 2000.
19 Deikman, 20001, pp.87-89.
20 Baron-Cohen, 2003, p.37.
21 In Wilber, 1995, p.610.
22 James, 1899/1995, pp.315-6.
23 Pascal, 1966, p.67.
24 In Bullock, 1998, p.47.
25 ibid.
26 Partridge, 1919, p.23.
27 ibid., p.15.
28 DeMeo, 1998.
29 Prescott, 1975, p.15.
30 ibid., p.12.
31 McCarthy, 1991, p.116.
32 Ehrenreich, 1996.
33 McCarthy, 1991, p.116.
34 ibid.
35 Malinowski, 1932; Elwin, 1968; Turnbull, 1993.
36 Boehm, 1999.
37 In Heinberg, 1989, pp.68-69.
38 In Wilson, 1985, p.169.
39 Griffith, 2001, p.116.
40 Recent research has suggested that illiteracy may be the biggest root cause of crime of all. For example, a study of Scottish prisoners showed that 48% of them had dyslexic tendencies. ("Undiagnosed Dyslexics..." *TES*, 2000) People with undiagnosed dyslexia are liable to have behavioural problems at school, low self-esteem, and to become ostracised from mainstream society, possibly leading to criminal behaviour (Osmond, 1993).
41 Daly & Wilson, 1983, p.38.
42 Archer, 1991.
43 ibid., p.133.
44 Baron-Cohen, 2003.
45 Wilson, 1985, p.666.

9. The Origins of Social Chaos 2 – Patriarchy
1   Goldberg, 1973.
2   Wrangham & Peterson, 1996, p.233.

3   Wilber, 1996, p.3.
4   Baron-Cohen, 2003.
5   Gray, 1992.
6   Baron-Cohen, 2003.
7   Wareing, 1999.
8   Baron-Cohen, 2003, p.52.
9   ibid.
10 ibid., p.1.
11 ibid.
12 Macoby, 1990.
13 Rhode, 1990.
14 Baron-Cohen, 2003.
15 Daly & Wilson, 1983; Archer, 1991; Baron-Cohen, 2003.
16 In Baron-Cohen, 2003, p.38.
17 Wilber, 1995, 1996.
18 Griffith, 2001, p.24.
19 Wilber, 1995.
20 This is one of the problems with democracy as we know it in the modern world. The people who go into politics are those (most often men) with the strongest drive to gain power and status. And these are precisely the people who should *not* be given any power. As this book has hopefully made clear, the desire for power goes hand in hand with aggression, selfishness, and a lack of empathy. This is why political leaders – such as George Bush and Tony Blair – are usually so ready to go to war, and usually have no sense of environmental responsibility. As happens in hunter-gatherer bands, people who want to have power and status should be sanctioned against, and barred from getting any. People shouldn't choose to be politicians; they should be chosen.
21 Baring & Cashford, 1991, p.513.
22 Warner, 1976.
23 ibid.

10. The Origins of Social Chaos 3 – Inequality and Child Oppression

1   Pinker, 1997, p.504.
2   Wilson, 1995, p.190.
3   Cashdan, 1980.
4   Gluckman, 1965.
5   Ember & Ember, 1981; Wilber, 1981.
6   Boehm, 1999, p.37.
7   Service, 1978.
8   Boehm, 1999, p.64.
9   ibid., p.181.
10 ibid., p.83.
11 Service, 1978, p.81.
12 ibid., p.191
13 DeMeo, 1998, p.59.
14 Briggs, 1970, pp.4-5.
15 Kleinfeld, 1994, p.153.
16 Liedloff, 1989, p.97.
17 Hewlett, 1991.
18 Malinowski, 1932, p.17.
19 Briggs, 1970, p.42.
20 DeMause, 1974, p.40.
21 DeMeo, 1998.
22 ibid., p.340.
23 DeMause, 1974; DeMeo, 1998.
24 Liedloff, 1989, p.24.
25 Service, 1978, p.102.
26 ibid., p.212.
27 Liedloff, 1989.
28 Liedloff suggests that in-arms deprivation may be the root cause of a range of psychological disorders. It means that most of us carry around a basic sense of lack, which we might try to fill with materialism, drugs, or chasing after success and status. In other words, she suggests that a sense of lack is *produced*, whereas in this book I'm suggesting that it's a more fundamental part of our psyche. My own view is that the innate sense of lack caused by our strong sense of ego may be intensified by in-arms deprivation. Even if our children were brought up in exactly the same way as primal peoples, there would still be a certain sense of lack inside us, although not as strong.
29 Piaget & Inhelder, 1956.

11. The Origins of God

1   Eliade, 1967, p.6.
2   Evans-Pritchard, 1971.
3   Boyer, 2001, p.160.
4   Eliade, 1967.
5   Lenksi, 1978.
6   Evans-Pritchard, 1967. p.6.
7   Levy-Bruhl, 1965.
8   ibid., p.17.
9   Idowu, 1975, p.174.
10 ibid.
11 Hamilton, 1995.
12 Freud, 1946.
13 Narada, 1997.
14 Evans-Pritchard, 1967, p.113.
15 Lawrence, 1950, p.197.
16 Eisler, 1987; Gimbutas, 1982, 1991.
17 Berman, 2000, p.130.
18 Taylor, 1996, p.159.
19 DeMeo, 1998, p.167.
20 Eisler, 1995, p.57.
21 Baring & Cashford, 1991, p.xi.
22 Hamilton, 1995.
23 Frazer, 1959.
24 Cassirer, 1970, p.97.
25 ibid., p.91.
26 Baring & Cashford, 1991, 152.
27 ibid., p.xii.
28 Wilber, 1981.
29 Novak, 1996, p.275.
30 Lawrence, 1971, p.88.
31 Wright, 1992, p.101.
32 Service, 1978, p.64.
33 In Heinberg, 1989, p.12.
34 Marx, 1959.
35 In Hamilton, 1995, p.58.
36 Freud, 1946.

12. Separation from the Body

1   Genesis 3.
2   Lawlor, 1991.
3   ibid., p.173.
4   Malinowski, 1932, p.47.
5   Ryan, 2003.
6   Service, 1978, p.167.
7   Malinowski, 1932; Elwin, 1968.
8   Elwin, 1968.
9   Malinowski, 1932.

10 Ryan, 2003, p.128.
11 Bolton, 1973; Ryan, 2003.
12 Holmberg, 1950.
13 Lawlor, 1991.
14 Ryan, 2003, p.100.
15 ibid., p.101.
16 Cowan, 1992, pp.99-100.
17 Marshall, 1971.
18 Goodenough, 1973.
19 Ryan, 2003, p.98.
20 Wade & Tavris, 1994.
21 Herdt, 1984.
22 Evans-Pritchard, 1971.
23 Patron, 1995.
24 Hawkes, 1968, p.136.
25 ibid.
26 Rudgley, 1998, p.196.
27 Rudgley, 1998.
28 ibid.
29 Service, 1978.
30 ibid.
31 Turnbull, 1993, p.169.
32 ibid.
33 Lawlor, 1991, p.206.
34 In Wilber, 1981, p.61.
35 Lawrence, 1968, p.490.
36 Griffith, 2001, p.32.
37 ibid.
38 DeMeo, 1998.
39 Accad, 1978, p.20.
40 James, 1899/1985.
41 DeMeo, 1998.
42 In DeMeo, 1998, p.241.
43 Walker, 1983, p.911.
44 Accad, 1978, p.20.
45 Griffith, 2001; DeMeo, 1998.
46 Khanna, 2002, p.58.
47 ibid., p.49.
48 Demeo, 1998, p.302.
49 ibid.
50 Eisler, 1995, p.207.
51 DeMeo, 1998.
52 ibid.

13. The Origins of Time

1   Schopenhauer, 1930, p.56.
2   Lawlor, 1991, p.37.
3   In Service, 1978, p.173.
4   In Hall, 1984, p.86.

5   ibid.
6   ibid., p.37.
7   ibid., p.29.
8   ibid.
9   Bloch, 1977, p.288.
10 Service, 1978, pp.257-58.
11 Wilber 1981, p.66.
12 Dressler, 1999.
13 Neumann, 1973, p.281.
14 Grant, 1980.
15 Jaynes, 1976.
16 Ecclesiastes 1.
17 Macbeth, Act 5 Sc. 5.
18 In O'Neill, 1988, p.1172.
19 Keats, 1993, p.40.
20 Pascal, 1966, p.43.
21 Csikszentmihalyi, 1992.
22 Lawrence, 1990, p.667.

14. The End of Nature

1   Lynas, 2004.
2   *The Earth*, 2002.
3   *ibid.*; Elgin, 2004.
4   In Crowley, 1994, p.35.
5   Another way of looking at this is in terms of different worldviews. As Wilber (1995/2000b) sees it, there are a number of possible worldviews human beings can have, corresponding to different levels of consciousness. At the lowest level, there is the egocentric worldview, where we see everything just from our own point of view and nothing matters apart from our own desires, needs and problems. Then there is the ethnocentric (or sociocentric) worldview, where we see everything from the point of view of our social group or our country. Good means what's good for your country, and you don't care what happens outside it, to other people in the world or to the environment. Then there's the worldcentric view – a much wider and more inclusive outlook, where we see beyond race and nationality and identify with the whole human race and are as concerned with global problems as with our own personal problems. And beyond this there are the transpersonal or spiritual levels, where our circle of identity and concern spreads not just to all human beings, but all living beings – and further, when we identify with all reality, or all manifestations of spirit.

Obviously, ecological awareness is only possible with the last three worldviews. Only these three include foresight too, since caring about all human beings – or all living beings or all reality – equally implies caring about the living beings of the future. But unfortunately it seems that most present-day human beings only have an egocentric or sociocentric outlook. Research cited by Wilber (2001) suggests that only 10% of people have a worldcentric worldview. As far as 90% of Americans and Europeans are concerned, then, it doesn't matter if the environment falls to pieces and most of the world's other species are killed off, as long as they've got jobs and enough food to eat and enough money to go out and enjoy themselves. Rich countries like theirs will be able to build high sea walls and come up with scientific solutions to the problems anyway, while poorer countries are flooded and their soil turns to desert. And if environmental problems do affect us, it probably won't be until after we're dead anyway, so why should we care?
6   Sheldrake, 1991.
7   Roszak, 1992, p.226.
8   Heinberg, 1989.
9   Josephy, 1975, p.37.
10 Jaimes Guerrero, 2000, p.48.
11 Connors, 2000, p.148.
12 Thompson, 1916/1991, p.179.

13 In Crowley, 1994, p.36.
14 Eliade, 1967, p.139.
15 In Swain, 1992, p.134.
16 Bryan, 1996.
17 Baring & Cashford, 1991.
18 Snyder, 1999.
19 In Perry, 1992, p.78.
20 ibid.
21 In Baring & Cashford, 1991, p.543.
22 Sheldrake, 1991, p.27.
23 In Eisler, 1995, p.116.
24 Wilber, 1995, p.715. There are, however, a number of difficulties with Wilber's analysis of the ecological crisis. For example, he makes the strange assertion that primal peoples were/are no more "environmentally conscious" than we are. As he puts it, "the primal/tribal structure per se – in itself – did not necessarily possess ecological wisdom, it simply lacked the means to inflict its ignorance on larger portions of the global commons" (1995, p.713). He believes that the development of the ego was actually a step towards environmental awareness, since it brought about formal-operational thinking, which makes you capable of "grasping mutual interrelationships." However, whilst it's true that this would bring a form of ecological awareness, Wilber completely disregards what is surely the major type of ecological awareness: the awareness that comes from actually experiencing a shared sense of being with natural phenomena (an intersubjectivity) and being able to sense their aliveness, and to see them as a manifestation of Spirit.

In a similar way, Wilber believes that the ecological crisis cannot be overcome by "regressing" to a state of oneness with nature, but through the human race's evolution to a higher level of consciousness with increased perspective and rationality, which would enable us to clearly see that we are connected to the rest of the biosphere, and also enable us to clearly recognise the disastrous consequences of our ecological destruction. In other words, our outlook would become "worldcentric" and we would attain a new kind of "wide angle" vision, together with greater powers of foresight. There's no doubt that this would create greater ecological awareness, but it's difficult to see how this would be effective enough without a sense of connection to the natural world, and a sense of its aliveness.

As Wilber sees it, the root cause of the ecological crisis is not that the ego became "split off" from the body (and also from nature). He sees the development of the ego as an evolutionary advance – the point where the ego began to be differentiated from the body. He believes the problem is that this process of differentation went too far, became dissociated from the body. But it's not clear here what the difference is between differentiation and disassociation. And, in any case, the assumption that primal peoples did not have any sense of ego – and were not part of the noosphere – is, I believe, false. The problem is that with the Ego Explosion the sense of ego became too developed. For primal peoples the ego was not dissociated from the body and from nature; it was integrated and in harmony with them. But for Saharasian peoples the development of the ego went too far, and did create a mind-body and mind-nature division.

25 In Crowley, 1994, p.35.
26 Lawlor, 1991, p.40.
27 Ember & Ember, 1981.
28 ibid.
29 Hamilton, 1996.
30 Prescott, 1975.
31 Ember & Ember, 1981, p.326.
32 In Hamilton, 1995, p.110.
33 Ember & Ember, 1981.
34 DeMeo, 1998.
35 ibid., p.335.
36 ibid., p.336.
37 Teilhard de Chardin, 1965.
38 Maddox, 1999.
39 Chalmers, 1996.
40 McGinn, 1993, p.160.
41 Chalmers, 1995, p.210.
42 Forman, 1998, p.185.

15. The First Wave

1 The Upanishads, 1990, p.117.
2 In Happold, 1986, p.146.
3 In Hume, 1990, p.428.
4 ibid, p.116.
5 Eliade, 1967, p.13.
6 The Dhammapada, 1995, p.42.
7 In Spenser, 1950, p.79.
8 Feuerstein, 1990, p.132.
9 Griffith, 2001.
10 In Heinberg, 1989, p.95.
11 In Spenser, 1950, p.101. It's
    possible that there was a more
    direct link between the pre-Fall
    traditions and the post-Fall spiritual
    traditions of China and India.
    Rather than being completely new,
    the latter may have used and
    adapted surviving knowledge from
    pre-Fall traditions. The American
    scholar Joseph Needham suggested
    that Taoism sprang from the
    shamanic and nature-worshipping
    practices of Aboriginal villagers,
    before they were overrun by
    invaders (Griffith, 2001.) More
    contemporary Chinese scholars
    have suggested this too. According
    to Min, for example, "The
    philosophy of Taoism stems from
    the matriarchal society of the
    southern Xia nationality living in
    the Yangze basin" (ibid., p.188).
    Similarly, some scholars have
    suggested that ancient Indian
    spirituality (or yoga) may have been
    a mixture of the shamanic
    traditions of the indigenous
    Dravidians and Indo-European
    religious lore. Feuerstein, however,
    believes this theory is problematic,
    although he suggests that the roots
    of yoga may go back to the pre-
    Indo-European Harrapan
    civilisation of northern India
    (Feuerstein, 1990).
12 In Spenser, 1950, p.157.
13 In Happold, 1986; Spenser, 1950.
14 Sandbach, 1975.
15 Novak. 1996, pp.275-76.
16 Stace, 1964/1988, p.117.
17 Hardy, 1979, p.62.
18 In Stace, 1964/1988, p.117.
19 Underhill, 1911/1960, p.204.
20 ibid., p.212.
21 Waddell, 1986.
22 Narada, 1997, pp.416-7.
23 ibid., p.171.
24 In Spenser, 1950, pp.148-9.
25 Graf, 1977.
26 In Happold, 1986, p.195.
27 In Spenser, 1950.
28 Sandbach, 1975.
29 In Happold, 1986, p.195.
30 Prabhavananda, Swami &
    Isherwood, 1969.
31 In Spenser, 1950, pp.214-25.
32 ibid., p.91.
33 In Wilber, 1995, p.352.
34 Khanna, 2002, p.51.
35 Spenser, 1950, p.338.
36 ibid, p.305.

16. The Second Wave

1 Hibbert, 1966.
2 ibid; Garrett, 2000.
3 Winzer, 1993.
4 Hibbert, 1966, p.44.
5 Baron-Cohen, 2003, p.23.

6 Jaimes Guerrero, 2000; Keck, 2000; Wright, 1992; Ryan, 2003.
7 Garrett, 2000.
8 Allison et al., 1984, p.620.
9 Shelley, 1994, p.450.
10 Allison et al., 1984, p.614.
11 ibid., p.525.
12 Earley, 2002, p.120.
13 Wilson, 2004.
14 ibid., p.326.
15 Wright, 1992.
16 Keck, 2000.
17 According to Robert Keck (2000), by the middle of the twentieth century the nature of war began to change. Wars of conquest were no longer legitimate – now wars were mainly fought for liberation, independence and freedom. In the second half of the twentieth century, Keck suggests, three out of four wars were wars of liberation rather than of conquest. The present US-led war on Iraq bucks this trend in that it's a war of conquest masquerading as a war of liberation. It can be seen as a regression to an earlier more "fallen" mentality by a regressive government, who also want to reverse some of the other trans-Fall trends, such as the movement towards more democracy and social equality and a more positive attitude to sex and the body.
18 www.un.org
19 Boehm, 1999, p.257. In the light of this, it's not surprising that the present US administration is so opposed to the UN.
20 Eisler, 1987, p.82.
21 In Keck, 2000, p.105.
22 ibid., p.105.
23 ibid., pp.213-14.
24 Eisler, 1987, pp.198-99.
25 ibid, p.199.
26 Capra, 1997.
27 Tetry, 1966, p.446.
28 Russell, 1984.
29 Teilhard de Chardin, 1965.
30 Roudi-Fahimi & Moghadam, 2004.

17. A Question of Time

1 Barfield, 1957.
2 Wilber, 1981, p.303.
3 Gould, 1979.
4 Huxley, 1979.
5 Sheldrake, 1981.

BIBLIOGRAPHY

Accad, E. (1978). *The Veil of Shame*. Sherbrooke, QU: Editions Naaman.

Allison, W.A. et al. (Eds.) (1984). *The Norton Anthology of Poetry* (3rd Ed). New York: W.W. Norton & Company.

Anderson, A.A. (1968). "Discussion Part III: Analysis of Group Composition." In R.B. Lee and I. De Vore (Eds.), *Man the Hunter*, 150-55. Chicago: Aldine

Archer, J. (Ed.) (1991). *Male Violence*. London: Routledge.

Argyle, M. (1987). *The Psychology of Happiness*. New York: Methuen.

Argyle, M. (1989). *The Social Psychology of Work* (2nd Ed.). London: Penguin.

Atchley, R.C. (1985). *Social Forces and Ageing: An Introduction to Social Gerontology*. Belmont, CA: Wadsworth.

Attar, F.A. (1990). *Muslim Saints and Mystics*. London: Arkana.

Atwood, B. (1989). *The Making of the Aborigines*. Sydney: Allen and Unwin.

Barfield, O. (1957). *Saving the Appearances*. London: Faber.

Baring, A & Cashford, J. (1991). *The Myth of the Goddess: The Evolution of an Image*. London: Arkana.

Barnard, A. & Woodburn, J. (1988). "Property, Power and Ideology in Hunter-gathering Societies: An Introduction." In Ingold, T., Riches, D. & Woodburn, J. (Eds.). *Hunters and Gatherers, Vol. 2: Property, Power and Ideology*, 4-31. Oxford: Berg.

Baron-Cohen, S. (2003). *The Essential Difference: Men, Women and the Extreme Male Brain*. London: Allen Lane.

Bartlett, B. (1968). *Familiar Quotations*. Boston: Little Brown.

Bartlett, F.C. (1923/1970). *Psychology and Primitive Culture*. Westport, Connecticut: Greenwood Press.

Becker, E. (1973). *The Denial of Death*. New York: Free Press.

Berman, M. (2000). *Wandering God: A Study in Nomadic Spirituality*. Albany, NY: State University of New York Press.

Bernt, R. & C. (1963). *Sexual Behavior in Western Arnhem Land*. Melbourne: Viking Fund Publications in Anthropology no. 16.

Bewley, R. (1994). *Prehistoric Settlements*. London: Batsford.

Bloch, M. (1977). "The Past in the Present." *Man* (N.S.), 12, 278-292.

Boehm, C. (1999). *Hierarchy in the Forest*. Cambridge, MA: Harvard University Press.

Boesch, C. & Boesch-Achermann, H. (2000). *The Chimpanzees of the Tai Forest: Behavioural Ecology and Evolution*. Oxford: Oxford University Press.

Bolton, R. (1973). "Tawanku: Intercouple Bonds in a Qolla village." *Anthropos*, 68, 245-55.

Boyer, P. (2001). *Religion Explained*. London: Vintage.

Brickman, P., Coates, D., & Janoff-Bulman, R. (1978). "Lottery Winners and Accident Victims: is Happiness Relative?" *Journal of Personality and Social Psychology*, 36, 917-27.

Briggs, J.L. (1970). *Never in Anger*. Cambridge, Mass: Harvard University Press.

Briggs, J.L. (1998). *Inuit Morality Play*. New Haven and London: Yale University Press.

Bryan, W.L. (1996). *Montana's Indians: Yesterday and Today*. Helena, MT: American & World Geographic Publishing.

Bullock, A. (1998). *Hitler and Stalin: Parallel Lives*. London: Fontana.

Burch, E.S. & Ellanna, L.J. (1994). "Editorial." In Burch, E.S. & Ellanna, L.J. (Eds.), *Key Issues in Hunter-Gatherer Research*. Oxford: Berg.

Campbell, J. (1959-1968). *The Masks of God*. New York: Viking.

Capra, F. (1997). *The Web of Life*. London: Harper Collins.

Cashdan, Elizabeth A. (1980). "Egalitarianism Among Hunter and Gatherers." *American Anthropologist*, 82: 116-120.

Cassirer, E. (1954-7). *The Philosophy of Symbolic Forms*. New Haven: Yale University Press.

Cassirer, E. (1970). *An Essay on Man*. New Haven: Yale University Press.

Chalmers, D.J. (1995). "Facing up to the Problem of Consciousness." *The Journal of Consciousness Studies* 2, 3, 200-19.

Chalmers, D.J. (1996). *The Conscious Mind*. Oxford: OUP.

Chapman, J, (1999). "The origins of warfare in the prehistory of central and eastern Europe." In Carman, J. & Harding, A. (Eds.). *Ancient warfare: archaeological perspectives*. Trowbridge, Wiltshire: UL Sutton Publishing

Connors, S. M. (2000). "Ecology and Religion in Karuk Orientations Toward the Land." In

Graham Harvey (Ed.), *Indigenous Religions*. London and New York: Cassell.

Childe, V.G. (1952). *New Light on the Most Ancient Near East*. New York: Praeger.

Childe, V.G. (1958). *The Dawn of European Civilization*. New York: Alfred Knopf.

Childe, V.G. (1964). *What Happened in History*. Baltimore: Penguin.

Cotterell, A. (2000). *World Mythology*. Bath: Parragon.

Cowan, J.G. (1992). *The Aborigine Tradition*. Shaftesbury: Element.

Crawford, H. (1991). *Sumer and the Sumerians*. Cambridge: Cambridge University Press.

Cross, S. (1994). *Hinduism*. Shaftesbury: Element.

Crowley, V. (1994). *Phoenix to a Flame: Pagan Spirituality in the Western World*. London: Thorsons.

Csikszentmihalyi, M. (1992). *Flow – The Psychology of Happiness*. London: Rider.

Csikszentmihalyi, M. (2004). "Materialism and the Evolution of Consciousness." In Kasser, T. & Kanner, A.D. (Eds.), *Psychology and Consumer Culture*. Washington: American Psychological Association.

Daly, M. & Wilson, M. (1983). *Homicide*. New York: Aldine de Gruyter.

Davidson, B. (1996). *African Kingdoms*. New York: Time-Life.

Deikman, A. (2001). "A Functional Approach to Mysticism." The Journal of Consciousness Studies 7, 11-12, 75-93.

Deikman, A. (2002a). *Deautomatization and the Mystic Experience* available at http:/www.deikman.com/deautomat.html, accessed 05/05/02.

Deikman, A. (2002b). *Experimental Meditation* available at http:/www.deikman.com/experimental.html, accessed 05/05/02.

DeMause, L. (1974). "The Evolution of Childhood." In DeMause, L. (Ed.), *The History of Childhood*. New York: Psychohistory Press.

DeMeo, J. (1998). *Saharasia. The 4000 BCE Origins of Child Abuse, Sex-Repression, Warfare and Social Violence in the Deserts of the Old World*. Oregon: OBRL.

DeMeo, J. (2000). *The Origins and Diffusion of Patrism in Saharasia, c4000BCE: Evidence for a Worldwide, Climate-Based Geographical Pattern in Human Behavior*. http://www.orgonelab.org/saharasia.htm, accessed 13/07/01.

DeMeo, J. (2002). "Update on Saharasia: Ambiguities and Uncertainties about 'War Before Civilisation.'" In DeMeo, J. (Ed.), *Heretic's Notebook (Pulse of the Planet #5)*. Ashland, Oregon: OBRL.

The Dhammapada (The Buddha's Teachings) (1995). Ed. and trans. Juan Mascaro. London: Penguin.

Diamond, J. (1987). "The Worst Mistake in the History of the Human Race." *Discover* (May 1987), 64-66.

Diamond, J. (1992). *The Third Chimpanzee*. New York: Harper Collins.

Diamond, J. (1997). *Guns, Germs and Steel*. London: Jonathon Cape.

Diamond, S. (Ed.) (1969). *Primitive Views of the World*. New York: Columbia University Press.

Diamond, S. (1974). *In Search of the Primitive*. New Brunswick: Transaction Books.

Divale, W. (1973). *War in Primitive Society: A Bibliography*. Santa Barbara.

Dolkhanov, P.M. (1999). "War and Peace in Prehistoric Eastern Europe." In Carman, J. & Harding, A. (Eds.), *Ancient Warfare: Archaeological Perspectives*. Trowbridge, Wiltshire: UL Sutton Publishing.

Dressler, R. (1999). *Time: A Dimension of Consciousness or Actual Reality?* Available on scimednet.com, accessed 30/3/2001.

Earley, J. (2002). "The Social Evolution of Consciousness." *The Journal of Humanistic Psychology*, 42, 107-32.

Eckhart, Meister (1996). *From Whom God Hid Nothing*. David O'Neal (Ed.). Boston: Shambhala.

Eckhart, Meister (1979). *German Sermons and Treatises*, Vol.1, (trans. M. Walshe). London: Watkins.

Ehrenreich, B. (1996). *Blood rites: Origins and History of the Passions of War*. New York: Metropolitan Books.

Eisler, R. (1987). *The Chalice and the Blade*. London: Thorsons.

Eisler, R. (1995). *Sacred Pleasure*. Shaftesbury: Element.

Elgin, D. (2004). "The Gathering World Storm and the Urgency of our Awakening." *What is Enlightenment?*, 24.

Eliade, M. (1967). *From Primitives to Zen*. London: Collins.

Elwin, V. (1968). *The Kingdom of the Young*. Bombay: Oxford University Press.

Ember, C.R. & Ember, M. (1981). *Anthropology*. Englewood Cliffs, NJ: Prentice-Hall.

Endicott, K. (1988). "Property, Power and Conflict among the Batek of Malaysia." In

Ingold, T., Riches, D. & Woodburn, J. (Eds.). *Hunters and Gatherers, Vol. 2: Property, Power and Ideology.* Oxford: Berg.

Evans-Pritchard, E.E. (1967). *Nuer Religion.* London: Oxford University Press.

Evans-Pritchard, E.E. (1971). *The Azande.* London: Faber and Faber.

Ferguson, R.B. (1995). *Yanomami Warfare: A Political History.* Santa FE: School of American Research Press.

Ferguson, R.B. (1997). "Violence and War in Prehistory." In Martin, D. & Frayer, D. (Eds.), *Troubled Times: Violence and Warfare in the Past.* New York: Gordon and Breach.

Ferguson, R.B. (2000). "The Causes and Origins of Primitive Warfare." *Anthropological Quarterly,* 73.3, 159-164.

Ferguson, R.B. (2003). "The Birth of War." *Natural History Magazine,* July/August.

Feuerstein, G. (1990). *Yoga: the Technology of Ecstasy.* Wellingborough: The Aquarian Press.

Fischer, R. (1971). "A Cartography of Ecstatic and Meditative States.' *Science,* 174, 897-904.

Forman, R. (1998). "What does Mysticism have to teach us about consciousness?" *Journal of Consciousness Studies,* 5 (2), 185-201.

Fortune, R. (1963). *Sorcerers of Dobu.* London: Routledge and Kegan Paul.

Frazer, J. (1959). *The New Golden Bough.* New York: Criterion.

Freud, S. (1946). *Totem and Taboo: Resemblances Between the Psychic Lives of Savages and Neurotics.* New York: Vintage Books.

Fromm, E. (1957/1974). *The Anatomy of Human Destructiveness.* London: Jonathon Cape.

Fromm, E. (1995). *The Art of Loving.* London: Thorson's.

Gabriel, R. (1990). *The Culture of War: Invention and Early Development.* New York: Greenwood Press.

Gardiner, H., Mutter, J.D., Kosmitzki, C. (1998). *Lives Across Cultures: Cross-Cultural Human Development.* Boston: Allyn and Bacon.

Gardiner, H.W. & Mutter J.D. (1994). "Measuring multi-cultural awareness and identity: A model." *Paper presented at the twenty-third annual meeting of the Society for Cross-Cultural Research,* Sante Fe, NM.

Garrett, A. (2000). "Introduction." in Garrett, A. (Ed.), *Animal Rights and Souls in the Eighteenth Century.* Bristol: Thoemmes Press, v-xxiv.

Geertz, C. (1973). *The Interpretation of Culture.* New York: Basic Books.

Gell, A. (1992). *The Anthropology of Time.* Oxford: Berg Publishers Limited.

Gellar, S. (1995). "The Colonial Era." In Martin, P. & O'Meara, P. (Eds.), *Africa.* Bloomington, Indiana: Indiana University Press.

Gimbutas, M. (1973). "The Beginning of the Bronze Age in Europe and the Indo-Europeans." *Journal of Indo-European Studies* 1.

Gimbutas, M. (1977). "First Wave of Eurasian Steppe Pastoralists into Copper Age Europe." *Journal of Indo-European Studies* 5.

Gimbutas, M. (1980). *The Early Civilization of Europe.* Monograph for Indo-European Studies 131, University of California at Los Angeles.

Gimbutas, M. (1982). *The Goddesses and Gods of Old Europe, 7000-3500 B.C.* Berkeley and Los Angeles: University of California Press.

Gimbutas, M. (1991). *The Civilisation of the Goddess: The World of Old Europe.* London: Thames and Hudson.

Gluckman, M. (1965). *The Ideas in Barotse Jurisprudence.* New Haven: Yale University Press.

Goldberg, S. (1973). *The Inevitability of Patriarchy.* New York: Wm Morrow.

Goodenough W.H. (1973). "Premarital freedom in Truk: Theory and practice." *American Anthropologist,* 51, 615-619.

Gould, S.J. (1979). *Ever Since Darwin: Reflections on Human Nature.* New York: W.W. Norton.

Graf, D. (1977). "The Pagan Witness to the Essenes." *Biblical Archeologist,* September 1977, 125-129.

Grant, J. (Ed.) 1980. *The Book of Time.* Newton Abbot: Westbridge Books.

Gray, J. (1992.) *Men are from Mars, Women are from Venus.* New York: Harper Collins.

Griffith, B. (2001). *The Gardens of their Dreams: Desertification and Culture in World History.* London: Zed Books.

Gross, P. (1996). *Psychology: The Science of Mind and Behaviour.* 3rd Ed. London: Hodder and Stoughton.

Haas, J. (1990). *The Anthropology of War.* Cambridge: Cambridge University Press.

Haas, J. (1999). "The Origins of War and Ethnic Violence." In Carman, J. & Harding, A. (Eds.), *Ancient Warfare: Archaeological Perspectives.* Trowbridge, Wiltshire: Sutton Publishing.

Hall, E.T. (1984). *The Dance of Life.* New York: Anchor Press.

Hallett, J.P. & Relle, A. (1973). *Pygmy Kitabu.* New York: Random House.

Hamilton, M.B. (1995). *The Sociology of Religion.* London: Routledge.

Happold, F.C. (1986). *Mysticism.* London: Penguin.

Hardy, A. (1979). *The Spiritual Nature of Man.*

Oxford: Clarendon Press.

Harman, W. & Sahtouris, E. (1998). *Biology Revisioned*. Berkeley, CA: North Atlantic Books.

Harris, M. (1977). *Cannibals and Kings*. New York: Random House.

Harris, M. (1980). *Cultural Materialism: The Struggle for a Science of Culture*. New York: Vintage Books.

Hawkes, J. (1968). *Dawn of the Gods*. New York: Random House.

Hawkes, J. (1973). *The First Great Civilisations: Life in Mesopotamia, the Indus Valley, and Egypt*. New York: Alfred Knopf.

Hayden, B. (1994). "Competition, Labor and Complex Hunter-Gatherers." In Burch, E.S. & Ellanna, L.J. (Eds.), *Key Issues in Hunter-Gatherer Research*. Oxford: Berg.

Heinberg, R. (1989). *Memories and Visions of Paradise*. Wellingborough: the Aquarian Press.

Heinberg, R. (1995). "The Primitivist Critique of Civilisation." *Paper presented at the 24th Annual meeting of the International Society for the Comparative Study of Civilisations*. Dayton, Ohio.

Herdt, G. (Ed.) (1984). *Ritualized Homosexuality in Melanesia*. Berkeley: University of California Press.

Hewlett, B.S. (1991). *Intimate Fathers: The Nature and Context of Aka Pygmy Paternal Infant Care*. Ann Arbor: University of Michigan Press.

Hibbert, C. (1966). *The Roots of Evil*. London: Penguin.

Hildebrand, M. von (1988). "An Amazonian Tribe's View of Cosmology." In P. Bunyard and E. Goldsmith (Eds.), *Gaia, the Thesis, the Mechanisms and the Implications*. Wadebridge Ecological Centre, Camelford, Cornwall.

Holmberg, A.A. (1950). *Nomads of the Long Bow: the Seriono of Eastern Bolivia*. Washington D.C: US Government Printing Office.

Hume, D. (1990). *The 13 Principle Upanishads*. Oxford: OUP.

Hume, L. (2000). "The Dreaming in Contemporary Aboriginal Australia." In Harvey, G. (Ed.), *Indigenous Religions*. London and New York: Cassell.

Huxley, J, (1979). *Essays of a Humanist*. London: Pelican.

Idowu, E.B. (1975). *African Traditional Religion*. Maryknoll, New York: Orbis Books.

Ingold, T., Riches, D. & Woodburn, J. (Eds.). (1988). *Hunters and Gatherers, Vol. 2: Property, Power and Ideology*. Oxford: Berg.

Jaimes Guerrero, M.A. (2000). "Native Womanism: Exemplars of Indigenism in Sacred Traditions of Kinship." In Graham Harvey (Ed.), *Indigenous Religions*. London and New York: Cassell.

James, W. (1899/1985). *The Varieties of Religious Experience*. London: Penguin.

Jaynes, J. (1976). *The Origins of Consciousness in the Breakdown of the Bicameral Mind*. London: Pelican.

Jilek, W. (1989). "Therapeutic Use of Altered States of Consciousness in Contemporary North American Indian Dance Ceremonials." In C. Ward (Ed.), *Altered States of Consciousness and Mental Health: a Cross Cultural Perspective* (pp. 167-85). London: Sage.

Johnson, Dr. (1905). *Lives of the Poets*, Vol. 3. (Ed. G.B. Hill). Oxford: Clarendon.

Josephy Jr., A.M. (1975). *The Indian Heritage of America*. London: Pelican.

Joyce, J. (1992). *Ulysses*. London: Minerva.

Kasser, T. (2002). *The High Price of Materialism*. Cambridge, MA: MIT Press.

Kasser, T. et al. (2004). "Materialistic Values: Their Causes and Consequences." In Kasser, T. & Kanner, A.D. (Eds.) (2004), *Psychology and Consumer Culture*. Washington: American Psychological Association.

Keats, J. (1993). *A Pocket Poet*. London: Grange Books.

Keck, L.R. (2000). *Sacred Quest: The Evolution and Future of the Human Soul*. West Chester, PA: Chrysalis Books.

Keegan, J. (1993). *A History of Warfare*. London: Pimlico.

Keeley, L. (1996). *War Before Civilization*. New York: OUP.

Keim, C.A. (1995). "Africa and Europe Before 1900." In Martin, P. & O'Meara, P. (Eds.), *Africa*. Bloomington, Indiana: Indiana University Press.

Kelly, M. (1977). "Papua New Guinea and Piaget: An eight-year study." In P.R. Dasen (Ed.), *Piagetian Psychology: Cross-cultural Contributions*, 169-202.

Khanna, M. (2002). "The Goddess-Woman Equation in Sakta Tantras." In Ahmed, D.S. (Ed.), *Gendering the Spirit: Women, Religion and the Post-Colonial Response*. London: Zed Books.

Kleinfeld, J. (1994). "Learning Styles and Culture." In Lonner, W.J. & Malpass, R., (Eds.), *Psychology and Culture*. Boston: Allyn and Bacon.

Knauft, B.M. (1991). "Violence and Sociality in Human Evolution." *Current Anthropology* 32, 4, 391-409.

Konner, M. (1982). *The Tangled Wing*. New York: Holt, Rinehart & Winston.

Kramer, S.N. (1969). *The Sacred Marriage Rite*.

Bloomingtom: Indiana University Press.

Kroeber, C.B. & Fontana, B.L. (1986). *Massacre on the Gila*. Tucson: University of Arizona Press.

LaChapelle, D. (1996). *D.H. Lawrence: Future Primitive*. Denton, Texas: The University of Texas Press.

Lachman, G. (2003). *A Secret History of Consciousness*. Great Barrington, MA: Lindisfarne Books.

Lamphear, J. & Falola, T. (1995). "Aspects of Early African History." In Martin, P. & O'Meara, P. (Eds.), *Africa*. Bloomington, Indiana: Indiana University Press.

Lancaster, B. (1991). *Mind, Brain* and *Human Potential*. Shaftesbury, Dorset: Element.

Laurendeau-Bendavid, M. (1977). "Culture, Schooling and Cognitive Development: A Comparative Study of Children in French Canada and Rwanda." In P.R. Dasen (Ed.), *Piagetian Psychology: Cross-cultural Contributions*, 123-168. New York: Gardner Press.

Lawlor, R. (1991). *Voices of the First Day. Awakening in the Aboriginal Dreamtime*. Rochester, Vermont: Inner Traditions.

Lawrence, D.H. (1950). *Selected Essays*. (Ed. Richard Aldington). London: Penguin Books.

Lawrence, D.H. (1968). *Phoenix*. London: Heinemann.

Lawrence, D.H. (1971). *Fantasia of the Unconscious and Psychoanalysis and the Unconscious*. London: Penguin Books.

Lawrence, D.H. (1971). *Mornings in Mexico*. London: Penguin Books.

Lawrence, D.H. (1979) *Apocalypse and the Writings on Revelation*. (Ed. Mara Kalnins). Cambridge: Cambridge University Press.

Lawrence, D.H. (1990). *Poems*. London: Penguin.

Lee, R.B. & DeVore, I. (Eds.) (1968). *Man the Hunter*. Chicago: Aldine.

Lenski, G. (1966). *Power and Privilege*. New York: McGraw-Hill.

Lenski, G & J. (1978). *Human Societies* (2ⁿᵈ Ed.). New York: McGraw-Hill.

Lenski, G. & J. & Nolan, P. (1995). *Human Societies* (7ᵗʰ Ed.). New York: McGraw-Hill.

Levy-Bruhl, L. (1965). *The Soul of the Primitive*. London: Allen and Unwin.

Liedloff, J. (1989). *The Continuum Concept*. London: Arkana.

Lorimer, D. (1990). *Whole in One*. London: Arkana.

Lynas, M. (2004). *High Tide: News from a Warming World*. London: Flamingo.

Macoby, E.E. (1990). "Gender and Relationships: A Developmental Account." *American Psychologist*, 45, 513-520.

Maddox, J. (1999). *What Remains to be Discovered*. London: Macmillan.

Magesa, L. (1997). *African Religion*. New York: Orbis.

Malinowski, B. (1932). *The Sexual Life of Savages*. London: Routledge and Keegan Paul.

Malinowski, B. (1964). "An Anthropological Analysis of War." In Bramson, L. & Goethals, G.W. (Eds.). *War: Studies from Psychology, Sociology and Anthropology*. New York: Basic Books.

Mallory, J.P. (1989). *In Search of the Indo-Europeans*. London: Thames and Hudson.

Mann, C.C. (2002). "The Real Dirt in Rainforest Fertility." *Science*, 297, 920-923.

Markus, H. & Kitayama, S. (1991) "Culture and the self: Implications for cognition, emotion and motivations." *Psychological Bulletin*, 98, 224-253.

Marshall, D.S. (1971). "Sexual Behavior on Mangaia." In Marshall, D.S. & Suggs, R.C. (Eds.), *Human Sexual Behavior*. New York: Basic Books.

Marshall, L. (1976). *The !Kung of Nyae Nyae*. Cambridge, MA: Harvard University Press.

Marx, K. (1959). *Capital and Other Writings*. New York: The Modern Library.

Mbuta, J. (1975). *Introduction to African Religion*. London: Heinemann.

McCall, J. (1995). "Social Organization in Africa." In Martin, P. & O'Meara, P. (Eds.), *Africa*. Bloomington, Indiana: Indiana University Press.

McCarthy, B. (1991). "Warrior Values." In Archer, J. (Ed.), *Male Violence*. London: Routledge.

McCreedy, M. (1994). "The Arms of the Dibouka." In Burch, E.S. & Ellanna, L.J. (Eds.), *Key Issues in Hunter-Gatherer Research*. Oxford: Berg.

McGinn, C. (1993). "Consciousness and Cosmology: Hyperdualism Ventilated." In Davies, M. & Humphreys, G.W., *Consciousness*. Oxford: Blackwell.

McTaggart, L. (2000). *The Field*. London: Thorson's.

Mead, M. (1964). "Warfare is only an Invention." In Bramson, L. & Goethals, G.W. (Eds.), *War: Studies from Psychology, Sociology and Anthropology*. New York: Basic Books.

Mearns, L. (1994). "To Continue the Dreaming: Aboriginal Women's Responsibilities in a Transformed World." In Burch, E.S. & Ellanna, L.J. (Eds.), *Key Issues in Hunter-Gatherer*

Research. Oxford: Berg.

Mellaart, J. (1967). *Catal Huyuk: A Neolithic Town in Anatolia*. London: Thames and Hudson.

Mellaart, J. (1975). *The Neolithic of the Near East*. New York: Scribner.

Mitchell, W.E. (1978). "On Keeping Equal: Polity and Reciprocity among the New Guinea Wape." *Anthropological Quarterly*, 51: 5-15.

Morgan, D. & Sanz, C. (2003). "Naïve Encounters With Chimpanzees in the Goualougo Triangle." *International Journal of Primatology*. April.

Murphy, M. (1992). *The Future of the Body*. Los Angeles: Tarcher.

Myers, F. (1997). "Burning the Truck and Holding the Country: Property, Time and the Negotiation of Identity among Pintupi Aborigines." In Ingold, T., Riches, D. & Woodburn, J. (Eds.), *Hunters and Gatherers, Vol. 2: Property, Power and Ideology*. Oxford: Berg.

Narada Maha Thera (1997). *The Buddha and his Teachings*. Singapore: Singapore Buddhist Meditation Centre.

Neumann, E. (1973). *The Origins and History of Consciousness*. Princeton: Princeton University Press.

Newcomb, W.W. (1950). "A Re-Examination of the Causes of Plains Warfare." *American Anthropologist* 52: 317-330.

Novak, P. (1996). "Buddhist Meditation and the Consciousness of Time." *The Journal of Consciousness Studies*, 3 (3), 267-77.

Nyanaponika Thera, (1973). *The Heart of Buddhist Meditation*. New York: Weiser.

Oates, J. (1986). *Babylon*. London: Thames and Hudson.

Oliphant, M. (1992). *The Atlas of the Ancient World*. London: Ebury.

Park, R.E. (1964). "The Social Function of War." In Bramson, L. & Goethals, G.W. (Eds.), *War: Studies from Psychology, Sociology and Anthropology*. New York: Basic Books.

O'Neill, E. (1988). *Collected Plays*. London: Jonathon Cape.

Osmond, J. (1993). *The Reality of Dyslexia*. London: Cassell.

Partridge, G.E. (1919). *The Psychology of Nations*. New York :Macmillan.

Pascal, B. (1966). *Pensees*. London: Penguin.

Patron. E.J. (1995). "Heart of Lavender: In Search of Gay Africa." *Harvard Gay and Lesbian Review*, Fall 1995.

Perry, M. (1992). *Gods Within: A Critical Guide to the New Age*. London: SPCK.

Phillip, H. & Kelly, M. (1974). "Product and

Process in Cognitive Development: some Comparative Data on the Performance of School Age Children in Different Cultures." *British Journal of Educational Psychology*, 44, 248-265.

Piaget, J. & Inhelder, B. (1956). *The Psychology of the Child*. London: Routledge & Kegan Paul.

Pinker, S. (1997). *How the Mind Works*. London: Penguin.

Platon, N. (1966). *Crete*. Geneva: Nagel Publishers.

Power, M. (1991). *The Egalitarians, Human and Chimpanzee: An Anthropological View of Social Organisation*. Cambridge: Cambridge University Press.

Prabhavananda, Swami & Isherwood, C. (1969). *How to know God: the yoga aphorisms of Patanjali*. New York: Mentor.

Prescott, J.W. (1975). "Body Pleasure and the Origins of Violence." *The Bulletin of the Atomic Scientists*, November, 10-20.

Raphael, B. (1984). *The Anatomy of Bereavement*. London: Hutchinson.

Reddy, G.P.(1994). "Hunter-Gatherers and the Politics of Environment and Development in India." In Burch, E.S. & Ellanna, L.J. (Eds.), *Key Issues in Hunter-Gatherer Research*. Oxford: Berg.

Rhode, D.L. (Ed.) (1990). *Theoretical Perspectives on Sex Differences*. New Haven, CT: Yale University Press.

Rice, M. (1990). *Egypt's Making: The Origins of Ancient Egypt 5000-2000 B.C.* London: Routledge.

Rose, H. & Rose, S. (Eds.) (2000). *Alas, Poor Darwin: Arguments Against Evolutionary Psychology*. London: Jonathon Cape.

Rosenberg, E.L. (2004). "Mindfulness and Consumerism." In Kasser, T. & Kanner, A.D. (Eds.), *Psychology and Consumer Culture*. Washington: American Psychological Association.

Rostow, W.W. (1960). *The Stages of Economic Growth*. London: Cambridge University Press.

Roszak, T. (1992). *The Voice of the Earth*. New York: Touchstone.

Roudi-Fahimi, F. & Moghadam, V.M. (2004). *Empowering Women, Developing Society: Female Education in the Middle East and North Africa*. Available on www.prb.org/pdf/empoweringwomeninMENA.pdf.

Rudgley, R. (1993). *The Alchemy of Culture*. London: British Museum Press.

Rudgley, R. (1998). *Lost Civilisations of the Stone Age*. London: Century.

Rudgley, R. (2000). *Secrets of the Stone Age*. London: Random House.

Rudmin, F.W. (1994). "Property." In Lonner, W.J. & Malpass, R., *Psychology and Culture.* Boston: Allyn and Bacon.

Russell, P. (1984). *The Awakening Earth.* London: Ark.

Ryan, C.P. (2003). *Human Sexual Behavior in the Pleistocene: A Challenge to the Standard Model of Human Evolution.* Phd Thesis, Saybrook Graduate School, CA.

Sahlins, M. (1968). "Notes on the Original Affluent Society." In Lee, R.B. & DeVore, I. (Eds.), *Man the Hunter,* 85-89. Chicago: Aldine.

Sahlins, M. (1972). *Stone Age Economics.* New York: Aldine de Gruyter.

Sandbach, F.H. (1975). *The Stoics.* London: Chatto & Windus.

Schopenhauer, A. (1930). *The Essays of Schopenhauer.* London: Walter Scott Press.

"The Secret of El Dorado." bbc.co.uk/science/horizon/2002/eldorado.shtml, accessed 12/7/04.

Scott, C. (1997). "Property, Practice and Aboriginal Rights among Quebec Cree Hunters." In Ingold, T., Riches, D. & Woodburn, J. (Eds.), *Hunters and Gatherers, Vol. 2: Property, Power and Ideology.* Oxford: Berg.

Service, E.R. (1966). *The Hunters.* Englewood Cliffs, NJ: Prentice-Hall.

Service, E.R. (1978). *Profiles in Ethnology.* New York: Harper and Row.

Sheldrake, R. (1981). *A New Science of Life.* London: Blonde and Briggs.

Sheldrake, R. (1991). *The Rebirth of Nature.* London: Rider.

Shelley, P. B. (1994). *The Works of Shelley.* London: Wordsworth.

Shields, W.M & L.M. (1983). "Forcible Rape: An Evolutionary Perspective." *Ethology and Sociobiology* 4: 115-645.

Silberbauer, G.B. (1981). "Hunter gatherers of the Central Kalahari." In *Omnivorous Primates: Gathering and Hunting in Human Evolution,* Harding, R. & Teleki, G. (Eds.), 455-98. New York: Columbia University Press.

Silberbauer, G.B. (1994). "A Sense of Place." In Burch, E.S. & Ellanna, L.J. (Eds.), *Key Issues in Hunter-Gatherer Research.* Oxford: Berg.

Sindima, H. (1990). "Community of Life: Ecological Theology in African Perspective," in C. Birch et al. (Eds.), *Liberating Life: Contemporary Approaches to Ecological Theology.* Maryknoll, New York: Orbis Books.

Smith, H. (1964). "Do Drugs Have Religious Import?" *The Journal of Philosophy,* LXI, 517-530.

Snelling, J. (1990). *Buddhism.* Shaftesbury: Element.

Snyder, G. (1999). *The Gary Snyder Reader.* Washington DC: Counterpoint.

Solomon et al. (2004). "Lethal Consumption: Death-Denying Materialism." In Kasser, T. & Kanner, A.D. (Eds.), *Psychology and Consumer Culture.* Washington: American Psychological Association.

Sorin, V. (1992). "Last of an Ancient People." In *Cultural Survival Quarterly,* Winter Issue.

Spencer, S. (1950). *Mysticism in World Religion.* London: Penguin.

Stace, W. (1964/1988). *Mysticism and Philosophy.* Los Angeles: J.P. Tarcher.

Stacey, J. (1983). *Patriarchy and Socialist Revolution in China.* Berkeley: University of California Press.

Stern, P. (1969). *Prehistoric Europe from Stone Age Man to the Early Greeks.* New York: W.W. Norton.

Stone, M. (1976). *When God was a Woman.* New York: Harcourt Brace Jovanovich.

Sumner, W.G. (1911/1964). "War." In Bramson, L. & Goethals, G.W. (Eds.), *War: Studies from Psychology, Sociology and Anthropology.* New York: Basic Books.

Sussman, R.W. (1997). "Exploring our Basic Human Nature: Are Humans Inherently Violent?" *Anthronotes – National Museum of Natural History Bulletin for Teachers,* 19, 3.

Swain, T. (1992). "Reinventing the Eternal: Aboriginal Spirituality and Modernity." In Habel, N. (Ed.), *Religion and Multiculturalism in Australia,* 122-36. Adelaide: Australian Society for the Study of Religions.

Taylor, C.F. (Ed.) (1991). *The Native Americans.* London: Salamander Books.

Taylor, G.R. (1953). *Sex in History.* London: Thames and Hudson.

Taylor, S. (1999). "The Elan Vital and Self-Evolution." *New Renaissance,* 8, 4.

Taylor, S. (2000). "Choosing the Future." *New Renaissance,* 9, 3.

Taylor, S. (2000). "From the Unreal to the Real: The Reality of Higher States of Consciousness." *New Renaissance,* 10, 1.

Taylor, S. (2002). "Where Did it All Go Wrong? James DeMeo's Saharasia Thesis and The Origins of War." *The Journal of Consciousness Studies* 9, 8, 73-82.

Taylor, S. (2003). *Out of Time: The Five Laws of Psychological Time and how to Transcend them.* Nottingham: Paupers' Press.

Taylor, S. (2003). "Primal Spirituality and the

Onto/Phylo Fallacy: A Critique of the Claim that Primal Peoples were/are less Spiritually and Socially Developed than Modern Humans." *The International Journal of Transpersonal Studies*, 22, 61-76.

Taylor, S. (2005). "D.H. Lawrence and the Fall." *The Journal of the D.H. Lawrence Society*, 2004-5.

Taylor, T. (1996). *The Prehistory of Sex*. London: Fourth Estate.

The Earth (2002). London: The Guardian in Association with Action Aid, August 2002.

Teilhard De Chardin, P. (1965). *The Phenomenon of Man*. London: Collins.

Tetry, A. (1966). "Evolution." In Rene Taton (Ed.), *A General History of the Sciences*, Vol. 4, 443-452. London: Thames & Hudson.

Thompson, L. (1916/1991). *To the American Indian: Reminiscences of a Yurok Woman*. Berkeley CA: Heyday Books.

Thornhill, R. & N.W. (1983). "Human Rape: An Evolutionary Analysis." *Ethology and Sociobiology* 4: 137-73.

Thorpe, N. (1999). "The Origins of Violence: Mesolithic Conflict in Europe." Paper presented at European Association of Archaeologists meeting, Bournemouth, UK.

Thorpe, N. (2000). "The Origins of War: Mesolithic Conflict in Europe." *British Archaeology*, 52.

Tuden, A. (1966). "Leadership and the Decision-making Process." In Turner, V.W., Swartz, M. J. & Tuden, A. (Eds.), *Political Anthropology*, 275-283. Chicago: Aldine.

Turnbull, C.M. (1965). *Wayward Servants: The Two Worlds of the African Pygmies*. London: Eyre & Spottiswoode.

Turnbull, C.M. (1972). "Demography of Small-scale Societies." In Harrison, G.A. & Boyce, A.J. (Eds.), *The Structure of Human Populations*, 283-312. Oxford Clarendon Press.

Turnbull, C.M. (1978). "The Politics of Non-aggression." In Montagu, A. (Ed.), *Learning Non-Aggression*, 161-221. New York: OUP.

Turnbull, C. (1993). *The Forest People*. London: Pimlico.

Underhill, E. (1911/1960) *Mysticism*. London: Methuen.

The Upanishads (1990). Ed. and trans. Juan Mascaro. London: Penguin.

'Undiagnosed Dyslexics are more likely to go to Prison." *Times Educational Supplement*, 21 July 2000.

van der Dennen, M.G. (1995). *The Origin of War*. Groningen: Origin Press.

van der Dennen, M.G. (2001). Review of "The Lucifer Principle" by Harold L. Bloom, available on http://rint.rechen.rug.nl/rth/dennen/bloom.htm, accessed 14/11/2001.

van der Merwe (1992). "Reconstructing Prehistoric Diet." In Jones, S., Martin, R. & Pilbeam, D. (Eds.), *The Cambridge Encyclopaedia of Human Evolution*, 369-372. Cambridge: Cambridge University Press.

Vencl, S. (1999). "Stone Age Warfare." In Carman, J. & Harding, A. (Eds.), *Ancient warfare: archaeological perspectives*, 57-72. Trowbridge, Wiltshire: UL Sutton Publishing.

Versluis, A. (1994). *Native American Traditions*. Shaftesbury: Element.

Waddell, H. (1986). *The Desert Fathers*. Ann Arbor: The University of Michigan Press.

Wade, C. & Tavris, C. (1994). "The Longest War: Gender and Culture." In Lonner, W.J. & Malpass, R. (Eds.), *Psychology and Culture*. Boston: Allyn and Bacon.

Wallace, A. (1966). *Religion: An Anthropological View*. New York: Random House.

Walker, B.G. (1983). *The Women's Encyclopaedia of Myths and Secrets*. New York: Harper & Row.

Walsh, R. (2003). "Entheogens: True or False?" *The International Journal of Transpersonal Studies*, 22, 1-6.

Ward, K. (2002). *God: A Guide for the Perplexed*. Oxford: One World.

Wareing, S. (1999). "Language and Gender." In Thomas, L. & Wareing, S. (Eds.), *Language, Society and Power*. London: Routledge.

Warner, M. (1976). *Alone of all her Sex*. London: Weidenfield & Nicholson.

Weisfield, G. (1991). "Aggression and Dominance." In Archer, J. (Ed.), *Male Violence*. London: Routledge.

Werner, E.E. (1979). *Cross-Cultural Child Development*. Belmont, CA: Wadsworth.

Werner, H. (1957). *The Comparative Psychology of Mental Development*. New York: International Universities Press.

White, L.A. (1969). "The World of the Pueblo Indians." In Diamond, S. (Ed.), *Primitive Views of the World*. New York: Columbia University Press.

Whitman, W. (1892/1980). *Leaves of Grass*. New York: Signet Classics.

Whyte, L.L. (1950). *The Next Development in Man*. New York: Mentor.

Wilber, K. (1980). *The Atman Project*. Wheaton: Quest Books.

Wilber, K. (1981). *Up From Eden*. Wheaton:

Quest Books.

Wilber, K. (1995). *Sex, Ecology, Spirituality*. Boston: Shambhala.

Wilber, K. (1996). *A Brief History of Everything*. Boston: Shambhala.

Wilber, K. (2000a). *One Taste*. Boston: Shambhala.

Wilber, K. (2000b). *Integral Psychology*. Boston: Shambhala.

Wilber, K. (2001). *A Theory of Everything*. London: Gateway.

Wildman, P. (1996). "Dreamtime Myth: History as Future." *New Renaissance*, 7(1).

Wilson, C. (1972). *New Pathways in Psychology*. New York: Taplinger.

Wilson, C. (1985). *A Criminal History of Mankind*. London: Grafton.

Wilson, C. (2004). *Dreaming to Some Purpose: An Autobiography*. London: Century.

Wilson, E.O. (1995). *On Human Nature*. London: Penguin.

Winzer, M.A. (1993). "Disability and Society before the Eighteenth Century: Dread and Despair." In Davis, L.J. (Ed.), *The Disabled Studies Reader*. New York: Routledge.

Woodburn, J. (1981/1998). "Limited Wants, Unlimited Means." In Gowdy, J. (Ed.), *A Reader on Hunter-Gatherer Economics and the Environment*, 87-110. Washington D.C.: Island Press.

Woodburn, J. (1982). "Egalitarian Societies." *Man*, 17, 431-51.

Wordsworth, W. (1950). *Poems*. London: Penguin.

Worthington, I. (2004). *Alexander the Great*. London: Longman.

Wrangham, R. & Peterson, D. (1996). *Demonic Males: Apes and the Origins of Human Violence*. London: Bloomsbury.

Wright, H.T. (1977) "Recent Research on the Origin of State." *Annual Review of Anthropology* 6, 379-397.

Wright, H.T. (1986). "The Evolution of Civilization." In Meltzer, D.D. et al. (Eds.), *American Archaeology Past and Future*, 323-365. Washington DC: Smithsonian Institution.

Wright, H.T. & Johnson, G.A. (1975). "Population Exchange and Early State Formation in South-Western Iran." *American Anthropologist* 77:267-289.

Wright, R. (1992). *Stolen Continents*. Boston: Houghton Mifflin.

Yalom, I.D. (1980). *Existential Psychotherapy*. New York: Basic Books.

Xu, H.M. (1996). *The Origin of the Olmec Civilisation*. Enid, OK: University of Central.

INDEX

AFTERWORD: THE FALL REVISITED (2018)

It's fitting that I'm writing this afterword to a new edition of *The Fall* shortly after the publication of my latest book, *The Leap*, which is in many ways a sequel to *The Fall*. *The Fall* is mainly about the human race's past. It's about how we fell 'asleep' – how we 'fell' out of a natural state of harmony and connection into discord and separateness. *The Leap* is about the corrective process to this. It's about the transcendence of discord and separateness, and a return to harmony and connection. It describes how, individually and collectively, we are 'waking up.' So in a sense, *The Fall* and *The Leap* complete each other.

I started to write *The Fall* in the summer of 2001. I have a very vivid memory of taking a break from writing Chapter 4 of the book, switching on the radio and hearing about the terrorist attacks on the World Trade Center in New York. However, I had been researching the book for a long time before then. For several years, I had been reading books on anthropology and archaeology and making notes in my journals. I had always been intrigued by the psychological differences between indigenous peoples (like American Indians, Australian Aborigines or the tribal peoples of Polynesia) and modern western or 'civilised' peoples. Most notably, I was struck by their different relationship to the natural world – indigenous people's respectful attitude to nature, their sense of its sacredness and aliveness, and their awareness that it was pervaded with a spiritual force, compared to modern people's exploitative attitude to it. Indigenous peoples seemed to have a sense of connection to nature which we have lost. We seem to exist in separation from the natural world, whereas they were intimately bonded with it.

I began to sense that a major psychological shift had occurred at some point in human history: the development of a new sense of separation and individuality. The more I read, the more evidence I found for this. I had an experience that I've never had with any other book – *The Fall* came into being very easily and inevitably, almost as if I was being helped and guided. I felt that I was being steered in the direction of all the material I needed. The structure of the book took shape so naturally that it felt as if it had already been arranged. Ideas and theories streamed into my mind more quickly than I could write them down. As a result, the book was easy to write. I felt like it was coming through me, rather than from me. Perhaps it had been forming in my subconscious mind for many years, and so was ready to emerge.

The book's reception has justified my faith in it. It has sold consistently well in the UK and US, and has been translated into several languages. Even now, I regularly receive appreciative e-mails from readers, telling me that the book has changed their lives, made them understand the human race better, and made them feel more optimistic about the future. I never expected that the book would have such an impact – although deep down, I sensed that I was 'on to something' and was delivering a message that needed to be heard.

RECENT SUPPORT FOR THE IDEAS OF *THE FALL*

Since it's now almost thirteen years since *The Fall* was published, one of the things I would like to do in this Afterword is provide an update. The foundation of the book is my argument that prehistoric human beings lived in a naturally spiritual and harmonious state, with a strong sense of connection to nature, in groups that were egalitarian and peaceful, without male domination or hierarchy. It was only once the 'Ego Explosion' occurred – when some human groups developed a strong sense of individuality and separation from their environment – that pathological traits such as warfare, the oppression of women, and hierarchical unequal societies developed. Thirteen years can be a long time in the scholarly world though. How does this argument hold up in the light of recent research?

I am pleased that a lot of new evidence has accumulated that supports the idea that early human beings were peaceful, and that warfare didn't become common until relatively recent times. In 2013, for example, the anthropologists Jonathan Haas and Matthew Piscitelli surveyed descriptions of 2900 prehistoric human skeletons from scientific literature. Apart from a single massacre site in Sudan (in which two dozen people were killed), they found only four skeletons with signs of violence – and even these signs were consistent with homicide rather than warfare. This dearth of violence completely contrasts with later periods when signs of war become obvious from skeletal marks, weapons, artwork, defensive sites and architecture. As Haas and Piscitelli wrote, 'The presumed universality of warfare in human history and ancestry may be satisfying to popular sentiment; however, such universality lacks empirical support.'[1]

Also in 2013, another anthropologist, Brian Ferguson, carried out a detailed survey of archeological findings from Neolithic Europe and the near East, and found almost no evidence of warfare. Indications were that warfare only became common in these areas around 3500 BCE. In the Levant – an area which includes present-day Jordan, Syria, Israel and Palestine – there was also no sign of warfare until 3500 BCE, even though the area had been densely populated and farmed since 9000 BCE. As Ferguson summarised, 'By considering the total archaeological record of prehistoric populations of Europe and the Near East up to the Bronze Age, evidence clearly demonstrates that war began sporadically out of a warless condition, and can be seen, in varying trajectories in different areas, to develop over time as societies became larger, more sedentary, more complex, more bounded, more hierarchical.'[2]

In *The Fall,* I looked at evidence showing that contemporary hunter-gatherer groups – particularly those living what anthropologists have a called an 'immediate return' way of life, meaning that they consume their food almost straight away, without storing surpluses – are peaceful and egalitarian. The logic here is that, since these contemporary groups follow the same way of life – with the same social systems and arrangements – as our prehistoric ancestors, then it is likely that they shared the same fundamental patterns of behaviour. In 2014, a study of 21 contemporary hunter-gatherer groups by the anthropologists Fry and Söderberg provided evidence for this. The study found a striking lack of evidence for inter-group conflict over the last hundred years. There was only one society (an Australian Aboriginal group called the Tiwi) who had a history of group killings.[3] Other recent research on contemporary hunter-gatherer groups has shown that men and women tend to have equal status and influence, leading to the suggestion that sexual inequality was also a relatively recent social development.[4]

In other words, this recent evidence strongly suggests that warfare (or indeed, male domination) is not innate, and has only been present for a small proportion of the time that human beings have lived on this planet. In the past, some of the most fervent support for the idea that human beings are innately – and have always been – war-like came from evolutionary psychologists. The idea that war is 'natural' fits in well with the view of human life as a struggle for genetic survival and reproduction. However, in recent years this view has become more and more untenable. The notion of prehistoric peace has gained more evidence, and become more widely accepted amongst anthropologists and archaeologists – to the point where even an orthodox evolutionary psychologist such as David Barash has agreed that early human groups were highly unlikely to be war-like because 'nomadic forager social systems [i.e. the social systems of our prehistoric ancestors] in particular predispose against violent interpersonal competition.'[5]

Group Conflict Amongst our Primate Cousins

Further evidence for the idea that human beings are actually innately peaceful rather than war-like comes from recent studies of the behaviour of our primate cousins.

Group conflict amongst chimpanzees has been seen as evidence for the innate war-likeness of human beings, since they are closely related to us as a species. However, as I mention in Chapter 1 of this book, there have always been doubts about how common chimpanzee group violence is. And since the book's publication, these doubts have intensified. Recent studies have found that chimpanzee killings are very infrequent. One study tracked 18 chimp communities for an average of 23 years per community, and observed only 15 intergroup killings, equivalent to one every 28 years.[6] Other studies have clarified that reports of chimpanzee violence – though never particularly high in any circumstances – are often inflated due to the fact that most research takes place in sites that are affected by human encroachment and disruption. Disruptive factors can include loss of habitat, poaching and hunting, disease, tourism, and demographic disruption. Studies of other chimpanzee groups in more undisturbed and natural environments show even lower levels of aggression. Over many decades of observing chimps, the zoologist Frances de Waal has concluded that depictions of chimpanzees as 'killer apes' are extremely distorted, ignoring their benevolence and altruism, as well as the peacemaking strategies they often employ.[7]

It is significant that human beings are as closely related to bonobos are we are to chimpanzees. It has always been accepted that bonobos are extremely peaceful – in fact, modern researchers have never observed a single incidence of group conflict or murder amongst them. Male bonobos do not dominate their groups, and their societies show no signs of hierarchical arrangements. Bonobo social interactions are typically amicable. If they show any signs of aggression, or any signs of social tension or disputes, it is often diffused by sexual activity. Bonobos frequently display empathy and altruism, not only to members of their own groups, but to strangers, and even to members of other species (e.g. helping injured birds).[8] And Frances de Waal believes that bonobos are actually *more* representative of human beings than chimpanzees. This contradicts the idea that we have inherited our supposed innate war-like behaviour from killer-ape ancestors.

The Greatest Mistake

Another aspect of this book that has become more widely accepted is the idea that the lives of prehistoric human beings were much easier, healthier and happier than those of later peoples. I suggested that – as well as being free of warfare, male domination and social hierarchy – prehistoric hunter-gatherers had a good diet, were largely free of illness and had long lifespans. The notion that for early human beings, life was 'nasty. brutish and short' is a myth, as is the related idea that human history has been a story of constant gradual progress, from a state of savagery towards increased sophistication and civilisation. These are the myths that the colonists of 18th and 19th century Europe used to justify their oppression and exploitation of less technologically advanced groups around the world. An early commentator of *The Fall* bizarrely accused me of 'new-age racism' for my views, while others suggested that I was perpetuating the myth of the 'noble savage.'

Of course, there was already a lot of evidence for the 'non-progressivist' view of human history at the time I wrote *The Fall*. As far back as 1968, the anthropologist Marshall Sahlins called prehistoric hunter-gatherers the 'original affluent society,' while in 1979, the anthropologist Richard B. Lee published his famous study of the !Kung people of Africa, describing how they would only spend around 15 hours a week collecting food, and had an abundance of leisure time. Although well known to anthropologists, these ideas have taken a long time to filter through to the wider public consciousness – probably because the myth of human progress has been so entrenched.

However, now this different view of human history (or prehistory) has been widely accepted. The idea of the 'noble savage' now seems less much less fantastical than the colonial myth of primitive savagery. One of the best-selling non-fiction books of recent years was *Sapiens: A Brief History of Humankind* by Yuval Noah Harari, which portrays prehistoric life as a period of abundance and leisure, and sees the advent of agriculture as 'history's biggest fraud.' According to Harari, farming broke down the symbiotic relationship between human beings and nature and led to alienation, greed, inequality and warfare. For almost all peoples who underwent the shift from foraging to farming, it wasn't an advance but a terrible mistake, which meant harder work, an inferior diet (with a greater risk of starvation), more disease, more crowded living conditions, and many other problems. Another recent book, *Against the Grain*, by the political scientist James C. Scott, also portrays the agricultural revolution as a disaster.

Scott argues that the cultivation of cereals was responsible for the formation of the first states (because it made taxation possible), and therefore indirectly led to warfare, slavery and hierarchy. Finally, a similar argument was put forward by the anthropologist James Suzman, in his recent book *Affluence Without Abundance: The Disappearing World of the Bushmen*. Suzman spent years living the bushmen of southern Africa, who he sees as a remnant of the human race's ancient past, and a reminder of the 'primitive affluence' and the egalitarianism which existed until the beginning of farming.

This isn't exactly the argument I put forward in *The Fall*. I don't equate the advent of male domination, intensive warfare and social inequality with the end of the hunter-gatherer lifestyle, and the advent of agriculture. In Chapter Two, I point out that there wasn't an abrupt shift from hunter-gathering to farming – initially, most groups adopted a 'simple horticultural' lifestyle, cultivating small gardens, and using hoes rather than ploughs. I summarise evidence showing that during this 'horticultural' phase – which lasted from roughly 8000 to 4000 BC – peaceful conditions continued, and groups were still relatively egalitarian, with an attitude of reverence to nature and the feminine form.

More recent archaeological research supports this view, showing that there was a time lag between the adoption of 'sedentism' – that is, living in settled communities – and the beginning of agriculture. The first phase of the Neolithic era included the domestication of plants and animals, but did not feature farming as we know it. Real farming – and the attendant problems of greed, alienation from nature, warfare and social hierarchy – came later. It clearly was associated with the fall, although I don't believe that farming actually *caused* the fall, as authors such as Harari, Scott and Suzman effectively suggest. I would reverse the causal relationship and say that farming was the consequence of the fall. The intensified sense of ego brought about a new sense of alienation from nature, a new desire to own land and accumulate property and goods, and to gain power and status. All of these were factors in the shift to farming – as well as in the fall into warfare, social hierarchy and the development of city-states.

THE LEAP

In the last part of this book, I suggest that over the last three centuries or so, a 'trans-Fall' phase has been underway: a collective, gradual movement beyond the separateness of the Ego Explosion.

And I feel that that the 'trans-Fall' movement has intensified over the last decade. Interest in spiritual teachings and spiritual practices has increased massively. It seems that more and more people are feeling the impulse to transcend our strong sense of ego, and re-connect with nature and the cosmos. In my research as a transpersonal psychologist, I have been amazed to find how common cases of spiritual awakening are. My research has mainly focused on spiritual awakening triggered by intense psychological turmoil, as described in my book *Out of the Darkness*. I have found that this experience most often happens to ordinary people who know nothing about spirituality. (As a result, it sometimes takes them a long time to understand what has happened to them.) It's almost as if our normal 'sleep' state is losing its hold over us as a species, and slipping away, and a new, higher-functioning awakened state is slowly emerging in its place.

One interesting piece of evidence for this view (which I wasn't aware of even when I wrote *The Leap*, but would certainly have referred to if I had been) is research suggesting that spiritual or mystical experiences have become more common over the last few decades. In a 1962 Gallup poll, just 22% of Americans reported that they had 'ever had a religious or mystical experience.' In 1994, 33% of people answered yes to the same question, while by 2009, the figure had risen to 49%. Research by the Pew Research Center in the US has shown a similar trend. In 2007, 52% of Americans reported that they regularly felt a 'deep sense of spiritual peace and well-being.' In 2014, the figure had increased to 59%. In 2007, 39% of Americans said that they regularly felt a 'deep sense of wonder about the universe' – a figure which had increased to 46% in 2014.

In the UK, the surveys of the Religious Experience Research Centre (originally set up by Sir Alister Hardy) have had similar findings. In a 1969 survey, the question 'Have you ever experienced a presence or power, whether you call it God or not, which is different from your everyday self?' was answered affirmatively by 29% of people. In 1978, the figure had risen to 36%, and then to 48% in 1987. In 2000, there was a further steep rise to 75% – a 27% increase in 13 years (which was, coincidentally or not, exactly the same figure by which church attendance declined over the same period).

Of course, right at the present time, it seems as if – in some countries at least – many 'fallen' characteristics are growing more prevalent, such as nationalism, inequality, lack of compassion for marginalised groups, lack of concern for the environment, and so on. But even these trends may not be wholly negative. As I suggested in both *The Fall* and *The Leap*, when a new phase begins, it's natural for the character-istics of the previous one to become more rigid and entrenched, in response to the threat of their demise. These characteristics try to assert themselves more strongly, in the same way that immigrant communities sometimes become more conservative, to try to defend their traditions and conventions against those of the wider community they are a part of. (This was also the view of the Swiss philosopher Jean Gebser, who suggested that human consciousness has evolved through different structures over history, and that the characteristics of structures become more rigid and overt as they are being superseded.) So even these seemingly negative developments may be a sign that change is underway.

Here it's also important to consider the potential awakening effect of psycho-logical turmoil. As I showed in *Out of the Darkness*, it's not uncommon for people to shift into a state of permanent wakefulness following intense episodes of suffering brought on by bereavement, a diagnosis of cancer, alcoholism and other traumatic events. The collective turmoil we are presently undergoing as a species may be having a similar effect – that is, spurring on the process of collective awakening.

In Mahayana Buddhism, there is an interesting concept of the 'reverse Bodhi-sattva.' Bodhisattvas are saint-like enlightened beings who devote their lives to helping others to attain enlightenment, often by relieving suffering and encouraging spiritual development. However, there is a special class of 'reverse Bodhisattvas' who have a frightening appearance, and try to enlighten others by creating challenges and hard-ship. They purposely create negativity in order to further people's spiritual develop-ment. This expresses very clearly the awakening potential of psychological turmoil – and I can think of a few present world leaders who would fit the description of reverse Bodhisattvas!

CONCEPTS OF SPIRIT-FORCE IN JAPAN AND KOREA

Let me mention a couple of other pieces of information I've become aware of which are relevant to the argument of *The Fall*.

Since writing the book, I have become even more aware of how common concepts of an all-pervading spiritual force were to the world's indigenous peoples. I have yet to find a Native American group who didn't have a term for 'spirit-force.' In other examples I have become aware of since writing the book, the Tlingit of the Pacific North-West called spirit-force *yok*, the Dakota called it *taku wakan*, the Haudenosaunee called it *orenda*, the eastern Algonquians called it *manitou*, and so on. Although these terms are sometimes translated as the Great Spirit, it is more accurate to refer to them as the Great *Mystery*. One of the best descriptions of the Great Mystery is from a Christian missionary called Reverend Stephen Riggs, who spent more than forty years living with the Dakota in the 19th century. He described *taku wakan* as:

> supernatural and mysterious… It comprehends all mystery, secret power and divinity. Awe and reverence are its due, and it is as unlimited in manifestation as it is in idea. All life is *Wakan*; so also is everything which exhibits power, whether in action, as the winds and drifting clouds; or in passive endurance, as the boulder by the wayside. For even the commonest sticks and stones have a spiritual essence which must be reverenced as a manifestation of the all-pervading, mysterious power that fills the universe.'[9]

At the same time, I have become aware that a sense of the aliveness and sacredness of the natural world (and the awareness of a spirit-force pervading it) is by no means confined to indigenous and prehistoric peoples. Such worldviews are still common amongst the most technologically developed peoples of East Asia. In Japanese culture, the natural world is believed to be alive with *kami*, non-physical forces (sometimes translated as 'spirits') that are manifestations of *musubi*, the interconnecting creative spiritual force of the universe. Similarly, in Korea, the world is perceived to be alive with *shin*, and the terms *haneullim* or *hwanin* refer to an all-pervading divine force or principle. (Literally, *haneullim* means 'source of all being.') Significantly, East Asian cultures are generally much less individualistic and more communally-oriented than modern western cultures. According to one anthropologist, in Vietnam, the concept of an 'individual' didn't enter into language until the 20th century, and then only in a negative sense, to describe selfish behaviour.[10]

This suggests that such cultures have retained aspects of the 'unfallen' state of being, and have never fallen so deeply into egoic separateness as western cultures. It seems more and more clear to me that the western de-spiritualised vision of the world – which sees nature just as a supply of resources, and living beings as nothing more than chemical machines – is an aberration, produced by a pathological state of separation.

SWEDENBORG AND GERALD HEARD

In recent years, I have become aware of two other authors who developed strikingly similar ideas to *The Fall*. One of these is the Swedish mystic and scientist Emmanuel Swedenborg, who died in 1772. Swedenborg divided the history of the human race into five 'great ages.' The first was the 'most ancient' era of prehistory, which Swedenborg associates with the human race's 'infancy.' This was a celestial age of innocence and harmony, in which human beings felt a direct connection to the divine, and all things were seen as its manifestation. In other words, this was the 'pre-Fall' era.

After this came what Swedenborg calls the 'ancient era.' This was when egoic self-consciousness began. Human beings lost a direct awareness of the divine and the first simple religions and myths became necessary, to help us maintain a spiritual sensibility. (Swedenborg associates this with the human race's childhood.) This was followed by what Swedenborg calls the 'Jewish' era (in that it was the period of history covered by the Old Testament). During this phase, we continued to lose our connection to the divine, and religions become rigid and external, based on obedience to precepts and laws. (This corresponds to a shift from polytheism to monotheism, which I describe as the second more intense phase of the Fall.)

After this a regeneration began. The love and compassion of Jesus's teachings (and the wisdom and scholarship of the early Christian church) heralded a re-emergence of true spirituality, and a new connection to the divine. And eventually, during Swedenborg's own lifetime, this led to what he called the 'new spiritual age.' Swedenborg saw this as a return to the celestial vision of prehistory. There was a much more direct link between the material world and the spiritual world, and individual spiritual experience became more important than external religion. It was a return to the spirituality of the most ancient era, but incorporating wisdom and self-awareness. This is the stage of the human race's 'maturity.'

This is exactly how I described the trans-Fall era in relation to the pre-Fall era – the same basic spiritual awareness but with a new conceptual maturity and heightened intellectual abilities. But to me the most interesting aspect of Swedenborg's ideas is that he specified the precise year when the New Spiritual Age began: 1757. I was startled when I read this, because in *The Fall* I suggest that the trans-Fall movement began (or at least first became overt) in the second half of the 18th century. This was the time of the Romantic movement in poetry and music, of the ideals of democracy and egalitarianism (leading to the French Revolution and the American constitution), the beginning of many progressive movements (women's rights, animal rights, anti-slavery etc.), more humane treatment of criminals, and so on. All of these were signs of a new movement beyond ego-separateness.

I find it quite remarkable that Swedenborg's chosen date corresponds so closely with my own timeframe. And in fact, I've become aware that the second half of the eighteenth century has been highlighted as a significant period by other historians. For example, in his *History of the World*, J.M. Roberts identified the middle of the 18th century as a time of 'great acceleration,' when 'the whole world more changed in [one] lifetime, than in the previous thousand years.'[11]

Another author who developed ideas that correspond closely with *The Fall* was the mid-twentieth century author Gerald Heard, a now little-known philosopher and mystic who was close friends with Aldous Huxley and Christopher Isherwood. In 1939 Heard published a book called *Pain, Sex and Time*, in which he put forward an evolutionary spiritual vision of the human race's past and future. Although his survey of human history only stretched as far back as ancient Sumer and Egypt, Heard noted that at the earliest stages of these cultures, there were signs of 'a pre-individualised society' and that there was a later point when 'individualised man is being crystallised out of organic society' and a 'new, self-conscious creature is created.'[12] Heard recognised that this sudden psychological change resulted in imbalance and turmoil, with a new sense of solitariness and disconnection. It brought about a new kind of ego that was, in his words, 'isolated completely from the deeper layer of mind'[13] and made the world appear alien and mechanical. However, Heard was aware that this ego was just a transitional stage, and that there is a higher consciousness that transcends it.

In connection with this, Heard recognised the importance of what I call the 'first wave' – the wave of mystical practices and contemplative traditions that arose from around 600 BCE. He saw these as an attempt to transcend the constricted ego, or to 'take part consciously in a new expansion of consciousness, to advance to a condition of mind as superior to self-consciousness as that condition is superior to the undefined, restricted awareness of the animal.'[14] This was the beginning of true sanity and freedom. Heard was very clear that our individual spiritual development is connected to the evolution of our whole species, and that one day the mystic's expansive state of being will be common to the whole human race. This was the next stage of our evolution. As he wrote, 'The whole purpose of our evolution and existence is the advancement into a higher and more extended consciousness.'[15] If we fail to achieve this, Heard believed, we are doomed, both individually and collectively.

As with Swedenborg, the similarities with Heard's ideas and my own are striking. To my mind the fact that such ideas have arisen spontaneously in so many different contexts vouches much for their veracity.

Apart from such additions, I think the only other change I would make if I wrote *The Fall* now would be to de-emphasise the environmental factors which I suggest may have caused the Ego Explosion – that is, the desiccation of large parts of the Middle East and central Europe from around 4000 BCE. There is a lot of evidence for this environmental change, and it's certainly very striking that the groups who first exhibited 'fallen' traits such as patriarchy, hierarchy, warfare, theistic religion etc. stemmed from these areas. However, in retrospect, I feel that the exact *causes* of the Ego Explosion aren't so important, and that I spent a little too much time focusing on them.

Overall though, I have no desire to change *The Fall*. I'm happy with the book as it was, and as it is. I'm happy that it has attracted a great deal of interest over the years, and that it is still being discovered by new readers. The book has struck such a deep chord in so many people that I feel it must be confirming knowledge that was already inside all us – truths that we have forgotten but that were always part of our collective unconscious. Perhaps we all sense, deep down, that the fall was an aberration, and that human beings' true nature is not to be full of discord and to create so much conflict. Perhaps we all sense, deep down, that the present bleak and chaotic phase of human history is only temporary, and that we are entering a new, brighter, more harmonious phase – a new spiritual age indeed.

Hopefully, when I write another Afterword for this book, perhaps in another thirteen years, this will have become even clearer.

Steve Taylor, February 2018.

Notes/References

1. Haas, J. & Piscitelli, M. (2013). 'The Prehistory of Warfare: Misled by Ethnography and Ethology.' In War, Peace, and Human Nature, edited by Douglas P. Fry, pp. 168-190. New York: Oxford University Press, p.184.

2. Ferguson, R. B. (2013). 'The Prehistory of War in Europe and the Near East.' In War, Peace, and Human Nature, edited by Douglas P. Fry, pp. 473–7. New York: Oxford University Press, p.116.

3. Fry, D. & Söderberg, P. (2014). 'Myths about Hunter-Gatherers Redux: Nomadic Forager War and Peace.' *Journal of Aggression, Conflict and Peace Research 6* (2014.): 255-66.

4. Dyble, M et al. (2015) 'Sex equality can explain the unique social structure of hunter-gatherer bands.' *Science,* 15 May 2015: 796-798

5. Barash, D. (2012). *Homo mysterious: Evolutionary puzzles of human nature.* Oxford: Oxford University Press, p.30.

6. Wilson, M. L., Boesch, C., Fruth, B., Furuichi, T., Gilby, I. C., Hashimoto, C., ... & Lloyd, J. N. (2014). Lethal aggression in Pan is better explained by adaptive strategies than human impacts. *Nature, 513*(7518), 414-417.

7. De Waal, F. (2009). *Primates and philosophers: How morality evolved.* Princeton: University Press.

8. Furuichi, T. (2011). Female contributions to the peaceful nature of bonobo society. *Evolutionary Anthropology: Issues, News, and Reviews, 20*(4), 131-142.

9. In Griffiths, B, (1976). *Return to the Centre.* London, Collins, p.21.

10. Marr, D. (2000). Concepts of 'Individual' and 'Self' in Twentieth-Century Vietnam. *Modern Asian Studies, 34*(4), 769-796.

11. Roberts, J.M. (2007). The Penguin New History of the World. London: Penguin.

12. Heard, G. (2004). Pain, Sex and Time. Rhinebeck, NY: Monkfish, p.75.

13. ibid., p.79.

14. ibid., p.83.

15. ibid., 169.

BOOKS

Iff Books

ACADEMIC AND SPECIALIST

Iff Books publishes non-fiction. It aims to work with authors and titles that augment our understanding of the human condition, society and civilisation, and the world or universe in which we live.

If you have enjoyed this book, why not tell other readers by posting a review on your preferred book site.

Recent bestsellers from Iff Books are:

Why Materialism Is Baloney

How True Skeptics Know There is no Death and Fathom Answers to Life, the Universe, and Everything

Bernardo Kastrup

A hard-nosed, logical, and skeptic non-materialist metaphysics, according to which the body is in mind, not mind in the body.

Paperback: 978-1-78279-362-5 ebook: 978-1-78279-361-8

Brief Peeks Beyond

Critical Essays on Metaphysics, Neuroscience, Free Will, Skepticism and Culture

Bernardo Kastrup

An incisive, original, compelling alternative to current mainstream cultural views and assumptions.

Paperback: 978-1-78535-018-4 ebook: 978-1-78535-019-1